LANDSCAPE *with* FIGURES

AMERICAN

LAND & LIFE

SERIES

Edited by Wayne Franklin

LANDSCAPE *with* FIGURES
Nature & Culture in New England

KENT C. RYDEN

Foreword by Wayne Franklin

UNIVERSITY OF IOWA PRESS ᴪ IOWA CITY

University of Iowa Press, Iowa City 52242
Copyright © 2001
by the University of Iowa Press
All rights reserved
Printed in the United States of America
Design by Richard Hendel
http://www.uiowa.edu/~uipress

The publication of this book was generously supported
by the University of Iowa Foundation.

Printed on acid-free paper

Library of Congress
Cataloging-in-Publication Data
Ryden, Kent C., 1959–
Landscape with figures: nature and culture in New England /
by Kent C. Ryden; foreword by Wayne Franklin.
p.   cm. — (The American land and life series)
Includes bibliographical references and index.
ISBN 0-87745-787-5 (cloth), ISBN 0-87745-788-3 (pbk.)
1. Human ecology — New England.   2. Landscape assessment —
New England.   I. Title.   II. Series.
GF504.N45R93   2001
304.2'0974 — dc21   2001027988

01   02   03   04   05   C   5   4   3   2   1
01   02   03   04   05   P   5   4   3   2   1

TO PAT

Lifelong New Englander, and the

best guide anyone could ask for

CONTENTS

※❀※

A few hundred years is not long as human history is measured—let alone earth history—but, as Kent Ryden suggests in this thoughtful collection of essays on nature and culture in New England, it offers sufficient ground for raising a rich crop of insights.

I first read his meditations while sitting in an old farmhouse in the midst of the complex landscapes he explores. He opened my eyes to things I had learned while occupying the house without quite realizing it. The first is how many layers even the simplest fact can have. This house, the wood plaque on its façade proclaims, was built in 1762. The most recent local history states that it was erected by a Scots-Irish doctor and his wife, then in their forties. On arriving from County Antrim as a youth, John Dunsmoor probably lived with kin nearby in the old Massachusetts town of Lancaster, where he learned his trade, then moved to Lunenburg some years prior to Ruth Fisher. She hailed from the Connecticut Valley town of Hatfield, but also apparently had immigrated from Ireland. How they met isn't known, but with their marriage in Lunenburg in 1747, this town became their permanent home. After fifteen years of married life in some undetermined house elsewhere in town, where Ruth gave birth to their six children, they at last managed to erect this place on Northfield Road. Having moved in, they stayed until their deaths in the closing years of the eighteenth century. They are buried side by side in the town's North Cemetery, which can be reached by a lane leading through a small hemlock wood just across the street from their house.

As the couple's final home, the place draws regular visitors from across the United States who claim descent from them. Since I regard myself as merely the latest in a sequence of people who have nested here, I happily give visitors a tour of house and grounds, filling in what I know from books and oral tales. It's a big structure now, the sort that has become a New England icon. And the dwelling itself is dwarfed by the enormous nineteenth-century apple barn that, attached by a wing, hovers over its rear. Everybody in this rootless society has this image somewhere in their unconscious. We are a country mostly descended from modest outcasts, whatever our points of origin, but when we dream of our past we do not often seek out the marrow of that truth. Because the Dunsmoors' house probably began as a simple pair of rooms, upstairs and down, and then experienced several expansions over the decades, its appearance today hardly gives my dreaming visitors an accurate picture of how modestly their ancestors actually lived. Probably during the couple's later years here, the house was first doubled across the front, then had a back range of rooms added. Sometime in the 1870s, after the property had become the summer place of a grain merchant from the nearby city of Fitchburg, that large barn was built. At the same time, an old house frame from somewhere else was moved in and converted into the wing linking the two structures. A final three-story square structure that filled in a niche between wing and barn was the last addition, except for a relatively recent screen porch. The grain merchant and his daughter, whose own family lived here from 1911 on, tore out many original features and put in modern amenities, raised the height of the third floor to accommodate a dance chamber, and replaced the old central chimney stack with a pair of smaller flues, one of them to accommodate a central heating plant. The ultimate result was a house that has more than a dozen rooms, integrally linked to a clapboarded barn of truly massive proportions, all of it painted white and each of the sixty some windows adorned with a pair of dark green shutters.

Like many older houses, this one sits smack on the road, and its location as the visitors drive up tends to magnify its size. All of the Dunsmoors' descendants, eager to claim their rightful place in the nation's first scenes, comment on the mass of the resulting composition. They clearly like the idea that the family tree is rooted in such ground and, like the ancient sugar maples along the road out front, appears to have a kind of eternal dimension. For a time I gently avoid the truth. Then, perhaps because I simply inherited the place by dint of a heavy mortgage a few years back, and thus have (among other things) a consumer's relation to the structure, I come to regard as a bit silly the illusion I see all too clearly reflected in their moist eyes. I know the place, after all, not only as a home but also as a house—a piece of real estate. I know it as well, I might add, as something of a lesson in the interesting surfaces of home maintenance. You learn some things slowly with an old house, others smack in the middle of the first night. Right now, the piles of snow lie very deep on the ground outside the kitchen windows, where it lands after catapulting off the slate roof hours or even days after each storm, depending on a variety of factors. After several months avoiding the neck-breaking surprise that the barn slates deliver to the driveway that I finished clearing, say, thirty-one hours earlier, I noticed a slight *click* in the substructure of the living room at the front of the house just before the snow came down out back. That premonitory sound, faithfully repeated each time the snow is about to fall, is the sort of thing that these traveling descendants will never hear and — when they hear of it — are unlikely to savor.

So, eventually, I try to walk them back through the changes that separate them from the builders' day. I start the process in the living room, pointing out details that suggest changes in the structure since the 1760s. Let me share one. The summer beam, which used to run from the east wall to join the now missing chimney girt on the west, was cut short when the original stack was removed around 1910 and a big staircase was inserted where it had stood. Now, instead of holding up the second and third floors, the summer beam is suspended by a hidden iron rod that runs all the way to the new roof timbers two flights up. And spliced to the beam's now truncated west end is a three-foot piece of timber that serves largely to uphold old structural appearances, adding an engineering plausibility to the room. Otherwise, with its principal structural member ending several feet from the wall, the thing might seem precariously modernistic.

Contemplating that one change gets my visitors looking up at the exposed beam and floor joists. While they are doing so, it is easy to direct their attention to other details, including the size and shape of the timbers. When they have taken those details in, I generally lead them into an adjoining room which at first seems equally old. Here, though, they quickly see that the timbers were cut in a different manner from a different wood, and have quite different dimensions. In the chambers above each of these first floor front rooms, as they see in good time, exactly the same differences are duplicated, suggesting how the original over-and-under east rooms were duplicated beyond their west ends, but in a newer style suggestive of the 1780s. Perhaps by then, shortly before their deaths, the good doctor and his wife were enjoying more prosperous times. Although their children probably all lived here with them from the beginning, meaning that the new house was crowded at the outset, things became even more crowded in later years. Their youngest son Ebenezer and his wife Susannah stayed on in the place after their marriage in 1777 and began building their own family of ten children, the last of them born here in 1804. Doubtless the presence of all these people made the addition of new rooms necessary. But changing ideas about culture — the new emphasis placed on privacy and refinement, for instance — also made it desirable for the family members to have more adequate space for their own purposes and for entertaining guests. Houses became bigger in this period partly because of a new vision of domestic life.

Similar questions about values arise across the course of any old house's history. So, too, with the landscape. John and Ruth Dunsmoor certainly farmed their land. Their son Ebenezer, who lived in the house until his death in 1827, owned 187 acres in 1798, when the house was appraised at the sizable sum of six hundred dollars. In 1803, when he was a lieutenant in the militia, Ebenezer made at least part of his living as a teamster hauling goods to Fitchburg and Concord and Boston. And, to judge by his purchases of farming tools and seed from a local storekeeper, he continued farming then and afterward. But the real story of the farm as farm is a later and more complex one. Ebenezer and Susannah Dunsmoor's youngest son, Joseph, who never married, lived on the property with his mother until her death in 1840. For twenty-four years thereafter he stayed here virtually alone, evidently tilling what remained of the property, until at the age of sixty he sold the farm at auction and moved north to live out his days in the home of a nephew in Charlestown, New Hampshire.

It was then or soon after that Joseph Cushing, Fitchburg merchant, bought the Dunsmoor farm. Cushing, who at the age of eighteen early in the century had been the youngest (and reputedly the fastest) stagecoach driver in New England, never wandered far from the world of horses. After he retired from the road, he ran a livery stable in Fitchburg, then after the Civil War bought a big old stone cotton mill there and converted it to house his prosperous flour and grain business. He also ventured, comically, into railroads. Because his mill was five hundred feet beyond the end of the Vermont and Massachusetts Railroad line in town, he personally extended the tracks to his property. When this shortest of short lines was completed two years after the first transcontinental railroad opened, Cushing held his own fancy ceremony, smacking a gold spike into place with an enormous mallet as honored guests and a band on a platform car ever so slowly moved along the entire length of his rails. Waggishly, he printed complimentary passes for the Cushing Railroad and distributed them to the presidents of the largest lines in the country, who reciprocated without appreciating how lopsided the exchange was. One of those presidents, visiting Fitchburg, reportedly took Cushing up on the offer, only to be ferried on an ox-drawn flatcar over the whole distance while seated in a barber chair. Some gratuities are worth avoiding.

It may have been Joe Cushing's love of horses that led him to purchase the Dunsmoor farm. But he also must have had an interest in apples from the outset. He it certainly was who erected the enormous barn, which had ten horse stalls on the main floor, a piggery in the basement, a now removed cow stable running off the rear, and a third floor reachable for wagons (and even now by heavy trucks) by a ramp at one end. On that upper level, apples were sorted, packed, and stored. Because the barn's many sash windows were all framed in at the outset, as the timbers reveal, it is clear that plans for the fruit operation were part of the initial intent. Hay barns have no such openings, or only few of them, whereas those built for apple storage in the period typically used windows to promote vital air circulation, which controlled the temperature and released the ripening ethylene gas into the atmosphere. By 1882, listed as a nonresident in the town tax rolls, Cushing had nine horses on the property, along with twenty-two cows, two yoke of oxen, and eight swine. In addition to the house and two barns, he had a cider mill and an ice house on the total of just over one hundred acres that he owned. When he died late in the 1890s, some of his property went directly to his daughter Susan. But it was not until some years later, when she and her husband Charles P. Dickinson moved to the town from Fitchburg, that they began building the property into the image of what it became long after the Dunsmoors left it. Year after year, new structures went up and adjoining properties were added to the total, until by 1915 the couple owned an impressive collection of buildings (some twenty of them, including the two "pump houses and water works" from which they operated the local water company), and a total of nearly nine hundred acres of land, most of it in one piece centered on the brook that ran about a half mile behind the house. By the year of her death, 1926, Susan and Charles owned eleven hundred acres in town, most of it close to the old farm.

The property was the beneficiary of many other activities. Charles Dickinson, son of a bootmaker, had an uncanny sense of the new opportunities provided by the nation's economy in the twentieth century. He built several electric generating plants in New York, for instance, but he also had a keen interest in things aeronautical. With his son Arnold, who erected a second big house just down the street, he contacted Igor Ivanovich Sikorsky, the Russian-born aviation engineer, and founded the aircraft company named for him. The technical accomplishments of that entity were all achieved far from Lunenburg, although in two ways the landscape here was notably affected by those utterly modern developments. First, there is even today an old street near the house, bearing the name Cushing Lane, which in fact began as a landing strip for the Dickinsons' aircraft. And the 400-acre lake that now lies on what was for millennia a swampy lowland behind the house was built by Charles and Arnold Dickinson for their seaplanes. Ringed at present with summer houses — both the Dickinsons were real estate tycoons — Dickinson Reservoir, since gentrified as Hickory Hills Lake, floats other craft at present, pontoon boats and kayaks and canoes, for there is an eight-horsepower limit imposed on it by the private association that owns it. In the summer it provides cool water for the warm bodies of nearby residents. Ringed with large white pines and cut all around its basin with many coves and peninsulas, it seems as old as any other natural feature in the area — like Turkey Hill or Whalom Pond, both of them glacial leavings — but it is an artifact of American modernism pure and simple.

My visitors have a certain upper limit for anecdotes, as I often discover, so I try to keep from overloading their curiosity. But, as the readers of *Landscape with Figures* will I think come to agree, they would do well to regard with a somewhat doubting eye — and a somewhat enlarged sense of acceptance — the apparent truths of the American landscape. Things usually aren't what they seem. My little rural fantasy has depths of urban story below it, much as the placid lake I can almost see from the cupola of the apple barn owes its fish to the wealth produced by electric turbines and aircraft engines, before that to the railroads that planes have virtually outmoded — and before that to the horse economy the railroads killed. Like the layers of rock under this land, the levels of history on its surface are many and rich.

A book is a tree with an education, I suppose; taken from the forest, chewed up, and flattened into paper, the tree, studentlike, gets imprinted with all kinds of information, and those imprinted pieces of paper become bound into a volume that eventually stands on a shelf with a lot of other educated trees. Books about nature are thus almost kaleidoscopically complicated: reading one, you hold what was once a part of a forest in your hands, scanning it to learn someone's ideas about, say, some other forest somewhere, and all the while you could probably turn your head and look out the window at some trees much closer to home, trees that you likely have your own relationships with and opinions about. Ideas about nature, experiences in nature, material manipulations of nature — all of these and more swirl around the act of reading a book like this one. In thought, action, and memory, you and I are positioned in many ways at once toward the natural world even at the moment of writing or reading these particular words on this particular page. While it may be conventional for many of us to oppose "nature" to "culture," then, in practice it may be more difficult to maintain that separation than might at first appear. In fact, once we start looking closely at those landscapes in the world around us that we define as "natural," our sense of the integrity of the border between these two conceptual categories might begin to dissolve completely. Or, at least, these are some of the ideas I am going to explore in the coming pages of the former tree that you now hold in your hands.

Rather than locate these observations in the abstract, though, I want to literally bring them down to earth as much as I can by suggesting how they derive from a close reading of a particular place: in this case, the New England in which I have spent over two-thirds of my life. And I use the word "reading" advisedly, because I think it stands at the heart of my overall approach in this book, one that combines the interpretation of selected literary texts and specific New

England landscapes to come to some understanding of the ways that natural places and cultural processes have intertwined to shape the region both on the ground and in the mind. You can learn a lot about human relationships with the natural world from reading books, to be sure — at least, I hope you'll think so in the case of *this* particular book — but I also think you can learn just as much from bypassing the books and going directly to the trees they're made from and the landscapes in which they live, reading these things and places as texts in their own right for the implicit narratives they contain about the mutual interaction of people and their nonhuman environments. So I do both kinds of reading in this book, choosing throughout to approach "nature" not as an idea or as a conceptual category first and foremost, but as a field of experience. That is, in my examination of deliberately place-based writings and in my excursions into what have struck me as particularly suggestive corners of the New England landscape, I try to look at the world on the small scale and with the close familiarity through which New Englanders of the past and present have known their environment on an everyday basis, thinking about what "nature" has meant in their minds and how it has come through their hands. This region is rich with meaning, and while I focus largely on New England in these pages, I hope that some of the meanings I unearth will inspire readers both here and elsewhere to look at the world around them with slightly altered eyes, with an appreciation of what an interdisciplinary, historically informed approach can bring to our understanding of just what it is we're looking at when we're looking at nature.

My first chapter sets up much of the conceptual framework for the readings of literature and landscape that follow, so I don't feel any particular need to reiterate any of that material here by way of setting the scene. I will repeat one thing, though: I begin the chapter by saying that I would never have written this book if I hadn't spent my early childhood in Connecticut, and it's just as true that I would never have written this book if I had not become a faculty member in the American and New England Studies program at the University of Southern Maine. Not only have I had the opportunity — or, I suppose, given the name of the program, the professional obligation — to think, write, and teach about New England in particular and regionalism in general, I have also been able to develop many of the ideas and approaches that inform this book through regularly teaching courses in such fields as literature, environmental studies, and cultural landscape studies. Any students of mine who, having decided they need a little more Ryden in their lives, end up reading this book will recognize many of the texts, images, and interpretations I offer here, and I'd like to thank them all for their questions, their comments, their curiosity, and the ongoing intellectual collaboration of the seminar room. I teach in a great program. I'd also like to thank my colleagues in the program — Ardis Cameron, Donna Cassidy, Joe Conforti, Matthew Edney, and Nathan Hamilton — for their generosity in sharing ideas, perspectives, and encouragement, and for their part in creating and sustaining an intellectual and collegial atmosphere that supports wide-ranging interdisciplinary inquiry. I'm fortunate to be part of a fine community of teachers and scholars. Particular thanks go to Matthew for inviting me to give the opening lecture for the "Cartographic Creation of New England" exhibit at the Osher Map Library here at the University of Southern Maine in December 1996, a lecture that eventually grew to become chapter 4 of this book.

Gathering material is as important a part of a book like this as is interpreting that material, and I'd like to specifically thank those students who have provided me with research assistance in the time I've been working on this book or on the essays and papers that eventually went into it, including Mitzi Cerjan, Eben Blaney, Stacei Skowron, and Anna Berendt. And were it not for the efficient work and good humor of Casandra Fitzherbert and her staff in the interlibrary loan department at the USM library, I'd still be gazing wistfully at the bibliographical citations that those students had collected and wondering what the actual articles said. I'd like to also acknowledge the assistance of the staff at the Rhode Island Historical Society Library in helping me find the material on Philip Angell and the calamity at Simmonsville that appears in chapter 7, as well as that of Fred Bridge at the Little Compton (R.I.) Historical Society in filling in details on Sarah Wilbour and the Elizabeth Pabodie monument, also discussed in chapter 7.

Special thanks go to Dana Deering and his grandfather, Walter Hale, for their great generosity in showing me around their family property in Sebago, Maine, and explaining its story to me. Not only did they afford me a fascinating glimpse into a bit of Maine landscape history, they also provided me with a wonderful memory of a fine time had by all. A combination like that is hard to beat. I've also been fortunate to have good friends elsewhere with whom to share perceptions, test out bits of writing, get reactions and encouragement, or collaborate on the occasional conference panel to kick around some ideas in public. A list of them all might soon threaten to include everyone I've spoken to or written to about anything academically related in the last few years, so I'll forbear compiling a group acknowledgment that would be only partial at best. Such thanks are best given in person anyway. I do, however, want to offer thanks to Wayne Franklin for once more including a book of mine in the American Land and Life series. It's a good place to be.

The first section of chapter 1 originally appeared under the title "Big Trees, Back Yards, and the Borders of Nature" in the winter 2001 issue of the *Michigan Quarterly Review*, a special issue on "Reimagining Place," and chapter 2 originally appeared as "Landscape with Figures: Nature, Folk Culture, and the Human Ecology of American Environmental Writing" in *ISLE: Interdisciplinary Studies in Literature and Environment* 4: 1 (Spring 1997).

LANDSCAPE *with* FIGURES

ONE

Big Trees and Back Yards
Time, Landscape, & the
Borders of Nature

Iwouldn't be writing this book if I hadn't spent the first nine years of my childhood in New Milford, Connecticut. Our house sat on about an acre of ground, a plot that was shaped roughly like a right triangle: the hypotenuse was the road, the short leg was a hedge separating our yard from the neighbors', and the remaining side was a wall of trees. Although I haven't been back there for years, I remember those trees as being a mixed coniferous forest, blanketing the ground not with leaves but with needles, their verdure providing an annual green counterpoint to the blazing colors that distant Mount Tom splashed on our northern horizon every autumn. The trees extended for several minutes' worth of childhood tramping away from our yard, and then gave way suddenly to a broad expanse of tall grass, a meadow that marked a zone of transition away from the known and familiar world: the other side of that meadow seemed uncomfortably far from the house to a small child, as did the terra incognita we would enter if we strayed too far to the north or south of the patch of woods that extended straight east from our property line. Limited in extent as it may have been, the world on the other side of the yard's edge was a favorite haunt of my sisters and me, rivaled only by the East Aspetuck River just down the road. Some of my fondest memories of those years are not of specific events or episodes, but of patterns of activity in the wooded and watered landscape, repeated moments of contact and exploration and immersion: digging in a natural outcrop of sand where a rocky ledge broke through the meadow's grassy surface, revisiting a favorite shaggy-barked tree and marveling yet again at the odd and delightful texture of its skin (a texture that demanded that bits of it be pulled off and shredded and smelled), weaving a new route through the trees that I hadn't tried before, pulling apart the jointed snakegrass that grew along the river's edge, kicking off our shoes and wading into the swift shallow river itself on hot summer days. I learned to love that landscape, to the point where it became difficult to imagine my young self away from it: when my father gently broke the news to my sisters and me that we would be moving to Wisconsin, I remember crying hardest not because I would be leaving my friends, but because I would be leaving the woods.

It's probable that I would never have become interested in thinking and writing about the natural world as an adult if I hadn't accomplished the first nine years of my growing up in such close proximity to those woods, just up the hill from that river. In reflecting on his own path through life, the writer and biologist Robert Michael Pyle has noted that "when people connect with nature, it happens *somewhere*. Almost everyone who cares deeply about the outdoors can identify a particular place where contact occurred," he continues, and that place is usually not one that is storied, monumental, breathtaking, destined for calendar photos and official preservation and vacation visits, but is rather "unspectacular: a vacant lot, a scruffy patch of woods, a weedy field, a stream . . . — or a ditch," a reference to the High Line Canal that meandered through the Aurora, Colorado, of Pyle's youth and whose waters continue to nourish his days both personally and professionally: "Without a doubt," he believes, "most of the elements of my life flowed from that canal."[1] Likewise, a thoroughly unremarkable sliver of New England hillside field and forest — Mount Tom's poor cousin, the kind of landscape that the leaf-peepers drive through to get to the *worthwhile* woods — and a shallow rocky brook with no particular distinguishing marks somehow conspired to narrow my range of choices and preferences, to literally prepare the ground for many of the things I have come as an adult to think and write and care about, to subtly shape my ways of seeing: when I hike through New England forests now I am still shaded in imagination by my old backyard woods, and when I lean on a bridge railing to contemplate a stream I still hear quiet plashy echoes of the East Aspetuck. My life remains in many ways continuous with that time and place, rooted deeply in lands lying just outside a child's back yard.

And yet, despite this continuity, the way that I think about and understand those woods today has changed in at least one fundamental respect. When I was a child, in my mind the back edge of our yard was where tamed, domesticated space left off and something wilder, shaggier, more disordered, and more exciting began; in short, the line separating grass and trees represented the border between "culture" and "nature," between a humanized world and a world that was irreducibly nonhuman in its content, origins, and meaning. On our side of the line, my father kept the lawn carefully mowed, I not being old enough to have had that task handed over to me yet; in contrast to the green hulks of trees looming over them, the perpetually beheaded leaves of grass were ordered, made obedient, violently subjected to the will of my father and, behind him, the landscape aesthetic to which the entire family subscribed. While it would never have occurred to me to think of it in these terms at the time — mowing lawns was just something that dads did, and lawns were supposed to be kept short so kids could play on them — in contemplating the juxtaposition of lawn and woods, I can see the justice in Michael Pollan's observation that "a lawn [is] nature under culture's boot . . . a totalitarian landscape."[2] The back yard contained a swing set and a sandbox, both of which my sisters and I used energetically; it also sloped from the house up to the woods, providing an excellent sledding run on wintry New England days. To one side of the house, two willow trees had been planted by a previous landowner; their languidly drooping branches and their position near the house surrounded by carefully mowed grass clearly distinguished them in my mind from the bigger, wilder trees amassed nearby. Basically, the entire yard was nothing more than a big playground — a playground with different equipment and ground cover, certainly, but not that different in how I used and thought about it from the one I played on during recess at school. It contained natural objects, to be sure — cloned sheep aside, I'm still pretty sure that only God can make a tree, or a blade of grass for that matter — but it hardly qualified in my mind as "nature."

To find a *natural* landscape, I merely had to take a few steps up the hill. Stepping across the clean sharp border from lawn to woods, from culture to nature, was a profound and liminal experience, an immediate transition from one world to another, from a sphere clearly controlled and defined by human beings to a world in which I was a visitor, a guest. The forest grew in tangled disorder, nothing like the shorn green surface I could see over my shoulder through gaps in the trees. On the far side of the line, the world was not designed and furnished by and for human beings; instead, you had to fit your movements to its contours. And, being a rather timid child, if I brashly or carelessly wandered too far afield from the parts of the woods I was familiar with I could in short order become utterly terrified, literally "be-wildered" by the thought of being lost in what to me were trackless wastes. The felt quality of time changed in the woods, and not only in the sense that I would frequently have to be called after because I was going to be late for lunch or dinner. Unlike our yard, it seemed not to be a landscape that had any particular point of origin, a time when the house had been built and the willows planted and the lawn seeded, but rather a landscape that had always been there; only recently had a road been cut through it and a triangular house lot rudely wedged into it, modern intrusions into a place where human conceptions of time didn't seem particularly relevant.

Clearly I liked crossing that border, that line in my back yard where time and space changed. Gary Paul Nabhan and Stephen Trimble have echoed Pyle's observation about how "many naturalists start their journeys on ditchbanks, in empty lots — in any open space just beyond the backyard fence," and have expressed their concern "about how few children now grow up incorporating plants, animals, and places into their sense of *home*."[3] For me, the woods across the line were very near home, but they were not home themselves, and that was precisely the point; that perceived difference, that contrast vividly contained within a few feet of ground, was what gave them their significance, their excitement. To my way of seeing and thinking, nature was something that was physically separate from me and distant from me, even if that distance wasn't very far. Blazing Mount Tom on the horizon and the woods I saw every day from my bedroom window were conceptually the same thing; even if the backyard forest didn't share Mount Tom's spectacular colors, they were joined through the sense I had that the natural world was exceptional, a diversion from the everyday, a realm of experience that broke you out of the world that humans made and plunged you into a world in which you were subordinate, a world of strange and wonderful things that demanded new ways of thinking and feeling. This was a world that

Big Trees & Back Yards

fundamentally had nothing to do with me, while paradoxically having everything to do with the person I became.

Children are consistently among the most perceptive people I know, and I would not trade those early perceptions of mine for anything. I see in my past self what Nabhan sees in his own family when he observes that "a few intimate places mean more to my children, and to others, than all the glorious panoramas I could ever show them,"[4] and I learn in retrospective reflection what Nabhan learns from his kids: "wilderness is not some scenic backdrop to gaze at; . . . It is where you can play with abandon."[5] Children see the world differently from the way adults see the same world, he concludes, and the nature of immediate childhood experience in the landscape, getting hands dirty and cramming the senses and imagination full, can be a continual source of epiphany. I have seen this in children I have known — an unplanned experience setting their minds on fire. I spent a very instructive afternoon a few years ago with my young friend Donald Hefferon. I was visiting his family in Vermont, and one day he and I and his mother Lynne and his younger brother Alan went for a walk in some woods managed by the Audubon Society. Any walk in the woods makes a day special, and, as children seem to love running on excitedly ahead of big slow adults on such occasions as their parents desperately try to keep up, at one point I found myself lagging slightly behind the little group of Hefferons. A flash of bright orange at the edge of the trail caught my eye, and I squatted down and saw a newt, sitting so still that at first I half-wondered if it was a plastic toy that someone had dropped. Then it moved. I kept it in sight and called for Donald and Alan and Lynne to come back. The boys clustered around the newt; like me, they had never seen such a thing before, and they kept it under close and amazed observation until it scuttled away under the fallen leaves. Seeing this unprecedented iridescent amphibian seemed to change the quality of the day for Donald: he was quick to spot some frogs when the hiking trail passed through a swamp, and when we later came to the bank of a stream he was delighted when I pointed out some small fish to him in a pool. Upon turning away from the pool, he charged up a nearby hillside, intent on discovering if, in his words, "there was more nature up there."

At first Donald's comment amused me. He was completely surrounded by woods and water, but at that moment such commonplace things seemed no longer to qualify as "nature." That word was now reserved for rarer and more stirring sights: a frog kicking its way along under water, a fish skittering away from his shadow, a newt of a color he had never dreamed an animal's skin could be. He could see trees in his back yard; he could see plenty of water every time his parents took him near Lake Champlain. Nature, however, was something exotic, something extraordinary, something you had to travel to and have pointed out to you; while Donald's examples, the newt in particular, were admittedly more eye-catching than my own childhood example of "nature," I would have agreed with him in that "nature" was defined primarily through the contrast it offered to what you generally saw through the windshield, through the kitchen window, or in the company of lots of other people. It wasn't nature unless it suddenly made the world feel a little bit stranger and more wonderful, and unless you went and saw it on its own turf. And then it occurred to me that Donald (and I, for that matter) couldn't have come up with this definition of "nature" on his own, that it would have had to be taught to him somehow. We have to learn that nature is strictly separated from culture, both conceptually and spatially; its exceptional quality has to be explained to us until we believe it. And we do learn, and we do believe: the ways in which many of us structure our self-conscious interactions with the natural world continually reinforce these lessons. We travel far from our homes to visit national parks, strictly demarcated segments of the landscape that are set apart by virtue of their manifest and spectacular natural wonders from the more pedestrian landscapes around them (if they were high-quality nature, they'd be in the park too, right?). We watch televised nature programming that focuses on the lives of exotic animals of the sort that we will never see nibbling on our vegetable gardens. Some of us agonize over right whales and bison, canyons and clear-cuts, in places far from our own urban or suburban neighborhoods. Donald may have been on to something: to find nature, it seems, you have to go out and look for it. Everything else is one big back yard, tamed and mowed and put to human use, on the "lawn" side rather than the "woods" side of the line. If it's not nature, it must be something else; it must be culture.

As I mentioned before, though, I now think in a different way about the world I entered when I used to cross the line into nature. While I do not want to negate or repudiate that earlier way of seeing, or lose what is good in it — my awareness of being a guest in some way, my feeling of having to shape my actions to the land rather than the other way around, and above all my sense of wonder — I do want to qualify it fundamentally. What had appeared to me as a strict, sharp border now strikes me as vague and indistinct, blurred perhaps almost to the point of erasure; to see one side of the line as "nature" and the other side as "culture" is false, unfaithful to the history that the landscape — in New Milford, everywhere in the country — has seen. I'm told that a little learning is a dangerous thing, and I now know that my backyard woods, like just about every other forested landscape in New England, were at least second growth; what looked to me like a timeless green world had actually grown back on land that was once cleared for fuel, building material, or agriculture. It looked the way it did only because of the way that people had used it in the past; far from being exempted from culture and history, the wooded landscape was saturated with culture and history, with past land-use practices and attitudes about appropriate behaviors toward the environment. It is now also clear to me that what I simply thought of as "the woods" was undoubtedly someone's property, carefully surveyed and mapped and accounted for in official documents somewhere. In someone's mind other than mine, it was not a green and deeply known landscape but a spatial and monetary abstraction, a discrete and defined object, a lifeless thing. Also in retrospect, I am surprised by how much I was able to willfully ignore in the process of defining the world beyond the line as "nature," particularly the fact that straight through the middle of the meadow ran a high-voltage power line (which answers the question of who owned at least part of the landscape). One of the power-line towers stood squarely in the middle of the tall grass, but it somehow didn't count in my overall assessment of the landscape, and I managed to mentally erase it from the scene in order not to complicate my feeling of having left the world of culture behind (a process that may have been aided and made more urgent by the fact that I was afraid of the tower and its warning signs, convinced that I'd be instantly incinerated and reduced to a small heap of smoldering ash if I so much as accidentally brushed against it). Similarly, the East Aspetuck River was bordered on one bank by Paper Mill Road, and while the eponymous mill had long since vanished, its dam still spanned the river and its spillway was blocked off each summer by the owners of a nearby camp to create a swimming pond. We noncampers swam there too, but since we were swimming in river water in the middle of woods it felt very different from being at a pool or a public beach. It still counted as nature, as did the river downstream, even though its flow was still at least partially controlled by the relict dam. While I may have felt sure when I was leaving culture and entering nature, the nature that I was entering had people's fingerprints all over it: it had been defined and controlled, shaped and bounded, objectified and manipulated by many, many human beings long before I arrived on the scene. It may have appeared strictly natural on the surface, but the world I entered when I crossed over the border was as much the result of cultural processes as the back yard I left behind me. What I thought was a strict, sharp line now vanishes the closer I look at it.

One other thing becomes clear as I think back on those woods: when I picture that landscape to myself today, I can't envision it without including myself squarely in its midst. It is now, as it was then, a landscape with figures — in particular, the three small figures of my sisters and me. While I may have valued the woods superficially because they represented "nature" to me, a world exempted and distinct from human influence, in reality I had deeply humanized the little patch of forest behind the house, placed myself in its center, mapped it and named it and imaginatively made it my own. While I would occasionally give way to the explorer's urge and blaze a new trail, on most of my forays into nature I followed well-remembered paths of my own making, arranged among specific landmarks: protruding rocks, open spaces, gaps between trees. Certain areas of the landscape had their own designated uses in my mind: one small flat rock in a shady opening surrounded by tall pines was for sitting on when I wanted to be alone; the edge between the woods and the meadow was for walking along when I wanted to take the long way home and still come out at the far corner of our yard. Over time, I constructed a thickly detailed mental map of those woods, one whose most prominent markings are still legible after thirty-two years' absence. I had gotten my mind around the woods, gotten an imaginative handle on a small piece of nature, converted it into a meaningful object that I could carry around in my head as well as navigate through on the ground. This in its own way represented a conversion of the natural landscape into a thing fitted for human use — if not as obviously domesticated as our back yard, at least a space that I myself had tamed with my head if not with my hands. Just as much as had those shadowy people in the past who had logged off the hillside and dammed the river, I had essentially turned what looked like natural woods into something deliberately shaped and manipulated for human purposes, into a cultural artifact.

While those woods stood for pure unsullied nature to my childhood self, they stand for a different kind of nature to me now, one that is more complex than that earlier view and at the same time equally as stimulating to my imagination. They are a metonym for the rest of the earth's surface in that I doubt that a single inch of that surface does not somehow bear human toolmarks either directly or indirectly, has not been converted, however subtly, into a crafted artifact. Pollutants can be found even in the remotest polar reaches; global climate change affects plant growth and hydrologic cycles worldwide. In our own country, deliberate or accidental reshaping of the landscape has been ongoing since the first humans arrived on the continent; it is difficult to conceive of an inch of the earth's surface that has not at one time been built on, paved, plowed, planted, burned off, flooded, grazed, logged, mined, infiltrated by introduced plant and animal species, or gained mental control of by more subtle means: naming, mapping, surveying, painting, photography. Much recent scholarship has attempted to make the point that, contrary to the way we usually think about it, nature is not an ahistoric unsullied realm held apart from the world of human activity, standing separate and green and pure until people inevitably mess it up; instead, that common view of nature is itself a cultural construction. It takes a deliberate and ongoing effort of the imagination to abstract humans from the natural world and to see the meaning of nature as separate by definition from the meanings of things that people have made and done, and this effort strikes me not only as false to the history of human residence on the land, inaccurate in view of the reasons why the landscape looks the way it does, but also as not even particularly useful or necessary. Indeed, William Cronon has controversially argued that the commonly accepted dualism between humans and nature in fact does more harm than good: if we set aside and venerate particular pieces of the landscape as "wilderness," then we implicitly write off the rest of the landscape as irrevocably cultural, surrendered to human influence, not worth focusing our environmentalist energies on.[6] We all know that *real* nature is out there somewhere, on the other side of the line, and so we may as well just continue abusing the landscape that's on our side, secure in the knowledge that we still have wilderness to go visit whenever we want.

Do not get me wrong: to say that "wilderness" is an invented idea, and that there is no such thing any more as virgin land that has never been altered by human activity, does not mean that the cause is lost, nature doesn't exist, and we may as well sign over all the national parks to the oil companies. Human might is manifest everywhere, but might does not make right in this sphere just as it does not anywhere else. The benefits that people receive from visiting — or even simply thinking about — lands lightly touched by human hands are not invalidated by the fact that humans have laid their hands there, nor should those hands be allowed to do any more damage to the earth than they already have. And that damage is real, widespread, and lasting. In 1989, in fact, Bill McKibben threw up his hands and proclaimed "the end of nature," arguing that, because of the inescapable influence of human activity over the surface of the planet, nature as we have always pictured it and thought we have known it — wild, pristine, apart from humans — no longer exists. Because of increased atmospheric gases, even "temperature and rainfall" are "in part a product of our habits, our economies, our ways of life. . . . The world outdoors will mean much the same thing as the world indoors, the hill the same thing as the house."[7] McKibben's view, like mine, also sees the line between the domesticated back yard and the shaggy green woods up the hill as having been erased, but to particularly chilling and distressing effect: the woods have been co-opted, overrun, their wildness drained out of them. The most spectacular and awful examples of environmental change and degradation are conceptually no different from the most subtle and easily overlooked, and a quick look around the American landscape reveals that the idea of nature having been converted into an artifact is in many cases nothing to be proud of. Given our dualistic view of nature and culture, poor Donald Hefferon seems to have sent himself on a wild goose chase: there is no more nature up there, or anywhere else for that matter.

And yet, I wonder if it's possible to turn that idea around. Maybe the fact of human shaping doesn't mean that nature doesn't exist anymore but that nature needs to be redefined: it is not absent but *everywhere*, close to home as much as in remote wilderness areas, in the city as well as in the countryside. Perhaps it seems defeatist to think of

Big Trees & Back Yards

nature as an artifact, tantamount to admitting that the occupying army has won, but I believe that thinking in that way is more faithful to the history of the landscapes around us, and ultimately need not change their meaning drastically: does the world really look all that much different to you now after having read this essay? Will you enjoy the woods less, feel less exhilarated by the sight of a mountain or the movement of wind over prairie grass? Perhaps such a shift of vision can help break down the potentially pernicious separation we maintain between humans and nature, help complicate the widespread beliefs that the really important and valuable nature is distant and spectacular rather than immediately under our feet, and erase the borders between nature and culture in ways that make us more attentive to our impact on every inch of the planet. If we begin to see ourselves and the natural world as everywhere intermingled, then doesn't it make sense that we should be better able to locate nature within ourselves as well as to identify our impact on nature, to see these conventionally distinct spheres as seamlessly joined and to therefore possibly change our aggressive behavior toward a world of which we are an irreducible part? Nature, it turns out, isn't over there across the backyard frontier: our physical and imaginative encounters with nature can and should begin in the back yard itself. We don't have to travel far from home to find a field for our caring; all we have to do is walk out the door. That's where our connection with the planet begins, and that's where a mutually healthy relationship with the planet begins.

I currently have a relentlessly historical back yard. Many figures other than mine have preceded me there, and their minds and hands have shaped its surface in ways that are still clearly visible. I've owned my house for two years, and at eighty-four years old it's the oldest house on the street; in 1913, the drawbridge leading over the river from Portland was completed, placing more land within easy commuting distance of the city, and by 1917 suburban development had overtaken the agricultural lands to the south of the bridge, lands that soon started sprouting bungalows instead of crops. My lot was once part of an apple orchard; three living trees and five stumps stand in the back yard in an evenly spaced pattern that includes the trees and stumps in the neighbors' yards as well. Thus I live in a prime example of the early suburbanization of America, the conversion of working landscape into residential and aesthetic landscape. The trees and stumps are surrounded by grass, which as I write is showing the effects of a dry summer. I tell myself that I am philosophically opposed to watering and fertilizing and generally doing much more to the lawn than mowing it, which may be another way of saying that I am cheap and lazy. Still, I do keep the lawn shorn, demonstrating some sort of allegiance to the national aesthetic that ordains that houses, even in places where water is much scarcer than it is in Maine, must be surrounded by grass and that grass must be kept neat and presentable, tame and carpetlike rather than shaggy and weedy and suspiciously natural. Around the edges of the carpet, though, various kinds of greenery grow in luxuriant, riotous abandon, and while I dutifully attack the grass on a regular basis I'm content to let this other green life flourish largely unmolested, once again out of principle or inertia. Near the back deck, a badly overgrown tangle of grape vines, the remnants of a former arbor, mingles with lilac bushes; near a side fence and a concrete slab where a garage once stood, thick hardy bamboo introduced here God knows when — it's certainly not native to Maine — grows so fast you can almost witness it getting bigger by the moment. (Actually, on the occasions when I've tried to dig it up, I've found that its roots are so deep and big that I suspect it of having grown straight through the center of the earth from Asia.) My entire back yard is a historic document, a record of domesticated and weedy plants introduced into the local ecological community from elsewhere, of changing land uses, of some of middle-class American culture's preferred ways of seeing and interacting with the surface of the earth. And I suppose it's also a record of domination in its way, of agriculture succeeded by suburban homeownership, of a once-continuous landscape carefully measured and surveyed and parceled out in small privately held pieces, of the monoculture of apples followed by the monoculture of grass, of humans deliberately or accidentally leaving non-native plants behind them wherever they go.

My favorite part of the yard, though, is a small rectangular strip at the very end of the lot, against the back fence. The ground here had evidently once been cleared, why I don't know; perhaps an earlier resident had planted a garden there. Now, however, that ground supports a thick vigorous tangle of plant life, a tiny landscape that, despite its location and its history, still looks fundamentally natural and wild. Much of that landscape right now is taken up by raspberry canes, that being one of the first plants that characteristically moves into cleared

Big Trees & Back Yards

and abandoned ground in this part of New England. A couple of small aspen trees have also taken hold, along with some bittersweet vines and a range of other plants that lie outside my feeble and limited stock of botanical knowledge. I can look out the window of my second-story writing room and witness ecological succession taking place before my eyes, land that people have used being allowed to revert to whatever happens to end up growing there. Patterns run throughout our lives, and I am back where I began: gazing across a mowed lawn to the natural, wild lands beyond.

And yet, I know just how artificial that little strip of wildness is. It wouldn't be there at all if the ground that supports it hadn't been disturbed in the first place, and humans have added and subtracted so many plants in the local ecosystem (as in all local ecosystems) that its current appearance is likely far different from the way a similar piece of ground would have looked four hundred or more years ago. It's an artifact; an accidental artifact, to be sure, but one that humans still played a fundamental role in shaping and creating. So I look at the green space beyond this back yard differently from the way I used to look at the one in New Milford: it no longer represents where culture ends and nature begins, but is itself a product of human activity. The line between the grass and the raspberry plants is no longer an abrupt and rigidly patrolled frontier, but rather a zone of transition between two places where the marks of cultural process are more or less obvious, more or less intensive. The same history encompasses both sides of the line. At the same time, though, zones of transition work both ways, and what looks from one direction like a continuum from more to less culture may look from the other direction like a continuum from less to more nature. If both sides of the line encompass history, they also encompass green life that, even if it has been influenced by humans, can still be — and should be — noticed, respected, learned from, and lived with. We don't occupy foreign countries on opposite sides of an impermeable border; this back yard belongs to both of us.

If I ever lose sight of this joint occupancy, I'm reminded of it every time I catch sight of the woodchuck who also lives back there. I don't grow vegetables, so it doesn't bother me and I'm content to live and let live, and I think it feels the same. I know where both ends of its burrow are as well as its midtunnel escape hatch in the middle of the grassy yard, and knowing this makes me realize that what to me is a lawn that must be mowed is to it a comfortable underground home, a notion that renders my suburban homeownership pretty irrelevant; surrounded by both green and furry life, I'm just the guy whose name is on the deed, a fact that they neither know nor care about. I occasionally see the woodchuck lumbering and nibbling its way across the lawn, and as I look around I don't seen any borders between us. I give it a neighborly nod: woodchuck, I say, we're all in this together.

❧⚘☙

Almost a year has passed since I wrote the first part of this essay, and I am looking out the window of my writing room at my back yard once more. In many ways, the scene seems to have changed very little if at all over the past several months: the raspberry canes are once more bearing fruit, the grass still grows until some vestigial sense of responsible homeownership goads me into giving it a trim, the clumps of bamboo are still maddeningly vigorous. Undoubtedly the trees and bushes have grown a little taller since last year, new green shoots are gaining a foothold here and there, the old apple tree stumps have decayed a bit more on their way to becoming soil, but these changes happen at such a slow rate and with such subtlety that they do not register in my visual experience of the landscape. I haven't seen the woodchuck lately, though; perhaps it died over the winter, or perhaps it decided it didn't like living next to me and moved into a better neighborhood, one where people have the decency to plant convenient, tasty vegetable gardens. Its absence aside, the view from the back window looks virtually the same as it always has at this phase of the year, offering a vision of a green world that seems reassuringly constant, resistant in some fundamental way to the passage of time.

With one major exception. This year, when I look out the window I can see much more of the back yard than I could before: a large branch of one of the apple trees that used to arc across my field of vision is no longer there. Last January, a massive ice storm bulled its way across central and southern Maine, coating the landscape and the things in it with insupportably heavy shells of ice, tearing down branches if not entire trees, dropping electrical lines to the ground, leaving people without light and heat and water for up to two weeks. I actually was not affected by the major storm; the strip of land immediately along the coast, in which I live, received more liquid rain than frozen precipitation, so while my trees did receive a thin shell of ice, it wasn't enough to cause any damage. A couple of weeks later, though, in the sort of event that could almost convince you that nature does indeed possess a sick sense of humor, another ice storm moved up the coast, hitting only those southern Maine communities that had escaped unscathed the first time. Sitting in a silent chilly house after having awakened to a dark and lifeless bedside clock and its accompanying feeling of annoyance and frustration, I heard a sound I'd never heard before, a ripping, shattering combination of rending fiber and breaking glass. Then eerie silence again, followed a short time later by a repetition of the same sound. I looked out the window and saw a heap of wood lying on the ground near the house where a heap of wood had not been before; when I went outside later, I confirmed that two of the three main branches off the trunk of the old apple tree nearest the house had collapsed under the weight of the ice they bore. The entire visual character of the back yard was oddly changed: it seemed more open, more barren somehow, as the interplay of wood and shadow overhead was replaced by nothing but sky. I had always liked the embowering feeling that the overarching leaves and branches had created in that part of the yard during the summer, and felt angry at the loss, knowing that I would miss an aesthetic experience that, I now realized in the moment of its vanishing, I valued very much in my daily life. And I do miss it. The remaining part of the tree is still alive, but it arcs away from the house rather than shading the grass near the back deck, and as I turn my head from my computer now and look out my window my visual experience is very different from what it used to be. I can see more of the yard and sky, more of that green landscape that appears to my casual eye to be unchanged from last year and the years before, but I can see these things now only because of one very fundamental change that occurred in the back yard with a haunting crashing sound in a few seconds last January.

Events like the Ice Storm of '98, as it's now known in Maine, remind us in a particularly dramatic way that any sense of constancy and timelessness that we may be inclined to read into a landscape is misleading and illusory. When we look at nature, we are looking directly at time, not at the absence of time; far from comprising a realm exempt from history, each natural landscape stands as the unique product of its own tangled history, a process of ceaseless change over both the immediate and the long term. Nature is endlessly, unpredictably dynamic, and any scene that falls within our vision can best be understood as a freeze-frame glimpse of a very different looking past landscape transmogrifying into a very different looking future land-scape. A meteorological phenomenon such as an ice storm or a hurri-cane provides a vivid example of how one particular time-bound event can completely alter a landscape's short-term history, scrambling its surface, evicting some biotic populations and inviting others in, so that the way that landscape looks in the future is far different from how it would have looked if the storm had simply blown out to sea. My back yard isn't the only place in Maine that lost tree branches, of course; thousands of acres of wooded terrain were affected across a broad band of the state, and those acres are even now transforming — I was going to say "healing," but that implies that they are on their way back to looking just like they did before, as your arm does after it's gotten a cut or scrape, and that the ice storm somehow constitutes an injury, a hiatus from health and normal function. Ice storms and hur-ricanes have happened in the past, however, and will continue to hap-pen in the future, and so it seems unnecessarily anthropomorphic to say that Maine's forests are "injured"; they are simply forests that have had happen to them one of the sorts of things that have *always* hap-pened to forests. Disturbance is to be expected in wooded terrain, and by no means are all traumatic disturbances in natural landscapes caused by humans. Maine's forests are now simply undergoing the processes that always occur after a disturbance of this magnitude, and those processes may not necessarily lead over the next decade to the growth of forests that look virtually indistinguishable from the ones that blanketed the landscape before the storm.

In the short term, certainly, the green world in much of Maine has been turned upside down. The most obvious visual changes are those that I experienced in my back yard: the loss of branches and entire trees, the absence of obvious things that used to be there. With these losses comes further change; removing bits of the forest is not simply like snipping people out of a group photo with scissors, but instead has effects on the entire biological makeup of the surrounding land-scape.[8] The downed wood on the forest floor, for example, provides habitat for a variety of insect and animal species, which may in turn provide food for yet further species, so that the altered forest comes to harbor new populations and combinations of fauna that it did not when it was built differently. The new gaps in the forest canopy let in more light to the forest floor, enabling the growth of plant species that favor sunny conditions; new trees will grow tall in these gaps, nurturing more shade-tolerant species beneath their canopies, species that may eventually outgrow and shade out the earlier growth in their turn as the structure and the appearance of the forest continue to change over time. While observers may be inclined to mourn the loss of forest trees, as I mourn the loss of part of my apple tree, the forest they miss looked the way it did only because of past disturbance — storms, clearance by humans, a combination of the two—and it will continue to develop into a new forest, different in appearance perhaps but equally pleasing to the eye. Last year's forest was a sliver, frozen in time, of a long, ongoing dynamic process, just as is this year's collection of snags and litter. And the transition from the former to the latter emphasizes that landscapes can be transformed literally overnight — that, just as in human history, some significant events in a landscape's natural history can be precisely dated.

At the same time, landscape change takes place at a variety of time scales, and just as my back yard or a forest full of ice-downed branches reveal obvious alterations that take place over the course of a single day and press themselves insistently on the observer's attention, so do other landscapes bespeak much larger changes that occur over much longer periods of time, or that happened long in the past. One recent November, after twenty-four years' cumulative residence in New England as both a child and an adult, I finally visited Cape Cod for the first time. Writers from William Bradford to Robert Finch had familiarized me with many aspects of the Cape's history and topography as they had known it over the last four hundred years; now, experiencing the landscape directly for the first time, setting aside its literary overlay as best I could, I was fascinated by what felt to me to be the tenuousness of its physical fabric, by its exposure and ephemerality. Certainly Cape Cod's is a well-settled landscape, and its status as the place where Bradford's Puritan company first set foot on North American soil has given it an air of great antiquity, establishing it as a significant physical origin point in Euro-American history. And yet it was clear to me that the land that underlies that human history and the present-day built environment wants to move. The sand dunes that threaten to encroach on the highway into Provincetown are an obvious sign that, left unimpeded, the winds that blast this exposed spit of land would quickly reshape its contours into something new; the distinctive hooked shape of the end of the Cape is itself a sign that alongshore ocean currents are doing the same thing, moving sand from one place and depositing it somewhere else, gradually altering the shape and length of the peninsula. If storms rebuild landscapes in the short term, erosion does the same thing in the long term; this sandy cradle of New England and American history has a natural history of its own, one that dwarfs the span of years from Bradford's visit until mine.

As I wandered up and down the hills of Truro, where I was staying, I couldn't get over the knowledge not only that I was walking around on something that was moving, or at least trying to move, but that I was spending my Thanksgiving weekend on what was little more than a big heap of sand and gravel that had been left behind in recent geological time by a glacier — rather an impermanent foundation for someone used to living on the famously rockbound coast of Maine. Cape Cod is a terminal moraine marking the farthest point reached by the Wisconsinian Ice Sheet before it began retreating about thirteen thousand years ago, the most recent of several episodes of continental glaciation in the earth's geologic history; ironically, one of the oldest places in Euro-American history is among its youngest pieces of land. Here too is another aspect of the landscape's long-term changefulness: millennia ago, a glacier completely altered the face of the land in this place, covering the surface with a thick layer of ice, eradicating the life that had been there previously, building new landforms in the process both of its advance and its melting (the Great Lakes as currently configured are a prominent example of another glacial creation, as are Long Island and the offshore islands of southern New England); then, as it withdrew, the landscape changed further, with the climate warming as the ice withdrew, thereby enabling the successive establishment of different types and communities of plant life over periods of centuries as ice gave way to tundra and tundra changed to boreal and then temperate forest in the latitudes of New England.

None of this change would have been obvious from day to day or year to year, of course; as Mark Twain found out when he tried to travel in the Swiss Alps via moving glacier — "I stood there some time enjoying the trip, but at last it occurred to me that we did not seem to be gaining any on the scenery"[9] — those big blocks of ice don't move very fast. But the vicinity of what we know today as Massachusetts looks very different now from the way it looked in previous phases of our postglacier era, as well as from its appearance before the ice sheet arrived — and not only because the glacier created the Cape, but because the nature of the forest cover today is different from what occupied the land before the ice bore down on it. Again, the landscape did not really "heal" to its previous condition once the ice melted, resuming once more its exact preglacial forest cover: as ecologist Daniel Botkin points out, "Pollen records from England, where the history of the trees has been studied for six interglacial periods, show that the pattern of migration of species does not repeat itself from one ice age to another." He argues that the evidence is similar for North America, and he concludes, as I do, "that nature undisturbed is not constant in form, structure, or proportion, but changes at every scale of time and space. The idea of a static landscape . . . must be abandoned, for such a landscape never existed except in our imagination."[10] As we walk around on the Cape today, or anywhere in forested New England for that matter, we are looking at scenes that are unprecedented in the landscape's long-term history, both in their geologic form and in the composition of the green life that they sustain; we are looking at what is only the current phase in a process of endless dynamic change, which means that the far future will see yet new landscapes. I'm not nervously looking over my shoulder, waiting for the next glacier to pop into view on the horizon, but I also remember the old joke about the New England farmer being teased by the tourist. The tourist remarks that the farmer's field is sure full of stones. The farmer allows that that's true. The tourist asks where all the stones came from. The farmer says, "Glacier brought 'em." The tourist says, "Glacier, eh? So where's the glacier now?" The farmer replies, "Went back for more stones." I think the farmer is right.

🦋

If in this chapter I'm writing primarily about small places that I've seen and walked through in my life — a back yard, a patch of woods, the hills of a Cape Cod town — it's because I'm trying in this book to think about the way that people experience natural landscapes in their daily living: by glancing out the window, by taking a walk, by driving down the road, by seeing and looking. I'm trying to think about nature on the small scale in which people confront it every day, a scale limited by the frame of a window or windshield, the direction of a path and the spring in their legs, the nearness of the horizon. If I want to say something about the meaning and interpretation of nature, that is, I want to try to do so not in the abstract but at the spatial scale and through the modes of encounter by which people habitually experience nature. At the same time that I'm framing my inquiries within a human spatial scale, though, I want to also call attention to something important that people *don't* see within that scale. I want to try to confound another central aspect of human experience with nature by getting beyond the *temporal* scale in which we habitually encounter the natural world: the immediate moment. Unlike a building, say, or an obviously crafted landscape like a farm field or a formal garden, natural landscapes tend not to bear signs of origins or histories; they cannot be dated according to their style, have no obvious toolmarks or symmetries or flourishes. Being "natural" instead of "cultural," they look like they simply developed the way they did according to physical and biological processes, through the action of water and sunlight, of rainfall and erosion and photosynthesis. It seems not to make sense to think about where the small-scale landscapes that we encounter "came from" in anything but evolutionary or geological terms; "nature" is what exists, and has always existed, until cultural things come along to replace it. We tend not to think of natural landscapes as historical, as having pasts fundamentally different from their presents, as being traceable to origins. And yet, as I am trying to suggest, any landscape that we see or traverse is the result of a temporal process, a cumulative response to a series of events and disturbances both large and small. By restoring a sense of time to the natural places that we encounter on a human scale, we gain a fuller understanding of just what it is we're looking at when we're looking at nature — an understanding, I will argue, that has deep implications for many areas of human thought and action that take "nature" as their focal point.

As I've been thinking about these issues, I've found that rephotography projects provide a particularly striking means for contemplating the presence and meaning of time and history in natural landscapes. In the process of rephotography, the photographer tries to duplicate as closely as possible the viewpoint and conditions of a photograph taken in the past, positioning the camera as closely as possible to the original photographer's camera position, bringing the same segment of earth within the viewfinder, even taking the photograph on the same day and at the same time of day if possible. The resulting photograph pairs, while providing documentation of a particular landscape at two different times, also allude to something greater and more intriguing: they speak subtly of the time that has passed between them, the intervening decades and the changes that those decades have wrought on the land. Taken separately, each photograph captures a view of a landscape only as it existed at the moment of its taking, the sort of immediate vision with which each of us confronts the world around us every day; taken together, they show a dynamic landscape, one in which alteration is intrinsic, even if only subtly. Rephotographer Mark Klett has referred to his photographic pairs as being "like single frames picked from a time-lapsed film; when they are viewed in succession they give the appearance of time in motion, of continuous change." In Klett's view, his photographs "seem to extend beyond their own time frameworks and refer to an intervening period without actually describing a specific course of events."[11] *Some* course of events has intervened between past and present, though, and that seems to be precisely the point that rephotography reveals and reinforces — in nature, something is *always* happening: some sort of "movement," in the words of Klett's partner JoAnn Verburg, "the growth, development, and dissolution that occurred after the [original] photographers made their pictures."[12] Much of this movement is slow, perceptible over decades rather than days, but taking in visual evidence from beyond our immediate experience in nature helps us realize that the workings of time are an inherent part of any landscape.

Most published American rephotography projects focus on the West, primarily because government and military surveys in the nineteenth and early twentieth centuries provided an ample supply of photographs to compare with present-day landscapes. Klett's "Second View" project, for example, rephotographed dozens of scenes taken by government photographers in what are now the states of Colorado, Arizona, New Mexico, Utah, Wyoming, and Idaho in the 1860s and 1870s. Other western projects, such as Peter Goin's rephotographs in his book *Stopping Time*, examine a landscape that was not visited by any of the major nineteenth-century surveys but that nevertheless has been extensively photographed over time by a variety of professionals and amateurs — in Goin's case, Lake Tahoe.[13] (The best example of a project that focuses in large part on rephotographing eastern scenes, Thomas and Geraldine Vale's *U.S. 40 Today*, follows the route taken by George Stewart in his 1953 book *U.S. 40* and thus focuses almost exclusively on changes in the roadway itself and in its roadside built environment; unlike the nineteenth-century surveyors of the American West, Stewart traversed a world that had been obviously and extensively humanized long before he got there.)[14] The most immediate and eye-catching scenes in Klett's and Goin's photograph pairs are those in which there has been an obvious cultural intrusion, the addition of a blatant artifact built by people in the intervening decades: an interstate highway where no transportation path had existed before, a house standing scant feet from where the original camera placement had been — or, as is often the case in Goin's pictures of the long-settled and long-visited Tahoe region, a bigger and better road replacing a more primitive one, or a cluster of casinos having displaced a small humble settlement. Nevertheless, many of the pairs that these photographers present seem at first glance to be unchanged, different printings from the same negative. Only a closer view and a more painstaking comparison reveals some sort of movement, some addition to or subtraction from the scene: a fall of rock, a vanished tree, a denser growth of scrub. While human beings have been busy in the foreground, the background seems almost constant, exempt from their activities, changed only by gradual biological and geological processes.

The Canyon Revisited: A Rephotography of the Grand Canyon, 1923/1991, by Donald L. Baars and Rex C. Buchanan with rephotography by John R. Charlton, is a particularly interesting example of a western American rephotography project (figs. 1 and 2). The older photographs in Charlton's pairs were taken on a 1923 expedition down the canyon led by Claude H. Birdseye, chief topographic engineer of the U. S. Geological Survey, the goal of which was to map the canyon and survey for potential dam and reservoir sites. At the time of this expedition, only twenty-nine Americans had ever traveled as far down the canyon as Birdseye and his men went; thus, "preceded by so little river traffic, Birdseye's survey crew traveled a canyon untouched except by American Indians who had visited there for centuries,"[15] and their photographic record provides a valuable benchmark for assessing changes that have come to the canyon floor between then and now, when some twenty thousand people travel the canyon by boat and raft each year.[16]

Despite the density of modern river traffic and the canyon's popularity as a tourist destination, on the surface the 1991 photographs imply that cultural influence on the landscape has been very slight, limited to some footprints on beaches where rafting parties have camped

1. Algonkian Gorge above Hance Rapid, August 16, 1923. Courtesy R. C. Moore Collection, KU Archives, Spencer Research Library, University of Kansas.

overnight. Aside from the book's first picture, which now shows the Navajo Bridge spanning the upper canyon, built intrusions on the landscape are absent. Instead, the photographic pairs seem to reveal natural change taking place on two different time scales. The rock faces of the canyon are an insistent presence in each picture, and geologist Baars comments that "geologic change has been negligible since 1923,"[17] there being an "almost complete lack of change in gross aspects of canyon geomorphology";[18] the lithic strata of the canyon rise and fall and dissolve on a schedule infinitely slower than anything that two photographs taken over a span of sixty-eight years could suggest. The obvious changes have taken place immediately along the banks of the Colorado, beneath the impassive rock. Beaches have eroded along the canyon walls, plant life has taken root and grown; whatever change has occurred is a simple function of moving rivers doing what rivers do when they encounter soft malleable materials, of the normal interaction of seeds and water and sunlight.

And yet, as the book's authors emphasize, these changes are ultimately an effect of a huge cultural intrusion into the canyon landscape that took place upstream from the sites of their photographs: the

2. Algonkian Gorge above Hance Rapid, September 13, 1991. Courtesy John Charlton, Kansas Geological Survey, University of Kansas.

building of the Glen Canyon Dam in 1963. Before the dam plugged and controlled the river, annual spring floods regularly tore down the Colorado, scoured the banks of vegetation up to the high-water marks, and replenished beaches by moving sediment from the bed of the river onto its banks. Since 1963, the river's flow has been carefully regulated, with small daily fluctuations being geared toward meeting the power demands of the many western cities and towns that depend on Glen Canyon Dam for electricity; natural flooding has been all but eliminated, and the river's flow never comes remotely close to reaching the high-water marks of the freshets of the past. The impact on canyon beaches has been dramatic: not only does the dam impound the sediment that the Colorado would normally have carried into the canyon, depleting the supply of beach-building sand, but the river below the dam both eats away its own beaches to meet its sediment-carrying capacity ("In human terms, the Colorado River 'wants' to carry a certain amount of sediment"[19]) and never moves fast enough to keep the sand that it does carry from settling to the riverbed instead of being stirred up and redeposited along the river's sides. As a result, not only have beaches narrowed or vanished since Birdseye's crew came down the river — actually, since 1963 — but, in the absence of scouring floods, plants have been able to take root and thrive in places along the banks where they would have been forcefully uprooted in the past. (Ironically, the most aggressive plant revealed by the 1991 photographs is tamarisk, a tree not even native to the region but introduced by humans; in a landscape ultimately shaped by human activity, the dominant green component is present only as a result of human activity.) Yes, beach erosion and plant growth are natural processes, but this particular river moves sand in the way it does only because its flow is rigorously controlled by humans; these plants exist only because the conditions for their propagation and survival are ultimately set by the people whose hands are on the dam's valves. Despite the lack of obvious new cultural features, Baars and Buchanan conclude that, given the state of the canyon's flora and riparian topography, "in the brief time since Birdseye and company traversed the Colorado, human impact has been dramatic,"[20] even if that impact is indirect. The Colorado is a tamed river, made to do what people tell it to do, and the canyon's life and landscape have been forced to adjust accordingly. The river and its banks are handmade things in an important sense, artifacts shaped by human tools, showing everywhere along their length the evidence of human agency and intention.

The Grand Canyon is thus a landscape of forceful and insistent ironies. Vacationers trek to the floor of the canyon to view a fantastic geological wonder, the product of millions of years of erosion, the ultimate embodiment of nonhuman nature;[21] when they glimpse the river, though, they actually see something that has been carefully engineered, about as devoid of human influence as the water that comes out of their faucets at home. Claude Birdseye and his crew were among the first white Americans to see and travel on the Colorado through the canyon, at a time when it could legitimately be called pristine; given the dam-locating purpose of their survey, the Glen Canyon Dam and its effects seem eerily and causally related to the photographs they took, with Charlton's 1991 pictures not only showing changes from the earlier photographs but documenting differences that can be interpreted as a historical outgrowth of the actions of the men who took them and their government colleagues who advanced their work in later years. In late March and early April of 1996, a further change took place in the canyon landscape, as the Department of Interior sanctioned a week-long release of flood-level waters from

Glen Canyon Dam precisely to undo some of the effects of the dam's presence: to rebuild beaches, scour riverbanks, and break up debris jams caused by flash floods from the canyon's tributary creeks, actions that would improve habitat and breeding conditions for the canyon's native fish and other fauna — while also, of course, improving navigation and creating better campsites for rafters. (Many species of fish in the river not only need shallow pools behind sandbars to spawn in, but also relatively warm water; since the dam releases water from the bottom of its reservoir, Lake Powell, instead of from the top, the water temperature in the canyon below the dam is a constant forty-five degrees — as controlled as the flow of the river.) Some journalistic coverage of the artificial flood attempted to convey the impression that natural conditions had been restored to the canyon, at least temporarily — as in one article that stated that "concerns about adverse effects on the Grand Canyon's ecosystem prompted an interagency team of scientists to play Mother Nature with the depleted river,"[22] or another that discussed "the possibility of regulating the riparian environment by imitating the course of nature"[23] — but the scientists involved recognized that their activities were anything but natural, that they were engineering a solution to problems caused by the unforeseen consequences of past engineering; in the words of U. S. Geological Survey scientist Julia Graf, "the river is never going to be like it was before the dam."[24] The flood could not be seen as a resurgence of nature, that is, but only as an adjustment or fine-tuning of an already modified system.

Interestingly, the debate over whether or not to implement the flood revealed one further irony: some environmentalists expressed concern because they feared that the flood might damage the habitats of certain endangered species of birds and snails in the canyon, species that, in some cases, had "come to rely on vegetation that spread down to the river after the end of the regular floods."[25] In other words, in the years since 1963 an entirely new ecosystem had been created in the canyon, with the dam-caused alterations to the canyon bringing with them habitats for species and groups of species who might not have been able to survive there otherwise. The state of nature in the canyon had changed greatly since Birdseye saw it in 1923, and a decision to release floodwaters thus amounted to little more than having one humanly shaped configuration and interaction of water and flora and fauna and mineral deposits replaced by another. One group of scientists has tried to rationalize the effects of the flood (and possible regular controlled flooding in the future) on the new populations of endangered species by interpreting it within the larger context of natural processes, downplaying its environmental effects on the current canyon by arguing that "floods were part of the natural cycle of the Colorado River in the past, and many species, both common and endangered, have adapted to this process as long as there has been a Grand Canyon — for about five million years."[26] Out of those five million years, though, only since 1996 has that process been controlled by someone sitting in the control room of a dam with his finger on a button. The new species in the canyon are occupying a niche opened and held open by humans, living in a landscape that, despite its natural appearance, is fundamentally cultural and artifactual.

Thinking about the bottom of the Grand Canyon as being in some measure an artificial thing is sobering — if we can't contemplate a nonhuman world there, of all places, is there any place left where we can? Even those all-but-unchanged hillsides of scrubby vegetation in the backgrounds of western American rephotographic pairs may demand another look: in discussing the history of vegetation change in the remote southeastern Arizona borderlands, for example, Conrad Bahre concludes that "any attempt at understanding vegetation dynamics must begin with the assumption that the landscape has been disturbed until it can be demonstrated that the assumption is false"[27] — and, further, "that the most conclusive, long-term directional changes . . . have resulted from sustained and/or catastrophic human disturbances," including grazing, woodcutting, fire suppression, agricultural clearing, logging, construction of irrigation works, and the intentional or accidental introduction of exotic plants.[28] If this is true of the seemingly wild West, the suspicion grows that my various New England back yards are not the only places where it is futile to separate "nature" from "culture," to think of them as separate places or categories of places. Everywhere on this continent, we see the intentional or accidental effects of human activity. When we look at what we think of as a natural landscape — at the bottom of the Grand Canyon, in the middle of an Arizona desert — we look at a scene that has grown and been shaped as it has because of conditions that humans have set in the past and present. When we look at nature, we are looking at more than nonhuman processes of growth and decay, of weather and erosion, and we are looking at more than a single moment in the dynamic passage of time. We are looking at a world that we, collectively, have made.

⁂

None of the conclusions that I'm reaching here will be particularly astonishing to scholars in some contemporary disciplines, of course. Ecology in particular is a field that, especially in recent years, has come to understand natural landscapes to be characterized not by stasis but by disturbance and change; it sees and interprets nature as dynamic, as contingent, as depending for its form and appearance from place to place not on the inexorable workings of timeless laws but on the shaping influences of unique historical events, be those events caused by humans or not.[29] For much of this century, though, the consensus view within the field was very different: influenced most notably by the work in the 1920s and 1930s of Frederic E. Clements, ecologists believed that landscapes in different regions developed inevitably to achieve a "climax" condition, depending on such spatial variables as climate and soil type.[30] In this view, all plant communities were believed to grow through predictable stages of succession to a final structure, dominated by certain kinds of trees or plants, which they would maintain indefinitely if left undisturbed. Disturbance, in fact, was seen as more or less unnatural in this model, the exception rather than the rule, a complicating factor in an otherwise smoothly running system but a factor whose effects were ultimately temporary rather than having a fundamental shaping influence on the landscape's further development. That is, if a landscape was disturbed by anything from an ice storm to a group of men with chain saws and bulldozers, once the disturbance ceased the landscape would gradually undo the effects of the traumatic event, growing once more through its predictable successional stages to its determined climax. Given enough time, according to this model, it would be as if the disturbance had never occurred; within each piece of land that had been reshaped by people or weather or some other external factor lurked a climax landscape patiently waiting to get out.[31] Nature in this view is fundamentally ahistorical, tending always toward an ideal state not affected by the unique events of linear time, resisting and erasing and undoing history rather than reflecting history.

This is quite a common and comfortable view of nature, and one that has been strongly reflected in popular environmental attitudes. In everyday speech, we talk about respecting and restoring "the balance of nature," a phrase that implies that nature's essential tendency is toward stable points of equilibrium where it will rest forever unless and until something bumps into it hard enough to knock it off-kilter. And since nature is fundamentally balanced by definition, as a matter of logic it can only be non-natural forces that disrupt its equilibrium: that is, the forces wielded by humans. This view received one of its earliest and most influential expressions in this country in George Perkins Marsh's 1864 *Man and Nature*, in which he argued that "nature, left undisturbed, so fashions her territory as to give it almost unchanging permanence of form, outline, and proportion, except when shattered by geologic convulsions; and in these comparatively rare cases of derangement, she sets herself at once to repair the superficial damage, and to restore, as nearly as practicable, the former aspect of her dominion."[32] To Marsh, Mark Klett's western rephotography project would have been pointless, as he understood natural landscapes to be incapable of interpretation or appreciation within human time frames: "in countries untrodden by man, . . . the distribution of vegetable and animal life [is] subject to change only from geological influences so slow in their operation that the geographical conditions may be regarded as constant and immutable."[33] It is the constant rock of the Grand Canyon wall that defines and characterizes nature in this view, not the visible human-made changes taking place on the canyon floor, and Marsh goes on to explicitly exempt humans from nature, to argue that not only their acts but they themselves have no place in our definitions of nature and our understanding of how nature works — that is, through maintaining its timeless balance: "But man is everywhere a disturbing agent. Wherever he plants his foot, the harmonies of nature are turned to discords. . . . The fact that, of all organic beings, man alone is to be regarded as essentially a destructive power, and that he wields energies to resist which, nature — that nature whom all material life and all inorganic substance obey — is wholly impotent, tends to prove that, though living in physical nature, he is not of her."[34]

Marsh's view, with its emphasis on a balanced nature and its placement of humans in an inevitably and unavoidably antagonistic relationship with the natural world, remains familiar today, and it also
bears resemblances to the assumptions guiding much ecological research in recent decades. If "disturbance was thought to be an exceptional occurrence," point out ecologists S. T. A. Pickett and Richard S.
Ostfeld, then "the primary goal of ecological studies could be the understanding of undisturbed systems. As a result, ecologists emphasized pristine and apparently 'natural' systems," ignoring "such systems that were burned or blown down, populations apparently not
regulated internally, managed landscapes," and above all those landscapes most obviously altered by humans: "Humans were often pur-
posely left out of ecology because they introduced multiple states to
systems, acted as disturbance agents, transported materials and or-
ganisms beyond their usual distributions, acted as external regulators
of ecological systems, and prevented orderly, deterministic succes-
sions." Here too humans are specifically and deliberately excluded
from the world of nature, their activities seen as inimical to the functioning of natural systems and processes. To study nature and understand how it works, you have to get as far away from humans as possible, seeking out some remnant of untouched wilderness safely
removed from their fields and factories, their cities and clear-cuts. An
event such as Maine's ice storm would have been interesting only insofar as it could suggest "the return of systems from a disturbed state
to the single point of equilibrium," [35] the effacement of a temporal,
historical event by the return of the climax community, wiping out the
marks of 1998 and replacing them with a green surface of the kind that
had been there for millennia and would continue to be there, temporary disturbances aside, for millennia to come. "History" is a suspiciously human notion, one conventionally applied to areas of specifically human thought and action rather than to the world of
animals, vegetables, and minerals; people can have ideas about nature,
and can behave toward the natural world in changing ways through
time, but, as Alice E. Ingerson has commented, it seems counterintuitive to entertain the notion "that history might exist within nature, as
well as in the relations between nature and culture," or to focus on
"finding history — defined as unique sequences of contingent events
that shape entire social and ecological systems — within both nature
and culture." [36] As traditionally practiced, ecology as a science has

largely excluded contingency and the unraveling of unique temporal threads from its field of inquiry; here, as in its focus on the ostensibly pristine and undisturbed in its definition and study of the natural world, ecology has contributed to the firm separation of nature and culture in our thinking about and experience of the world around us.

Since the mid-1980s, though, ecology as a discipline has seen a fundamental shift in the framework through which it understands and approaches both nature as a whole and the individual landscapes upon which researchers focus in their work, one that Pickett and Ostfeld argue should replace the popular metaphor of "the balance of nature" with a new one: "the flux of nature." "The term *flux* highlights variation, fluidity, and change in natural systems," they point out, "rather than stasis, which is implied by the term *balance*."[37] Ecologists have come to recognize change, disturbance, and unpredictability as intrinsic to natural landscapes, not as anomalous and somehow alien to natural processes, and to attempt to account for it and understand it in their work. As Daniel Botkin summarizes this new ecological view of the natural world in contrast to the one that it replaced, "Wherever we seek to find constancy we discover change. . . . We see a landscape that is always in flux, changing over many scales of time and space, changing with individual births and deaths, local disruptions and recoveries, larger scale responses to climate from one glacial age to another, and to the slower alterations of soils, and yet larger variations between glacial ages."[38] What was previously thought to be a deterministic landscape now appears to contain a large element of chance: succession in any one place, rather than progressing through predictable stages at nature's stately pace, is often influenced by local factors including seed sources, rainfall or drought, the size of the local herbivore population at any one time, the frequency of fire and windthrow, the presence or absence of disease, and other such unpredictable matters. The kind of ground cover that occurs in any one place after disturbance, while certainly influenced by climate and soil type, is thus never a simple matter of clearing the ground and knowing exactly what kind of forest or grassland will be there in a certain number of years; too much can happen to favor one kind of growth over another, to make some plants thrive while others die — and, moreover, something almost always *does* happen. There seems to be no such thing as a stable, finished state of nature, it turns out, because every landscape develops in its own way under the influence of unique historical circumstances, continually in the process of becoming, continually recovering from the most recent disturbance. As ecologist Norman L. Christensen points out, "it is now generally recognized that natural disturbance cycles, involving such agents as fire, wind, or pathogens, are a normal part of most landscapes and that few ecosystems ever achieve a steady-state climax."[39] Large regions may have superficially similar kinds of vegetational cover, but on the ground, on the human scale of visual and kinetic experience, those regions are made up of innumerable small patches of landscape that have been shaped by the unique physical circumstances of time and space — just as a human society, while consistent and describable in the aggregate, is made up of particular individuals, each with his or her own life story. Or perhaps a mosaic provides a better metaphor—a unified composition made up of small, discrete pieces with their own particular sizes, shapes, and colors. And yet natural landscapes are not inert, hard, and lifeless, like pieces of clay or glass. Landscapes live in time, develop in time, have idiosyncratic pasts and unknown and unknowable futures. So do humans, of course, and this commonality provides one way in which we might "see, and discuss, nature and culture as qualitative variations along a single spectrum rather than as an either/or dichotomy," suggests Ingerson, for "history also occurs on both sides of the border."[40]

Current ecological thought and practice blurs this border in one other significant way as well. Botkin describes the case of the Hutcheson Memorial Forest in New Jersey, purchased by Rutgers University in the 1950s and preserved as the sole known remaining virgin forest in the region (purchased by a settler in 1701, it had never been cut, but kept as a woodlot). According to contemporary ecological thinking, the forest was understood to be a climax community, and therefore would remain fundamentally unchanged indefinitely: "As the old trees died, they would be replaced by vigorously growing younger trees, and so on, so that the view of the forest at any one time would be identical to the view at any future time." Contrary to these expectations, though, it became increasingly clear in the 1960s that the forest was in fact changing, its old and dying oak and hickory trees being replaced not by younger versions of themselves but by sugar maple saplings. Scientists eventually determined by examining growth rings on fallen trees that fire, either lightning-caused or set by Native Americans, had been very common in the forest prior to European settlement in 1701, but it had been consistently suppressed in the long time since then. Oak and hickory had predominated in the forest because they were more resistant to fire than sugar maples; now, in the long-term absence of fire, sugar maples were increasing in numbers. "The forest had taken more than 200 years to respond to the suppression of fire in a way that people could recognize," but the change finally became obvious, a change that was ultimately attributable to human agency, to the desire of landowners not to have their property destroyed by fire. Ironically, Botkin concludes, "the forest primeval was revealed as, in part, a human product"— even more so, it turned out, because several exotic plant species not native to North America, let alone New Jersey, were increasingly taking hold in the forest, having been originally brought to this continent to serve primarily as decorative plantings: "Once they were established in the New World, their seeds were transported by natural means — wind, birds, or mammals — and spread into Hutcheson Forest. The future forest would be one that no one had ever seen, dominated by native and introduced maples and dense with exotic species."[41]

Not only did the forest's development confute some of the central tenets of conventional ecological theory, then, but the course of its unexpected changes, as well as its current structure and composition, were directed by human activity; this island of nature in the middle of the eastern megalopolis was revealed to have been firmly shaped by cultural processes. Interestingly, these processes were not direct, the result of immediate physical intervention in the landscape via planting or harvesting or any act of deliberate cultivation or removal; rather, the effects of human hands in the landscape were indirect, the result of deciding not to let a fire burn in the forest but to let the trees remain unmolested, the product of people elsewhere deciding to import and plant new trees and seeds from those trees being disseminated far afield, beyond the scope of deliberate human intention. It is easy enough to find examples of places in this country where people have worked directly on the landscape with their minds and hands, piling earth into new forms, replacing green things with built things, making water go places it had never gone before, cutting down some kinds of plants and deliberately growing and harvesting others. But we could always go someplace where culture didn't hold sway if we wanted to, someplace where landscapes existed apart from our designing minds and our guiding or crippling hands. The example of the Hutcheson

Forest, though, suggests something new: that actions in one place can have distant spatial consequences, that actions in the past can bear strange fruit in the present, that no ostensibly natural place on earth has not been shaped — even if only through a very indirect causal chain, even in ways that are so obscure as to amount only to the substitution of one kind of green life for another — by the hand of human culture.

꽃

In recent years, a growing scientific and historical literature has begun assessing and documenting the effects that human activity has had on North American landscapes and ecosystems. "Human impact on the land is ubiquitous," notes historical ecologist Emily Russell, "although it differs in kind and intensity from one place to another, from one time to another," and this ubiquity "means that it is very difficult, if not impossible, to find systems that are devoid of human influence."[42] The process of altering local environments on this continent began when humans first crossed the land bridge from Asia; Europeans may have believed that they were confronting an untouched wilderness when they sailed across the Atlantic and set foot on the new land mass for the first time, but as William Denevan points out in arguing against what he calls "the pristine myth," "by 1492 Indian activity throughout the Americas had modified forest extent and composition, created and expanded grasslands, and rearranged microrelief via countless artificial earthworks. Agricultural fields were common, as were houses and towns and roads and trails. All of these had local impacts on soil, microclimate, hydrology, and wildlife."[43] Native peoples had reshaped the world around them in a variety of ways: through cultivation, through building, through hunting, and perhaps most extensively through the controlled use of fire. Prior to European settlement, natives in a wide variety of North American settings periodically burned areas of the landscape around them for a variety of purposes: to foster the growth of certain kinds of plants that they could either eat themselves or use to attract game animals; to clear undergrowth from forest floors to make travel and hunting easier; to keep woody growth from encroaching on grasslands, again to foster a favorable environment for hunting. Fire is, of course, set by lightning as well as by humans, and Native Americans had learned to shape the ecosystemic effects of fire to their own purposes; in this sense, the

Big Trees & Back Yards

structure of the Hutcheson Forest may have been just as influenced by humans before European settlement as after, with one artificial fire regime simply replacing another after 1701, both having the goal of guiding the landscape's form in order to best serve the domestic economies of the people who lived within it. Prior to European contact, Native Americans were very skilled at manipulating the environments around them in order to make them fit their needs and desires, to make them produce more of the foods they wanted and make them more efficient to live in, and those manipulations left marks on the physical world around them, unintelligible as those marks may have been to Europeans entering those landscapes for the first time.

Aside from such obviously cultural and hand-wrought features as buildings and earthworks, the aboriginal impact on the North American landscape was subtle rather than obvious, a matter of adjusting extant ecosystems to alter their composition and structure in selected ways rather than eradicating them completely in favor of an imposed cultural vision of the way the world *should* be. As Richard White has written about the Salish populations of what is now Whidbey Island, Washington, "This was a land shaped by its inhabitants to fit their own purposes. . . . Through observation and tradition, Indians altered natural communities to fit their needs without, in the process, destroying the ability of those communities to sustain the cultures that had created them."[44] Like native peoples elsewhere in North America, they had turned their landscape into an artifact of sorts, but it was a matter of rearranging in a limited way the landscape elements that were already there, adjusting their culture to their natural surroundings while also adjusting those surroundings to better serve the needs of their culture. Then, of course, Europeans arrived; they not only accelerated and expanded the pace and scale of environmental alteration, they introduced a new degree of change, intent on reproducing on North American soil the physical and biological world they left behind. Historian Alfred W. Crosby has referred to much of the United States and Canada as a "neo-Europe," marked not only by a climatic similarity to Europe but by a biotic similarity as well, a function of the fact that European settlers, in an ongoing act of what Crosby calls "ecological imperialism," brought their agricultural systems across the ocean with them.[45] Instead of adjusting their cultures to the landscape in which they found themselves, Europeans remade the surface of the continent according to the image of the world that they carried with them in their heads; they imported domesticated animals and food crops, divided the land according to European conceptions of property and agricultural productivity — and, significantly, introduced European pathogens against which native populations had no defenses, decimating those populations and making their occupation of the land much easier than it would have been otherwise. Other introductions, such as weed seeds, were unintended, but were no less influential in changing the face of the landscape; in fact, since weedy plants are best adapted to disturbed and exposed soil, by introducing a system of agriculture based on cleared and plowed land the European settlers guaranteed the success of a wider variety of non-native plant species than they had originally bargained for.[46]

As Euro-American settlement expanded across the continent and as individual communities grew, the surface of the land was cut down, torn up, heavily grazed, or plowed under; as Michael Williams has chronicled, almost all of the eastern forests were cleared at one time or another for agriculture, fuel, and building material,[47] and it has been estimated that 99 percent of the tallgrass prairies in America were lost in the creation of the midwestern agricultural landscape. The land surface has been engineered to create landscapes that topography and climate would not otherwise allow, as in the paradoxical history of standing and flowing water in America — marshes and swamps in the East and Midwest have been ditched and drained to create more farmland, while massive irrigation projects in the West allow cotton to bloom in the desert. In a relatively short time, the North American landscape has been completely transformed from its precontact state as people have looked at it, compared it to the landscape that they brought with them in their heads from some eastern place, brought in their tools and seeds and domesticated animals, and made the world out there match the ideal pattern as closely as they could, getting rid of the unwanted parts and adding new things and combinations of things. In this sense, the whole continent is an artifact, a designed object, a cultural product made out of the selected and manipulated materials provided by nature: water, soil, plant life. Aboriginal peoples may have started this process, but it has exploded in the past several centuries to the point that, as ecologist Gordon G. Whitney concludes, the landscape "represents a blend of the past and the present, of the human environment and the natural environment. The landscape is a historical document, a cumulative record of man's impact on the natural world."[48]

Over the past twenty years or so, and increasingly in recent years, environmental historians have shifted from focusing on the history of ideas about nature and on the origins and development of what we think of as the environmental movement, as in Roderick Nash's classic *Wilderness and the American Mind*, to looking as well at environment as history, to examining the material effects of ideas once they are put into effect in shaping the land itself, to looking at landscape as the end result of a series of historical acts, of culture-bound material behaviors in particular times and places. They trace a reciprocal process, one in which both nature and humans have agency; as William Cronon puts it in his attempt to "locate a nature which is within rather than without history," "Environment may initially shape the range of choices available to a people at a given moment, but then culture reshapes environment in responding to those choices. The reshaped environment presents a new set of possibilities for cultural reproduction, thus setting up a new cycle of mutual determination."[49] Gordon Whitney, in his aptly named *From Coastal Wilderness to Fruited Plain*, provides an overview of this process for temperate North America, while other authors have told similar stories for more focused parts of the country: some good examples include Cronon's work on colonial New England, Timothy Silver's study of the colonial South, Richard White's examination of the landscape history of Island County, Washington, Jack Temple Kirby's book on tidewater Virginia and North Carolina, and Dan Flores's meditation on what he calls the Near Southwest.[50] Most of these studies focus on origins and transitions, on the shift from the aborigine's world to the farmer's, from a lightly touched world to one that became almost completely transformed. Their emphasis is on the work of the mind and the plow and the ax, on the replacement of one ecological complex with another, as a world lightly inhabited by humans was remade into something that was obviously a product of cultural design, a world of buildings and fences and roads, of felled trees and grazed pastures and straight plowed furrows. As such, they focus on worlds that seem more cultural than natural; while their work is informed by the insights of contemporary ecology, as historians they look at the peopled landscape, not at the uninhabited world that lies on the penumbra of settlement, the plains and forests and swamps and mountains and deserts into which the settled world inexorably eats. And yet, as the Hutcheson Forest revealed, even that world is not as contrastive as it might seem, exempted from the bustling cultural transformation going on around it. Some quite untouched looking landscapes turn out to owe their existence directly to human activity, as in the Alcovy River swamps that Stanley Trimble studied in Georgia, the result of sediments washing off of plowed fields and clogging the waterway on the valley floor over the last two centuries, such that "the flora and fauna of these swamps have developed to the point that the swamps are now mistaken to be 'natural' and to be thousands of years old."[51] These swamps were not designed in the way that the fields uphill from them were, of course, but they demonstrate that the cultural manipulation of the landscape may have far-reaching effects elsewhere, creating natural-looking scenes that are ultimately as artificially derived as the worlds that the farmers and loggers and builders have made; the difference is in degree rather than kind. (Even the "natural" landscapes of our national parks are carefully shaped and controlled; some of them had their native white and Indian populations removed in order to foster an impression of untouched "wilderness," and many of them owe much of their appearance today to the work of landscape architects.)[52]

Historical ecologists and landscape ecologists thus supplement the work of environmental historians in demonstrating the ways and extent to which, as Norman Christensen puts it, "even segments of a landscape that have not been directly disturbed are influenced by the human factors affecting surrounding areas."[53] Appearances are deceiving, and recent work takes human impact into account as a matter of course, particularly work that focuses on landscapes at the spatial scale in which people encounter them every day. Landscape ecology is a new field that, as Joan Iverson Nassauer describes it, "investigates landscape structure and ecological function at a scale that encompasses the ordinary elements of human landscape experience: yards, forests, fields, streams, and streets. From the beginning, it has included the insistent and frequently destructive behavior of human beings as essential to understanding."[54] In this view, understanding any landscape becomes impossible without including cultural impacts: to look at a forest or field or stream is to look at the end result of people interacting with their environment just as much as looking at an obviously shaped space like a yard or street is. In this sense, a knowledgeable viewer can essentially "read" a landscape as a historical document, deciphering from its structure and composition the cultural influences, both intentional and accidental, that have intertwined with the local environment to contribute to its present form. Environmental historians account for the ways in which humans have entered North American environments and sculpted them into new built worlds of their own design; historical ecologists and landscape ecologists show us that even those parts of the landscape that we would conventionally describe as "natural" are also shaped by cultural activity — and, moreover, that the process of their shaping is inherent in their form, available for reading by those who know the code. Nature is not only an artifact; nature is a text as well.

Now, I am not an ecologist, nor do I count myself professionally as a historian. The past few pages represent what feels like a very sketchy redaction of reading that I've done recently, reading that corroborates the impressions that I've garnered from my own unremarkable encounters with landscapes that I've known while also shaping my reflections on those experiences. Sensing the presence of the past in nature provides a way of seeing that I find rich and rewarding, increasing the complexity and fascination of my visual and kinetic encounters with the natural world; it also feels more "real" somehow, truer to the way that the landscape developed, more cognizant of the histories that are intrinsic to any piece of the earth's surface. I'm also aware that some environmentalists are uncomfortable with this way of seeing, especially insofar as it sees human disturbance and influence as omnipresent, as inextricably involved in the structure and function of ecosystems. Gordon Whitney notes that "the realization that disturbance is a natural part of the environment and that ecosystems have enormous powers of recovery has led a number of investigators to minimize humankind's effects," with those investigators feeling that "at the worst human disturbances simply mimic natural disturbances." [55] The fear of some is that if human interference is widely believed to be inherent in the natural world, then there can be no logical argument against preventing humans from interfering in their environments in any way that they feel like. Of course, this argument ignores matters of degree: clearly some human impacts are more frequent and severe than others, and therefore to say that a hurricane blowdown and a massive program of clear-cuts are functionally equivalent and morally equal is simply wrong: one is a matter of weather, the other is a matter of choice. Ecosystems have evolved and developed gradually to accommodate fire, windthrow, beaver-caused flooding, and other nonhuman disturbance: the changes that humans have brought to the continent have occurred so quickly and on such a large scale that there has been no possibility of adjustment, so the health of landscapes under heavy assault has no chance to adjust. Nonhuman change does not destroy habitat in the way that so much anthropogenic change has. Still, the objections remain: William Cronon has met fears that the work of historians like him will "point toward a world in which anything goes, in which everything becomes relative to our own ideas and there is no stable ground on which we can hope to make a stand in defending the natural world" — to which he responds that "the answer, of course, is that not everything is up for grabs, and not all ideas or uses of nature are equally defensible."[56] Daniel Botkin reflects that "to abandon a belief in the constancy of undisturbed nature is psychologically uncomfortable. As long as we could believe that nature undisturbed was constant, we were provided with a simple standard against which to judge our actions, a reflection from a windless pond in which our place was both apparent and fixed, providing us with a sense of continuity and permanence that was comforting. Abandoning these beliefs leaves us in an extreme existential position."[57] If we give up nature as a moral touchstone, if there is no pristine and sacred wilderness against which to judge the rightness or wrongness of our actions toward it, what basis is there for ethical behavior toward an admittedly fallen world?

I feel obliged to acknowledge these fears and arguments, both because positions like the one I'm taking here tend to attract them and because I take them very seriously at a time when our environment is under constant and increasing stress and in a national popular and political climate that does not always look very kindly on environmentalism. (Around the time of a recent Maine referendum to put severe limitations on the forest industry's clear-cutting practices, I once saw a bumper sticker that said, "Save a Job — Kill an Environmentalist.") Ecologists answer that, given the human presence in nature and the ill effects that that presence has so often had, informed and sensitive land-use planning and landscape architecture, motivated by what Nassauer calls an "aesthetic of care,"[58] is key to maintaining the ecological health of landscapes in the future — if we live in a humanly shaped world, only further human shaping can fix it. Historians say that

Big Trees & Back Yards

knowing of past abuses and the effects of past thought and behavior will lead toward more responsible habitation in the future. I would add a couple more points to these arguments. First, I believe that acknowledging history, contingency, and disturbance in nature actually increases our moral responsibility toward nature rather than leading to a sort of moral relativism or an absence of ethical obligation. If we believe in a stable, steady-state nature leading to an inevitable point of balance regardless of local disturbance history, then we can basically do anything we want to the land, secure in the knowledge that the landscape will eventually "heal" once we are gone, becoming once more what it had been before we got there. If we understand that our actions have irreversible consequences, though, that the things we do today will live on into the future, influencing not only the landscape but the people who live in that landscape, then we are obliged to think long and hard about what we do before we do it. The ways in which we shape the landscape matter, and they matter long into the future. Nature is historical just as we are, existing in time, deflected by contingency and consequence, and we have to live in the history that we create in the landscape just as we inhabit the individual and collective histories that we forge with our lives.

My second point is more personal — and yet, I hope, more universal as well. In each of the landscapes I've discussed in this chapter, one of the histories I read there is *my* history, one that I hope resonates with those of my readers. While aspects of my sensibility may have changed over time as I move through the world, exploring new patches of green and revisiting old ones, some things have remained constant: the aesthetic delight I've found in nature (very few things are more beautiful than sunlight filtering through leaves in deep forest), the urge I sometimes feel to get out of the house or even out of the city altogether and go hang out with some trees, the companionship — there's no other word — that certain places have provided me throughout my life and that I keep with me always in memory. None of that has changed or been diminished in any way because I've realized that a certain patch of woods wasn't always there, but only grew back when some farmer moved away. *All* of that would change, though, if those woods were cut down, if some imported pest killed the trees, if air pollution turned vibrant green trees to withered brown sticks. Landscapes are not just material objects, explicable by some chronology of events in combination with the local climate and soil, but are presences that matter in human lives; they are experienced not only visually and kinesthetically, but aesthetically and emotionally as well. Seeing natural landscapes as historical, as artifactual, helps me understand them better, to know just what I'm looking at when I'm looking at nature. And it encourages me to put myself into the historical process, to understand myself as just one actor who will help determine what the histories of those landscapes will become, what these artifacts will look like if shaped with care rather than with avarice, violence, or indifference. Anyone who has ever loved a forest, a back yard, or even a single tree should feel the same way.

TWO

Landscape with Figures
Land & Tradition in American Nature Writing

✿✿

I occasionally wonder about what shape American environmental writing and ecocriticism would have taken if Henry Thoreau had decided that, on the whole, he got much more enjoyment from making pencils than from walking around outside, or if he had never developed an interest in writing about his experiences and reflections. To take one notable recent example, Lawrence Buell's sweeping *The Environmental Imagination* adopts Thoreau and his writings as its dominant motif for the simple and unavoidable fact that, to Buell (and to countless others), "no writer in the literary history of America's dominant subculture comes closer than he to standing for nature in both the scholarly and the popular mind."[1] The mind of one representative scholar, Scott Slovic, has taken the same starting point, setting out in *Seeking Awareness in American Nature Writing* to examine certain of "Thoreau's followers in the tradition of American nature writing," finding his legacy so powerful that "virtually all nature writers in Thoreau's wake perpetuate" certain of his practices and patterns of thought.[2] The path is clear: to study American environmental writing, you have to start in or go through Thoreau's Concord, and to write environmental nonfiction, you end up positioning yourself, wittingly or unwittingly, in Thoreau's footsteps. It is even difficult to escape Thoreau when simply enjoying the New England outdoors, at least if your head is stuffed as full of books as mine is: I hike through the Maine woods and find Thoreau everywhere ahead of me, tingeing the landscape with his words and ideas.

While I may see shadowy Henry tramping the trails ahead of me, however, he wouldn't necessarily have been happy had he turned around and seen me following him, at least if we are to take him at his word. As he notes in his essay "Walking," he has a predilection for strolling off "to some portion of the earth's surface where a man does not stand from one year's end to the next,"[3] and here too he sets the tone for subsequent writers and critics: the books and essays that the writers produce, and the interpretations that the scholars derive, tend to be largely unpopulated by humans — or, at least, those people who do occupy the landscapes in question and fall within the authorial sightlines take a decidedly secondary role to the nonhuman nature that the author and, after him or her, the critic has set out to explore and ponder. This comes as no surprise; the job of a nature writer or an ecocritic would seem to be, by definition, to write about flora and fauna, water and rocks, ecosystems and bioregions, and to do so is laudable and necessary. Through this work, perhaps we can learn a few things about improving our selves, our planet, and that planet's future, as when Barry Lopez suggests that humans might "find a dignity that might include all living things" and "bring such dignity to one's own dreams," making their lives "exemplary in some way," through "pay[ing] attention to what occurs in a land not touched by human schemes, where an original order prevails."[4] Moreover, there is a sense of justice in this focus on nonhuman nature: just as the oppressed and dispossessed in human society have increasingly come to find a voice and an advocacy in literature and criticism, so too has the abused and distressed earth gained the opportunity to present its experience, its perspective. Environmental writers give nature a voice, the ability to speak in the face of an exploitative culture; critics take it upon themselves to attend to and interpret that voice. In the context of this literary project, human voices other than the author's come to seem irrelevant at best, suspect or antagonistic at worst.

Here again the trail leads back to Thoreau. Sharon Cameron argues that, in his *Journal*, "Thoreau's descriptions of nature bring us closer to nature than does any other work of writing,"[5] and, moreover, that he is not just writing about nature or describing it closely but is in fact attempting to "voice nature or be nature's voice," to "incarnate its articulating will," a project that amounts to a "subversion of the human."[6] Others have also adopted the conceit that, through the nature writer, nature itself is writing, that the author serves as interpreter or amanuensis to the mute nonhuman world; Paul Brooks's study of "literary naturalists from Henry Thoreau [!] to Rachel Carson," for example, is entitled *Speaking for Nature*,[7] while Stephen Trimble, in the introduction to his nature writing anthology *Words from the Land*, argues that "contemporary natural history writers speak for the earth," that they "choose places to live and then listen to those places," that "what they hear in the earth are the voices of what Henry Beston called the 'other nations' of the planet," and that their literary works are "translations of these voices."[8] There is a sense that humans have done enough talking, not to mention exploiting and befouling; it is time for nature, the "other," to tell its side of the story without any people on stage competing for the microphone.

Of course, in any work of nature writing the author's persona appears either implicitly or as a full-fledged character, one of the two actors in the writer's literary attempt to solve, as Sherman Paul puts it, "the standing problem of our relatedness to nature." To Paul, however, humankind plays a decidedly secondary role in this drama: the nature writer's task is to find not only "how to reenter the world, participate in it, and recover respect for it," but also "how to express the experience and significance of encounters of this kind without, by means of language itself, displacing the world."[9] Nature is to retain center stage; while human language is necessary, the language-using human should try to remain as transparent as possible. Scott Slovic retains a closer focus on the author, examining how nature writers explore "relationships between the human mind and the natural world" and arguing that nature writing is "concerned, and perhaps primarily so, with interior landscapes, with the mind itself."[10] In both of these approaches, the nature writer comes across as primarily an observer or reporter, either of the natural world or of his or her own consciousness (or both)— not as a denizen, not as someone intimately involved with the rhythms of the landscape. Nature must be kept at some distance so it can be watched and learned from; the writer is *among* the creatures and landscapes he or she is writing about, but is not *of* them. Literary scholars by and large seem to concur with this tendency to keep the human separate from the natural; there is a strong sense among both writers and critics that, when we consider and write about nature, we are — and moreover, as a matter of respect and moral obligation, should consciously be — contemplating something that is ineluctably separate from us, a world apart.[11]

Speaking as a resident of New England, however, I find that my ability to keep nature and people conceptually separate is quickly confounded every time I step into the woods. During ten years' residence in Rhode Island, I was a faithful explorer of that tiny state's surprisingly large amount of preserved lands, and it was a common experience on my walks to find ample evidence of prior occupancy and use of the landscape over the last two or three centuries, evidence in the form of stacked or worked stone: walls, foundations, fragmentary dams, collapsed millraces. These episodes were always among the high points of my walks; each time, I would linger over the lithic remains as travelers have always done over ruins, rebuilding a departed community and way of life in my mind — and realizing, moreover, that this piece of land that had been officially set aside as a nature preserve had been in the relatively recent past a working agricultural landscape. What was now labeled, and considered in the public mind, as "nature" had in fact attained its current form only after the strenuous operations of human culture.[12] I have since moved to Maine, but you don't study the environmental history of New England for very long before you learn that up to three-fourths of the region, from Maine to Vermont to Rhode Island and all points in between, had been deforested by the middle of the nineteenth century, and that the trees that now thickly blanket the area are second-growth forest that gradually reclaimed the landscape only after the general failure of New England agriculture and wholesale abandonment of farmland in the mid-1800s.[13] Even northern Maine, which contains almost nothing but trees — which contains whole townships that have never even been named, but are still officially known as Township X, Range Y — has been logged intensively since the earliest days of settlement in the seventeenth century. Virtually all of New England's natural landscapes, even those that appear most wild, bear the direct marks of human involvement and manipulation, subtle though those marks may be. The entire region is a handcrafted cultural artifact.

Once this realization about the nature of nature in New England is made, interpretations and value judgments soon follow, most assuming some sort of conceptual division — an estrangement, an antagonism — between the land and the New Englanders who used that land. The old New England farmers looked upon nature as an object to be exploited ruthlessly, argue the historians — "a resource to be

Landscape with Figures

mined until it was exhausted," in the words of William Cronon;[14] cultivating the same walled-in fields year after year, rarely rotating crops or letting a field lie fallow, they depleted the land's fertility in short order and found themselves unable to compete with the more fecund lands being settled in the Midwest. Since they had neither understood nor respected the land, agricultural failure was seemingly no more than the New England farmers deserved. Today, the Northern Forest of Maine, New Hampshire, Vermont, and upstate New York is a point of grave environmental concern. Much of that land, including all but 5 percent of the forest land in Maine, is owned by private lumber and paper companies who, driven by the bottom line, have recently expanded their reliance on environmentally harmful forestry practices, such as large-scale clear-cutting, and have also increased sales of cleared-off land for second-home development; once more, nature is seen as nothing more than an economic resource, a commodity.[15] In this sort of situation, it is easy to cast humankind as villains, not only separate from but contemptuous of nature. The nature writers are correct, it seems: in considering the landscape and the life within it, why take account of the people in that landscape — the ax-wielding, plow-dragging people — except to denounce them?

Such a broad and critical approach, however, obscures a fact that is important to keep in mind, especially in thinking about the densely and longtime settled East: in a place where nature is inextricable from human life and culture, many individuals and small communities, beneath and between the workings of the corporations, do manage to live on the land in ways that are respectful, sustainable, and — crucially — directed and constrained by the cycles and capacities of the local environment. (Even nineteenth-century New England farmers, to be fair, were not the sworn agents of some vast cultural conspiracy, not cut-and-run industrial agriculturists; while they may have been environmentally blind, they were undoubtedly puzzled and disappointed when their farming traditions gradually failed to support them.) In their recent book about the landscape and people of New England's Northern Forest, journalists David Dobbs and Richard Ober comment that, throughout their interviews and interactions with the men and women who work and hunt in that forest, "we were moved again and again by their care and respect for the land and for their communities, and by their understanding of the vital connections between the two." Even among people whose job it is to harvest trees from the forest, and despite the attitudes and practices of those workers' distant bosses, Dobbs and Ober find noteworthy "the knowledge and care residing in the people who live here, and who struggle each day to use these lands well. Most of these people care deeply about the land. They try to give back more than they take."[16] Such a statement may fly in the face of popular stereotypes concerning residents of America's less-developed lands and their attitudes toward nature, particularly in these days of environmental backlash, "Wise Use" organizations, and grass-roots property-rights movements. As New Hampshire environmentalist Jeff Fair comments, however, "Look. Locals . . . have goals much more similar to the environmentalists than people think. They might have a different idea on how to achieve them, but they're basically the same: to keep it like it is. The locals care just as much about wildlife and conservation as folks from Audubon. They just don't want to be preached to."[17] Despite appearances, despite the us-vs.-them and them-vs.-environment tone of much environmental discourse and debate today, there is an intermingling, an inextricable connection, of people and environment in pockets of northern New England—and in other parts of our admittedly abused continent — a realization that has important implications for the practice of American environmental writing, and should affect its study as well. The fact is that, in some places, an understanding of the environment implies an understanding not only of natural processes but of the human lifeways — often subtle, often traditional — that those processes have informed and shaped over time. The two are not always divisible, even when headlines, history books, and — yes — works of nature writing make them seem irreconcilable; the "eco" in ecocriticism should make room as appropriate not only for natural ecology but for its accompanying human ecology as well.

To repeat: what we think of as the natural landscape, especially but not exclusively in the East, is to some extent an artifact, shaped by human hands and intentions, brought into use to meet certain purposes and achieve certain designs. And like any other artifact, the landscape has not achieved its form and acquired its uses through whim or accident, but as the result of a sequence of deliberate choices. Artifacts enact and encode culture; what they look like, how they are made, and how they are used are strongly influenced by their maker's sense, shared with his or her community, of what constitutes a right appearance, an appropriate use, a proper method of construction. To be sure, when we think of human manipulations of nature we often think first of aesthetically and morally jarring examples on a large industrial scale: clear-cut forests, dammed rivers, open-pit mines, suburban sprawl, and the like. These examples speak primarily of our nation's urban-industrial economic culture, with executives making decisions in distant windowless offices and workers carrying out their duties to earn a paycheck, and they have rightly attracted the attention and provoked the alarm of nature writers and ecocritics. Our culture, the cry goes up, is at war with nature, concerned only with human needs and desires, and it is imperative that literary rear-guard actions be fought. On one level this is absolutely true; we may modify this conclusion, however, if we look beyond industry and consumerism to the level of folk culture, specifically folk technologies and traditional uses and modifications of the natural environment. The industrial manipulator of nature uses heavy equipment to mold the landscape according to the dictates of a single question: how can it be made to yield profit? The folk manipulator of nature, on the other hand, uses traditional tools and techniques in order to subtly shape the landscape and gather from it material and aesthetic benefits that accord with traditional standards and practices. No good comes from radical innovation, from the pursuit of exclusively personal gain, or from destroying or depleting the landscape: not only will the individual attract the censure of the community for deliberately flouting local tradition, but despoiling the landscape effectively brings traditional uses of that landscape to an end, removing not only the material on which hands can act but also the body of knowledge and appreciation that guides and restrains those hands. In order to ensure the continuance of a valued way of life, then, the folk manipulator and user of landscape must let his or her material practices be shaped and constrained by the limits, capacities, and rhythms of nature, observing closely, never taking more than can be replenished, melding human practice with natural process. Insofar as it is an artifact, nature is shaped by culture; at the same time, within many folk communities, culture is shaped by nature as well. The boundaries become blurred; to study nature is perforce to study the people within it.

Scholars of material culture tell us that artifacts embody the processes — the decisions and material practices — by which they were produced, and when we look at a clear-cut or a strip mine the process behind it is sadly apparent. When we look at natural land-scapes that are used in traditional ways by local communities but on which human hands have rested lightly, however — so lightly that evidence of human interaction with the landscape may be all but invisible—we may better understand it by applying the folklorist's notion of "praxis," which Simon Bronner defines as "the customary nature of making, using, and doing things." To look at the folk artifact is to gain an understanding of the "everyday behaviors and thoughts" behind it; as Bronner argues, "the praxic emphasis on customary ways of making, using, and doing things suggests that people directly reveal themselves and their social, psychological, and physical realms in their evocative, expressive, and responsive behavioral encounters with the material world along the path of life and experience."[18] Traditional users of the landscape reveal through their actions an understanding of the properties of that landscape learned through both personal experience and the shared knowledge that they have acquired through membership in the local community; they reveal their understanding of their symbiotic relationship to that landscape, defining themselves individually according to the mirror that nature provides; and they demonstrate their sense of affiliation with the community, a community that gains its identity at least in part according to its interactions with, and absorption in, the natural world around it. Folklorist John Michael Vlach argues that "the essential characteristics of folk things stem from their communal nature" and that studying them "puts us in touch with their wider public who use crafted objects . . . to express a shared worldview, a communally shared perspective on life,"[19] and if we consider America's natural landscapes as "folk things" and examine the traditional communities whose lives are embedded within them, we find people who are both in and of the landscape, whose worldview is predicated not on the exploitation and destruction of nature but on understanding, respect, and preservation.

To bring this discussion down to earth, so to speak: scholars of material folk culture have come to pay increasing attention to the ways in which traditional uses of and practices within the natural landscape also comprise means of identifying with that landscape, as well as of interpreting the local natural environment, of appreciating and translating its capacities and complexities. The person in the landscape adjusts himself or herself to its demands, priorities, and idiosyncrasies, rather than the other way around. In discussing fur trapping in the Missouri Ozarks, for example, Erika Brady finds that, contrary to the image that many may have of hunters as irresponsible predators who cultivate an adversarial relationship with wildlife, the trappers she studied enter the landscape in a spirit of "explicit identification with the fellow mammal: the ability not only to think like an animal but to interpret information in field and on riverbank through its eyes." "You can learn a lot from them — they're smart little critters," says one longtime trapper, demonstrating an understanding of his activity as, in Brady's words, "a reflective intellectual and physical pursuit that demands intimate identification with and respect for an animal," one that raises and answers "ethical questions involving appropriate relations between men, animals, and the environment." Brady's subjects do not emerge as resource-depleting exploiters driven solely by profit, but rather trap for the sake of the activity itself and its long-standing role in defining the region's culture (and thus defining themselves); lest the tradition end, each trapper is careful to be "a responsible husbander of a renewable but limited natural resource."[20] In her study of the folklife of the New Jersey Pinelands, Mary T. Hufford finds that "all things that are crafted out of the imagination's encounter with the land and its resources — recipes, songs, poems, paintings, crafts, tools, technological processes, rituals, festivals, recreational activities, and landscapes," amount not only to uses but also to interpretations, traditional means by which residents cultivate and perpetuate "an ability to make sense of the environment, not only to tell what is there, but to understand the relationships between environmental elements."[21] Thus the region's locally developed "tools for clamming, oystering, and eeling, for example, reflect the varied nuances of 'bottom' — some geological, some seasonal — below the region's diverse waters," while the area's distinctive type of boat, "the Barnegat Bay sneakbox, . . . effectively synthesizes the observations of generations of baymen of water, land, air, man, and mud," being designed to operate effectively in all possible conditions thrown at their users by the swampy local environment.[22] In their many traditional interactions with the natural landscape, the residents of the Pinelands demonstrate a deep and complex understanding of the environment that surrounds them, and have shaped their expressive material and verbal culture — and thus, by extension, their sense of who they are as individuals and a community — according to the specific conditions of nature as experienced in their particular place on earth.

Folklife studies like these make a point that nature writers and critics, in light of their concern with giving nature a voice and with counteracting the many harmful effects of human interaction with the natural environment, might tend to overlook. In many places in America, on a small and intimate scale, human culture is incorporated intimately into nature, shaped by it and shaping it in ways that, while they are interdependent and mutually informing, depend ultimately on the conditions that nature sets. Understanding and writing about nature realistically in these places means more than attending to the flora and fauna, landforms and waterways, and other nonhuman elements found in the local landscape; it means understanding the praxis of landscape use as well. Where appropriate, such an awareness can and should inform the practice and criticism of nature writing, providing as it does a supplementary facet to that understanding of the relation of people to nature that such writing aims to elucidate — a facet that, moreover, might be seen as providing some basis for hope and a general, environmentally sensitive model of right living for the future. If occasionally we wonder about the efficacy of nature writing and ecocriticism in bringing about change — if, as Scott Slovic comments, we "share the commonplace and frequently unexamined assumption that awareness will lead directly to corresponding action,"[23] a wishful assumption made necessary because, as teachers and writers, we are largely limited to raising consciousness and hoping for the best — then discussing places whose residents have developed traditions of landscape use in cooperation with and deference to nature may provide readers and students with ideas, at least, on where to begin.

In the remainder of this essay, I want to explore some ways in which contemporary American nature writers have taken as their subject the intersection and intermingling of nature and culture in traditional landscape use, beginning briefly with Robert Finch and then discussing John McPhee's *The Pine Barrens* and Gretel Ehrlich's *The Solace of Open Spaces* in detail as examples — one from the eastern United States, one from the much more sparsely populated and lightly manipulated West — of works that demonstrate that focusing on material folk culture as it has developed within a particular landscape is not inimical to the role and purpose of the nature writer, but is in many cases essential to achieving a full and accurate understanding of a specific slice of the natural world. Robert Finch is someone whose nature-writing bona fides are in excellent order, and whose work suggests well the potential tensions involved in incorporating local human cultures into American environmental prose. The author of three books about the landscapes and seascapes of Cape Cod, where he makes his home, Finch was also the editor (with John Elder) of the *Norton Book of Nature Writing*, and in much of his work he settles himself comfortably into the wonted stance and role of the eco-conscious American nature writer as outlined earlier in this essay. The introduction to the Norton anthology, noting once again that Thoreau is the central figure in the field because "he both touches the genre's roots and anticipates its flowering in this century," posits that much of Thoreau's influence derives from the fact that he brought "an ironic awareness to his nature writing, continually recognizing in his wry style that by focusing on nonhuman nature we objectify and abstract it" [24] — that is, he sets the writer alone in the landscape, excluding other people from his vision, keeping himself intellectually separate from nature the better to describe it and ponder its meanings. The selection from his own writings that Finch includes in the anthology finds him walking by himself around a Cape Cod pond on a clear, still winter night, attending carefully to "the hardest of all sounds in nature to hear: the silent assertion of a landscape itself," opening his senses to rocks and trees and water and ice and appreciating how "nature's unstrung voices made themselves heard in the dark silence" [25] — taking on, that is, the traditional role of nature writer as translator, hearing the landscape explain itself in ways that less sensitive observers would overlook, providing a voice and an advocacy for a natural world that is ordinarily mute, taken for granted, defenseless.

So far, so conventional. At the same time, however, Finch is very aware that his Cape Cod is by no means a pristine natural landscape, that it bears no resemblance to the "desolate wilderness" that William Bradford perceived when he landed on the Cape in 1620,[26] but rather that it has been lived on, altered, rearranged, and used heavily by the good people of Massachusetts for 381 years (leaving aside, for both writers, the question of Native American uses and alterations prior to European contact). Rather than dismissing this fact as some sort of alien intrusion upon or desecration of nature, however, Finch recognizes that, on Cape Cod at least, human beings have become as rooted in the soil as the native trees, and to study the natural world that surrounds him is perforce to study the ways in which human culture has adapted itself to that world, to appreciate the way in which nature and culture have grown together into a symbiotic unit. The landscape in which he has chosen to live, he notes, is "a very natural-looking landscape that is actually a resultant of human activity and natural processes,"[27] and this intermingling centrally informs his perceptions, his predilections, and his writing; thus, for example, he admits in a 1988 public dialogue with Terry Tempest Williams that "my personal perspective is that the most interesting landscapes are those in which there is some human presence" (Williams, the westerner, notes in response that "I find just the opposite").[28] While adhering to what has emerged as a strong American nature-writing tradition in his editorial and authorial performances in the Norton anthology, then, Finch has at the same time developed a great sensitivity to "the local culture which I have tried to incorporate into a lot of my writing," a culture that he characterizes as "the long-rooted continuum of living with the land," as "knowing what it took to make a living on the land."[29] The result of this conception of the nature and meaning of the Cape Cod landscape is a book like *The Primal Place*, which is essentially an elaboration on Finch's realization that, "despite the landscape's wild aspect, there is hardly a square foot of ground in the immediate vicinity that does not bear, directly or indirectly, marks of the past hand of man."[30] He writes of the annual alewife migration up Stony Brook, and the traditional fishery that has long accompanied it, not only because it is a fascinating natural phenomenon but because the fish "have been with us so long that they now form part of our own local identity and . . . we would feel incomplete without them."[31] "How well-used these long, low flats have been!" he remarks of his favorite clamming grounds, noting that "everywhere over their dark, wet plains are spread the artifacts of past human use"; at the same time, he also comments on "how remarkably unscathed they have remained, even today, despite the increasing intensity of human activity."[32] Finch may find it important to discern "the silent assertion of a landscape itself," but the voices he passes along to us in his Cape Cod books are human just as often as they are natural—or, rather, the voices of both parties blend together in an indistinguishable harmony.

Of all American writers working today, John McPhee most fully and assiduously explores the melding and interdependence of the hu-

Landscape with Figures

man and the nonhuman in the natural world, a pursuit that he achieves not only through his choice of subject matter but also through his technique. While this shape-shifting author has written about subjects as various as oranges, Arthur Ashe, and the Swiss army, he has firmly established his nature-writing credentials through such books as *The Pine Barrens*, *The Crofter and the Laird*, *Encounters with the Archdruid*, *The Survival of the Bark Canoe*, *Coming into the Country*, and *The Control of Nature*. Even his quartet of books on geology —*Basin and Range*, *In Suspect Terrain*, *Rising from the Plains*, and *Assembling California*— can be seen as books of nature writing, only this time training their focus beneath the natural landscape rather than upon its surface. McPhee shows up in the *Norton Book of Nature Writing* and Stephen Trimble's *Words from the Land*, and such critical attention as he has attracted tends to emphasize the prevalence of environmental themes and issues in his books.[33] In a typical critical appraisal of his work, David Espey finds that "whether he is in Alaska, or the canyons of the Colorado River, or the Pine Barrens of New Jersey, McPhee has the same preoccupation — the clash between man's exploitation of the land and his reverence for the wilderness."[34] Given American ecocritical history, it should come as no surprise that Espey places McPhee in a Thoreauvian tradition, pointing out that "like Thoreau, McPhee is a river traveler, a naturalist, and a fact gatherer," and asserting that "McPhee's celebration of natural beauty and wilderness around his home [in Princeton, New Jersey] recalls the preindustrial Northeast of Henry David Thoreau."[35] Yet it would be facile and misleading to assume that, like Thoreau, McPhee positions himself as a solitary observer of natural, nonhuman phenomena and that those phenomena — especially in contradistinction to the harmful effects of human culture — make up his primary concern and focus, as Espey implies when he says of *The Pine Barrens* that, in its pages, McPhee "finds true natural wilderness in this overpopulated hub of the eastern urban world" and "emphasizes the resilience and vitality of natural forces despite urban encroachment."[36] As McPhee himself explains, he may write frequently about nature, but "the common thread in all of my work is people — and what they're up to, as it's expressed through their work."[37] Insofar as that work takes people into the natural landscape, and insofar as those people work with nature — with its rhythms and constraints, according to its suggestions and promptings — rather than against it, so does McPhee as nature writer take as his subject not the untouched land but the natural world as it has become entwined with the praxis of landscape use.

Part of this emphasis is a result of the fact that, like Robert Finch, McPhee lives in and thus writes frequently about the long- and thickly settled East, where cultural fingerprints and the effects of work are everywhere on the natural landscape. Yet he trains this focus on other, more remote parts of the continent as well: for example, the greater part of his book about Alaska, *Coming into the Country*, is not a Barry Lopez-style meditation on Arctic landscape and wildlife but an examination of life in and around the small town of Eagle, while in an essay entitled "North of the C. P. Line" he explores the unpopulated Maine woods not by tramping through them alone but by flying above them with a Maine game warden and avid outdoorsman, a doppelganger also named John McPhee.[38] Instead of being a simple function of place and time, McPhee's interest in the commingling of nature and local culture grows inevitably out of his characteristic means of approaching his subject matter: not solely through his own perceptions and experiences, but also through the activities and explanations of a traveling companion, a longtime indigene of the place in question and/or expert in whatever field McPhee happens to be writing about. All of McPhee's books find him tagging along with one or more figures who come to act as guide and teacher for both author and readers, be it environmentalist David Brower in *Encounters with the Archdruid*, geologist David Love in *Rising from the Plains*, farmer Donald McNeill in *The Crofter and the Laird*, or any similar figure in any other of his books. As Espey describes this technique (without fully exploring its implications), each of McPhee's books is a "character study of an expert combined with an exploration of the expert's terrain," with the result that "the trip becomes a journey into the character as well as a movement through space and time."[39] The signature of McPhee's technique, then, is that he does not take in the natural world simply through his own senses, does not strike out on his own and move quietly in hopes of hearing nature's voice, but filters the landscape and interprets its meaning through the eyes, hands, mind, and life of a second person — and it so happens in McPhee's writings that this person is someone who has come over a period of many years to live on terms of comfortable intimacy and cooperation with that landscape, who has crafted a life shaped by the qualities and capacities of the natural world. Nature is not a separate realm in McPhee's writings; given his chosen technique and approach — his reading of landscape through people and understanding of people insofar as they work in the landscape — the blending of the human and natural worlds that he portrays is as inevitable as it is true to life.

The Pine Barrens best exemplifies both the way in which McPhee conceives of the natural world and the method through which he demonstrates and elaborates that conception on the printed page. This book, an examination of the last extensive undeveloped area in the northeastern urban corridor, is framed in such a way as to establish its subject in the reader's mind as a natural landscape that is both unspoiled and threatened. This region of thick forests underlain by an aquifer of nearly pure water, McPhee informs us at the outset, "is still so undeveloped that it can be called wilderness." [40] A view of the Pinelands from a fire tower at their center, a view that extends twelve miles, reveals nothing but trees reaching to the horizon and beyond. McPhee associates the Pine Barrens with other, better-known American natural landscapes by pointing out that the area "is nearly as large as Yosemite National Park," almost the same size as Grand Canyon National Park, and "much larger than . . . most of the national parks in the United States" (5). At the same time, this remarkable wilderness is threatened with obliteration. The all-but-uninhabited Pine Barrens sit in uncomfortably close proximity to America's most densely populated areas: they are "so close to New York that on a very clear night a bright light in the pines would be visible from the Empire State Building," while "the halfway point between Boston and Richmond — the geographical epicenter of the developing megalopolis — is in the northern part of the woods" (5). With population pressures come development pressures; as McPhee puts it near the end of the book, "the simple facts of all that space and all that subsurface water increase in importance with each new nail that goes into the megalopolis of which the Pine Barrens are the geographical center" (148). In his last chapter, McPhee underscores the extent of the threat to the wilderness by describing a proposed airport and planned city that developers hoped to construct in the heart of the region (but that, as it turns out, were never built), and he concludes pessimistically that, because of continuing smaller-scale development, the Barrens "seem to be headed slowly toward extinction. . . . At the rate of a few hundred yards or even a mile or so each year, the perimeter of the pines contracts" (156–57). The structure of the book, then, sets up through its opening and conclusion a familiar opposition: the integrity of nature versus the destructive demands and practices of humanity. As a writer and concerned citizen, McPhee feels obliged to explore the region before people gnaw it away completely: as he admits early in the book, "I was in the pines because I found it hard to believe that so much unbroken forest could still exist so near the big Eastern cities, and I wanted to see it while it was still there" (12). *The Pine Barrens* is his report on that "unbroken forest."

The minute he begins his exploration, however, it becomes clear that his interest, his sense of what must be taken account of and reported on in order to write honestly and comprehensively about the Pine Barrens, is not limited to the woodlands and their ecosystems, but takes in as well — and as a matter of course — those human communities that have traditionally gathered their living from the natural landscape of the region. McPhee is in no danger, as it were, of being unable to see the forest for the trees; those trees, while fascinating and important in their own right, have since colonial times helped formed the backbone of a local human culture that has learned to use the forest landscape so extensively, and yet with so light a touch, that natural and human ecology have long ago blended together. Forest and people are so inextricable that the locals even refer to themselves as "pineys," taking their identity and their name from their wooded surroundings. After his opening description, McPhee descends from the fire tower to find "the center of the pines," and from his experience and the testimony of maps he "would judge that the heart of the pine country is in or near a place called Hog Wallow" (6), one resident of which is Fred Brown, a garrulous old man living in an unpainted house without electricity or central heating. Fred Brown, both geographically and thematically, is the true center of the Pine Barrens, the heart of the country, its *genius loci* — it is through him, rather than through an examination of the landscape itself, that we come to grasp the meaning and significance of the region. Through Fred and his friend Bill Wasovwich, McPhee and his readers learn about the "yearly cycle" (42) through which pineys have traditionally gotten their living, a cycle set to nature's clock and dependent on materials that nature makes available: gathering sphagnum moss in the spring, picking blueberries in the summer, harvesting cranberries in the fall, cutting wood and making charcoal in the winter, each practice demonstrating both an expertise in and a reliance on the local landscape that shows how attuned local residents have become to the capacities and potentials of the natural world as it is found in their place. Pineys like Fred and Bill are completely at home in their landscape, habituated to its subtleties, happily adapted to its contours and demands: Bill, for example, is fond of "setting out cross-country on long, looping journeys, hiking about thirty miles in a typical day," and while his "long, pathless journeys" are completely unplanned, "Bill always emerges from the woods near his cabin — and about when he plans to." "Almost no one who is not native to the pines could do this," McPhee marvels (9). The elderly Fred no longer spends much time in the woods, but accompanies McPhee in his car on the unmapped sand roads of the Pine Barrens, pointing out places where he and his friends have lived and worked, logged and hunted, "picking fragments of the past out of the forest" (20) — and, like Bill, Fred "always knew exactly where he was going" (19). The forest that McPhee experiences, and that his readers view and understand, is the forest as mediated by the Fred Browns who live within it as comfortably as the many animals that it shelters. It is a forest filtered and given meaning through human lives, and through which those lives have been filtered and given meaning at the same time in an endless reciprocal process.

Throughout the book, a sense of human involvement in and adaptation to the natural landscape is intrinsic to McPhee's vision. To be sure, several of its chapters carefully describe the flora, fauna, and geological peculiarities that contribute to the Pine Barrens's uniqueness — its twenty-three kinds of orchids, its quaking bogs and rare tree frogs that are found almost nowhere else in the country, its sandy soil that holds "a natural reservoir of pure water that, in volume, is the equivalent of a lake seventy-five feet deep with a surface of a thousand square miles" (14), its recurrent fires that have resulted in the natural selection of tree species that "are not only highly flammable but are able to tolerate fire and come back quickly" (118), its puzzling groves of dwarf pines; on the whole, McPhee provides a wealth of natural description that not only offers a comprehensive picture of nonhuman nature in this ecologically unique region but also indicates its fragility and vulnerability and the importance of assuring its preservation. Intermingled with these descriptions, though, is an equally comprehensive historical account of the many ways in which people have used the forest's resources since the earliest days of colonial settlement — and not only through working the yearly cycle of harvesting naturally available materials. McPhee describes the colonial iron industry in the pines, which drew naturally occurring iron oxide from the sandy soils and produced from it a variety of iron products. He devotes one chapter to "The Vanished Towns" of the Barrens's ironmaking past, and writes in another of life today in "The Capital of the Pines," the tiny crossroads of Chatsworth. The oral traditions of the region, the practices of hunters and firefighters — all aspects of human life in the pines get the same exhaustive treatment as does natural life. Here too, McPhee implies, is an element of the forest that is increasingly under threat and that must be preserved. It has been, and continues to be, a unique and fragile ecosystem in its own way, one intimately tied to and derived from the landscape. While clearly an environmentalist tract, one that brings the reader imaginatively and emotionally in contact with a natural landscape and that argues passionately in that landscape's defense, *The Pine Barrens* demands that we refine our understanding of exactly what makes up the environment; when we read this book to discover the otherwise unheard voice of nature, the voice we bring away with us may well be that of Bill Wasovwich summarizing a life's experience of the forest by saying "there ain't no place like this left in the country, I don't believe" (13), or of the unnamed piney, standing for Fred and Bill and all the rest, who remarks to McPhee that "it's a privilege to live in these woods" (58).

As noted earlier, the act of nature writers' seeing and discussing landscapes as cultural artifacts seems more appropriate in— indeed, may seem possible only in — the thickly settled and heavily manipulated East of Finch and McPhee, as opposed to the open spaces and sparse human habitation of the West. As Bill McKibben has observed, "American heads jerk to the west when we think about nature,"[41] to images of towering mountains and yawning canyons, to the nation's largest and best-loved national parks, to breathtaking big-sky vistas without a human being in sight. The East, as represented by those wooded hills of New England where failed farmsteads are now overgrown with new generations of forest, where the ruins of a past agricultural landscape have been covered by a blanket of green, is a place where, in John Elder's words, "human vestiges and the region's nonhuman life have begun to fade together, lost in an emerging balance of wilderness and culture," where "what began as an opposition has slowly turned into a balance."[42] In the rural West, by contrast, that opposition still seems very much in force, with the natural world holding itself aloof, by virtue of its scale, its demanding terrain, and the harshness of its climate, from the small, widely scattered human populations that try to get a living from it as best they can. This opposition informs western environmental writing as well; as critic Glen Love has argued, this specifically regional writing "is characterized, to no small degree, by its recognition of a natural otherness, a world of land and sky and organic life which exists outside human life, yet seems to command its allegiance."[43] Allegiance, perhaps, but not alliance: this is a world in which nature and culture are not in balance, but in which individuals and small local communities have traditionally had to work very hard simply to maintain themselves in the face of a stark, indifferent natural world.

Certainly this is the image of Wyoming that Gretel Ehrlich presents in her 1985 book *The Solace of Open Spaces*. Ehrlich first came to Wyoming in the late 1970s to work on a film project. During the course of this project she suffered a deep personal tragedy, the death of her lover. In the aftermath of her loss, she decided to stay in Wyoming, trying first to lose herself, and then finding she was healing herself, through a prolonged confrontation with the state's broad arid vistas. As with other nature writers, Ehrlich takes as her primary task and goal a direct encounter with the nonhuman world, seeking to understand it as best she can on its own terms: having come to what appears to many as "a landscape of lunar desolation," she realizes that, having done so, "I was able to take up residence on earth with no alibis, no self-promoting schemes," no predetermined cultural intentions and frameworks.[44] Also like other writers, she sees herself as attempting to somehow incorporate nature directly into her writing, giving it a voice and an immediate literary presence, bringing to "the page the same qualities as earth: weather would land on it harshly; light would elucidate the most difficult truths; wind would sweep away obtuse padding" (x). The nature she confronts, however, is not a fecund green world, not a sustaining landscape in the manner of Thoreau's Concord, but one more closely aligned with the unsettling rocky terrain that Thoreau found near the top of Katahdin: stark, harsh, off-putting, indifferent. This is a world that on the surface seems inimical to human culture and concerns, even threatening to human life. Wyoming's winters are unremittingly, deadeningly cold: "This white bulk is sometimes dizzying, even nauseating, to look at. At twenty, thirty, and forty degrees below zero, not only does your car not work, but neither do your mind and body. The landscape hardens into a dungeon of space. . . . In the silence that such cold creates I felt like the first person on earth, or the last" (1–2). Summer brings blistering heat and a choking aridity punctuated by torrential lightning storms and floods from the mountains' melting snow cover — "Westerners," says Ehrlich, "are ambivalent about water because they've never seen what it can create except havoc and mud" (78). "Spring weather is capricious and mean" (7), and in all seasons an "earth-dredging wind" (7) blasts through the ranches on the state's eastern plains. Living in this bleak elemental place, however, has a tonic effect on Ehrlich, renewing her, sweeping away her pain, connecting her through the workings of nature to a more basic and less encumbered level of existence. "The arid country was a clean slate," she realizes. "Its absolute indifference steadied me" (4). While winter may bring "the deep ache of this audacious Arctic air" (72), it also brings "refreshment — snow on flushed cheeks and a pristine kind of thinking"; in this white frozen world, "a reflection of mind appears, sharp, vigilant, precise" (74). Wyoming's terrain emerges as "nearly uninhabitable land" (9), resisting the human touch and the workings of culture, and through its harsh integrity it provides for Ehrlich the sort of guidance, awareness, and inspiration that writers have traditionally sought in the natural world.

As the book progresses, however, it quickly becomes apparent that, despite appearances, the Wyoming landscape is deeply implicated in traditional patterns of work and ways of life. From the time she first moves to Wyoming, Ehrlich lives and works on sheep ranches, eventually buying a small place of her own with her new husband. These ranches provide the standpoint and perspective from which she comes to contemplate the natural world around her. Most of the encounters she has with that world take place during the course of such activities as herding sheep or accompanying friends and neighbors as they go about their work; most of the landscapes she traverses on horseback or in pickup trucks are grazing land for the area's ranches. The Wyoming landscape, harsh and elemental though it may be, also emerges in Ehrlich's writing as basically an enormous outdoor workplace for cowboys, herself included. Her landscape is in the end a peopled landscape, widely spaced though those people may be; it is also a landscape that becomes filtered through the eyes, minds, and activities of ranch hands following a way of life that has been pursued there for well over a hundred years. This attentiveness to humanity, this desire to see a populated terrain, emerges as an important part of the local culture, a response to that same stark openness that so invigorates Ehrlich: at some point, all that blank, cold, dry space becomes too much to contemplate. People seek each other out as if through a gravitational force: "A common sight," she points out, "is two pickups stopped side by side far out on a range, on a dirt track winding through the sage" (5), their drivers sharing coffee and a cigarette, while in the midst of a bleak Wyoming winter "our connections with neighbors — whether strong or tenuous, as lovers or friends — become too urgent to disregard" (72). At the same time that Ehrlich establishes her own personal relationship with the natural world, then, she also immerses herself in a particular, local, cultural relationship with that world, one that — through the exigencies of work and the psychological pressures of climate and terrain — etches human beings and their patterns of life onto that landscape in sharp relief.

Traditional western patterns of work attract Ehrlich's attention throughout the book. She attends a rodeo, a stylized ritual display of traditional ranch tasks that "stands for the western way of life and the western spirit" (96); in an elegiac chapter entitled "Obituary," she observes an auction at a bankrupt sheep ranch and is heartened by a final realization that "the West, however disfigured, persists. Cowboys still drift from outfit to outfit, . . . making fifty-mile circles during fall roundup; and year round, the sheepherders — what's left of them — stay out with their sheep" (31–32). The conjunction of person, animal, and landscape embodied by cowboy and herder becomes a prominent motif throughout the book; Wyoming is mediated to Ehrlich to some extent through ranch workers' eyes and lives, while Ehrlich herself mediates her perceptions and understandings of the world around her through her experiences as a neophyte rancher, through the process of losing her outsider's status and becoming acclimated to and grounded in a local land-based economy and culture, a world where "a person's life is . . . a slow accumulation of days, seasons, years, fleshed out by the generational weight of one's family and anchored by a land-bound sense of place" (5). Wyoming's valleys, prairies, and mountains become deeply known places for the people who work in them, homes in a sense despite their forbidding size — in discussing one sheepman she knows, Ehrlich hints at this combination of large scale and intimate domesticity by noting that "to put 100,000 miles on his pickup in three years and never leave *home* is not unusual" (2; my emphasis). Some ranchers actively alter and domesticate their landscapes through irrigation projects, making them more amenable to human use; at the same time, even in the farthest, most rugged reaches of a ranch's grazing land, the landscape is brought firmly within the scope of human intention, with herders expertly leading their sheep up onto the mountains and down into the valleys in response to the year's cyclical changes in weather, water, and vegetation. In Ehrlich's descriptions, the ranching culture is not destructive and exploitative, not based on opposition to and oppression of the natural world, but is instead a sort of symbiosis, humans and animals and land merging into a single cooperative unit: on buying her own place, she comments that "if I was leery about being an owner, a possessor of land, now I have to understand the ways in which the place possesses me" (90). When she is traveling away from home, the shorthand image of Wyoming that she carries in her mind is not one of unpopulated mountains — the standard western calendar picture — but rather one of people working on the land, not in tension but in harmony: "What I'm aching to see is horseflesh, the glint of a spur, a line of distant mountains, brimming creeks, and a reminder of the ranchers and cowboys I've ridden with for the last eight years" (49). This is, for Ehrlich, the essence of Wyoming's open spaces — a landscape that is invigorating in its scope and starkness while at the same time made subject to traditional uses and interpretations; a landscape that, through work, is converted into a cultural artifact while retaining, through its force and power and harsh extremities, its chilling indifference to the workings and intentions of human beings.

In the end, though, this balance is not quite as even as it might seem. In Ehrlich's Wyoming, in the peopled, working landscape that she sees surrounding her, it is nature that finally sets the conditions of the relationship, nature that keeps the upper hand. Ranching depends crucially on rainfall and snowmelt so that animals will have enough to eat and drink, but "waiting for water is just one of the ways Wyoming ranchers find themselves at the mercy of weather" (76). An unexpected snowstorm at the wrong time of year, for instance, "can act like fists: trees are pummeled, hay- and grainfields are flattened, splayed out like deer beds; field corn, jackknifed and bleached blond by the freeze, is bedraggled by the brawl" (126). In the face of this powerful and capricious natural world, Wyoming ranchers have reacted not by resisting nature, not by attempting to harness or tame it, but by accommodating themselves to it. They understand it and ride out whatever it throws at them; patiently, not resentfully, they set out to complete their tasks as best they can. In this light, the traditional silent determination of the western ranch worker emerges not as ornery stubbornness, but as a wise environmental humility. The rural Wyoming resident, though he or she may see the landscape as one big workplace, learns that the best way to work in that landscape is to allow nature to follow its inscrutable dictates and to fit into the spaces and patterns that it allows as best one can, to ride the relentless wind rather than fight it. "Traditionally, at least," notes Ehrlich, "ranch life has gone against materialism and has stood for the small achievements of the human conjoined with the animal, and the simpler pleasures. . . . The toughness I was learning was not a martyred doggedness, a dumb heroism, but the art of accommodation" (43–44). In the end, Ehrlich presents a vision and understanding of western nature and a traditional western culture not at odds, not in irreconcilable opposition, but forming a single, intermingled entity in which human beings and their work ultimately become subsumed to, absorbed into, the natural world. To understand nature here is to understand the culture that depends on it; to participate in that culture is to become immersed and entwined, by virtue of the very fact of living and working, in the fundamental processes of nature, no matter how stern and forbidding that nature may be: "Implicated as we westerners are," Ehrlich notes, "in this sperm, blood, and guts business of ranching, and propelled forward by steady gusts of blizzards, cold fronts, droughts, heat, and wind, there's a ceremonial feel to life on a ranch. It's raw and impulsive but the narrative thread of birth, death, chores, and seasons keeps tugging at us until we find ourselves braided inextricably into the strand" (103). Ehrlich's Wyoming may be far different from John Elder's New England of balanced wilderness and culture, but in her pages too the balance of nature and culture — or, more properly, the adaptation of culture to nature — is inescapable.

Lives like those of Ehrlich's ranch workers and McPhee's pineys — lives that are rooted in, dependent on, and shaped to the nonhuman environment — are a subtle, intrinsic part of natural landscapes throughout America. Insofar as any landscape is a folk artifact — a material object that, through the shared, traditional ways in which it is used or shaped, embodies and enacts culture — its significance cannot be fully and accurately gauged in isolation from the human beings who live within it. And insofar as those human beings allow their traditional culture to be guided and circumscribed by the rhythms and capacities of the natural world, they must be understood, not as separate from nature and inherently antagonistic to it, but as, in essence, part of the local ecosystem, an important element — but by no means the sole determining element — in making the landscape what it is. Many nature writers demonstrate in their works a sensitive awareness of this symbiosis, taking on the role not only of naturalists but of folklorists as well, listening carefully to people in order to understand their traditional uses and interpretations of the landscape, examining the landscape itself as providing clues to human culture. In so doing, they bridge the gap between the human and nonhuman that looms so large in American nature writing and ecocriticism; while fully aware of the deep and widespread harm that human beings have done to the natural world, they also examine individual landscapes on an intimate scale, showing how communities have constructed mutually sustaining partnerships with nature, suggesting through their literary examinations that humans can live wisely and well on the earth if only they will let nature take a guiding role in the development of culture.

THREE

Sea Green

Ethics & Environment in
New England Coastal Fiction

I n Wallace Stevens's poem "The Idea of Order at Key West,"
the speaker and his companion, listening to a woman singing
by the ocean, attempt to distinguish her voice from the sounds
made by the sea itself. "It may be," he says, "that in all her
phrases stirred / The grinding water and the gasping wind; / But it was
she and not the sea we heard." He continues:

> If it was only the outer voice of sky
> And cloud, of the sunken coral water-walled,
> However clear, it would have been deep air,
> The heaving speech of air, a summer sound
> Repeated in a summer without end
> And sound alone. But it was more than that,

he concludes, and realizes that when the woman sang, "the sea,

> Whatever self it had, became the self
> That was her song, for she was the maker. Then we,
> As we beheld her striding there alone,
> Knew that there never was a world for her
> Except the one she sang and, singing, made.[1]

In these lines, Stevens suggests a central problem and paradox confronted by anyone who attempts to write about the ocean or any other
component of the natural environment, and, by extension, by anyone
who attempts to critically analyze such writings. As an element of
nonhuman nature, the ocean does not inherently mean; it owes its
existence to no human agency, but ebbs and flows and creates its

sounds — its "constant cry," in Stevens's words, "Inhuman, of the veritable ocean" — regardless of who may be observing it or what they may be thinking about it. At the same time, in order for it to become the stuff of literature, the ocean as subject must be filtered through a writer's mind, sensibility, values, and learning, and thus it reaches the reader not as water and wave but as idea, as symbol, as meaningful presence. Nature becomes spoken for, its inhuman cry — "The meaningless plunges of water and the wind," in another of Stevens's phrases — translated into a sequence of human words according to whatever framework of interpretation the author brings to bear on it; it is, in the end, she and not the sea we hear.

Ironically, even to identify something as natural, as by definition nonhuman, is to bring it within the shaping influence of the human mind, is to convert it into a sort of cultural artifact. As Eric Zencey says in his book *Virgin Forest: Meditations on History, Ecology, and Culture*, the very notion of virgin forest, a seemingly straightforward concept, is filled with ironic complexities: while

> for many people virgin forest symbolizes the antithesis of our culture, . . . the concept of forest virginity is not a natural but a cultural category, a template we lay upon the arboreal ecosystem, an idea that we import to nature. To call a forest "virgin" credits it with having its own natural, non-human "disturbance history," and so takes note of the forest for having maintained its otherness, its continuity outside the most obvious graspings of human culture. . . . By elevating to the status of distinguishing criterion our failure to disturb, we draw the virgin forest firmly into our history, for we use our history as the base against which its exception is measured.[2]

The human framework of interpretation becomes the overriding source of the forest's meaning, so that even the slightest alteration, the cutting of a single tree, changes its identity completely and irrevocably: cut that tree, and "the forest around immediately falls, losing in that instant its purity, becoming just another old growth forest."[3] This despite the fact that the huge majority of the fabric of the forest continues unchanged. So it is with the ocean; to write about it at all makes it into a human construct, a cultural artifact, a text rather than a cold amorphous congeries of hydrogen and oxygen and salt — leaving out, for the moment, the extent to which human activity has changed the physical ocean itself, raising its level through practices that contribute to global warming, altering its chemical makeup with pollutants, changing its biotic populations through fishing and whaling.

Stevens's poem, and observations like Zencey's, have important implications for the ways in which we think about and experience the natural world — and therefore, by extension, for the field of ecocriticism, a relatively new addition to the academic lexicon that I used here and there in the previous chapter but that might repay some closer scrutiny at this point. According to Cheryll Glotfelty, in the introduction to *The Ecocriticism Reader* (1996), which she edited with Harold Fromm, "Simply put, ecocriticism is the study of the relationship between literature and the physical environment. . . . Ecocriticism takes an earth-centered approach to literary studies,"[4] she continues, drawing parallels between this literary endeavor and the efforts of feminist and Marxist critics to incorporate issues and perspectives of gender and class into their work. As I have tried to imply in these pages, though, the relationship between literature and environment is anything but straightforward and transparent, regardless of how uncomplicated it may sound to mute the human voice and focus on the meanings and perspectives of the earth itself. Glotfelty moves on to refine her definition, outlining ecocriticism's special place within the broader field of literary studies: "Literary theory, in general, examines the relations between writers, texts, and the world. In most literary theory 'the world' is synonymous with society — the social sphere. Ecocriticism expands the notion of 'the world' to include the entire ecosphere."[5] In so doing, Glotfelty again implies a shift in focus away from human priorities, activities, and consciousness, advocating a criticism marked by the attention it pays to the physical, ostensibly nonhuman world not as background, not as stage set for human activities and relationships, but as central and equal actor and moral presence within the text; "as a theoretical discourse," Glotfelty says, "it negotiates between the human and the nonhuman,"[6] with the emphasis on the nonhuman, moving it into the critical spotlight in the place of the dominant group just as other theoretical discourses have done with women or members of the working class. To pay too much attention to the cultural, human aspects of nature would seem to defeat the purpose of such an ecocritical project.

This focus on the nonhuman "other," exempt by definition from the workings and shapings of culture, has been central to much of the early groundbreaking theoretical work in the field of ecocriticism. In

1990, for example, Glen Love published an essay called "Revaluing Nature: Toward an Ecological Criticism," which has become one of the most widely cited pieces in the field. In decrying "our discipline's limited humanistic vision, our narrowly anthropocentric view of what is consequential in life," Love encourages his readers

> to outgrow our notion that human beings are so special that the earth exists for our comfort and disposal alone. Here is the point at which a nature-oriented literature offers a needed corrective, for one very important aspect of this literature is its regard — either implicit or stated — for the non-human. While critical interpretation, taken as a whole, tends to regard ego-consciousness as the supreme evidence of literary and critical achievement, it is eco-consciousness which is a particular contribution of most regional literature, of nature-writing, and of many other ignored forms and works, passed over because they do not seem to respond to anthropocentric — let alone modernist and postmodernist — assumptions and methodologies.[7]

The literatures to which such an approach would redirect our attention, then, are those that get as far as possible outside of the author's head, that tune out the chatter of human characters, and that turn their attention firmly to the ground under the author's feet, to the animals and vegetables and minerals that surround any people who may be included in the book as well. Love then directs the bulk of his remarks to advocating the study of what we conventionally think of as nature writing — nonfiction prose involving a first-person narrator's encounters with the flora and fauna of some segment of the earth's surface far from buildings and pavement and other people — and particularly that associated with the American West, a region whose landscape, as I noted when I opened my discussion of Gretel Ehrlich, encourages observers to see around them little more than "a natural otherness, a world of land and sky and organic life which exists outside human life, yet seems to command its allegiance."[8]

Glen Love's purpose in writing his article is not only theoretical but avowedly political: he argues that an ecologically informed criticism and a higher valuation put on nature writing can be important to, as he puts it, "the acknowledgement of our place within the natural world and our need to live heedfully within it, at peril of our very survival;" as he says at the end of his article, "the most important function of literature today is to direct human consciousness to a full consideration of its place in a threatened natural world."[9] I agree completely and wholeheartedly, and have no desire to gainsay or undercut any of the value in this position or any of the cultural and practical work that criticism like this has taken as its mission. Rather, I want to reexamine some of the perspectives, priorities, and limitations of the approach outlined by scholars like Glotfelty and Love, supplementing them in order to make them not only theoretically broader and more widely applicable but, by extension, even more useful as a means of rethinking our environmental attitudes and our behavior toward the planet on which we live.[10] As such, having tried to complicate what is meant by "ecocriticism," I also want to continue my questioning of what is meant by "environment" in the field of ecocriticism; in addition, having looked at nonfiction in the previous chapter, I want to test the applicability of this theoretical discourse to realistic fiction set along New England's shores, a kind of writing that is not only set far away from the big skies of the West but that also features casts of human characters who, while they live and work on the ocean and its margin, resolutely refuse to get off the stage, absorbing the bulk of authorial attention and interest.

First, as I have implied earlier, not only is any literary treatment of the environment passed through a system of cultural filters as it leaves the writer's head and enters the reader's, but I've been arguing throughout this book so far that what we think of as the natural world is itself a cultural artifact, shaped, even if only subtly and indirectly, by human activity and intention, by the work of hands and minds together. Few if any spots on the earth's surface have escaped the effects of human disturbance, actions that have molded the very shape of the land as well as the composition of the animal and plant life that it sustains. The world is everywhere thickly smudged with human fingerprints, and certainly the landscapes and seascapes of New England have been so heavily used since European colonization and before that it makes no sense to think of them as in any way virginal, standing outside culture by their very essence. What we think of as "environment" has not only been passed through cultural lenses as people have perceived it, but has been deeply implicated in the physical and economic business of survival, of getting a living. Any theoretical discourse that aims at an earth-centered approach must take this implication, this embeddedness and interaction, into account if it is to bear any relation to environmental reality, if it is to focus on *actual* landscapes and seascapes rather than on *ideas* about those landscapes and seascapes.

At the same time, such a discourse must transcend a narrow focus on particular literary subgenres and take in as broad a spectrum of writing as possible if it is to escape being marginalized academically and is to have as wide an impact as possible both inside and outside the academy. As such, I want to look at three novels by two writers that, while they focus on the lives of fishermen and are set on the New England coast and the Atlantic Ocean, seem on their surface not to have what we might think of as a conventional environmental emphasis but to remain within an emphatically anthropocentric world: *Candlemas Bay* and *The Weir* by Maine's Ruth Moore, published in 1950 and 1943, respectively, and John Casey's *Spartina*, winner of the National Book Award for fiction in 1989, which is set on and along the southern coast of Rhode Island. Not only are the main characters of these novels fishermen, commercial exploiters of the sea's resources and therefore by definition the enemy in much environmental rhetoric, but there is no sense of environmental crisis in these books either: the waters are clean, the fish are plentiful if occasionally difficult to find, and not a tree is hugged from beginning to end. The action of all these books focuses on such matters as the inner lives and torments of their characters, interpersonal conflict, and questions of identity, not on the fate of the fishery or questions of environmental sin and salvation. While all three novels interest me because they focus on ethical matters, on right and wrong behaviors and personal integrity, these seem on the surface to be matters of *human* ethics rather than some version of Aldo Leopold's famous land ethic: "A thing is right when it tends to preserve the integrity, stability, and beauty of the biotic community. It is wrong when it tends otherwise" — an ethic that, as Leopold puts it, "changes the role of Homo sapiens from conqueror of the land-community to plain member and citizen of it." [11] There is little in these books that suggests such a common biotic membership, that challenges a view of nature as being anything other than hierarchical and instrumental, there for humans to use as best they can. Casey and Moore create characters who make their living by killing as many fish as they can and who do not apologize for it — indeed, within the fictional worlds of their books, have no need to apologize for it. These examples of New England coastal fiction, then, hardly seem to be "nature writing," and indeed seem on the surface to be indifferent if not antagonistic to the ideology and topical focus of such writing — and yet, I want to argue, in their way they are as "green" as anything that Henry Thoreau or Annie Dillard have written, as amenable as they are to a positive ecocritical reading once we make the necessary adjustments to the definition of "eco" and thus to the focus of "criticism."

The work of environmental historian Richard White offers an important means for assessing the environmental knowledge, behavior, and awareness of fishermen of the sort who appear in Moore's and Casey's books. In an essay entitled "'Are You an Environmentalist or Do You Work for a Living?': Work and Nature," White comments critically on the phenomenon whereby, as he puts it, "most environmentalists disdain and distrust those who most obviously work in nature. Environmentalists have come to associate work — particularly heavy bodily labor, blue-collar work — with environmental degradation. This is true whether the work is in the woods, on the sea, in a refinery, in a chemical plant, in a pulp mill, or in a farmer's field or a rancher's pasture. . . . Nature seems safest when shielded from human labor."[12] By contrast, environmentalists themselves tend to encounter nature most typically through play and leisure activities — hiking, canoeing, camping — and to do so in landscapes, such as parks and so-called wilderness areas, that seem on the surface not to have been obviously worked or shaped or altered, which bear human toolmarks lightly if not all but invisibly. This tendency, in White's view, only serves to contribute to "a larger tendency to define humans as being outside of nature and to frame environmental issues so that the choice seems to be between humans and nature."[13] Not only is this a false distinction in light of the ubiquitous cultural reworking of the earth's surface, as I have noted above and as White also argues, but the attitude behind it denigrates and denies a fundamental means by which humans have typically encountered and understood their physical environs: the fact that "work itself offers both a fundamental way of knowing nature and perhaps our deepest connection with the natural world."[14] White elaborates: "Work that has changed nature has simultaneously produced much of our knowledge of nature. Humans have known nature by digging in the earth, planting seeds, and harvesting plants. They have known nature by feeling heat and cold, sweating as they went up hills, sinking into mud. They have known nature by shaping wood and stone, by living with animals, nurturing them, and killing them. Humans have matched their energy against the energy of flowing water and wind. . . . They have achieved a bodily knowledge of the natural world."[15] Thus, in this view, it is workers in nature — fishermen, loggers, farmers, miners, and the like — who achieve the most intimate, detailed knowledge of nature: not a mystical, spiritual kind of knowledge, but one born of experience, of the necessity of assessing and adapting to or reacting against the particular physical properties of earth and wind and water and flesh in a specific time and place; not the result of uplifting leisured visits to the natural world, but of immediate, difficult, daily, full-body immersion in that world; a knowledge of force and slope and texture and resistance that is carried in the memory, joints, and muscles. True, this sort of knowledge does not necessarily result in responsible environmental behavior — as White points out, "a connection with the land through work creates knowledge, but it does not necessarily grant protection to the land itself"[16] — but recognizing the interconnection of work and nature, and the very presence of workers in nature, can not only help break down barriers between parties who are conventionally aligned on opposite sides of environmental debates, but can also help blur the conceptual boundary between the human and nonhuman worlds that prevails in our culture and that is so strongly acknowledged and policed by many environmentalists and writers, thus perhaps leading to new approaches to environmental problems and concerns.

It is dangerous, after all, to conflate the environmental effects of practices and policies carried out by industrial corporations with the perspectives and perceptions of workers on site, which may run counter to the views of distant bosses and which may see the acts that workers are required to perform as a sort of betrayal of their environmental experience and the ethic that that experience has inspired. In their book *The Northern Forest*, for instance, journalists David Dobbs and Richard Ober quote Maine slasher operator Rick Irish as saying, while looking at a clear-cut, "The landowners are just squeezing it for all it's worth. . . . It's a shame to walk in the woods and see something like that. I just don't like to see it. But I have to feed my kids, and that's what buys my biscuits at the end of the week. I make a living at this. But I don't have to like it."[17] According to Dobbs and Ober, this sort of attitude is increasingly common among

Maine loggers, growing out of their uneasiness over seeing "signals that long-term economic, aesthetic, and biological integrity is being sacrificed for short-term profits."[18] Out of environmental knowledge gained through work rather than through leisure and literature, perhaps, can come a sort of environmental wisdom and responsibility, yet one that does not bring with it a corresponding desire to sweep working people off the landscape completely.

In the two novels I want to start with, John Casey and Ruth Moore depict characters who have come to know the ocean, the shoreline, and the life that these environments contain through exactly the sort of work processes on which White focuses in his article. Dick Pierce, in Casey's *Spartina*, and the three generations of fishermen in the Ellis family — Grampie, Guy, and Jeb — in Moore's *Candlemas Bay* are all portrayed as skilled and successful fishermen, their success deriving from the detailed knowledge of tide, wave, current, ocean bottom, and fish and crustacean behavior that they have developed over time since they began working as boys. And yet their environmental knowledge emerges as secondary to other elements of characterization and plot: Dick Pierce and the men in the Ellis family are all coming to terms with the loss of family position and property over time, some more angrily or adaptively than others. While their status as fishermen is central to the identity of each of these characters, fishing is not really what these two books are about; the novels have much more to do with personal and familial connections to place than with economic relationships with place, and in that sense fishing is just something that these characters do to earn money while they are simultaneously working out larger questions of identity and negotiating comfortable emotional and imaginative relationships with the places where they live, places where they have long yet steadily diminishing family histories. And yet, as these characters work out their problems, in one important sense their work-derived environmental knowledge, and their fidelity to that knowledge, remains central to the resolutions at which they arrive. In the pages of their novels, Casey and Moore use environmental awareness within the context of work to establish the ethical status of their characters in general: the more a fisherman pays attention to, conforms his work practices to, and remains within the limits enforced by the shifting vagaries of sea and shore, both developing knowledge through work and using it responsibly, the more his moral standing is enhanced in the book as a whole, in personal, social, and economic terms as well as in environmental terms, and the more satisfactorily are his personal crises resolved. So, while none of these characters seems particularly interested in saving the whale, and while the ocean and shore on which they earn their livings are unsentimentally portrayed as workplaces more than anything, in an indirect way these works of coastal fiction, while possibly seeming to challenge many conventional ecocritical precepts, nonetheless carry a powerful "green" message: through knowing nature, albeit doing so through work rather than contemplation, in the end comes salvation.

John Casey's *Spartina* is by no means a polemic, like so much of what is conventionally considered to be nature writing; instead, Casey elaborates his environmental ethic through the unfolding of the plot and through revealing the confused, bitter thoughts swirling through his protagonist's head. Dick Pierce is a Rhode Island fisherman who is struggling angrily with his diminished economic circumstances. At one time his family owned all of Sawtooth Point, but after his uninsured father died after a long and expensive illness Dick had to sell off most of the family land to developers and second-home builders, an unfortunate necessity that has filled him with anger: he must always choke back "his feeling of bitterness that the old man's dying had stripped away the rest of the point, leaving his son and grandsons bare." [19] Much of the book has to do with Dick's efforts to finance and build his own fishing boat, *Spartina*, which would not only ease his chronic financial straits but would also, in his mind, help compensate for the loss of the family land: "Okay — he wouldn't get the point back. He'd get the goddamn boat built. It'd all go into the boat — the little piece that the old man had left and whatever scraps and crumbs could still come off the point from the new owners" (47–48). Some of the money comes from doing menial jobs like organizing a clambake for the summer people, but much of it also comes from Dick's share of the income derived from successful swordfishing runs in which he participates as a crewman on someone else's boat. For all his faults and anger, Dick is gifted at finding and catching fish, a talent that over the years has become second nature to him to the point where he feels a sort of affinity with the ocean waters and the life within them: as he tells another character at one point, "When I was a kid, I had two knacks that impressed my father. One was I could get in our skiff to go after stripers and I'd get a feeling. I'd get out to the sandbar and I'd get a kind of nervousness along the inside of my forearm. It would be one side or the other. That was the side the fish were on. . . . Wasn't anything mystical. What it probably was, was there was so many little clues I couldn't figure them out one by one, so I just got one general feeling." As to Dick's other knack, "I could feel the tide. I still can, just not as well. I'd be in school and I'd start thinking about the tide and I'd know — . . . I didn't calculate. I didn't remember what I'd seen in the morning and then count the hours. I just felt it. Especially if the tide was coming in. I'd feel it rising up in me. Up my arms and chest." This too Dick does not attribute to any mystical agency, but to an ingrained environmental attentiveness: "it mattered to me, so I kept track without knowing I was keeping track" (174–75). Through a lifetime of fishing—fishing not for leisure and recreation but because his life literally depended on it—Dick has internalized so much information about the water and salt marsh in which he works, and the life that those environments contain, that his sense of identity derives as much from his location as from his sense of bitterness and grievance: "Dick loved the salt marsh. Under the spartina there was black earth richer than any farmland, but useless to farmers on account of the salt. Only the spartinas thrived in the salt flood, shut themselves against the salt but drank the water. Smart grass. If he ever got his big boat built he might just call her *Spartina*, though he ought to call her after his wife" (3). He eventually does name the boat *Spartina*, of course, signaling what to him is the most important relationship in his life, and so his boat emerges as an expression not only of his accumulated anger but of his environmental affiliation and expertise.

And yet, over the course of the book that anger leads him to betray his knowledge, not using it consistently as a means of gaining a legitimate livelihood but perverting it in the service of various illegal money-making schemes, all with the goal of getting his boat built and thus salvaging his pride. Early on in the book, Dick borrows a friend's tractor, drives it into a protected wildlife refuge in the marsh over a nineteenth-century farmer's long-abandoned causeway that only he knows about, and poaches clams from the beach. More seriously, Dick gets involved in a cocaine-running scheme with his shady friend Parker, using his knowledge of the labyrinth of navigable passages through the salt marsh to bring Parker to a rendezvous with his buyer. The plan goes awry, Parker's connection fails to show up, federal agents begin searching the area, and Parker and Dick end up hiding deep in the marsh, hoping desperately that they won't get caught. They manage to escape, thanks to Dick's detailed knowledge of the terrain: "In his mind, Dick could see the marshes—one marsh really, laced with creeks and dotted with ponds, divided by fingers of high ground. The whole marsh fringed by beach to the south. The chart of the problem was clear to him." At the same time, though, Dick realizes that he has come to his current hiding place at the high cost of his integrity:

> But what he saw more insistently, as he pictured the marsh from above, was the hummock where he and Parker lay beside the skiff. Himself dissolving. Not dissolving with fear, though he admitted that possibility. He could put that off for the moment. What was dissolving was something more important than nerve. It wasn't that there was that much wrong with bringing in some coke, . . . but there was something wrong with how *he'd* got there. And something else in him was being leached into the mud. It wasn't Parker's fault. This stuff didn't do Parker any harm, it was part of Parker's way of cutting through Parker's kind of life. But Dick saw himself leaking into the hummock. (108–109)

This dissolution of all that is best in him, this use of environmental knowledge in a morally dubious cause, is the most serious crisis that Dick faces in the novel. It signals the beginning of a long dark period for him, intensified shortly thereafter when he embarks on an adulterous affair with Elsie Buttrick, a member of one of the local wealthy families and an employee of the state Department of Natural Resources, two aspects of her life that pertain centrally to Dick's motivations and misguided purpose: "Could it be that he'd gone to bed with Elsie Buttrick because she was part of Sawtooth Point? Because she was one of the Buttricks, the Perryville School, the life of tennis courts and sailboats that had overgrown the point, squeezed him up Pierce Creek to an acre of scrub? Of course, it had squeezed him into a concentrated purpose too" (215). Still, this purpose, this monomania, has come at the cost of warping his relationship with his natural surroundings, and Dick's illicit sexual liaison with a representative of Natural Resources is therefore perhaps symbolic and symptomatic of how far from his best and truest self he has strayed — to be crude about it, he's screwing the natural resources rather than feeling wedded to them. Dick knows that he is straying, but seems powerless to stop himself: "He'd blasted himself loose. That's what he'd been doing all summer. Even that half-assed clam poaching. Going out with Parker, going along with Parker. . . . He'd blown himself out of all that, without knowing what he was doing. Or maybe he'd known. But he'd damn well done it, and he'd better look out where he was going now. Adrift or under way, he was afloat on his own" (187), at the mercy of circumstances, no longer in control of who or where he is.

Dick's regeneration comes when he stops drifting, when he once more fits himself to his environmental circumstances, literally saving himself through applying all that he knows about ocean, wind, and wave. His turning point comes after he finally finishes his boat: a hurricane is moving up the coast just as he gets *Spartina* into the water, and, since his insurance coverage will not go into effect until the next day, he knows he has to take the boat out to sea all night and try to outrun or at least ride out the storm if it is not to be lost with no possibility of rebuilding it. Before he sets out, another captain reminds him, "If you do get caught, don't fight. You understand? More power isn't the answer. The shape of your boat is the answer. If you punch hard against a big wave, it's harder for her. If you let her yield, she'll move right. The wave is a wall if you run at it. If you move with it, it's a wave" (255). Dick does get caught and badly battered by the storm, but, through adapting himself to the storm rather than fighting against it, he and his boat survive, a fact that he realizes is attributable to his own expertise as a boatbuilder, the way that he has been able to construct a vessel that is exactly suited to its environment, the way he has drawn on the knowledge that is most intrinsic to his identity, the best and deepest part of him: "He'd made her. He'd made her, but now she was the good one. She was better than him. It wasn't alarming to hear this news, it was deeply, thickly soothing. She was lightened of a dangerous disabling weight" (263). She was better, at least, than the person Dick had become, but at the same time she came out of the person that Dick had always been, the Dick whose sense of who he is comes out of where he is, in a healthy and not an angry relationship: "He'd been a son of a bitch, he'd been bitter and hollow and stupid, but not about *Spartina*. *Spartina* had come through him untouched" (318).

After riding out the hurricane, Dick begins to return to himself, realizing that "feelings already in him had been laid bare to himself by the storm, some bare rock of what he really cared about" (283), and this return to health and integrity is expressed through Dick's renewed perception of and sense of relation to his local land- and seascape after the maelstrom subsides. Returning to the harbor, he gets a clear view of the shoreline, and sees that

> the air was scrubbed so clean, the wind had winnowed the dead brown away so completely, the green was so bright in the morning light that particular blades jumped across the water to his eyes. . . . Just this place, the shore from Green Hill to Galilee, the upland from the beach to the Great Swamp, the Matunuck Hills, and Wakefield, just five miles wide and five miles deep, was just about all the land he knew. He hadn't known it could come on him like this. It was as if he'd been blown clean as the marsh grass, been scoured even more than *Spartina*'s wheelhouse. . . . Each time he looked on this stretch of land, the green came into him like a stroke of paint on parched clean wood. (278)

Both Dick and his environment have been cleansed and purged, emptied of useless dead detritus by the force of wind and rain, renewed by their ability to adapt themselves to the physical circumstances of the world surrounding them. As such, Dick becomes conceptually linked to the local environment itself: not only has Dick built the perfect boat for the waters off Rhode Island, but the green spartina grass, as he has recognized earlier, is able to thrive despite its saline environs, drinking the water while shutting out the salt. The book's last passage finds Dick renewing his personal, imaginative connection with his environment. Having resisted one last temptation with Elsie, "He closed his eyes and saw the marsh, the salt pond at high water, brimming up into the spartina. . . . He could forget everything he'd thought here, this night, in the middle of his life. Let it ebb, and it would flow back. He felt like the salt marsh, the salt pond at high water, brimming" (375). Dick will resume his life, emptied of anger and bitterness, captain of his boat and of his life once more. That boat will continue to catch as many fish as possible — while not an industrial employee like the Maine loggers mentioned earlier, an independent fisherman like Dick still must sell to a wholesaler and thus is firmly embedded in a larger resource-exploiting economic structure — and Dick himself doesn't seem the type who would subscribe to any sort of conventional environmentalist agenda. But the story of his crisis and redemption makes clear that he is saved by his environmental knowledge, the abuse of which first led him astray but the return to which gets him back on course — a knowledge that derives, first and last, from his life as a worker getting his livelihood from the ocean and its fringing landscape.

Dick Pierce's boat is a cultural artifact that amounts to an eloquent interpretation of the environment in which it is meant to operate, shaped by the distillation of a lifetime's professional experience in ocean waters, mediating between nature and culture — or, more properly, blurring the boundaries between the two, embodying culture as given form by the guiding influence of nature. In Ruth Moore's novel *Candlemas Bay*, that artifactual interpretation of nature is enacted more literally in the form of an annotated sea chart that has been handed down through generations of fishermen in the Ellis family since 1871. "This was a man's work-sheet, and not only one man's. There were navigation notes here that had been handed down from times before the coast was mapped. Ellises had been Candlemas Bay fishermen when the U. S. Coast and Geodetic Survey was a gleam in its founder's eye. And if you planned to be like them, this was your work-sheet, too, from a record that went a long way back into time."[20] The chart is a cumulative map of personal, experiential knowledge, both a guide to the environment and a chronicle of family history, as exemplified by several notations written by Captain Malcolm Ellis, whose chart it originally was, that catch the eye of the teenaged Jeb Ellis early in the book:

> *"Hell in a Northeaft Snowstorm,"* Great-Grandfather had written in one place, and *"Muddy Bottom, God Blaft!"* in another. Little Nubble Shoals had *"an old baftard of a tiderip;"* and there were other epithets elsewhere, explicit and unprintable, in green ink now faded to a pale bile.
> *Chandler's Ledge. The Weaver. Red Rock. Grindstone.*
> *"Crofs currents. Ebb tide sets here southeaft by southe.*
> *Eben killed, Dec. 24, 1880.*
> *John loft, Jan. 12, 1888."*
> Eben, Gramp Malcolm's brother. Died of cold and exhaustion trying to row home against the tide and a northwest gale. They found him frozen to his skiff on Christmas Eve.
> Great-Uncle John, Malcolm's youngest son. He had been setting a load of lobster traps off Little Nubble Shoals in a dory. They never found anything of him. (4)

This chart summarizes the environmental experiences and observations of many men who have worked the waters that it diagrams, and the way that characters in the novel treat the chart, and either maintain fidelity to the knowledge that it contains or fail to do so, becomes a measure not only of their fitness as fishermen, but of their moral strength and standing as well. As in *Spartina*, the ocean is viewed primarily as a workplace, a storehouse of seafood, and a system of navigational problems and challenges; yet also as in that book, paying attention to that environment, respecting it, acknowledging it as central to your identity and as the primary shaping force in that identity, can determine if you will be saved or lost both literally and spiritually.

Young Jeb pores reverently over the chart every chance he gets, absorbing its lessons and savoring the sense of palpable connection with earlier generations of his family that it inspires in him: "No, there was nothing unreal about Great-Grandfather Malcolm, Jeb thought, his hands on the limp texture of the chart. That might be his gray, blurred fingerprint alongside the compass-rose. Those brown stains, there, you might take for extra islands, if you didn't know that was where his thumb had bled, once when he stuck it with a mackerel-jig" (7). Jeb's father, Guy, on the other hand, is the most troubled and tragic character in the book, a Dick Pierce who never manages to turn himself around, and his sad fate seems clearly related to his indifference to the sea chart and what it represents both as an aid to navigation and as a family artifact summarizing a lineage of blood, knowledge, and attachment to place. The old map is in Guy's possession as the novel opens, but "Guy never used the chart. . . . What he liked to keep [it] for, was to show to the summer people, when he had a sailing party aboard, as he had, sometimes, in the season. 'Now, here's something might interest you,' Guy would say, sliding it out of its oilskin case. 'My grandfather's chart, dated 1871, with all his navigation notes on it. He was quite an outspoken old party, so maybe you'd better not show it to the ladies.' . . . Oh, he could really lay himself out for the summer people" (2–3). This cavalier behavior, this conversion of family knowledge and history into something quaint to thrill tourists with, deeply offends Jeb: "No, Great-Grandfather's notes weren't anything to hold up as a curiosity to strangers, unless you showed them with pride and told what was behind them. The way Guy made it out, Malcolm had been an eccentric old character, who wrote down cusswords on his chart just for the heck of it. But Capt. Malcolm Ellis, in his day, had gone from a rowboat to a pinky to a mackerel schooner, and finally to a fleet of mackerel schooners, all earned with his own hands. And there was a lot more on his chart besides cusswords" (4–5). This lack of respect shown to the past and, by extension, to the ocean environment itself is echoed by the lack of respect that Guy shows to himself and everyone around him. Guy is improvident, continually spending money that his family doesn't have; he is an alcoholic; and he is violent, drunkenly attempting to beat his own son Jeb in the novel's most harrowing scene. The sea chart, in both its physical and its symbolic dimensions, figures centrally in Guy's violent behavior toward Jeb: Guy has forbidden Jeb to be on his boat while it's moored in the harbor, but Jeb sneaks on anyway to study the chart, an act that enrages Guy when he finds out about it. Not only does he renounce his own heritage in the way that he treats the sea chart, he attempts to cut the next generation off from its family history and its close traditional working relationship with the waters of Candlemas Bay.

The basis of Guy's anger and self-loathing is the fact that he feels he's been driven to fishing for a living rather than having chosen it freely; he'd rather be doing anything *but* fish, but his family's circumstances have kept him within the family trade despite his greedy ambitions and sense of entitlement to something better. Like Dick Pierce early in *Spartina*, Guy nurses a grievance, a deep feeling of injury and outrage. The Ellis family, having founded the settlement of Candlemas Bay, had long been the area's richest and most prominent family, but their money and status had dwindled over time due to poor investments and the Great Depression, a run of bad luck that Guy takes as a personal affront: "Things weren't always the way they are now . . . ; most of the Ellises poor as pot-water, and he, Guy, the poorest of the lot. Time was, he had traveled high, wide, and handsome, with plenty to spend and a future coming up. . . . He could have been a big man in Candlemas Bay; or even the state. Hell, he'd had the brains to be president of the country, and would've been something like that, if he'd only had the breaks. If the old man hadn't lost the money" (33). In the end, this selfish attitude, this resentment of rather than connection to his lineage, proves to be Guy's undoing and costs him his life. Returning in his boat one night from a nearby town, where he had watched a movie about a bank robbery, Guy is so distracted by greedy fantasies about money and restoring what he sees as his lost birthright that he loses track of where he is on the water and runs aground on the Weaver Ledge. Any Ellis with any amount of environmental knowledge in his head would have avoided such an accident, but Guy has amply demonstrated his estrangement from what the family sea chart represents, and thus, lost in his own thoughts, makes a stupid navigational error: "The south spur [of the Weaver] wasn't marked, but it was always awash, in plain view, at ordinary high tide. A spring tide would put it under. Even then, there was generally some movement of water over it to show where it was. Besides, everybody knew the Weaver" (36). By taking his knowledge of the bay for granted, by not paying careful attention to the surface of the water, by not aligning himself with the relationship with the environment that his forebears and his own son have, Guy literally forgets where he is and, unable to swim, drowns after his boat sinks, a fitting end, perhaps, to a vain, angry, self-centered life, a life notable for its lack of respect for the people and the environment around him. Through ignoring the chart, ironically, Guy earns himself a place among its annotations of Ellis family deaths at sea.

After Jeb and Guy's father, Grampie, having heard Guy's distress call on the radio, try and fail to find him, Jeb dives down to Guy's boat, now lodged underwater on a lower ledge of the Weaver, and rescues the old sea chart from the cabinet where Guy kept it. If Guy stands at one ethical pole in the novel, the generations on either side of him stand at the opposite one, as Jeb's salvaging of the chart implies. By the end of the novel, Jeb is well on his way toward becoming a successful fisherman himself and is recognized as the true heir of the Ellis lineage: as he and Grampie are out on a fishing trip,

> Grampie said, "It's been a good summer. About the best time I ever had in my life. But I don't doubt it's made a sucker out of you for going on the water, Jebby, same as, time was, was made out of me."
>
> "Not only this summer, Grampie."
>
> "That's right. I guess it would be a good many summers, not only yours and mine."
>
> He means Gramp Malcolm, Jeb thought. And the others, back along.
>
> Against the stillness, he heard his mind say their names. (297)

Grampie dies on this trip, expiring quietly in his bunk after going below to rest, but Jeb's final thoughts in the book are that "the way

Grampie went was as good a way as there was for a man to go, right in the middle of his work, at the top of his skill and nothing lost, knowing he had just done, and still could do, a good job. It was time, not to forget him, but to look ahead; not to put out of your mind the men of the old times, . . . but to see now what was best to do with the time to come" (308). Jeb's final act in the novel is to mark the date and place of Grampie's own death on the family chart, a chart that he seems certain to continue to use as a guide for his identity as an Ellis and for his work as a fisherman. Guy's fate demonstrates the cost of failing to pay attention to and respect the ocean, of assuming that he is in control of where he is rather than recognizing that the sea can snatch his life away at any time if he ignores it, but it is a fate that Jeb seems certain to avoid: while dedicating his life to harvesting the sea's resources, to working in the same way his grandfather did, he knows that the only way to do that safely is to acknowledge the power of the ocean, to understand it as best he can, and to take what it gives him.

Interestingly, in the only overtly environmentalist passage in the book, Guy and Grampie find themselves on opposite sides of an argument: Grampie accuses Guy of overfishing and rails about the pollution in the harbor inlet and the absence of Atlantic salmon, while "Guy would grin. 'There'll be fish when I'm dead. If there ain't, Christ, I won't know it. . . . We got a nice little fish-packing business here in Candlemas Harbor, making work for people, and, by God, the more it stinks, the better I like it. A good stink means a lot of fish coming in. I'd rather smell it than flowers. Who cares for a few salmon? Taste better out of a can'" (12). It's not surprising that these two men with such opposite attitudes toward the chart and the ocean it interprets should have such divergent attitudes toward the health of local fish populations and the purity of the water, although it could also be argued that this is simply the difference between a sustainable and a nonsustainable use of a resource with no sense of nonanthropocentric environmental ethics being expressed at all. While environmentalist polemics are hardly what the novel is about, though, it nevertheless manages to portray a vivid sense of the way that environmental knowledge can be gained through work while also arguing implicitly for the value of conforming one's actions to the limits and constraints imposed by the nonhuman world. As Dick Pierce also learns, certain relationships to the environment can enhance ethical health in all aspects of life, while others can drag you to your doom.

I want to stay with Ruth Moore here for a bit, not only to give more space to an unfortunately neglected regional novelist but to tease out more of the ecocritical implications of her work. Having been herself a member of a fishing family as well as a fifth-generation native of Great Gott Island — just off the southwestern corner of Mount Desert Island, where Bar Harbor and Acadia National Park are located — Moore focused almost exclusively on work and community life in Maine's island settlements and coastal villages over the course of her forty-year writing career, portraying them with a partisan's fondness while at the same time avoiding sentimentality and simplistic celebration. As an adult, Moore lived and wrote on Mount Desert itself, but her sensibilities — and certainly her *environmental* sensibility — seemed to remain firmly located in her childhood home. Since the establishment of Acadia in 1908, Mount Desert has been drawn into the national parks model of how nature should be seen and experienced, its scenic panoramas and natural wonders standing in clear contrast to the shops, restaurants, and resort attractions of the neighboring town of Bar Harbor. This is "nature" as separated out from "culture," the sort of pristine and spectacular stuff that you have to drive to the far corners of the country to see. (A misleading impression, to be sure: much of the land in the park had belonged to the Rockefeller family prior to the park's establishment, and the system of carriage roads that they had built still offers one of the most popular ways for hikers, bicyclists, and equestrians to see the park.) Moore, however, remained faithful to her experiential, historical understanding of the mutual involvement of humans and the natural environment along the Maine coast, portraying and evaluating each through the quality and character of its interaction with the other. Hers remained a Great Gott view rather than a Mount Desert view, seeing natural places and the processes of human life as inextricably intermingled.[21]

And while *Candlemas Bay* nicely encapsulates Moore's novelistic understanding of the natural world and its place within a work-based system of environmental knowledge and ethics, and of the way that system shapes allegiance and responsibility not only to nature but to other people as well, that book in itself doesn't capture the full range of her thought about the meanings of natural environments and the ideal lives of the people who live and work within them. In her very first novel, *The Weir* (1943), Moore not only anticipates some of the concerns and conclusions of *Candlemas Bay* but also uses the coastal environment itself, not simply the behavior of her characters toward and within that environment, as a central moral touchstone. Without drawing her lines sharply and simplistically, but rather taking into account the complexity of her characters as plausible and flawed human beings, Moore attributes virtue to physical location to a large extent, suggesting that residence on an island rather than on the mainland, and work on the ocean rather than in some more overtly commercial enterprise, is an important key to being a good and honorable person. To be sure, *The Weir* is by no means filled with stereotypically quaint and noble old salts, but rather reflects Moore's lifelong awareness that island residents are just like anyone else — you'd be hard-pressed to find anyone among the novel's hardworking people who doesn't also have his or her full share of anger, stupidity, blindness, and spitefulness. At the same time, though, Moore maps what I think of as a "moral geography" over the course of the book, a gradient of virtue that ties how people behave toward each other to where they live. The complexity of Moore's characters ensures that she doesn't suggest a naive environmental determinism, but the topography of her novel's moral mapping nonetheless carries with it a strong environmental component: within the small compass of the book's setting, the moral peaks lie within the bounds of rough, hardscrabble Comey's Island, while the low points are located in the onshore settlements of "the Harbor" across the channel and Bellport down the coast. By working this spatial dimension into her thought and writing, Moore expands her implicit environmental argument, subtly establishing a particular environment *itself* as a moral presence in addition to the people who live within it, one that can influence those people to a degree if they regard and approach it in the right way — and one, as well, that is by no means an alternative to or refuge from the corrupt human world, but rather is a central part of that world, heavily worked and cleverly manipulated to make sure it surrenders a steady supply of its edible resources.

When we first meet Hardy Turner, one of the book's protagonists, he comes across as a mixture of Guy Ellis and the early Dick Pierce without their sense of loss and entitlement. As with Dick and his "knacks," Hardy possesses a deeply ingrained, almost subconscious environmental awareness, an integration of the self and mind with the local physical world that grows out of many years of work on Comey's Island and its surrounding waters. A backward glance that

Hardy bestows on his house one day while walking down to the water suggests how deeply and literally rooted he is in the landscape of Comey's Island, a grounding that derives both from his own long-term residence and from his family's history in the place: "Years of snugging down on the sturdy stone foundations dug into the top of the low hill on which it was built, had blended it into the line of the hill, so that the eye followed the sweeping curve gently, with no sense of climax in the peaked gables of house and barn. From a distance it seemed almost as if the green turf, with a little extension of growing, could have closed over the roof, leaving no sign that a house had been there. Hardy's great-grandfather had built it, the same Andrew Turner whose date in the island cemetery was 1831."[22] While this image might suggest entombment or a new growth of lawn on a recently filled grave — an interpretation that, as we will shortly see, Hardy himself might embrace to a certain extent — it also suggests some fundamental characteristics of Hardy's relationship to the natural environment around him. Hardy's view of the house shows landscape and human presence blended into a single organic whole, with the artifact of the house becoming subsumed into the dirt and grass around and beneath it, a blended vision that fits human works and activities into the curves and constraints of nature rather than having human will reign supreme. This model of the ideal relationship between people and their natural surroundings is enacted in other aspects of Hardy's life as well, most notably in his awareness of natural cycles and processes. For example, Hardy shares Dick Pierce's near-instinctual grasp of the tides. Climbing into his dory at low tide after his walk from the house, Hardy notes that the boat is floating just clear of the bottom: "In his younger days he would have given himself some slight credit at having judged the tide exactly right. A subconscious time-schedule in his mind paid attention to the working of the tides for him now. Yet if he had been asked at what given time the water would cover any one of the familiar ledges about the Pool, Hardy would have glanced at the tide marks and told instantly" (66). Details and descriptions like these suggest that Hardy is living in the one true place where he belongs, a spot where he can work hard, care for his family, and live a good and satisfying life.

And yet, Hardy's growing dissatisfaction with that life leads him to drift away from his environmental knowledge, his allegiance to it, and his commitment to using it well. Although Hardy was a native of Comey's Island, he left home as a youth to pursue his education and transcend the fisherman's life that awaited him had he stayed, and his travels came to inspire in him a strong sense of ambition and an equally strong distaste for island life and the drudgery of fishing for a living. By the time he was twenty-six, he was an up-and-coming first mate on a freighter in the South American trade, and when he met and married his wife, Josie, on a visit back to coastal Maine they returned to Comey's Island as a stopgap until Hardy could save enough money to fulfill his dream: to own a business on the mainland, "a little store, or maybe a small hotel, and somehow get away from this dead hole of an island" (9). Despite his best efforts, though, he could never save much money through tending his lobster traps and his herring weir, a maze-like trap consisting of a system of nets attached to upright poles driven into the ocean bottom in shallow water. Hardy maintained his dream, but over time it turned sour and embittered him as it seemed less and less likely to come to fruition, and as a result he has become increasingly alienated from where he lives and the ways of life that that environment supports. By early middle age, all Hardy can feel is "disgust for his life and the way he was living it, for his work done day in and day out without much return, disgust for the island with its smallness and hemmed-in-ness and its everlasting monotony" (127). Early in his life, it seems, Hardy had allowed his allegiance to drift away from the island and settle elsewhere; just as his weir captures fish, he himself feels equally entrapped by the brushy maze — as his primary means of livelihood, the weir keeps him there against his wishes, a mantrap as well as a fishtrap.

Hardy's disgust with the weir and what it represents also shows itself in his increasing detachment from his surrounding world of land and sea, as his sense of historical and physical connection to the island and its waters begins to elude him; it's an environment that he no longer understands, in which he no longer seems to belong, and in Moore's world this sort of estrangement, this renunciation of fidelity to a deeply known environment, can lead only to disaster. One day while burning brush in his woodlot, which Turners had carefully managed and gathered fuel from for generations, Hardy is suddenly filled with a sort of exhausted bitterness, realizing how detached he now feels from both his family history and the natural world that has given them food and heat: "They put all that into it, he thought, and handed it on to me. And I don't even want it. . . . He turned his back on the fire and looked at the trees, trying to recover the lost gusto and hopefulness that in another time had made them mean something to a man. But they were only trees, soaring upward in secrecy and silence, and their solitude seemed to him only like an imprisonment" (241) — not unlike the weir, in fact.

Most significantly, and without seeming to realize how or why, Hardy loses his sense of the tide, his subconscious awareness of nature's rhythms and processes; he now seems as estranged from his environment as he once was embedded in it. While watching an approaching storm and deciding whether to take his weir nets down lest they be blown over by the wind and the weir destroyed,

> the problem nagging at him left him feeling foggy, so that the sense of wind and weather he had always depended on didn't seem to tell him anything.
>
> People had said that Hardy Turner could smell a storm three days away, and he'd always thought he could. Now, with the clouds rolling out over Canvasback and the combers beginning to put up their heads so you could see them over the outer ledges, the *feeling* of storm eluded him. . . .
>
> He stood uncertainly, a little stooped and weary in the drooping lines of his loose wet oilskins, trying to convince himself of the signs which now bewildered him. (148)

Hardy makes the wrong call this time, leaving the nets up only to find the weir partially destroyed in the morning. Perhaps showing a vestige of divided allegiance, as well as a lack of will and resolution to completely change the course of his life, Hardy rescues his nets and rebuilds the weir, and does so with such expertise, "all the trained skill of which he was master" (173), that he is rewarded with a rich bonanza: one day he checks the weir and finds that "the water was literally black with fish" (191), and he repeats this success regularly over the course of the summer, his knowledge of current and tide and fish finally paying off in a way it never had before. Hardy seems to regain some of his long-lost confidence and satisfaction as a result, becoming "the center of all, the important man, referred to and talked about, the man who was making money" (220). He even regains a measure of his environmental sensitivity, removing his nets for the season on a beautiful November day simply because he doesn't like the looks of the sky and being vindicated when a rough snowstorm blows in the next day. It seems that Hardy has reached a turning point in his life: having always hated the weir, he now works with it and with the ocean and sky as a single harmonious unit. Perhaps life on the island can be satisfying after all.

But Moore doesn't have this simple a solution in mind for Hardy: he has to betray himself one last time, emphasizing through his movements within the novel's moral landscape the full range of meanings and values that Moore discerns in her coastal environment. Hardy's fishing success allows him to put down a substantial payment on a grocery store in the Harbor belonging to his old friend and schoolmate Willard Hemple; ironically, his great success in working the ocean has allowed him to renounce the ocean completely. While Comey's Island is no paradise — Moore amply demonstrates in the novel that it's largely populated by small-minded, grudge-bearing gossips — the Harbor emerges as a bleak and ugly place, depending on fish-processing factories for its economic lifeblood and thus standing in a secondary, derivative relationship to the hard work and environmental knowledge of people like Hardy, that much farther removed from Moore's perceived source of virtue and worth. A source of both human and environmental degradation, the town even looks pathetic and soul-destroying; as Hardy's adult son, Leonard, realizes about the Harbor's many run-down houses when he accompanies Hardy there so he can arrange his deal with Hemple,

> They had gone beyond the stage where a man with a hammer and a few nails could do much good — uncared-for and forlorn, as if the people who lived in them were too tired and discouraged to mind that their houses weren't anything more than a place to eat and sleep and shelter.
>
> Below them, the tide twice a day went over the beaches, but even its scouring never quite cleaned away the refuse and grease spilled out from the vents of the sardine factory. The salt wind never quite blew away the heavy stench of frying oil hanging in the air over the town. (312)

The sense of foreboding created by the description of the town is fully borne out by Hardy's experience there: despite his unthinking assurance that he'll be treated fairly by his old friend — "I've known Willard for years. I'd just as soon take his say-so" (318) — Hardy gets cruelly cheated, as Hemple breaks his oral promise by stripping the store of its fixtures and using them to set up a rival establishment nearby. When Hardy confronts him, Hemple indignantly splutters out what seems to be the moral code of the mainland: after explaining that his word means "nothin' in a court of law" and that there were no witnesses to their oral transaction, Hemple says, "God, you'd think a man was a criminal jest because he's drove a good bargain. If you've come out the little end a the horn, Chrise, that was your lookout, warn't it?" (336–37). This is a far different ethic from that exhibited on the island, where, despite any bad feelings that people might have toward each other, residents work together when one is in trouble: when Hardy goes out to save his weir nets after the storm, every able-bodied man with a rowboat goes out to help him. "They're doing it for Hardy" (159), his wife, Josie, realizes, not for themselves. One gets the clear sense that it would not occur to the townsmen of Moore's fictional world to do the same.

Shattered and defeated at the end of the book, Hardy learns a difficult lesson, one that Moore keys closely to the ocean environment and the accompanying moral geography of the island and the town. Critiquing the sort of attitude whereby, in Leonard's words, "there isn't a one of us who didn't have a fire built under him the day he was born — to get some place, to be somebody" (341), Moore instead advocates a commitment to place despite any limitations that it may impose, particularly commitment to a place where one can work in nature, adapt oneself to the conditions and opportunities of one's environment, and thereby gain in integrity and achieve a healthy sense of community — and in Moore's life and work, that place is a strip of water and coast, a Comey's Island or a Candlemas Bay. The key to a good life is to synchronize with nature, not spurn it, to belong to a specific environment and to anchor one's life and identity there. As Leonard says angrily about his father at the end of the book, "Why didn't he stay over on the island where he belonged! . . . He was looked up to. He was a man on his own ground. Look at the way people always come to him when there was a tough job on! Look at the things he can do better'n anyone else!" (338). Leonard himself comes to the resolution that Hardy, it seems, should have, and thus is one of the few characters in the novel who seems to have a bright future: while he starts out as a restless young man who wants more out of life than the island can give, "something staunch and self-respecting kept protesting to him that if a man had something he did well, then that was the thing he ought to do" (186). And, like Hardy, Leonard is an excellent fisherman, one perfectly suited to his place and work; as his soon-to-be-fiancée, Alice, realizes at one point, "He was like a tool made especially for the work he was doing. He knew where he belonged, what he was fit for" (218). Leonard and Alice agree to marry at the end of the book and to move back to the old Turner house on the island that Hardy has just vacated — that same house that had settled so organically into the landscape. The implication is that Leonard will also settle in that way and be the better for it, abandoning his ambitions in favor of a renewed commitment to place and a renewed fidelity to his environmental knowledge. So, Moore implies, should we all. If the island represents the highest peak of her moral geography, it does so because it enables a particular working relationship with a particular environment, one whose benefits infuse the souls of its people as well.

(Any of you who have read *The Weir* have probably had an eyebrow raised for a few pages now, since you know that the novel's best fisherman and boatbuilder, Morris Comey, is also a moral monster. Sadistic, vindictive, and violent, he engineers the seemingly accidental death of a fellow fisherman who insults him in a tavern, and toward the end of the book he nearly kills one of his brothers in a fight, only to be thrown overboard to drown by his own mother as she comes to the brother's defense. Clearly Morris gains no moral benefit simply through environmental expertise or living on the island, the clearest refutation of any environmental determinism that may seem to inhere in Moore's moral geography. The difference between life on the island and life in the town, then, emerges as relative and not absolute. Still, the main source of Morris's spiritual corruption is the fact that he keeps himself radically isolated and insulated from any attachment to his fellow islanders. He prefers to work alone, is rude to everyone he meets, hates taking orders and suggestions, and generally treats the rest of humanity with scorn and contempt. Moore seems to suggest through Morris that it's not simply working in nature that represents a good and moral life — it's working *together* in nature that counts, forming a cooperative human community based on shared knowledge and careful use of natural places. While Morris is by no means an environmentalist, and while the events of the book as a whole don't necessarily lend themselves to looking at him through a green lens, I'm tempted to read into him a muted critique of the model of the individual encounter with nature that informs so much of the American nature-writing tradition and of many Americans' idealized interactions with natural scenes. Human communities in nature trump human individuals in nature, just as working in nature trumps playing in nature. Great Gott Island outweighs Acadia National Park once again.)

Now, while I'm trying to complicate conventional thinking about "nature" in this chapter, I still agree with Thoreau when he famously says "In Wilderness is the preservation of the World." I also know that not all fishing activity is benign, that overfishing is a serious problem in the North Atlantic. A couple of years ago here in Portland, for instance, there was a public hearing at which a federal official claimed that "the American lobster is a population at risk," despite protestations from local fishermen that they'd never seen so many lobsters in their lives.[23] And yet Zencey's observation about the phrase "virgin forest" is relevant here: to define something as "wild," as Thoreau does, is still to define it within a human framework, in terms of what it is not — it is not tamed, it is exempt from the workings of culture — and to believe that encountering nature requires walking off to unpopulated zones is to perpetuate the idea that nature is out *there* somewhere, far from buildings and pavement, that just as it is conceptually separated from culture, so is it geographically distant as well. This notion has potentially dangerous consequences: if nature is seen to be contained within the national parks, wilderness areas, and remote forests, then much energy goes into preserving those areas while the rest of the planet, non-natural by definition, can be ignored, given up as a lost cause, and allowed to continue to go to hell.[24] This attitude also denies the way in which most people actually experience and come to know about the natural world. Nature begins within our bodies and extends to the end of the universe, and we come to know nature as our bodies move through the world, walk down the street, work in the back yard, or even fish on the ocean. Nature is "here" as well as "out there."

And yet many ingrained cultural attitudes about people's relationship with the environment persist. For example, a *Maine Sunday Telegram* editorial in the wake of that public hearing on the lobster fishery was headlined "Lobster warning ignored at the peril of resource," and the editorial writer commented that "folks had a grand time telling the [government] scientist he didn't know what he was talking about — but he, too, was right," the editorialist concluded, going on to draw parallels between current lobster populations and the fate of the Plains bison in the nineteenth century.[25] The lobstermen are portrayed here as nature's shortsighted enemies, an attitude that only perpetuates the false dichotomy that Richard White warns against that contrasts leisured nature-lovers with evil, destructive workers in nature. While fishing does, by definition, kill living things and can deplete fish populations, novels like *Spartina*, *Candlemas Bay*, and *The Weir* remind us that there are many ways of knowing and understanding nature, that even unexpected texts can lend themselves to a rich ecocritical reading, and that any respectful encounter with wind and water and wave and tide can lead to environmental enlightenment, ethical reawakening, and the beginnings of responsibility. At the same time, reading these authors and thinking carefully about what they are saying may awaken us to new possibilities for reintegrating ourselves with nature through both our minds and our bodies — through work, through movement, through the realization that the places where the air meets our skin or the ground meets our feet are not frontiers between alien realms, but seamless continua within the natural world.

FOUR

"A Labyrinth of Errors"
Thoreau, Cartography, &
The Maine Woods

In Wendell Berry's novel *Remembering*, a character looks out of his airplane window as he leaves San Francisco, and Berry describes the view: "Afloat in fickle air, laboring upward, the plane makes a wide turn out over the ocean, and heads inland. . . . As they rise from it, the details of the ground diminish, draw together, and disappear. The land becomes a map of itself."[1] By juxtaposing and contrasting the terms "land" and "map," Berry implies a crucial point about mapmaking as a technology and about the relationship of that technology to both the landscape being depicted and the experiences and ways of life of the people who live on the mapped ground. The map is not the territory; any exercise in mapping requires acts of selection and simplification in order to convert a particular landscape into portable and legible graphic form, and as a result certain details get highlighted and others get left out. Thus, as Berry's traveler rises into the sky, "land" becomes "map": the rich and complex San Francisco landscape loses detail, resolves itself into its most visible large-scale features, and, through the frame of the airplane window, becomes a static thing that looks like it belongs in an atlas, a far cry from the ground-level view of the city and its environs as residents and visitors know it, an abstract image giving no hint of the true color and incessant movement of the ocean, the height of the hills, the species of the trees. Thus if the writing of a McPhee or a Moore is one way of getting a landscape or seascape down on the page, using the sensibility of the author or of a set of characters to simplify the scene and thereby make it both comprehensible and meaningful, cartography offers another way of translating the tangled, textured surface of the world into a form that people can easily read, one that brings with it intriguing qualities and problems of its own.

As a particular kind of print medium, maps occupy an interesting middle ground between nature and culture. They are humanly constructed artifacts that depend for their public acceptance on their perceived fidelity to the physical details of the earth's surface. While even the familiar and precise quadrangle maps produced by the U.S. Geological Survey cannot actually duplicate or reproduce the landforms and vegetation in the places they cover, the more "natural" these maps are, the better — the more accurate, the more scientific — they are seen to be. At the same time, though, those same maps pound the landscape flat, meld the complex composition of a forest into a single shade of green, freeze rivers and oceans in one place regardless of rapids or tides. They have a strong basis in nature, but make the land over into an abstraction, a symbol system. Thus it seems that maps, like landscapes themselves, represent an inextricable blending of the earth's non-human surface with the transforming force of human thought and action. Dependent on nature, they remain irreducibly cultural. Still, while the sort of distance and effacement of detail represented by Berry's lofty airplane — whereby the thickly textured world of local life and experience becomes replaced in the visual field by large landforms and broad spatial patterns — is common in most maps we see today, it is not necessarily inherent in the nature of maps, but only in maps as they are conventionally produced in the modern world. And perhaps no American writer knew this better than Henry David Thoreau.

Thoreau took three trips into the forests, lakes, rivers, and mountains of northern Maine in 1846, 1853, and 1857, thereby establishing himself as what John McPhee has called "in all likelihood, the first tourist into the Maine woods."[2] If not the first, he certainly hasn't been the last, and in writing about his excursions in three essays that were collected and published posthumously under the title *The Maine Woods* in 1864, he also located himself at the head of a long tradition of not only traveling through but writing about the region as well, a tradition that includes John McPhee's own book *The Survival of the Bark Canoe*, published in 1975. In addition to his journeys and his writings about those journeys, though, what may be most interesting about Thoreau in the Maine woods, and most intriguing in light of our discussions of how natural landscape and cultural process can mutually inform each other, is the fact that he was also a skilled and successful surveyor and mapmaker. He is the only major American writer that I know of who made a significant part of his living from measuring and defining tracts of land, and the literary critic Lawrence Buell, in reference to *Walden*, has called Thoreau "very likely the most skillful cartographer who ever penned a literary classic." [3] Moreover, he was not simply a surveyor and mapmaker who happened to pick up a pen every now and then; instead, his writing and his professional work were intricately implicated in one another. I want here to suggest some of the ways in which Thoreau's surveying, and his deeply ambivalent attitudes toward the practice and cartographic products of surveying, strongly influenced how he perceived and wrote about the landscapes around him, in Maine as well as in the more familiar precincts of Concord. He did no surveying or mapmaking in Maine as such, but the eye and sensibility with which he viewed and interpreted the terrain had been honed in part by looking through a surveyor's transit in Massachusetts, and the standards and expectations that he developed in his work led him to make some fairly pungent comments about the state of the Maine maps that were available to him in his travels. The essays in *The Maine Woods* amount in their own way to a mapping of the northern Maine landscape according to Thoreau's particular cartographic sensibility, one that tries as best it can to combine the practical and the poetic, the mathematical and the experiential. In so doing, they inscribe their own presence onto the geographical surface, one that later travelers and writers like McPhee take into account in accomplishing their own literary mappings.

We tend not to think of Thoreau as a professional surveyor and as a cartographer, if only because most of us know him through his written works and he tends not to call attention to that part of his life in his writings, and indeed sometimes actively obscures it. Early in *Walden*, for instance, in the course of distinguishing the course of his life from that of his fellow townspeople, Thoreau emphasizes the inutility of his daily pursuits, the extent to which he is ill-suited to the world of business concerns. "For many years," he says, "I was self-appointed inspector of snow storms and rain storms, and did my duty faithfully; surveyor, if not of highways, then of forest paths and all across-lot routes;" [4] he thus proclaims his imaginative allegiance not to lot boundaries, property lines, and well-traveled roads, but to the landscapes between the lines, the things that could be found off the beaten path. This comment seems a little disingenuous when we realize that, by the time *Walden* was first published in 1854, Thoreau was probably the busiest and most highly regarded surveyor in the town of Concord; he had been making most of his living from surveying for a good five years, if not necessarily during the period when he lived by Walden Pond from 1845 to 1847, and had been interested in the subject for many years before that. In 1840, as a twenty-three-year-old schoolteacher, Thoreau bought some simple surveying equipment for his students to use in order to introduce a practical element into their mathematics classes.[5] This approach suited the taste for precise observation that Thoreau brought to his later writings and his inspections of the natural world; it also appealed to his belief in the value of experiential knowledge, in the priority of the concrete over the abstract, a sentiment expressed most clearly in *Walden* when he said, "To my astonishment I was informed on leaving college that I had studied navigation! — why, if I had taken one turn down the harbor I should have known more about it" (95). And his familiarity with surveying also was to eventually provide him with a regular source of income. He tried his hand at the craft from time to time even while he was living in his cabin at the pond (a fact he mentions only briefly and tangentially in the "Economy" chapter of *Walden*), and in 1849, midway between his first two trips to the Maine woods and in the face of financial difficulties, he decided to advertise his services and pursue the profession on a regular basis, printing up a broadside that read:

LAND SURVEYING Of all kinds, according to the best methods known; the necessary data supplied, in order that the boundaries of Farms may be accurately described in Deeds; *Woods* lotted off distinctly and according to a regular plan; Roads laid out, &c., &c. Distinct and accurate Plans of Farms furnished, with the buildings thereon, of any size, and with a scale of feet attached, to accompany the Farm Book, so that the land may be laid out in a winter evening.

Areas warranted accurate within almost any degree of exactness, and the Variation of the Compass given, so that the lines can be run again. Apply to Henry D. Thoreau.[6]

While we might not habitually link the word "woods" with the phrase "regular plan" when we think of Thoreau, he himself made the conjunction as an acceptable way of spending his time and making some money.

Thoreau quickly made a name for himself as a surveyor. His work was noted locally for its accuracy and honesty. In 1850, he was hired to survey the new courthouse lot for the town of Concord, and he performed over twenty private surveys during the year as well. His account book for 1851 lists a further thirty jobs, and it was clear that Thoreau had hit on a source of income that he would be able to draw on for the rest of his short life.[7] At the same time, in many ways it was more than just a job, for surveying appealed to Thoreau in many ways both intellectually and personally. It was congenial in many ways to his general way of seeing: it provided another outlet for his penchant for precise, accurate, detailed, patient, empirical observation, the same way of engaging with landscapes and natural life that ultimately underlay the metaphysical speculations of works like *Walden* and also provided the matter for later ecologically oriented natural history essays such as "The Succession of Forest Trees" and "Autumnal Tints." In addition, surveying quite simply provided him with a convenient and remunerative way to spend a lot of time outdoors, in the natural world that he valued so highly and that provided his imagination with so much to work on.

This latter benefit appears most clearly in the journal that Thoreau kept for his entire adult life. By and large, surveying does not figure at all prominently in the journal — it clearly was not high on the list of things that Thoreau felt moved to observe and comment on from day to day. Insofar as he does mention surveying, it is as a means to other observations, a way of getting him physically to places where he could see and think, either to better understand the workings of the natural world or to draw philosophical or aesthetic conclusions from that world. The entry for November 18, 1851, illustrates the process by which, as Thoreau puts it, "the man who is bent upon his work is frequently in the best attitude to observe what is irrelevant to his work." The entry begins, "Surveying these days the ministerial-lot. Now at Sundown I hear the hooting of an owl," and he attempts to illustrate the sound: "hõo hoó hóo — hoorer — hóo." He continues: "It sounds like the hooting of an idiot or a maniac broken loose. This is faintly answered in a different strain apparently from a greater distance — almost as if it were the echo — i.e. so far as the succession is concerned." So far, he is trying to observe and record as accurately as possible, in the spirit of the selfsame survey that brought him out there. But he moves from there to speculate on the wider significance of what he has seen: "It is a sound admirably suited to the swamp & to the twilight woods — suggesting a vast undeveloped nature which men have not recognized nor satisfied. I rejoice that there are owls. They represent the stark twilight unsatisfied thoughts I have. Let owls do the idiotic & maniacal hooting for men. This sound faintly suggests the infinite roominess of nature — that there is a world in which owls live."[8] Two days later, he even suggests that the act of surveying not only puts him in contact with nature, but increases his openness to its influences: "Hard and steady & engrossing labor with the hands especially out of doors — is invaluable to the literary man — & serves him directly — Here I have been for 6 days surveying in the woods — and yet when I get home at evening somewhat weary at last, and beginning to feel that I have nerves — I find myself more susceptible than usual to the finest influences — as music & poetry — The very air can intoxicate me or the least sight or sound — as if my finer senses had acquired an appetite by their fast."[9]

And yet, while surveying was often able to satisfy him in so many ways, at the same time Thoreau often found both the effects and the larger implications of his work to be deeply troubling: it seemed to dull his "finer senses" as often as it whetted them, and he could not escape the fact that, by surveying woodlots and other parcels of private property, he was contributing to the process of shrinking that "vast undeveloped nature," that "infinite roominess" in which the owls lived. On December 12, only three and a half weeks after observing the owls, Thoreau complained that "I have been surveying for 20 or 30 days — living coarsely. . . . Indeed leading quite a trivial life — & tonight for the first time had made a fire in my chamber & endeavored to return to myself. I wished to ally myself to the powers that rule the universe — I wished to dive into some deep stream of thoughtful & devoted life — which meandered through retired and fertile meadows far from towns. . . . I wished to live ah! as far away as a man can think. I wished for leisure & quiet to let my life flow in its proper channels — with its proper currents. . . . Might do my own work & not the work of Concord & Carlisle — which would yield me better than money."[10] All too often, surveying left Thoreau feeling like he had to bracket or anesthetize his usual sensitivities in favor of concentrating on the job at hand, and at the same time he often found that job to be, in his opinion, unimportant and annoyingly petty: after accompanying the Concord selectmen on a perambulation of the town boundaries in 1851, he complained that he had been "dealing with the most commonplace and worldly-minded men, and emphatically trivial things,"[11] and in 1853 he commented in general that "all I find is old bound-marks, and the slowness and dullness of farmers reconfirmed."[12]

Even worse in Thoreau's eyes, by doing surveying that was often a preliminary to woodcutting or cultivation on the part of the people employing him, he found himself a party to the bounding and destruction of that same natural world that sustained him and to which he longed to escape. The fact of his aligning himself with the developers of Concord's wild lands was a troubling irony that he found difficult to reconcile; as he noted on May 1, 1859, after surveying the site of a new factory village, "With our prying instruments we disturb the balance and harmony of nature."[13] In fact, he feared that his complicity in defining land as property might warp his own vision, making it too completely material and erasing his sympathies with nature, as he confessed in his journal on January 1, 1858: "I have lately been surveying the Walden woods so extensively and minutely that I now see it mapped in my mind's eye—as, indeed, on paper—as so many men's wood-lots, and am aware when I walk there that I am at a given moment passing from such a one's woodlot to another's. I fear this particular dry knowledge may affect my imagination and fancy, that it will not be easy to see so much wildness and native vigor there as formerly. No thicket will seem so unexplored now that I know that a stake and stones may be found in it."[14] The implications of being complicit in having "*Woods* lotted off distinctly and according to a regular plan," as Thoreau himself had put it in his 1849 advertising broadside, came to be too much for him. In the end, Thoreau viewed his profession of surveyor with a profound and deep-seated ambivalence, in that it simultaneously sustained and destroyed the visual, spiritual, emotional, and imaginative relationships with landscape and nature that he valued so highly.

Surveying, of course, leads to mapmaking, and Thoreau's attitude toward maps and mapping — that paperbound view of the world that he feared he was coming to carry in his mind's eye — was as ambivalent as his feelings about its contributing science.[15] To a large extent, the literary and graphic products of Thoreau's pen show him to have been quite a map aficionado. Thoreau was a skilled cartographer, as befits a man with his eye for detail and his reputation for accuracy as a surveyor. He appreciated maps as artifacts and enjoyed creating and copying them, frequently doing so as a way of memorializing a journey he had made. Robert F. Stowell and William Howarth's

Thoreau Gazetteer includes a map that Thoreau drew of the route of the trip he made with his brother John in 1839 that provided the material for his first book, *A Week on the Concord and Merrimack Rivers*.[16] The map extends from Concord on its southern edge to Mount Washington in the north, and even includes what he calls "Sebago Pond" across the New Hampshire border in Maine. Thoreau also drew a careful map of the far end of Cape Cod, a region that he had explored extensively over the course of three visits in 1849, 1850, and 1855 and that he wrote about in his book *Cape Cod*.[17] Thoreau habitually studied maps before taking trips in addition to using them as a means of memorializing his travels, and on at least one occasion his thirst for cartographic study and ownership led him to a rather comic extreme. He traveled to Canada in 1850 without being able to study the terrain beforehand, since adequate maps were not available in Concord. One day after dining in Quebec, "remembering that large map of Canada which I had seen in the parlor of the restaurant in my search after pudding, and realizing that I might never see the like out of the country, I returned thither, asked liberty to look at the map, rolled up the mahogany table, put my handkerchief on it, stood on it, and copied all I wanted before the maid came in and said to me standing on the table, 'Some gentlemen want the room, sir;' and I retreated without having broken the neck of a single bottle, or my own, very thankful and willing to pay for all the solid food I had got."[18]

Not only did Thoreau enjoy making, possessing, and using maps for both practical and imaginative purposes, he had a lively interest in historical cartography as well, valuing the cartographic productions of the past more for their scientific accuracy than their aesthetic qualities. In *Cape Cod*, for instance, he spends many pages toward the end of the book summarizing the history of European exploration and cartographic representation of the Cape and of the New England coast in general, arguing that while "John Smith's map, published in 1616, from observations in 1614–15, is by many regarded as the oldest map of New England, [and] was the first that was made after this country was called New England, for he so called it," Samuel Champlain's map of the area, "made when it was known to Christendom as New France," not only predated Smith's map, but was a superior example of the cartographer's craft.[19] The French map's spatial extent, the wealth of "geographical, ethnographical, zoölogical, and botanical" information it contained, its attention to the variation of the compass, and the many separate charts and soundings of individual harbors it included, combined to make it "a completer map of the New England and adjacent northern coast than was made for half a century afterward, almost, we might be allowed to say, till another Frenchman, Des Barres, made another for us, which only our late Coast Survey has superseded" (268). In all, Thoreau concludes, "the explorations of the French gave to the world the first valuable maps of this coast" (273), and he attributes that value to the scrupulously careful observations and comprehensive attention to detail of explorers and mapmakers like Champlain, whom he quotes approvingly: "It seems to me that I have done my duty as far as I could, if I have not forgotten to put in my said chart whatever I saw, and give a particular knowledge to the public of what had never been described nor discovered so particularly as I have done it" (269). Insofar as Thoreau the surveyor valued accuracy in his own work, he seems to recognize in Champlain something of a kindred spirit.

To Thoreau, then, the French explorers and cartographers provided an ideal model for mapmaking, using their time wisely and well: the reason that the French charts were the best, in the end, was that "they went measuring and sounding, and when they got home had something to show for their voyages and explorations" (273). Along with his observations on Champlain, this comment indicates the extent to which Thoreau's cartophilia was tempered by the habitual primacy that he put on accuracy and detailed observation; in his eyes, a map had little value if it did not correspond to what he took to be observable facts, to the empirical realities of geographical experience, and therefore did not lend itself to efficiently serving some practical purpose, be it navigation or wayfinding or property delineation. As we will see momentarily, for example, on his Maine travels Thoreau summarily dismissed Moses Greenleaf's famous and popular map of the state as "a labyrinth of errors," not worth the paper it was printed on. To Thoreau, it seems, a map was valuable only insofar as it accurately reflected what was out there on the ground.

And therein lay the largest shortcoming that Thoreau found in maps, a fault similar to that which he found in the craft of surveying. Just as surveying made him fear that he would end up seeing only woodlots and not wildness, so was he dismayed by the very limited aspect of landscapes that maps could capture on paper, the way that, regardless of their scientific accuracy, they reflected only the smallest, most partial facet of geographical experience. The geographical world contained much more than distances, coastlines, place names, the boundaries of fields and townships: it contained wild plants and animals, light and sound and scent, emotional and spiritual truths, and the omission of these things was an inaccuracy that no amount of hard work with pen and paper could redress. As he commented in his journal on November 10, 1860,

> How little there is on an ordinary map! How little, I mean, that concerns the walker and the lover of nature. Between those lines indicating roads is a plain blank space in the form of a square or triangle or polygon or segment of a circle, and there is naught to distinguish this from another area of similar size and form. Yet the one may be covered, in fact, with a primitive oak wood, like that of Boxboro, waving and creaking in the wind, such as may make the reputation of a county, while the other is a stretching plain with scarcely a tree on it. The waving woods, the dells and glades and green banks and smiling fields, the huge boulders, etc., etc., are not to be found on the map, nor to be inferred from the map.[20]

And this complaint doesn't take into account those aspects of the landscape that are not even available to sense, let alone mappable — the moral lessons and metaphysical truths that Thoreau discerned in the facts of the natural world. While his comment in *Walden* about surveying forest paths and across-lot routes may have obscured the extent to which he was involved in the world of surveying and mapping, in another sense it fulfills Thoreau's demand for complete and comprehensive accuracy quite nicely: he knew that the really interesting things in the landscape happened beneath and between the mapped and mappable features, in the woods and on the short cuts between one measured boundary and another, and that they too inevitably fell within his surveyorly purview. As a result, his project as a writer and a human being became to reconcile his ambivalences as best he could, to simultaneously bring to maps and mapping both his strict technical and empirical demands and, through the very pursuit of those demands, his informing sense that gathering and checking and recording those details led directly to deeper understanding, that his job was not done to his satisfaction unless the map had been annotated somehow with experience and reflection.

Thoreau's best-known exercise in surveying and mapmaking, one that appears in the pages of *Walden*, provides one instance where he manages to successfully resolve his ambivalences, to inextricably combine exacting measurement and depiction with larger philosophical speculations rather than see the two exercises as inimically opposed. The attitudes toward surveying and cartography that he expresses here came to affect not only his assessment of the maps of Maine available to him on his travels, but his perception and evaluation of the Maine woods environment as a whole. In the chapter entitled "The Pond in Winter," Thoreau sets out to dispel myths and misconceptions about Walden Pond, particularly the popular belief that it was bottomless: "As I was desirous to recover the long lost bottom of Walden Pond," he writes, "I surveyed it carefully, before the ice broke up, early in '46, with compass and chain and sounding line. There have been many stories told about the bottom, or rather no bottom, of this pond, which certainly had no foundation for themselves. It is remarkable how long men will believe in the bottomlessness of a pond without taking the trouble to sound it" (333). To Thoreau, all speculations and conclusions about the natural world need a solid grounding in facts, in measurement and careful observation, or else they will be little more than flights of fancy, their reality anchored only in people's minds and bearing no necessary connection to the world around them: as he puts it, "The amount of it is, the imagination, given the least license, dives deeper and soars higher than Nature goes" (336). Consequently, he sets out to find the depths and heights of his own particular patch of nature so that he can better fit his thinking to its contours: he surveys the shores of the pond from its frozen surface, cuts holes in the ice so he can sound the bottom, and concludes that "I can assure my readers that Walden has a reasonably tight bottom at a not unreasonable, though at an unusual, depth"; far from its being bottomless, "I fathomed it easily with a cod-line and a stone weighing about a pound and a half," and he lists the depth as "exactly one hundred and two feet" (335). Thoreau took over one hundred soundings in all, and then mapped the pond at a scale of ten rods to an inch (fig. 3). He later made a more careful copy of that map; this map was later simplified and lithographed for publication in the first edition of *Walden* in 1854, and it has appeared in most subsequent editions as well. This piece of precise surveying and cartography appears a little anomalously in what is otherwise a very personal and meditative work, but it serves to remind readers that, whatever else the book is about, it derives first and foremost from Thoreau's

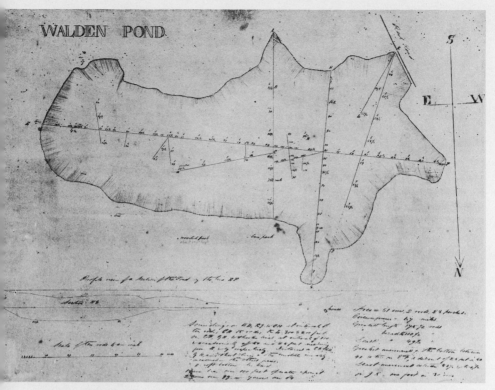

3. Thoreau's survey of Walden Pond. Courtesy Concord Free Public Library.

experience with a particular pond of specific dimensions nestled in the wooded landscape of Concord, Massachusetts.

Having made and recorded these measurements, though, Thoreau is led immediately to their larger implications, to what they can teach him and his readers about human life and conduct, exhibiting what critic William Howarth has noted as his constant attention to "the moral significance of facts." [21] After reporting his exact measurements of the pond's depth, he comments, "What if all ponds were shallow? Would it not react on the minds of men? I am thankful that this pond was made deep and pure as a symbol. While men believe in the infinite some ponds will be thought to be bottomless" (335). As he dismisses and corrects the inaccurate beliefs surrounding the pond, then, he does not do so at the expense of all imaginative engagement with that mysterious body of water, demonstrating his awareness that while nature is not purely symbolic, fodder for the philosophical imagination, nor is it simply material, its entire significance summarized in a few sketched lines and tabulated figures — while maps by definition must correspond as exactly as possible to the facts on the ground, the ground is not the only place where those facts lie.

As he maps and writes about the pond, then, we find Thoreau attempting to synthesize the two perspectives in a single way of seeing, scrutinizing his map carefully for what he can read in those symbolic depths, gauging not only its visible surface but its unseen foundation. "I laid a rule on the map lengthwise," he writes, "and then breadthwise, and found, to my surprise, that the line of greatest length intersected the line of greatest breadth exactly at the point of greatest depth" (337). Having extracted this observation from the map, he speculates as to whether he has discovered a new scientific law of limnology, a convenient formula of measurement. At the same time, he goes on to conclude that "what I have observed of the pond is no less true in ethics. It is the law of average. Such a rule of the two diameters not only guides us toward the sun in the system and the heart in man, but draws lines through the length and breadth of the aggregate of a man's particular daily behaviors and waves of life into his coves and inlets, and where they intersect will be the height or depth of his character" (339). A weighty conclusion for a simple map to bear, perhaps, but indicative of how Thoreau thinks a map is best read, as a guide to both the physical and the metaphysical, not only to landscape but to the human mind and heart, as when he refers to Walden and other ponds as "earth's eye; looking into which the beholder measures the depth of his own nature" (233)—as well as to the beauty, integrity, and ongoing life of the natural world itself.

Reconciling his divergent, ambivalent attitudes toward surveying and mapping — reading maps both for their accuracy and for the chance they afford to see deeply into the landscape and himself, putting objective fact and subjective perception on an equal footing — allows Thoreau to reconcile the uneasily coexisting aspects of his own modes of thought and expression as well. In discussing the moral lessons of his Walden map, he notes that most people "are conversant only with the bights of the bay of poesy, or steer for the public ports of entry, and go into the dry docks of science" (340), but he is both kinds of person in one, simultaneously a poet and a scientist. Through reading his own map not only for its accuracy in indicating the pond's bottom but for its poetic, symbolic value as well, Thoreau achieves a unified vision on the frozen surface of the pond, as in the instance at the end of "The Pond in Winter" where, "when the ice was covered with shallow puddles, I saw a double shadow of myself, one standing on the head of the other, one on the ice, the other on the trees or hillside" (341–42). It is this two-shadowed man, then, at once hardheaded surveyor and visionary transcendentalist, who took those trips to Maine in the 1840s and 1850s and wrote about them in the essays that make up *The Maine Woods*, a book that was shaped in many ways by Thoreau's emerging philosophy of cartography.

On the surface, maps appear to figure very little in the pages of *The Maine Woods*, with Thoreau occasionally and briefly mentioning them by name only to comment on their usefulness (or lack thereof) in his travels. In the book's first essay, "Ktaadn," an account first published in 1848 of his 1846 trip up the Penobscot to Maine's highest mountain, Thoreau and his party stop at a public house at Mattawamkeag, on the Houlton military road. He writes: "The last edition of Greenleaf's Map of Maine hung on the wall here, and, as we had no pocket map, we resolved to trace a map of the lake country: so dipping a wad of tow into the lamp, we oiled a sheet of paper on the oiled table-cloth, and, in good faith, traced what we afterwards ascertained to be a labyrinth of errors, carefully following the outlines of the imaginary lakes which that map contains. The Map of the Public Lands of Maine and Massachusetts is the only one I have seen that at all deserves the name."[22] Thoreau took his next journey to Maine in 1853, and in his subsequent essay "Chesuncook," first published in 1858, he writes of encountering this exemplary map again as he enters the saloon of the Moosehead Lake steamer at Greenville: "there, very properly, was tacked up the map of the Public Lands of Maine and Massachusetts, a copy of which I had in my pocket" (91). Still, soon even this map lets him down: he reaches the other end of the lake and portages over the Northeast Carry, accomplishing "a gradual descent to the Penobscot; which I was surprised to find here a large stream, from twelve to fifteen rods wide, flowing from west to east, or at right angles with the lake, and not more than two and a half miles from it. The distance is nearly twice too great on the map of the Public Lands, and on Colton's Map of Maine, and Russell Stream is placed too far down" (94). Here too the maps in Thoreau's possession seem as well suited for getting him lost as for helping him find his way through the woods.

Thoreau's final direct reference to particular maps comes toward the end of the book's last essay, "The Allegash and East Branch," which describes Thoreau's final trip in 1857 and which first saw publication when the book as a whole appeared in 1864. At one point on his way down the east branch of the Penobscot, he comments that "we could not find much more than half of this day's journey on our maps (the 'Map of the Public Lands of Maine and Massachusetts,' and 'Colton's Railroad and Township Map of Maine,' which copies the former). By the maps there was not more than fifteen miles between camps, at the outside, and yet we had been busily progressing all day, and much of the time very rapidly" (279–80). And not only did Thoreau correct his maps in print, he occasionally inserted corrections directly on the maps themselves, annotating them from his own experience: Stowell and Howarth note that Thoreau's own copy of the "Map of Public Lands of Maine and Massachusetts" was found to contain faint pencil notations including corrections of distances and areas as well as names for features not identified on the map.[23] Thoreau's first expectation of a map, then, his primary criterion for its even deserving the name "map," is that it faithfully reflect the verifiable facts of the geographical surface, that his spatial experience in moving through the landscape correspond to and corroborate the features and distances inscribed on the map's surface. To fail to do so invokes his wrath and calumny: he mentions maps directly in *The Maine Woods* only when he finds them to be wrong, when they conspicuously fail to do their job, and given his standards the phrase "labyrinth of errors" is perhaps the worst possible insult he could have directed at the fruit of Moses Greenleaf's labors.

Thoreau seems sincerely disappointed that his maps have let him down, and his complaints and cavils reveal a somewhat surprising failure to grasp or acknowledge that the quality and accuracy of maps is directly bound up with the circumstances of their production, as well as a naive expectation that maps, by definition, constitute direct reflections of the geographical surface. The way in which the information was gathered not only for Greenleaf's map of Maine but for other maps as well led almost inevitably to the sorts of distortions and omissions that so vexed Thoreau, and his remarks are an indirect commentary on the constraints under which surveyors and cartographers worked to produce these maps, maps of a much larger and less intimately known area than Thoreau had the luxury of being able to scrutinize in precise detail in Concord.[24]

The "Map of the Public Lands of Maine and Massachusetts," like the maps of Greenleaf and Colton to which Thoreau also refers, is a political map, depicting boundaries, rivers, and roads on a township-by-township basis, and it was compiled in a piece-by-piece format, through the cartographer's linking together township surveys drawn up by surveyors in the field, a process that by its very nature led to omissions of data and details. An example from the mapping of Maine will illustrate why these sorts of errors were inevitable: in this case, John Webber's 1833 survey of Soldier Town, which had been set aside to be granted to veterans of the Revolutionary War (fig. 4). In producing a map of this sort, surveyors would not necessarily have run every line in the grid. They would run only a certain number of lines and then interpolate not only the other lines, but the hydrologic features that they crossed. As one line crossed a river, and another line crossed what seemed to be the same river, the mapmaker would connect the two as best he could according to field observations and educated guesswork. Moreover, since the concern of surveyors was to run the lines and not bother with Thoreau's beloved "across-lot routes," they often had very little information to impart about the interiors of their surveyed squares; so estimation frequently played a large role in the final product, and these estimates were not always accurate: one small pond on Webber's map is shown as draining to the west, whereas later maps based on more extensive field observation would show it correctly as draining to the east. Finally, being first and foremost property surveys, township plats like these paid little attention to surface relief or features other than rivers and ponds, since those elements of the landscape had nothing to do with land divisions and sales and were thus irrelevant to the map's purpose. The result was a piecemeal, statewide sequence of maps like Webber's, blank stacks of smaller squares containing only a few lakes and rivers drawn in on the basis of fairly sketchy information.

Despite their limitations as comprehensive depictions of the earth's surface, survey maps like these provided the basis for the larger state maps that Thoreau consulted. Both Greenleaf's and Colton's maps of Maine trace their lineage back to Osgood Carleton's 1802 "Plan of the District of Maine," which incorporated its methodology—"drawn from several plans"—directly into its title in its 1795 manuscript form (fig. 5). When Carleton got the contract from the Massachusetts government to produce the official maps both of Massachusetts and its District of Maine, he compiled them from information contained in surveys that each town had sent of its territory, as well as from

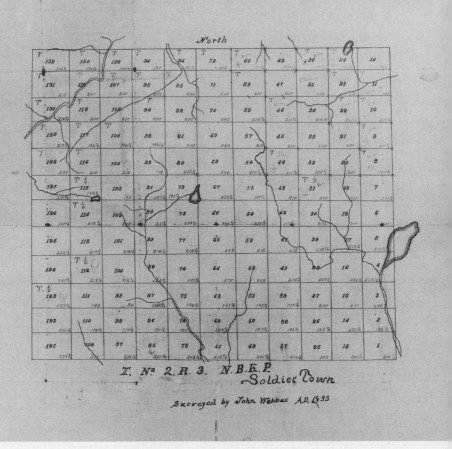

4. John Webber's 1833 survey of Soldier Town, Maine.
Courtesy Nathan Hamilton.

surveys for lands in Maine supplied by the Committee for Sale of
Eastern Lands. Carleton's final product was thus determined by the
amount and quality of material that he had been given to work with;
not only were the individual surveys not comprehensive over the entire surface of the area they depicted, but they varied in quality, requiring that Carleton do his own estimation and guesswork from time
to time in the face of incomplete or conflicting information. His final
map of Maine thus perpetuated any inaccuracies provided to him in
his source materials, and the as yet unsurveyed portions of the district
were by necessity left blank.

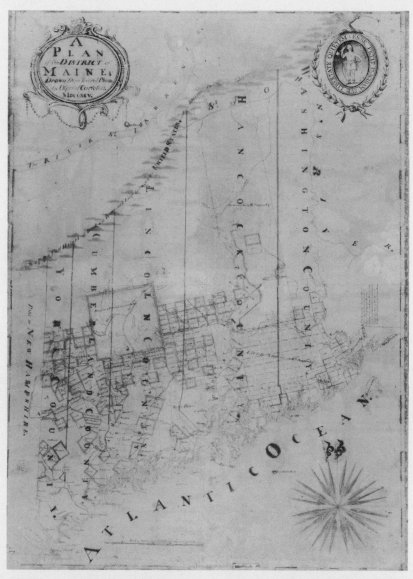

5. Osgood Carleton, "Plan of the District of Maine," 1795.
Courtesy Osher Map Library, University of Southern Maine.

In method and, to a large extent, in content, Carleton set the standard for cartographers of Maine for half a century to come. Moses Greenleaf's maps, both his 1815 "Map of the District of Maine from the Latest and Best Authorities" and his 1820 "Map of the State of Maine," were based largely on the information contained in Carleton's

Thoreau, Cartography, & The Maine Woods

6. Moses Greenleaf, "Map of the District of Maine from
the Latest and Best Authorities," 1815. Courtesy Osher Map Library,
University of Southern Maine.

map, with the addition of further details gathered in the intervening years (fig. 6). Greenleaf's map thus contains both more township squares and more hydrologic features than Carleton's, although Greenleaf was operating under the same methodological constraints that Carleton was and also perpetuated any inaccuracies that Carleton's original map contained. Given the circumstances of its production, then, when Thoreau copied Greenleaf's map and took it up the Penobscot with him, essentially field-checking it against experiential observation, it is not surprising that he pronounced it a "labyrinth of errors." Colton's "Railroad and Township Map of Maine," both the 1853 edition that Thoreau would have taken on his second trip and the 1855 edition that would have been available to him on his third trip, continued the process of statewide coverage, now containing at least the outline of all the state's townships, but Colton relied on the information contained in earlier maps as well as on the variable quality of township surveys, and so his products too, even though they were the latest available, came up short under Thoreau's critical scrutiny (fig. 7).

In subsequent years, as maps were improved as a result of better and closer field scrutiny, their comprehensiveness and fidelity to the facts on the ground increased significantly, a result as well of their being tailored specifically to the task of navigating through the forest instead of simply delineating parcels of property, geared toward movement through a continuous landscape rather than legal definition of discrete pieces of the landscape. Thomas Sedgwick Steele's 1880 tourist-oriented *Canoe and Camera* map of the Moosehead Lake region, for example, was much more detailed than any of the maps Thoreau used — and, incidentally, accurately reversed the drainage of that little pond in Soldier Town, showing it as a part of the Kennebec River watershed rather than the Penobscot River watershed (fig. 8). Steele's map would have likely satisfied Thoreau's navigational purposes as well as his standards of what qualifies as a true and worthy map, but it lay too far in the future for this pioneer among Maine tourists. When he made his forays into the forest, he was forced to rely on maps ill suited to his purpose and so corrected them with his famous crankiness, demonstrating an exacting standard of cartographic accuracy, but also either ignorance of or impatience with the circumstances under which maps of large areas were necessarily produced.

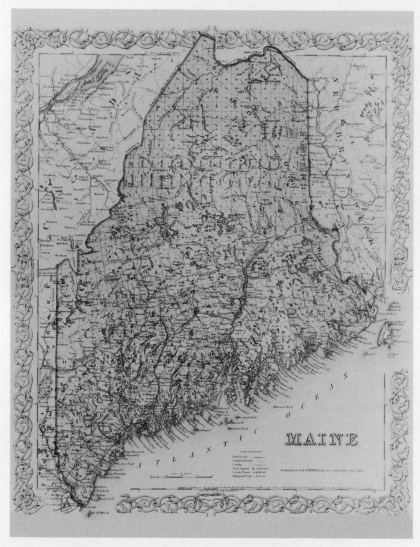

7. Colton's "Railroad and Township Map of Maine," 1853.
Courtesy Osher Map Library, University of Southern Maine.

His brother cartographers didn't have the luxury of being able to indulge a Thoreauvian standard of observation, deviating from lot
lines at will or taking more than a hundred soundings in a sixty-one-
acre pond.

The essays that make up *The Maine Woods* can thus be seen as a cor-
rection of the maps that Thoreau had available to him — or, perhaps

an alternative mapping project, an attempt on Thoreau's part to get down on paper as accurately and completely as possible, in language rather than lines and figures, *all* aspects of the forested Maine landscape as he experienced it and interpreted it, an enactment of the same general cartographic program and philosophy that he demonstrated in surveying and mapping Walden Pond; the book, finally, emerges as nothing less than a map in words, closely detailed and thickly annotated. The book's essays amply fill in the blank spaces on Thoreau's maps with close narrative descriptions of the various flora and fauna that he encountered on his journeys. To take one of dozens of possible examples almost at random, Thoreau notes in the "Chesuncook" essay, upon first embarking on the Penobscot River, that

> its banks were seven or eight feet high, and densely covered with white and black spruce, which I think must be the commonest trees thereabouts, fir, arbor-vitae, canoe, yellow, and black birch, rock, mountain, and a few red maples, beech, black and mountain ash, the common and rarely the large-toothed aspen, many civil looking elms now imbrowned along the stream, and at first a few hemlocks also. . . . The immediate shores were also densely covered with the speckled alder, red osier, shrubby willows or sallows, and the like. There were a few yellow-lily pads still left half-drowned along the sides, and sometimes a white one. Many fresh tracks of moose were visible where the water was shallow and on the shore, and the lily stems were freshly bitten off by them. (96–7)

Not only does Thoreau give his reader a sense of the complexity of riverside forest composition in northern Maine in passages like this, he also suggests just how dense and crowded those woods are with plant and animal life, just how much physical stuff there is on the ground that the maps of the state are simply unable to take account of. In an echo of the journal entry quoted earlier, these are things that "are not to be found on the map, nor to be inferred from the map."

In addition to descriptions like these, the final published version of the book included a detailed appendix that Thoreau had prepared listing all the trees, shrubs, other plants, birds, and quadrupeds that he had seen and been able to identify as well as the places where he found them, giving *The Maine Woods* something of the appearance of a reference book in botany and field biology, literally bringing to life the maps that Thoreau carried. At the same time, Thoreau makes no

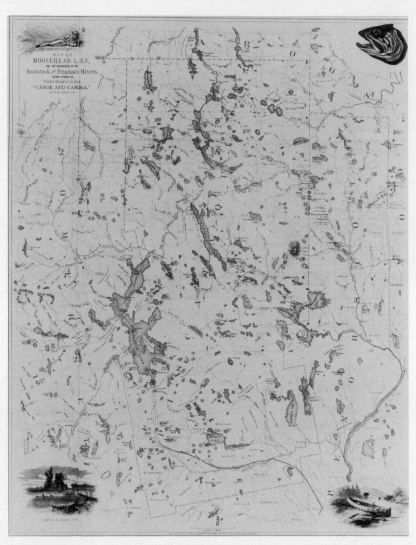

8. W. R. Curtis, "Map of Moosehead Lake" in Thomas Sedgwick Steele, *Canoe and Camera* (New York, 1880). Courtesy Nathan Hamilton.

claims of comprehensive description, of extrapolating his data over a large geographical space despite the particularities of the many individual patches of ground that make up that space, but limits his observations to only those things that he has verified himself — "I speak only of what I saw" (298) — and thus presents his readers with a lived and experienced landscape, not simply another abstract and potentially error-ridden "map" pieced together from incomplete informa-

"A Labyrinth of Errors"

tion. Thoreau's appendix also includes a description of "a good outfit for one who wishes to make an excursion of twelve days into the Maine woods in July, with a companion, and one Indian for the same purposes that I did" (318), listing what such a person should wear and carry as well as what provisions would be necessary and how much the whole kit should cost (about twenty-five dollars "if you already possess or can borrow a reasonable part of the outfit" [320]). Thoreau may have been the first tourist in the Maine woods, as John McPhee observed, but not only does he anticipate that many more people will be following in his canoe's wake, he seems to offer *The Maine Woods* as, if not a map as such, at least a guidebook, not only indicating where readers might want to go but briefing them accurately on what they will see and what kinds of things they might prepare themselves to look for along the route. (As he says at one point in the "Ktaadn" essay, before describing his party's progress through a sequence of small lakes and portages, "I will give the names and distances, for the benefit of future tourists" [46–47].) Here too, as with his prose descriptions of the woods environment, Thoreau enhances the cartographic aspects and implications of his book, getting down on paper a detailed version of the landscape that he seemed to hope readers would find more useful than he himself found the maps of Greenleaf and Colton.

At the same time, Thoreau's concern extends not only to assessing and rectifying his maps' topographical content and rendering a more useful "map" of his own for the benefit of future travelers, but to correcting the very purpose of those earlier maps. Recall that the maps he was using were political maps, emphasizing property divisions and displaying the grid of surveyed lines as one of their most prominent features. Not only were these lines obviously not visible on the ground, but even thinking about the woods in terms of property, Thoreau came to realize, was made irrelevant by the experience of directly encountering this wild forested landscape, and he sets out to correct the mistaken impression that the township lines might leave. Environmental historian Theodore Steinberg notes that "among the more problematic notions informing modern ideas of property is the belief that all land should have an owner. This notion is based on an economic logic that holds that the earth is put to its best use when a person claims it."[25] And claimed and owned land was precisely the kind that Thoreau became familiar with through his surveying work and everyday travels in Concord. By contrast, "Those Maine woods," he says at the end of "Chesuncook," "differ essentially from ours [in Concord]. There you are never reminded that the wilderness which you are threading is, after all, some villager's familiar wood-lot, some widow's thirds, from which her ancestors have sledded fuel for generations, minutely described in some old deed which is recorded, of which the owner has got a plan too, and old bound-marks may be found every forty rods, if you will search. 'Tis true, the map may inform you that you stand on land granted by the State to some academy, or on Bingham's purchase; but these names do not impose on you, for you see nothing to remind you of the academy or of Bingham" (152). These are not the amply surveyed and well-mapped lands that Thoreau knows so well in Massachusetts, and to think of them as property, even though they may be nominally owned by someone, is to distract the observer from their untamed characteristics, from the necessity of encountering and understanding them on their own terms.

Viewing the forest as property, the view that underlies and is encouraged by political maps such as those Thoreau used, is pernicious in another way as well, in that it is literally destructive not only of an appropriate way of seeing but of the land itself: to survey, bound, and sell these woods, in Thoreau's experience, is only a first step in logging them off, a practice that he finds increasingly distressing over the course of his three journeys. In the first essay, "Ktaadn," the sight of the lumber mills at Old Town leads him to lament, "Think how stood the white-pine tree on the shore of Chesuncook, its branches soughing with the four winds, and every individual needle trembling in the sunlight — think how it stands with it now — sold, perchance to the New England Friction Match Company!" He concludes that "the mission of men" in the Maine woods "seems to be, like so many busy demons, to drive the forest all out of the country, from every solitary beaver swamp, and mountain side, as soon as possible" (5). Regaining his optimism and idealism, Thoreau comes to temper this assessment over the course of the essay, characterizing the forest as seen from the high slopes of Mount Katahdin by saying that "it looked as though no one had cut as much as a walking stick there" (66). Here is that "virtually unmapped and unexplored" (83) country that Thoreau had come so far to see, just waiting for his glad embrace.

Still, at times Thoreau seems reluctant to fully immerse himself in that wild landscape, feeling somewhat ambivalent about scaling the mountain's slopes and finding "no man's garden, but the unhandselled globe" (70). While "Nature was here something savage and awful, though beautiful," that beauty doesn't completely outweigh the savage sense of threat that accompanies it: "Vast, Titanic, inhuman Nature" seems to say to human intruders "sternly, why came ye here before your time? This ground is not prepared for you. . . . Shouldst thou freeze or starve, or shudder thy life away, here is no shrine, nor altar, nor any access to my ear" (64). The upper reaches of Katahdin show Thoreau "pure Nature," and "Man was not to be associated with it. . . . There was there felt the presence of a force not bound to be kind to man" (70). While Thoreau's reactions to what he sees on Katahdin certainly hew fairly closely to the conventions of the Romantic sublime, critics today always seem divided as to whether his final retrospective exclamation about his mountain hike represents rapture or terror or something in between — "Talk of mysteries! — Think of our life in nature, — daily to be shown matter, to come in contact with it, — rocks, trees, wind on our cheeks! the *solid* earth! the *actual* world! the *common sense! Contact! Contact! Who* are we? *where* are we?" (71).[26] Thoreau certainly has grounds for exhilaration, having not only ascended out of the grasp of the New England Friction Match Company but into another realm of experience entirely, but at the same time his confrontation with an inhuman nature, perhaps not that dissimilar from the vision offered by Melville's "Whiteness of the Whale," is a sobering and somewhat disheartening one; in response, he stays on the grateful lookout for artifacts and ways of acting that, like maps, serve to place a human mark and inscribe human patterns and meanings on the inhuman landscape.

This search leads Thoreau to describe and assess certain of the things he sees on his trip in ways that might surprise us. Given his modern reputation, we might expect Thoreau to rail vehemently against the litter and detritus that earlier travelers have left behind, but his response to stumbling over an old logging camp is telling: "In the midst of a dense underwood, we noticed a whole brick, on a rock, in a small run, clean, and red, and square, as in a brick-yard, which had been brought thus far formerly for tamping. Some of us afterward regretted that we had not carried this on with us to the top of the mountain, to be left there for our mark. It would certainly have been a simple evidence of civilized man" (45). This passage is particularly interesting in light of Thoreau's feelings and observations about that mountain, as it indicates a desire to give human organization to that off-putting and alien place, to tame raw nature through the presence of culture. In its strictly geometrical form, obviously not "unhandselled" but looking like it had come straight from the factory, this brick resembles the titular artifact in Wallace Stevens's "Anecdote of the Jar," which was placed on a hill and "made the slovenly wilderness/Surround that hill," to the point where it "sprawled around, no longer wild." [27] As with maps, the brick could have potentially provided a human reference point, lending pattern to undifferentiated landscape. And even if Thoreau was not among the "some of us" who wish they'd added the brick to their luggage, he reports the wish without comment, perhaps thereby adding his implicit endorsement.

Moreover, and despite his earlier anger at those who would cut down the white pine tree, Thoreau speaks with admiration and approval of the woodsmen who are acting as his guides, lauding their ability to tame and control the unforgiving and intractable natural world. In describing the process of "warping" a boat upstream against rapids with poles and ropes, Thoreau admits that "I could not sufficiently admire the skill and coolness with which they performed this feat," and after his revelations on Katahdin he seems particularly impressed by these masters of the natural world: on the way back home, for example, Thoreau's party came to "the longest rapid in our voyage, and perhaps the running of this was as dangerous and arduous a task as any." The boatmen shot the rapids with no problem, though, leading Thoreau to note with no apparent irony or criticism that "after such a voyage, the troubled and angry waters, which once had seemed terrible and not to be trifled with, appeared tamed and subdued; they had been bearded and worried in their channels, pricked and whipped into submission with the spike-pole and paddle, gone through and through with impunity, and all their spirit and their danger taken out of them, and the most swollen and impetuous rivers seemed but playthings henceforth" (76–77). Certainly these boatmen are usually employed primarily by the lumber industry, and therefore are nothing if not emissaries of destruction. Still, this fact does not disqualify them from earning Thoreau's admiration: "It was easy to see," he admits, "that driving logs must be an exciting as well as arduous and dangerous business" (42). And at the same time, the woodsmen have carefully mapped the area's rivers and rapids in their heads, knowing just what path to take in order to avoid "being split from end to end in an instant" (76), organizing nature's spaces so they pose no threat but instead lend themselves to human movement and cultural control. These mental maps are not printed on paper like Greenleaf's map, but in the end Thoreau finds them impressively accurate — and, having just spent time in "primeval, untamed, and forever untameable *Nature*" (69), that accuracy seems particularly reassuring.

In the "Ktaadn" section of *The Maine Woods*, then, Thoreau exhibits a complex and somewhat ambivalent attitude toward maps, or at least toward the ways of thinking and seeing that characterize and accompany maps. While at first attacking the habits and customs of property that lead to the surveying of forests and the conversion of trees to matchsticks, Thoreau comes to approve the application of form and pattern to natural landscape lest it be *too* natural: one of his concluding observations about the Maine wilderness is that "it is even more grim and wild than you had anticipated, . . . The aspect of the country is universally stern and savage" (80), perhaps in need of some taming. Also, as we have seen earlier, in this section Thoreau also dismisses Greenleaf's map of Maine as "a labyrinth of errors," insufficiently true to the physical form of the landscape itself, an imperfect way of regularizing and organizing the geographical surface. Still, Thoreau also hints in this section at his ongoing awareness of the more fundamental inadequacy of maps of *all* sorts, the way they overlook the most important physical and imaginative components of the lands they map. Looking back from high on Kahtadin, he says, "There it was, the State of Maine, which we had seen on the map, but not much like that." At this elevation, Thoreau has the same sort of view as Berry's airplane passenger, but finds that view incomplete and misleading. The map may have charted the landscape, simplifying it into a pattern of symbols, but it could give no sign of the ground-level hiker's view of "immeasurable forest for the sun to shine on, that eastern *stuff* we hear of in Massachusetts" (66).

That forest is as important, if not more so, as anything else that the map might contain, and in the later two essays in *The Maine Woods* Thoreau more fully embraces the Maine wilderness despite his earlier reservations about its "stern and savage aspect," reverting to his original criticisms of the logging industry, acting consistently as the forest's advocate, speaking harshly of those who see the woods simply as material to be harvested and sold. In his third essay, "The Allegash and East Branch," Thoreau again attacks with sarcasm and great indignation not only the activities but the entire way of seeing of loggers, as when he describes how the wilderness "feels 10000 vermin gnawing at the base of her noblest trees . . . till, the fairest having fallen, they scamper off to ransack some new wilderness, and all is still again. It is as when a migrating army of mice girdles a forest of pines" (228). Continuing his outburst, he notes that "when the chopper would praise a pine, he will commonly tell you, that the one he cut was so big that a yoke of oxen stood on its stump. As if that were what the pine had grown for — to become the footstool of oxen!" (229). He is angered not only by the loss of forest, but by the entire attitude that lies behind that loss, an attitude that sees and admires trees only for their size and their economic utility: the logger "admires the log, the carcass or corpse, more than the tree," Thoreau notes sadly, and he "fells trees from the same motive that the mouse gnaws them — to get his living" (229). It is in the living tree, not the dead one — just as it is in the wilderness experience, not the surveyed grid — that Thoreau ultimately finds the greatest value.

As Thoreau writes, then, he attempts not only to correct the content and purpose of his political maps, but essentially to incorporate into his own verbal map the presence and perspective of the forest itself. He annotates the available maps not only with his own experience and reflections but with the ongoing experience and right to continued existence of nonhuman nature in the Maine woods, attempting both to fill in the trees and animals on those blank grants to Bingham and the academies and to give those species a public voice as well. He signals this purpose by essentially giving trees human standing as denizens of the mapped and bounded landscape, as deserving to have their names written there too: of the logger who admires the timber that he has just felled, he says, "What right have you to celebrate the virtues of the man you murdered?" (229), thereby conferring metaphorical human status on the fallen tree. This same elevation to full forest citizenship holds true for animals as well. In the essay "Chesuncook," Thoreau pays particular attention to the moose that live in the Maine woods, devoutly hoping to see one and participating willingly in a moose hunt. Upon seeing two moose at the edge of a meadow, though, he has a revelation: "They made me think of great frightened rabbits, with their long ears and half inquisitive half frightened looks; the true denizens of the forest, (I saw at once), filling a vacuum which now first I discovered had not been filled for me" (110). That is, not only do the woods truly belong to the moose, not only is the forest above all their home rather than someone else's, but Thoreau feels that they contain some essence of Maineness, constituting a presence, a geographical feature, that no map or description of the state would be complete and accurate if it did not include. As a result of this revelation, Thoreau is disgusted when he finally sees a moose shot: "one moose killed was as good, if not as bad, as a dozen. The afternoon's tragedy, and my share in it, as it affected the innocence, destroyed the pleasure of my adventure," he concludes, noting that hunting for sport "is too much like going out by night to some woodside pasture and shooting your neighbor's horses." Thoreau finishes his account of the moose hunt by reflecting again on "how base or coarse are the motives which commonly carry men into the wilderness," and decides that even hunters and explorers "have no more love for wild nature, than wood-sawyers have for forests" (119). Here too is a living presence that, Thoreau implies, has just as much tenure and right to continued occupancy as if it held one of those old deeds that define the landscapes of Concord.

Moreover, in the course of describing and defending the woods and inscribing them onto his conceptual map, Thoreau performs the same sort of transformation that he does with his map of Walden Pond, scrutinizing it carefully for the moral applications inherent within it, combining once again the role of the observer, the faithful recorder of landscape, with that of the philosopher and poet. Most people, he says, are content to see the pine tree "in the shape of many broad boards brought to market, and deem that its true success! But the pine is no more lumber than man is, and to be made into boards and houses is no more its true and highest use than the truest use of a man is to be cut down and made into manure. There is a higher law affecting our relation to pines as well as to men. A pine cut down, a dead pine, is no more a pine than a dead human carcass is a man. . . . Every creature is better alive than dead, men and moose and pine-trees, and he who understands it aright will rather preserve its life than destroy it" (121). Just as Thoreau carefully observes and delineates Walden Pond both in its own right and as a means of better understanding human nature, so does he assiduously reconceptualize and fill in the blanks of the Maine maps that he has encountered, incorporating the woods into them not as property or lumber but as living presences, as a means of extracting moral and ethical truths. Once again the surveyor and poet work together to constitute a single way of seeing—

for after all, as Thoreau says, "it is the poet . . . who makes the truest use of the pine, . . . who loves them as his own shadow in the air, and lets them stand. . . . It is the living spirit of the tree, not its spirit of turpentine, with which I sympathize, and which heals my cuts. It is as immortal as I am, and perchance will go to as high a heaven, there to tower above me still" (121–22).

In rewriting and annotating the maps of Maine, Thoreau had one additional source of information, perspective, and experience, one signaled in the description he gave of his "Chesuncook" essay to James Russell Lowell when Lowell published it in the *Atlantic Monthly*: it was about "the Moose, the Pine Tree, & the Indian."[28] While focusing his attention most closely on the nature and meaning of nonhuman life in "Chesuncook," in the book's third essay, "The Allegash and East Branch," Thoreau devotes a great deal of space to his Indian guide, Joe Polis, a Penobscot from Old Town, endeavoring as best he can to catch a glimpse of the landscape through Polis's eyes, gaining some measure of understanding of how its residents defined and interpreted the land long before it was mapped by Carleton, Greenleaf, and Colton; as he puts it, "Nature must have made a thousand revelations to them which are still secrets to us" (181). As the essay reveals, an important part of the knowledge that Thoreau seeks out is linguistic: he shows a growing interest in Indian place-names, coming to understand that the names scattered over a landscape compose a mapping of that landscape, a spatial arrangement of significant places, and that the names of those places often amount to summaries of communal perception and grounded experience, references to the ways in which the landscape has been known and felt by the people who have lived and traveled within it. Here is another significant component of the woods landscape that Thoreau's maps omit, which he has to learn and supply himself.

As best he could over the course of his trip, Thoreau made a careful study of Indian words and names, admitting early on to Polis that "I should like to go to school with him and learn his language. . . . I told him that in this voyage I would tell him all I knew, and he should tell me all he knew, to which he readily agreed" (168). As a result, Polis became something of a walking atlas and gazetteer to his visitor from Massachusetts. Thoreau ended up including and translating a long list of Indian words and place-names in his appendix to the book as a whole, indicating that he thought them to be as important and integral a part of the landscape as the flora and fauna that he also listed there, and he pays particular attention to place-names as facts and as concepts in the pages of "The Allegash and East Branch" as well. "So much geography is there in their names," he says at one point. "The Indian navigator naturally distinguishes by a name those parts of a stream where he has encountered quick water and falls, and again, the lakes and smooth water where he can rest his weary arms, since those are the most interesting and memorable parts to him. . . . And not less interesting is it to the white traveler, when he is crossing a placid lake in these out-of-the-way woods, perhaps thinking that he is in some sense one of the earlier discoverers of it, to be reminded that it was thus well known and suitably named by Indian hunters perhaps a thousand years ago" (270). Polis points out some of these significant spots on Maine's rivers from time to time, thereby revealing not only the density of the layer of place-names that he applies to the landscape, but the extent to which those names differ from those that are marked on the maps that Thoreau carries. "When we passed the Moose-horn," Thoreau notes, Polis "said that it had no name," evidently not figuring largely in his experience or his navigational requirements. Soon thereafter Polis came to a brook that "he called *Paytaytequick*, and said that it meant Burnt Ground Stream," a reference perhaps to a long-ago fire. A bit farther downstream, another lesson in toponyms and in identifying particularly useful stretches of water: "A reach some miles above Pine Stream, where there were several islands, the Indian said was *Nonglangyis* dead-water. Pine Stream he called Black River, and said that its Indian name was *Karsaootuk*. He could go to Caribou Lake that way" (195). Not only does Polis rewrite parts of Thoreau's map, then, he thereby reveals to him how Maine's rivers are experienced by, and therefore how they look and feel to, an Indian moving through them by canoe; this is a world where names are not assigned arbitrarily, but grow out of long-term contact and collective familiarity. He also demonstrates that the maps of Maine that Thoreau carries are misleading in more ways than simply their navigational shortcomings. What looks to Thoreau like featureless forest is anything but that when seen through Joe Polis's eyes—from the Indian perspective, it is as crowded as one of those old Concord deeds and surveys.

Not only had Polis mentally mapped the Maine woods with a system of communal place-names and agreed-upon travel routes, he organized the forest environment into a system of personal places as well, sites among the trees and on the riverbanks that had accrued deep experiential significance for him over the course of his life. Thoreau came to realize this most powerfully when the party left one river and entered another, "chang[ing] the civilizing sky of Chesuncook for the dark wood of the Caucomgomoc" (198), moving into a space that seemed to Thoreau to be particularly wild and forbidding. To Polis, however, it was not wild at all: he knew of a good campsite a short way up the Caucomgomoc, and upon arriving there, Thoreau "read on the trunk of a fir-tree blazed by an ax an inscription in charcoal which had been left by him. It was surmounted by a drawing of a bear paddling a canoe, which he said was the sign which had been used by his family always." Polis had left his mark on the shaggy landscape on his earlier travels, perhaps not unlike the brick that Thoreau had found on his way to Katahdin, and had conceptually claimed this spot of riverbank in the name of himself and his family, a spot that now possesses imaginative meanings that other similar woodland places don't and that he returns to now and again over time. An inscription accompanies the drawing, and Thoreau copies it into his notebook, interlining it with his English translation:

July 26,
1853.

Niasoseb
We alone Joseph
Polis   *elioi*
Polis   start
sia   *olta*
for   Oldtown
onke   *ni*
right   away.
quambi

July 15,
1855.
Niasoseb. (199)

And, in keeping with his customary practice, Polis updates the inscription, this time signing his name in English instead of his native language: "1857, July 26. Io. Polis."

Upon seeing this inscription, Thoreau realizes that "this was one of his homes. I saw where he had sometimes stretched his moose-hides on the opposite or sunny north side of the river, where there was a narrow meadow" (200). Not only had Polis mapped the woods in his mind, not only had he inscribed his name on the landscape (in a significantly different fashion from the way that Concord's property holders had left *their* names all over the town), he had literally domesticated the "dark wood of the Caucomgomoc." Thoreau's use of the word "home" in this context seems to point in two directions: it signifies here a place of residence, where Polis sets up camp on his hunting excursions and butchers and skins his moose, and also takes on the larger sense of "feeling at home," being in a place that is comfortable and familiar. In that sense, the entire Maine woods is Polis's address, a space that he knows intimately and feels perfectly acclimated to, as Thoreau realizes in a further conversation with him: "He sometimes, also, went a-hunting to the Seboois Lakes, taking the stage, with his gun and ammunition, axe and blanket, hard bread and pork, perhaps for a hundred miles of the way, and jumped off at the wildest place on the road, where he was at once at home, and every rod was a tavern-site for him" (201). Far from being the wildest places on the road, Polis's jumping-off spots were places he knew as well as he knew his metaphorical front hall, places carefully "mapped" and linked together in the particular spatial interpretation of the Maine woods that he, and only he, carried in his head.

In addition to Polis's domestication of the woods environment, his division of the landscape into a network of significant places, Thoreau is particularly interested in Polis's woodcraft, his facility in navigating the Maine woods by foot and canoe and in utilizing its plant and animal resources. As with his place-names and his many "homes," Polis's ability to traverse the thickly wooded landscape with ease indicates a deep familiarity with and long experience in the forest landscape, to the point where Polis finds it difficult to bring to conscious notice and articulate the principles by which he finds his way. At one point Thoreau "asked him how he guided himself in the woods. 'O,' said he, 'I can tell good many ways,'" whereupon he touches on a variety of visual and sensory cues that he uses: looking at the differential plant growth on the sides of distant hills in order to gauge north and south, examining trees and rocks for similar signs of northern or southern exposure, sensing wind direction, and so on. "'Sometimes I lookum side hill,' and he glanced toward a high hill or mountain on the eastern shore, 'great difference between the north and south, see where the sun has shone most. So trees, — the large limbs bend toward south. Sometimes I lookum locks' (rocks). I asked what he saw on the rocks, but he did not describe anything in particular, answering vaguely, in a mysterious or drawling tone, 'Bare locks on lake shore, — great difference between north, south, east, west side, — can tell what the sun has shone on'" (184). When Thoreau asks him if he could find his way back to Old Town after being dropped a hundred miles away in the woods in the dark and spun around twenty times, Polis admits that that's not a particularly original idea: "'O yer,' said he, 'have done pretty much same thing'" (184), whereupon he recounts an incident in which he and "an old white hunter at Millinocket" who "said he could go anywhere in the woods" chased a moose for half a day before they caught up to it and killed it. Then Polis challenged the white hunter to return directly to their camp. "'Don't go round and round where we've been, but go straight. He said, I can't do that, I don't know where I am. Where you think camp? I asked. He pointed so. Then I laugh at him. I take the lead and go right off the other way, cross our tracks many times, straight camp.'" Thoreau expresses amazement at this feat: "'How do you do that?' asked I. 'O, I can't tell you,' he replied. 'Great difference between me and white man'" (184–85).

Thoreau is tempted to condescendingly assume that Polis "found his way very much as an animal does," but finally concludes that he operates instead with "a sharpened and educated sense" (185), the result of long experience in reading the subtleties of the landscape. In reaching this conclusion, he also senses that Polis organizes space differently from white travelers, that the kinds of relationships among features on his mental map are as foreign to conventional cartography as the geography encoded in his place-names is unknown to the maps of Maine that Thoreau carries. He even seems to organize the conceptual categories of space and time differently from Thoreau, a habit of mind that Thoreau attributes to Indians as a group. Speaking of an earlier Indian guide, Joe Aitteon, in the "Chesuncook" essay, Thoreau notes that "he had noticed that I was curious about distances, and had several maps," certainly typical behavior for this surveyor and devotee of precise measurement. Thoreau continues: "He, and Indians generally, with whom I have talked, are not able to describe dimensions or distances in our measures with any accuracy. He could tell, perhaps, at what time we should arrive, but not how far it was" (131). Space and time seem to be much more closely linked for Aitteon than for Thoreau, as the Indian seems unable to conceive of distance without defining it in terms of his own movement over that distance; distance to him is a lived experience rather than an abstract application of arbitrary, conventional units. It is hours, not miles or rods, that matter to Aitteon; miles and rods, in fact, seem to be an irrelevant category for him, a puzzling fact to a traveler who quibbles so assiduously with the distances on his own maps and who spent so much of his time precisely measuring lines and acreages in Concord. "Great difference between me and white man," indeed.

His discovery of the nature of Joe Aitteon's spatial world is a particularly striking observation for Thoreau, one that leads him in "The Allegash and East Branch" to quietly question the nature and conventions of maps as he has drawn them and used them in the past, not just criticizing the particular errors and omissions of Greenleaf and Colton but realizing that the simple act of drawing or reading maps on paper does not provide unique access to truth and to geographical reality. His experience with Polis and Aitteon has opened his eyes to a new and equally valid perspective on geographical knowledge; looked at through their eyes, *any* map might seem like a "labyrinth of errors," in its conception if not in its details. As Thoreau puts it, "Often, when an Indian says, 'I don't know,' in regard to the route he is to take, he does not mean what a white man would by those words, for his Indian instinct may tell him still as much as the most confident white man knows. He does not carry things in his head, nor remember the route exactly, like a white man, but relies on himself at the moment. Not having experienced the need of the other sort of knowledge, all labelled and arranged, he has not acquired it" (185). Thoreau here seems to be deliberately critiquing conventional maps, drawing a distinction between "labelled and arranged" knowledge — a cartographic model of landmarks, familiar routes, and clear fixed relationships, by which one moves through the landscape by determining exactly where one is within a larger spatial system and then reading a map — and Polis's alternative system, which seems in Thoreau's description to depend not on fixed routes but on reading the landscape on a place-by-place basis within a context of shifting natural clues and an awareness of predictable natural relationships. And Polis's system works, often better than Thoreau's: on occasions when they had to portage around falls and rapids, Thoreau "observed that he could keep [the trail] almost like a hound, and rarely hesitated, or, if he paused a moment on a bare rock, his eye immediately detected some sign which would have escaped me. Frequently we found no path at all at these places, and were to him unaccountably delayed. He would only say it was 'ver strange'" (276–77). Polis is perfectly capable of using and reading conventional maps — as the travelers were planning their route home, "taking the map, he showed where we should be each night, for he was familiar with the route" (232) — but at the same time Thoreau locates Polis completely outside not only the information contained on the readily available maps of Maine, but outside the traditions and conventions of western cartography altogether. By focusing on Polis and his many ways of seeing in the book's third essay, looking at his names and "homes" and spatial knowledge, Thoreau takes perhaps his most radical and inclusive step in correcting the errors and omissions in the maps at his disposal.

In the years since its publication, and true to its partial stated purpose, Thoreau's literary mapping of the Maine woods has been available as a guide to other travelers and writers as they traverse the region's rivers and forests, and they in their turn, in a continuing process of mapping and revision, have had to adjust their vision to the particular ways in which the book has depicted the landscape. Thoreau is a particularly influential presence in John McPhee's 1975 book, *The Survival of the Bark Canoe*, which I mentioned at the beginning of this chapter, and that book will provide us with an appropriate place to end this cartographic excursion. McPhee's experience provides a useful coda to Thoreau's book conceptually as well as geographically: he suggests that no map is ever complete or definitive despite the care with which it is created, and that coming to a full understanding of any landscape does not depend solely on the skill of the mapmaker; it depends on the sensibilities of map readers as well, and particularly on their willingness not to read the map too literally but, like Thoreau, to annotate it and update it with what they themselves have found on the landscape.

McPhee's book focuses on Henri Vaillancourt, who makes birchbark canoes in New Hampshire in the traditional Indian fashion, and a canoe trip that McPhee and a friend, along with Vaillancourt and two of his friends, take on the same rivers and lakes that Thoreau had explored and described over a century earlier. Vaillancourt and his friends are avid readers of Thoreau, particularly *The Maine Woods*, and the trip is largely inspired by Thoreau's earlier adventures, with the young men intending to follow in his path. McPhee himself had been unacquainted with *The Maine Woods* prior to the trip, but, as he puts it, "read to catch up" in the intervals when he was not paddling.[29] Thoreau has thus mapped out the group's voyage in an important sense, providing a depiction of the landscape that guides, conditions, and mediates the travelers' expectations and experience of that landscape. He does this in several ways: he supplies a destination and route for the group; he shapes the anticipated experience of the group, in that Vaillancourt and his friends are driven into the woods by a desire to have an inspiring wilderness encounter similar to Thoreau's; and he provides a description of the landscape that McPhee can check against his own experience of that landscape as he travels through it 120 years later. And in many ways, Thoreau's "map" turns out to be quite accurate: as McPhee puts it, "The Maine of his bark-canoe trips was the deepest wilderness Thoreau would see in his lifetime. Today, astonishingly, it looks much the same as when he saw it. Lake and river, many thousands of miles of shoreline are unbroken by human structures and are horizoned only with the tips of spruce."[30] As McPhee compares the literary map to the physical terrain, as far as he can tell it is still a reliable guide, with no editing necessary — certainly not a "labyrinth of errors."

In other ways, however, the map turns out to be highly misleading, as the young men make the error of reading the experiential aspect of Thoreau's book, the unmappable aspect of the terrain that Thoreau found missing in conventional maps, as a guide to the sort of experience that they themselves will have — if it's in the book, after all, shouldn't they find it on the ground as well? This ends up not being the case at all: Henri Vaillancourt, avid reader of Thoreau, turns out to be astonishingly inept on the region's lakes and rivers, and the trip becomes much more frustrating than it does satisfying or enlightening, completely opposite to his and McPhee's expectations. Given Vaillancourt's expertise as a canoe maker, McPhee had made the unwarranted assumption that he was an expert canoeist as well, but it quickly emerges that Vaillancourt has never been into the Maine woods before, has never made a long canoe trip, has never even made a portage. His whole knowledge is derived from Thoreau's literary map, and his experience reveals the shortcomings of that map; as a result, McPhee's book becomes a revision of Thoreau just as Thoreau's book can be seen as a revision of Greenleaf and Colton.

And McPhee accomplishes that revision in the same way Thoreau did, through an unmediated encounter with the landscape itself, through taking the place on its own terms rather than on the map's terms; as he puts it toward the end of the book: "There is a time of change in a wilderness trip when patterns that have been left behind fade beneath the immediacies of wind, sun, rain, and fire, and a different sense of distance, of shelter, of food. We made that change when we were still in the Penobscot valley, and by now I, for one, would like to keep going indefinitely; the change back will bring a feeling of loss, an absence of space, a nostalgia for the woods."[31] Like Thoreau before him, McPhee learns to complicate other people's depictions and interpretations of the landscape with his own experience and evaluation of what's out there on the ground. At the same time, he enacts that perpetual fascination that I imagine many of us have: the fascination with maps of all kinds — graphic, yes, but verbal as well — and the ways that they connect us to the landscapes in which we live, leading us to contemplate our own understandings of and relationships to the world around us. Thoreau may have been concerned with correcting errors and omissions on the maps he had, depicting the woods as accurately as he knew how, but those maps, and the words that those maps ultimately inspired, are never finished: they invite all of us to look again not only at the maps and books but at the woods themselves, filling in the blanks according to our own geographical and imaginative journeys.

FIVE

A Walk in the Woods

Art & Artifact in a New England Forest

Thoreau isn't the only one who's ever enjoyed walking in the Maine woods, of course. I do too, and try to do it as often as I can. And I'm often driven to those woods by one of the same impulses that sent Thoreau there so many years ago: the desire to get away from other people, at least for a short time. Thoreau learned a lot from Joe Polis, to be sure, and was ultimately very glad to have recruited experienced rivermen as his traveling companions while approaching and leaving Mount Katahdin, but on the whole he always seemed taken aback when he came across other people and their works on his travels, as though they really didn't belong out there in the forest: on noticing "a ring-bolt well drilled into a rock" on the shore of a remote lake, he notes that "it was always startling to discover so plain a trail of civilized man there."[1] Like many walkers and hikers, I too prefer to avoid the ring-bolts when I take to the woods for an afternoon or a day. I go there to be alone, to think or to clear my mind. I go there to get outside my own crowded, noisy head for a while. I take plenty of walks in my residential neighborhood as well, but there's something about being away from cars and houses and other pedestrians that encourages the pieces of a particularly knotty writing problem to fall into place, say, or that allows me to replace my all-too-human concerns with an outward gaze at a rocky ledge breaking through the forest floor or a turtle surfacing in a quiet pond. If I'm going to spend a day being surrounded by distractions, I prefer them to be the unexpected sights and encounters I can find in a patch of forest, not the usual time-eating tasks

I can find in my office. There's value in having your most pressing concern be not losing the trail.

I particularly love a good view. There's something about getting some elevation under you and being able to take in a big chunk of space at a glance that cleans out the eyes and ventilates the soul. Sabattus Mountain, just outside Center Lovell near Maine's border with New Hampshire, is one of my favorite climbs these days. It's more like a big hill, really, not much of a mountain by western American or even Maine standards: a mere 1,280 feet, with a rise of only 500 feet from the base to the summit. You can climb it in twenty minutes at a leisurely pace. But its bald granite dome falls sharply off on its southern and western sides, offering views of the sort you might not think you quite deserve for so easy a climb. The view from Sabattus is one of those that allows you to indulge the illusion that you've ascended out of the humanized world completely into another, quieter, greener realm (fig. 9). From even that modest height, the forests on the ground below seem to draw together and fill in their gaps to hide everything that humans have added to the landscape. Everywhere you look, you see what seems to be a uniform blanket of treetops, broken here and there by a lake or pond and, very occasionally, a house or farm building, or a tiny clearing in which a microscopic cow or two is grazing. The road you drove in on has vanished completely, as have the various villages you passed through. Around to the west, the southern edge of the White Mountains corrugates the horizon. I can spend a long time just sitting or stretched out on the dome up there, choosing my spot carefully in order to stay away from anyone else who may have made the climb with the same idea I did, staring at soothing greenness or at stirring mountains or at nothing at all. Even though I know better, I like to imagine that, at least for a few minutes, I've traded one world for another.

And yet, being me, I also end up taking close looks at the forest itself, both on the way up Sabattus and from the summit. While there's therapeutic value in thinking of all those massed trees simply as "the woods," noteworthy because of the nonhuman meaning and value I find there, there's value of another kind in looking at them carefully as individual landscape compositions, as unique collections of particular trees. My first time up Sabattus, I sat there feeling impressed by just how unoccupied the surrounding expanse of Maine and New Hampshire looked from that vantage point, taking in what I could pretend

A Walk in the Woods

9. Looking south from Sabattus Mountain, Lovell, Maine.
2000 photograph by the author.

was a latter-day version of Thoreau's Maine where "it did not look as
if a solitary traveler had cut so much as a walking-stick." Before long,
though, my eye was caught by a patch of darker green in the verdant
surface immediately below me. Looking closer, I figured out that it
was a stand of white pine, its sharp if subtle borders separating it from
the prevailing hardwood forest surrounding it. There's a story there, I
thought. That green border probably is, or was, a property line of
some sort. Maybe that piece of land is being managed for pine, or
maybe it was left alone when the lands around it were cleared or
logged off at some point in the past. Or maybe something else. Either
way, people made that pattern in the green because of something that
they either did or didn't do. And as I was climbing the mountain, I had
noticed that the slender young trees of the forest covering the slope
had mossy old stumps scattered here and there among them, their
humped and shaggy shapes suggesting a kind of primeval force but
their even tablelike tops giving evidence of the chain saws that had
created them in the relatively recent past. There were stories there
too — stories of work, of logging and skidding. That hillside was once

alive with voices as well as trees; it rang with the noise of tools and trucks. My view as I climbed to the summit was shaped by old work, and it didn't take too much imagination to place the workmen back in the landscape as I made my way up. I was intending to see and hear nothing but miles of empty air from atop Sabattus, but it's never as easy to leave other people behind as you think, even people from the past. You're never alone in these Maine woods.

Of course, the woods on and near Sabattus aren't the only ones around here that have at some point been part of someone's working life. Just about every patch of New England forest today was once part of a farm, or has been lightly or heavily logged in the past, or both. That entire green landscape that I saw from Sabattus, extending to the horizon and beyond, holds histories, encodes memories, and refers to countless stories, the stories of the people who have lived and worked there and who, through those lives and that work, have contributed to making the forest what it is today. Of course, those stories are implicit in the landscape at best, largely unrecoverable; I didn't exactly see any old loggers sitting on those stumps offering to tell me how they cut down those particular trees, how they chose the ones they did, and what became of the logs once they came out of the woods. True, Maine is full of working forests (and forest workers) today, but the ones that hikers are likely to repair to when they seek solitude look the way they do precisely because they've gone into retirement, so to speak, their former occupants having long since left the scene. All we hear there may be wind and our own footsteps. But just because people have left the woods doesn't mean that they are gone completely. Those memories that the wooded landscape holds are still alive here and there in New England; those voices, while aging, can still be heard. Listening to them can help us bring one more layer to our understanding of just what it is that we're looking at when we're looking at nature in New England. As Thoreau learned when listening to Joe Polis, if we go to the woods guided by memory and story, we will see a changed world: what looks like a place to go to escape the human sphere emerges as a place that's been shaped and patterned by someone's mind and life in the past, a place deeply known, perhaps loved or hated, by a working person or a farm family. If reading Thoreau, or Casey and Moore, or McPhee and Ehrlich, can demonstrate to us some of the ways in which people's lives are implicated in natural places, humanizing those places in some important ways, then walking through a landscape in this region and listening to the voice of someone who knows it well can bring a more immediate human presence to our wooded surroundings, showing us a world that is not just an undifferentiated expanse of natural stuff but that has been structured both physically and imaginatively by the unremarkable everyday rounds of individual and collective New England lives. No matter *where* you look from Sabattus, there's a story there.

A few years ago one of my graduate students, Dana Deering, invited me for a walk in the woods with him and his grandfather, a gentleman named Walter Hale. These weren't just any woods, though; they were the second-growth forest cover of what had once been Mr. Hale's farm in the rural town of Sebago, Maine. The farm was first settled by one of Dana's forebears in 1830, ten years after Maine achieved statehood; Mr. Hale came there in 1927 as a fifteen-year-old hired hand to the farm's owner at the time, Dana's great-grandfather John Douglass. He eventually married Douglass's daughter Edna and stayed and farmed until 1948, when the old house and barn burned down and he took advantage of the opportunity to go into a better-paying line of work as a trucker. Knowing of my interest in New England landscapes, Dana had suggested that I might want to talk to his grandfather some time about the old farm, and the three of us agreed it would be a good idea for Mr. Hale and Dana to actually walk me around the property, essentially giving me a guided tour of the woods. We did so one cool September afternoon, and I brought along a camera and a tape recorder, clipping the microphone to my jacket and turning the recording level as high as I could to best pick up our voices as we walked along and paused here and there. I had told Mr. Hale that I was interested in the history of this piece of land as far as he knew it, and so as we walked our talk centered on what individual pieces of land had been used for and how they had been worked when Mr. Hale was first a hired hand and then a young farmer in his own right. Our words became a rambling, informal conversation that mirrored the rambling, informal nature of our walk, with Mr. Hale recalling stories and episodes and patterns of past work as we stepped over an old stone wall from one former field to another, or as we came to particular artifacts and other personal landmarks that had helped structure the farm landscape in Mr. Hale's mind when he lived there. I wasn't trying to piece together a definitive history of the property by any means, nor am I pretending to present such a history here. Rather, I simply wanted to listen to Mr. Hale talk. Walking through what to me was a homogeneous woodlot, I wanted to see a little bit of what the forest looked like through the eyes of someone whose presence there predated the forest itself; I wanted at least a glimpse of the stories and the voices that inhered in those woods and that were invisible to almost everyone but Walter Hale.

In the end, I heard what I had hoped to and more. Mr. Hale struck me as a pleasant and plain-speaking man, not a natural storyteller but someone who will patiently and fully give you all the information you ask for without necessarily doing so in long narratives or colorful word-pictures. But not everyone sees life as a sequence of stories, and while Mr. Hale's conversation may not have enlivened the woods with dramatic narrative, he nonetheless amply and effectively used his voice to reveal a compelling layer of meaning that was simply not evident or available in the mute forest itself. In talking about work on the farm and about the state and use of the landscape as he remembered it, Mr. Hale stripped away the trees that now cloak that landscape and rebuilt the old Douglass-Hale place with words, situating himself back in the middle of those fields and pastures and woodlots, suggesting to me not the seeming timelessness of the sylvan scene before me but a dynamic and bustling place, one marked by movement and annual growth and lots of hard work. And his words revealed something else as well. In the course of reconstructing for me the landscape as he saw it in memory, Mr. Hale showed that land uses were not allocated among various sections of the farm at random, but that different divisions of land were arranged in a particular ordered way around the house and barn, an order that historians have suggested was common and traditional in New England as a whole. And since forest structure and composition are strongly directed by the particular disturbance history of a piece of landscape, that means that the current forest cover of Mr. Hale's old farm also subtly follows the original patterns of the farm's fields. Listening to Mr. Hale made me realize that the shaggy woods that he and Dana were leading me through, while certainly wild and unplanned-looking, were in an important if indirect way a kind of cultural artifact, taking the specific form they did because of the ways the land under them was used in the past. And if those ways were repeated across the region, then maybe the New England woods aren't a particularly good place to get away from the human world after all. Given the great extent of reforestation following farm abandonment in New England, the entire wooded landscape might be seen as just one big folk artifact — not only a repository of oral narratives, but a traditionally shaped thing in and of itself.

One of the things that occurred to me most powerfully as we walked and talked our way through the woods was just how extensively used this now-quiet patch of earth had been in its previous incarnation, both for agriculture and for other income-generating activities. Everywhere we went, it seemed that Mr. Hale was able to recall some past bit of farmwork, work that sometimes even predated his tenure there. At one point we walked into what seemed to all appearances to be a natural clearing, and Mr. Hale explained that, in the nineteenth century, this spot had been a charcoal kiln, or "kill" as he pronounced it, where wood from the farm's woodlots was burned to produce charcoal to sell for extra farm income (fig. 10). The same spot was used for burning year after year, a process that affected the fertility of the underlying soil: Mr. Hale never plowed the land for cultivation while he was working on the farm, and even now, as he put it, "it seems to resist trees." At another point, in the middle of a particularly thick stretch of woods, we came across a heap of rocks filling a small gully, which Mr. Hale explained was one of the farm's stone dumps: each year, a new crop of rocks would be heaved to the surface of the farm's cleared fields by the winter's frosts, and they had to be removed as the field was being plowed in the spring. As a young man, it was frequently Mr. Hale's job to follow the plow and pick up stones, carrying them to the edge of the field where they could either be added to the bordering stone wall or picked up later and carted off to a gully like this one, a piece of land otherwise unusable in the farm's operations, to be dumped and forgotten (fig. 11). The forest was dotted throughout with places like the kiln and the stone dump, and in locating and explaining them Mr. Hale reanimated the landscape with scenes of past activity, navigating the woods according to a detailed mental map that saw the forest in terms of his regular movements there in the past, revealing in the process the extent to which so much of what I could see around me in this green and lonely place had been crafted by human hands.

In fact, as I came to learn, very little of the old farm landscape had managed to avoid becoming a site of work and human activity. Given

10. Site of former charcoal kiln on Walter Hale's old farm, Sebago, Maine. 1996 photograph by the author.

Maine's short growing season and relatively thin and rocky soils, farming in the state had never been an easy proposition, particular after regional and national transportation systems brought Maine farmers into competition with the larger farms and better soils of the Midwest and other parts of the country and world. Like most New England farmers historically, John Douglass and Walter Hale had followed a system of mixed agriculture, raising crops for sale while also keeping livestock — in Mr. Hale's case, a small herd of dairy cows — in an effort to maintain as diversified a system of production as possible. In order to make a living from his land, then, Mr. Hale was obliged to convert everything he could on his farm to cash income: at one point, while indicating a hillside that had been cleared of rocks and plowed despite its rather steep slope, he commented dryly that "if it was there, you'd use it." In fact, neither Mr. Hale nor his father-in-law was

11. The overgrown stone dump. 1996 photograph by the author.

able to make a full-time living simply from farming, from tillage and dairying. Up until two generations before him, Mr. Hale supposed that farmers could have "squeezed out an existence" from the land, but, as the site of the old charcoal kiln suggests, even they had to supplement their income through activities such as charcoal burning. John Douglass owned extensive woodlots in addition to his tillage fields and pastures, and to raise money he periodically sold stands of timber to lumber companies. In one memorable instance in 1934, he sold $10,000 worth of standing timber to the DuPont Corporation; DuPont erected a gasoline-powered sawmill in the woods and other support structures (the collapsed remains of the cookhouse are all that is now visible in the second-growth forest), and Walter Hale himself worked for them as a woodcutter, bringing sawdust back to the barn at the end of the day to use as bedding for the farm's dozen cows. Mr. Hale's memories made clear that this entire landscape, despite its current natural appearance, had been valued quite recently not for its aesthetic or therapeutic resources but for its productive capacity, its ability to make money through being put to whatever kind of use seemed practicable. If you went out for a walk on this property in Mr. Hale's day, you were probably heading someplace at a pretty brisk clip to get some work done.

And this was true not only for the cornfields, the hayfields, and the pastures. Even the farthest reaches of the farm, those that seemed most untouched and natural in contrast to the more heavily worked spaces on the property, were anything but pristine. Pretty much everything that grew on this acreage was potentially convertible to cash income, or could at least be put to use in some aspect of the farm's operation. Not only were the extensive woodlots valuable assets for possible sale to companies like DuPont, but they also provided material for sale to smaller local industries; Mr. Hale used to cut ash trees, for example, which he sold to a snowshoe factory in the nearby town of Norway, and he produced plenty of cordwood for sale to nearby townspeople. And the woodlots were not only saleable, but also sometimes provided food for the cows: in an echo of New England grazing practices in the years before walled-in pastures, Mr. Hale would occasionally turn the cows loose in the woods on his property to forage for themselves, finding them at the end of the day by listening for their cowbells. The milk and cream that the cows produced was generally sold to a local camp during the summer months and to a nearby creamery the rest of the year, another indication of the extent to which the farm was closely hooked into the local economy. Even the most unspoiled-looking elements of the farm landscape were integral parts of the farm's very intensive system of land use. Mr. Hale took me to a natural meadow on the property and explained how it was employed throughout the year (fig. 12). During the summer, the meadow's natural grasses were cut for hay, an arduous process that had to be performed by hand because the wheels of the horse-drawn haying machine would have sunk into the soft earth; the grass was then carried to other fields and laid out to dry. As cold weather approached, the outlet of the stream running through the meadow was dammed and the meadow flooded to a depth of about four feet. Once the flooded meadow froze sufficiently, Mr. Hale and a partner would cut blocks of ice and pack them in the icehouse that stood next to the barn, to be used for household purposes and to keep the milk cool in the dairying operation. When I saw it, fringed with trees just starting to show their autumn colors, the meadow could have posed for a New England postcard picture, displaying a natural beauty of the sort that

12. The meadow, formerly used in different seasons for mowing and ice cutting. 1996 photograph by the author.

Mr. Hale claims not to have noticed while he was scything hay or slipping through broken ice into chest-deep water. In contrast to my woods-walker's evaluation of the scene, being there for Mr. Hale had been just another part of the workday, just as the meadow itself was just another part of the working, economic landscape that constituted the entire farm property.

Our path to the meadow took us down an old lane bordered by stone walls that had once separated parcels of land but now enclosed nothing but trees. As we walked and talked our way along, Mr. Hale pointed out the different former fields and what they had been used for: some were old fields used primarily for growing corn, some had been pasture land, and some were used for growing and mowing hay and other fodder for the animals. At the time we took this walk, I hadn't yet read much about forest succession and disturbance histories and the like, so I was particularly intrigued when Mr. Hale began showing me that the woods within one stone boundary were different in their composition from those within another: fields used for growing corn have now grown up to open, parklike stands of pine with some interspersed oak and maple, he explained, while former hay-fields are dense and scrubby, containing a lot of gray birch. As I listened to Mr. Hale make these fine discriminations, the woods suddenly became more complicated to me, detailed and nuanced in a way I might not have suspected, or might have only dimly intuited, had I taken that walk on my own. This was not only a walker's natural refuge but a deeply *historical* forest, its past regimen of land use and subsequent abandonment encoded subtly but directly in its very form. A savvy expert in forest ecology could undoubtedly make out the broad outlines of these woods' land-use history on her own, sensing that some sort of farmer had been at work here at some point in the past to be determined by the age of the trees and the structure of the forest, but Mr. Hale was able to tell me the story himself in all its detail, a story that he himself directed. These woods were not just an instance of a specific kind of ecological process; they had a precise starting point, they grew not out of generic old fields but owned and known patches of land that were used in particular ways from year to year, and thus they encode a very particular individual and local history as well as a more general and generic one, a history that has everything to do with the way the landscape looks now but that is perhaps fully attainable only through oral history. Knowing this didn't make this walk in the woods any less enjoyable or exhilarating in my mind, any less a refreshing respite from my normal routine. Instead, having the forest filtered through Walter Hale's mind and voice made it even more interesting in a way, gave it a dramatic, narrative dimension, ratcheted up the fascination I always feel with the complexity of the natural world. For all that this landscape had been intensively used for agriculture for over a hundred years, it was amazing to see and understand how it had changed in such a short time.

While having completely transformed the landscape, though, seemingly changing cultural space to natural space, these woods nevertheless were human-made in an important sense, their current form constrained and conditioned by the agricultural uses that the lands from which they grow had been put to in the past. And that walk down to the meadow also made me realize that the woods were not only historical and artifactual in very particular ways, they were patterned as well; as Mr. Hale revealed, the spaces that they now occupied had originally been spatially arranged in very deliberate ways. As we gradually made our way down to the meadow, Mr. Hale led me first through the fields closest to the site of the old house and barn, fields that he and John Douglass had used alternately for growing corn and hay. Corn was the most lucrative crop in this part of Maine, and farmers in Mr. Hale's neighborhood grew it as often as they could. As the fields came into what Mr. Hale called "a run-out condition" through corn production, though, they would be sown with a combination of millet and grass. The millet would grow faster than the grass and act as a "nurse crop," shading out weeds and allowing the grass to become established. The millet would be cut at the end of the year, and the following year farmers could count on a lush field of grass. Farther from the house, we came to fields that had been dedicated strictly to hay; beyond those were the old pastures, still studded with rocks that had never had to be removed from the path of a plow, and farthest out from the house site were the old woodlots and the natural meadow, areas that were important to the farm's operation and economy but were least intensively grazed and cultivated compared to the fields and pastures. As he explained the former uses of the old fields that we traversed, Mr. Hale indirectly demonstrated that space on his farm expanded concentrically from the farmstead, moving from those regions that were domesticated most thoroughly through the activities of humans and livestock — areas that might be seen as conceptual extensions of the house and barn — to those that were roughest, seemingly most wild, that bore the marks of husbandry most lightly. The space was carefully patterned, laid out in a physically and conceptually organized way that didn't change much from year to year and that emphasized the extent to which the old farm landscape was not just a productive system but a deliberately handmade thing as well.

On the surface, this spatial arrangement seems a matter of common sense. Of course you're going to put the farmstead and the most intensively worked fields next to each other: if that's where you're going to spend a lot of your working time, why build in a lot of unnecessary travel? Why not keep your tools close to where you'll be using them; why not put the fields that need manuring right next to the barn? But common sense is not always as common or sensible as we think. As we'll soon see, Mr. Hale (and most of his New England farming brethren) worked all over the farm landscape at different times of the year; at times, it would have been much more convenient to have the woodlot right outside the back door instead of the cornfields. Of course people want their tools and artifacts to work well, even on the level of an entire farm. But there's choice involved as well as economic and ergonomic efficiency. Farms don't just appear; people make them, and they don't make them by whim or accident. A farm landscape not only has to perform its job, in its layout it also has to make conceptual as well as physical sense to the people who make and use it. As I like to point out to students in my folklore classes (who usually delight in telling me that they've seen an example that proves me wrong), in this country we tend not to put our vegetable gardens in our front yards. We *could*, but we don't. Through traditional means, through looking around at other houselots over the course of our lives, through learning by the customary example of family and neighbors, we learn what front lawns are *supposed* to look like; we internalize a general working definition of "lawn-ness" that helps us decide what kinds of plantings to put where. So front lawns might contain patches of flowers, but not tomatoes — unless you want the neighbors to talk about you.

And what applies to houselots also applies to old New England farm landscapes, generally speaking. All along the expanding frontier of agricultural settlement in the region from colonial times into the nineteenth century, people establishing farms did so largely through copying the models of agricultural space that they had seen in their former homes or on the property of their neighbors, modifying them according to the qualities of the specific sites that they had to work with. Over time, these designed spaces took on a kind of inertia, encouraging future farmers to maintain their customary uses: it was much easier to keep plowing a field that had been carefully cleared of stones than it was to prepare a new one, and once fieldstone became the most widely used fencing material in the region in the late eighteenth and early nineteenth centuries, the boundaries, and so the uses, of particular parcels of property became literally set in stone. Later occupants could make their own modifications to properties that they bought or inherited, but they did so within a spatial structure that had already been laid down; in that sense, reshaping a farm landscape would have been something like remodeling an old traditional Cape Cod house. Although it might seem odd to think of them in these terms, New England farmers through the nineteenth century were folk designers, a kind of artisan whom architectural historian Thomas Hubka characterizes as "operat[ing] in a narrow, culturally defined field of possibility that is structured by tradition. This field consists largely of the existing building examples available to each builder and the design repertoire contained within each builder's particular tradition."[2] As planned vernacular artifacts, then, New England farm landscapes came out of and expressed the particular range of spatial options that farmers carried in their heads, the physical and visual vocabulary that they picked up through living in face-to-face agricultural neighborhoods and seeing how other farmers went about arranging and using their spaces.

When Mr. Hale came to John Douglass's farm and married into his family, then, in a sense he inherited an old family artifact, a carefully shaped vernacular space made and maintained by earlier generations of his wife's family in ways that made particular cultural sense to them. And, as with other traditional handmade heirlooms like quilts or pieces of furniture, the farm landscape wasn't constructed idiosyncratically, but was an individual expression of a larger shared tradition — in this case, a tradition that accounted for much of the appearance of an entire regional landscape. The patterning of space on Mr. Hale's old farm corresponds to what Hubka, in his book on the connected farm buildings of New England, has described as the region's typical "four-field system" of crops, mowing, pasture, and woods moving progressively away from the house. This system, according to Hubka, "remained the basic pattern for a small, mixed-farming New England farmstead well into the twentieth century" and "was developed over many years of trial-and-error testing in the New World," at which point it lodged itself deeply in regional tradition.[3] The house and barn that burned down in 1948, which constituted just such a connected farm building as Hubka writes about, thus gathered working space about it in a way that had been customary in the region for generations. When I was able to correlate the descriptions and memories that Mr. Hale told on the way to the meadow with this larger story of regional land use, then, the woods appeared to me in yet another guise. I like to think of them not as a kind of replacement landscape, the vegetative equivalent of the dust that accumulates in an abandoned house, but as a new addition to the traditional artifact that was the entire farm landscape, growing directly out of the landscape pattern that it established, a pattern that was widely found throughout the region and that stood as a collective statement of how the world was most appropriately organized, of how the earth's surface was supposed to look. Certainly John Douglass did little to alter the farm's traditional aspect; he may have read the occasional farm paper, but, as his former farmhand Walter Hale commented with a humor drawn from experience, "he didn't go for many modern ideas," going so far as to keep using draft horses until his last horse died in the 1930s. Reading the woods through the words that Mr. Hale attached to them revealed them to be literally rooted in that same traditional world.

I learned something else in the course of the conversation that accompanied this walk: not only did the woods grow out of the traditionally structured spaces of the farm, but the entire farm landscape had once been deeply implicated in traditional structures of time as well. Time was lived out in the farm's spaces in annual rhythms and patterns, with particular tasks being carried out in particular areas of the farm according to the time of year. As he began telling me at the meadow, Mr. Hale performed his outdoor winter work in the areas farthest from the house, cutting ice in that selfsame meadow and chopping down trees in the woodlots. Weather would determine the next phase of work, work to be performed in the areas closer to the farm buildings. As the snow and ice began to melt and the ground began to thaw, Mr. Hale would cut firewood in the barnyard and store it for the next winter's heating needs. When the fields were clear and the ground was soft, it was time to shovel out the winter's accumulation of manure from beneath the barn and spread it on the fields; which fields would be corn and which would be hay was determined according to how they were used the previous year, with uses alternating on an annual basis to avoid exhausting the soil. After the manure was spread, it was plowed into the ground, and a new crop of rocks was added to the walls or hauled to the stone dump. Plowing was followed by harrowing, seeding, and cultivating, each operation performed with horse-drawn equipment and a two-man team. July 5 was the traditional day to begin haying, although this operation was suspended when the corn was ready for harvest and the local corn dealer let it be known that he was ready to receive deliveries. Haying continued through the month of October, at which point it was time for Mr. Hale to shoulder his equipment and head for the outer fringes of the farm once more to begin cutting wood again. And among all these activities, of course, the cows had to be taken care of on a daily basis, either taken out to and fetched from the pastures or woods or else fed in the barn during the winter.

The year on Mr. Hale's farm thus divided into a steady, structured pattern of work tasks that flowed into each other as determined by weather, traditional dates, and the demands of the local economy, work divided among particular zones of the farm; as Mr. Hale put it in talking about the nature of his farming life, "One thing would lead to another, which seemed to keep us busy." And in its temporal dimension as well as its spatial dimension, Mr. Hale's experience aligns itself with long-standing regional farming traditions, with "the cyclical nature of the farming enterprise," as Hubka puts it, "which was organized according to recurring daily, weekly, and seasonal activities."[4] Time was as much a vernacular object as space was in this world, patterned and shaped in regular, predictable, culturally significant ways. What now looks like undifferentiated forest and placid meadow thus grows not only out of what had been a meaningfully structured system of spatial units, but also out of the patterned structure of time as encoded and experienced in those spaces. Here too Mr. Hale's words led me to see the woods in a new way. There are at least three kinds of time hidden in that green landscape, I came to see: the movement through time of this particular piece of Maine, the kind of land-use story that I wondered about on Sabattus; the passage of time from the fields' abandonment to the present, demonstrated by the existence of the woods themselves; and the rhythmic temporal pattern of the way those fields were specifically used when they were part of a working farm, that same use that ultimately selected the specific kinds of forest that Mr. Hale introduced me to on our walk. The new green growth in the fields doesn't simply allude to the passage of those fifty-two unmolested years; it takes its current shape only because of the way those fields had been brought repeatedly through the cycle of the local agricultural year.

And the New England woods provide a great deal of aesthetic pleasure to people like me, both in their summer verdancy and in their fall colors. Even bare trees on a bright New England winter day carry a stark beauty of their own. But there's another kind of aesthetic presence here as well; in a very subtle way, I think we can see these woods not only as an artifact but as art. The geographer Stewart McHenry once wrote an essay called "Eighteenth-Century Field Patterns as Vernacular Art," in which he argues that "eighteenth-century field patterns are a unique type of vernacular art, bearing many similarities to vernacular architecture or building practices: they have a particular shape or form and are composed of specific materials; they have texture and color as well as regular variations of texture and color; pattern and design are clearly apparent in the rural landscape."[5] Using Vermont as his example and carefully examining six different sites within the state in order to determine the locations and patterns of old field boundaries in those locations, McHenry found not only that different places were marked by their own distinctive field sizes, shapes, orientations, and locations relative to other landscape features, but that these patterns correlated to the different social groups who first settled the study areas and laid out the fields: Dutch, French Canadian, or New Englanders from Connecticut, Massachusetts, or New Hampshire. Settlers didn't lay out their fields at random, nor did the concept of "field" mean the same thing to people all across Vermont. Instead, they shaped their agricultural spaces through making deliberate cultural choices, drawing on shared templates of what their landscape should look like that they had brought with them from their places of origin. As a result, McHenry concludes, "it is possible to say that the rural agricultural landscape can be viewed as a unique vernacular art form."[6] Individual fields are laid out according to traditional patterns and joined to neighboring fields just as squares of cloth are sewn together into a quilt, and if we believe that McHenry's observations about Vermont might be applied to other parts of New England, then much of the region's old agricultural landscape could be seen as nothing less than a work of folk art on an epic scale, a place where natural materials were reshaped according to the patterns held in human minds in order to not only do a job but to exhibit a sense of visual rightness, to inspire a sense of creative satisfaction in its makers and a degree of aesthetic pleasure in its viewers.

McHenry's argument is fascinating, but he doesn't really explore the implications of using the term "art" rather than "artifact" to talk about old farm fields. In fact, the idea does seem rather counterintuitive on the surface. How can we talk about a bounded-off patch of dirt as a work of art, an idea we usually reserve for paintings and sculpture and the like? As it happens, folklorists find that the categories of folk art and folk artifact or craft blend into each other to such an extent that it's difficult to talk about one without talking about the other. Even the most utilitarian traditional object, be it a house or a barn or a tool or a piece of furniture or a woven textile, is rarely lacking at least some kind of aesthetic component: ornamentation, symmetry and repetition in design, a particular manipulation of color or proportion. And in folk art this aesthetic component is traditional. What is valued is not artistic innovation but allegiance to the group's standards of what the world should look like; as folklorist John Michael Vlach puts it, "folk art is by definition a collective social expression."[7] As such, folk art has a specific audience: the fellow members of the community in which the maker lives, learns, and works. To make or see a piece of folk art, even something as utilitarian and unprepossessing as a farm field, thus brings a specific kind of aesthetic pleasure to both maker and user: the artist has demonstrated that he or she can successfully execute the aesthetic standards of the community by creating a particular instance of the shared pattern, and the audience feels the quiet delight we experience when we encounter another instance of a shape or form of the sort that our culture has taught us is attractive to look at. Together, they feel affirmed in their community and their culture, collectively creating a world that is at once functional, comprehensible, and beautiful.[8]

I think that the old fields on Mr. Hale's farm must have come out of just such a vernacular world, a world that fell away as the entire farm neighborhood was gradually abandoned over the years. My educated guess is that the fields were originally laid out according to some ideal visual and spatial template of the sort that McHenry talks about, and their arrangement in the traditional four-field system suggests more concretely that the farm Mr. Hale inherited showed clear evidence of shared pattern and design, a pattern and design that were as artistic and aesthetic as they were practical and utilitarian. Today's forest grows out of what could once have been seen as a piece of folk art, one small swatch of that big New England landscape quilt that generations of farmers wove and stitched together across the countryside. It's probably a stretch to locate that same artistic impulse behind the trees themselves, of course; the trees are the product of a specific disturbance-influenced process of forest succession, not of the culturally embedded decisions of a creative human mind. They showed up after the art was created, a green patina upon the sculpted surface. And yet, I think again of the view from Sabattus, of the subtle variations of tint and hue in the leafy landscape below me, the patches of lighter and darker green abutting each other across my visual field. Those patches exist only because of the ways that people designed and used the landscape in the past. There's a pattern in those trees down there, the quilt metaphor coming again to mind. And it's a pattern that couldn't exist if the ground itself hadn't been patterned in the first place. While from the ground the landscape may look simply like a tangle of trees, those trees collectively make up a kind of secondary, accidental artistic expression, subtly blurring the conventional opposition between the "artful" and the "natural." And some people think art looks even better when it's acquired a little character over the years.

This way of looking at the landscape is much more esoteric and recondite than Mr. Hale's own perspective, of course — this is what happens when you walk around in the woods after spending too much time in school. Mr. Hale didn't spend much time talking about the sculptural form or aesthetic value of the old farm landscape, focusing instead on his memory of the way the land was used to get a living. And yet he seemed to find his own kind of satisfaction and pleasure there, tied not to questions of art and culture but to the fond recollection of episodes of his own life as they had played out in those fields and forests. I've mentioned the subtle layers of time that inhere in these woods, and I came to see that the fields beneath the forests also encode time on a personal as well as a communal level: not only the cyclical time of farmwork as it was performed in southern Maine, but also the linear time of an individual man's life. What looked to me like a labyrinthine tangle of trees and undergrowth was easy for Mr. Hale to navigate as he led me decisively from place to place throughout the property. While well aware of the new forest growth that surrounded him, and marveling on occasion about how much the landscape had changed since his farming days, the past landscape remained clearly present in his mind. His vision penetrated and cleared the forest as he walked the old fields in memory, identifying them not only according to how they had been embedded in older local structures of use and time and space, but how, as well, he had spent twenty-one years of his working life within their bounds.

Particular sites in the woods continue to stand out as touchstones, in a literal sense, of personal and family experience. In explaining the woods and fields to me, Mr. Hale led me to two otherwise unremarkable stones, two named landmarks that helped give this space a kind of personal rather than communal shape and structure in his mind, a sense of spatial form that was much more immediate and meaningful to him than anything that might have motivated the men who built the landscape in the past. First we came to what he called Initial Rock, in which a Douglass relative had purportedly carved his initials sometime during the previous century, although I must admit that our careful scrutiny of the rock failed to turn up any initials. Shortly thereafter, we came to Target Rock, which Mr. Hale used to fire his gun at from a hundred yards away to make sure that it was shooting straight before he went hunting for deer — and not always in season; as he noted with a laugh, "The game laws didn't have too much effect on us" (fig. 13). Another part of the woods, which had been used by Mr. Hale as a hayfield, still bears the label of "The Other Place" in Mr. Hale's mind because it had been the site of the original 1830 cabin on the property; the cabin started being called "the other place" when the farmhouse that later burned was built in the mid-nineteenth century, and that part of the farm kept that name within the family even after all traces of the cabin had vanished. Although the woods are new, Mr. Hale continues to navigate them according to a detailed mental map, a document handed down from the past and added to through time, a chart thickly contoured with the experience of long working days, with family stories and traditional place-names, and with individual peaks of personal experience. And Mr. Hale's grandson Dana also knew of and was able to corroborate the location and significance of these old landmarks, indicating that they were part of a family tradition as well as an individual memory and suggesting the quiet and insistent power of the meanings that were lodged in this landscape for at least a few of its viewers.

None of this meaning is visible, though, to the uninitiated eye. And the old fields and farm spaces in which meaning was created and displayed are themselves disappearing from view beneath their wooded cover. Despite his years of experience in this landscape, there was really nothing to keep Mr. Hale there after the house and barn burned down in 1948. When Mr. Hale's attention is drawn to the current state of the fields, to the difference between the farm landscape that he navigates in his mind and the thick forest that clothes that landscape today, his reaction is unsentimental. He sees abandonment and reforestation as completely sensible; anyone with any brains would have left the land as he did, at the first reasonable opportunity. When I asked him what he felt when he looked at the fields today, he replied that it was "a sad sight," but "no way could you hammer a living out of it. No way." Of his decision to leave the farm, he said, "I would see other people making money doing different things and I thought, hell, I ain't going to work my life away here. So I didn't." When the farm

13. Target Rock. 1996 photograph by the author.

was no longer the best economic option, that is, it had outlived its usefulness in Mr. Hale's eyes; it had become a sort of worthless antique, fit to be obliterated, to be turned back over to the natural world out of which it had first been carved.

And yet that past remains everywhere present, brought alive by the sound of Mr. Hale's voice and by the very form of the forest itself. Just about every chunk of New England woods has had its Walter Hales, or has them still, and while it's not hard to find evidence of past human presence in those woods in the form of such things as old stone walls or cellar holes, that evidence also extends to the wooded landscape itself. Forests have oral histories, and they are also material culture, to be interpreted like any other artifact that humans make. They'll always be great places to take walks, but we can make those walks as simple or as complicated as we want them to be, either enjoying our solitude in a clearly nonhumanized place or inviting the whole ghostly gang of implicit past residents to join us in a world that they had a fundamental hand in shaping — or both at once; and that commingling of the natural and the cultural, of many simultaneous perspectives on and experiences in the landscape, is part of what makes the woods so fascinating. We may not have time to understand the whole story that surrounds us as we walk through the woods alone or with a companion, but we can still grasp or sense enough to know that the view from Sabattus, whatever form that view takes in each of our lives, reveals to us a surrounding green world of richness and complexity, of beauty and meaning, of time and memory. Not a bad vista at all.

Redesigning the River

Nature, Technology, & the Cumberland & Oxford Canal

One summer Maine day in the town of Gorham I drove down Hurricane Road, a narrow ribbon of two-lane blacktop winding its way downhill among the trees that closely crowded it on either side. Rounding one final bend, I came to Babb's Bridge, a covered bridge that spans the Presumpscot River and connects Gorham to the town of Windham on the other side. The original bridge on the site dated from 1839 but was burned by vandals in the 1970s; the current replica was rebuilt almost immediately thereafter and is marked on maps and noted in guidebooks as something that tourists and Sunday drivers might want to see, adding an extra touch of New England charm to their rambles through the countryside. The bridge attracts local people as well, but for recreational rather than aesthetic reasons. The riverbank immediately below the span is a popular swimming spot for families and teenagers, and as I pulled off the road and parked on a small sandy patch of ground at one end of the bridge I could see a small group of kids lounging in the sun next to the water, one or two swimming lazily in the slow current, the occasional brave member of the bunch climbing onto one of the bridge abutments and plunging into the river below, the whole scene forming a tableau of sheer youthful enjoyment of warm sun and cool water and fresh air. Leaving the bridge behind, I crossed the road and entered the surrounding forest on a path that followed the crest of a low wooded ridge. The river lay downhill to my left; to my right, the ground fell away several feet and then rose gradually uphill once more in a thick tangle of woods. The ridge I was walking on was level for the most part, sloping slightly downhill at one point for several yards, sloping again farther on as the path followed a narrow peninsula of sorts between the river and a small inlet of still water, about ten feet wide, that lay to my right. A man stood fishing near the end of this peninsula, savoring a summer afternoon in the outdoors just like the kids at the bridge, gratefully accepting nature's gifts in the form of fish rather than riverbank leisure, drawn like the swimmers to the sheer enjoyment of the natural world, of the depths and wooded banks of the freely flowing Presumpscot.

I walked past the fisherman to the end of the peninsula, and then broke through undergrowth and stepped between trees to get to that short narrow inlet paralleling the main channel of the river, where I squatted down and began carefully examining its edges and depths, looking for all the world like I had once dropped something in the water there and had come back to try to find it. This is what the fisherman thought, at any rate; with the slightly injured air of someone who resents having had his solitude invaded, he asked me what I was looking for. Basically, I was looking for the past, and I told him that the sliver of water that had interested me so much was not a naturally occurring feature, not a backwater somehow carved by river or glacier, but had been dug by human beings; it was in fact a long-abandoned segment of the old Cumberland and Oxford Canal, an artificial watercourse completed in 1830 that had connected the Portland waterfront to Sebago Lake over twenty miles away until its closure in 1872. Fascinated as always by New England's relict landscapes, I had been alerted by William Robinson's book *Abandoned New England* to places where remnants of the canal could still be seen, and that was what had guided me down Hurricane Road and brought me into the fisherman's presence this day.[1] The ridge that I had followed to eventually intrude on his piscatorial reverie was the canal's towpath, earth that had been displaced from the canal bed and carefully mounded between the canal and the river to provide a path for the horses that pulled the canal boats and the boys who guided the horses; the low ground to my right as I had walked along was the dry canal itself, now containing not water but trees and fallen leaves. The spot where the path had sloped downhill was once Upper Kemp Lock, where boats had been raised and lowered between two segments of the canal that stood at different elevations; close examination revealed that the sides of the ditch at this point were embedded with stacked fieldstone and rubble, all that now remains of the lock structure.

The watery inlet that I had begun examining when I got to the end of the path was Lower Kemp Lock, and I pointed out to the fisherman, who hadn't known about the Cumberland and Oxford Canal and was now showing interest, that its sides underwater were also walled with fieldstone. Three weathered upright logs stood in the water near the lock's side walls, the only remnants of the lining of wooden plank facing and supporting piles that helped keep the locks as watertight as possible (fig. 14). (Because of a small hydroelectric dam that had been built downstream after the canal had been abandoned, the level of this segment of the Presumpscot is higher than it had been in the mid-1800s; thus, the side walls of Lower Kemp Lock are now submerged, not exposed as they would have been during the canal's working life, and the canal ditch below the lock is also under water.) At one time, this peaceful spot next to the river would have been bustling with lock operators and horses and heavily laden boats; the canal stopped carrying traffic in 1872, though, and was largely allowed to go dry like the section above the Lower Kemp Lock. One segment of the canal was subsequently improved and now diverts water from the river to a small electrical power station; other sections are now drowned, still others have succumbed to development and other land uses, and in 1976 Robinson was able to identify only two abandoned dry segments of canal accessible to the interested public.[2] Today, it is difficult to tell that this piece of landscape off Hurricane Road was shaped by human hands if you don't know that fact ahead of time; wooded and watered, it looks to all appearances like just another section of the natural riverside, an eminently suitable place to leave the human world behind and just go fishing.

The fisherman soon left; the history lesson had piqued his curiosity, but evidently my presence provided a little more humanity than he was in the mood for. I remained behind, however, for I found this small piece of land- and waterscape to be intensely suggestive. To my mind it seemed to comprise two different kinds of space, each standing as the physical and conceptual opposite of the other. On one side of the towpath, this carefully piled and shaped ridge of earth, lay the flowing river, continually replenished by rain and snowmelt, continually emptying into the ocean, part of an ongoing cyclical hydrologic system having nothing to do with human intention.[3] On the other side lay the canal, which, while it also once contained water, was very much a planned and controlled feature of the landscape, its

14. The long-disused and flooded Lower Kemp Lock, Gorham, Maine. 2000 photograph by the author.

artificiality partially masked now through the effects of dereliction and new plant growth but nonetheless deeply evocative of human work and design—the work of the hundreds of unskilled laborers who dug and shaped the canal bed; the design of the civil engineers who planned and oversaw the canal, of the surveyors who mapped its route and maintained its level bottom, and of the masons, carpenters, and ironsmiths who built its locks. One side of my peninsular vantage point represented a realm whose processes would continue without any human interference; the other represented years of mental and physical effort on the part of human beings, an artificial thing forced into the landscape as the result of human will. If the view in one direction revealed a scene from the natural world, the view in the other was shaped by a desire to bring that scene, and especially the waters that lay at its heart, under firm human control.

In a way, it seems slightly absurd if not hubristic to think about taming something as protean as flowing water, a substance so changeable that even the Greek philosopher Heraclitus noted that you can't step into the same river twice. It takes a special effort of the imagination to believe that such a thing can be confined, contained, made into a constant and controllable object. Nevertheless, that imaginative exercise has been quite common on this continent; people have been altering the flow of rivers and streams, even if only inadvertently, at least since they discovered that beavers are good to hunt, removing them from the landscape and eradicating their dams and the wetlands that formed behind those dams.[4] Rivers have been used to power machinery from small colonial gristmills to huge complexes of textile factories; swamps have been drained and rivers channelized to create and safeguard agricultural land; flowing water has been impounded for purposes of irrigation, electrical power, flood control, and drinking water in situations from small New England reservoirs to massive dam projects on western rivers like the Colorado and Columbia. As Alice Outwater has chronicled, natural hydrologic cycles and water flows have been massively altered by engineering and the elimination of certain animal species like beavers, an ongoing exercise that has brought environmental costs: "By dredging, by damming, by channeling, by tampering with (and in some cases eliminating) the ecological niches where water cleans itself, we have simplified the pathways that water takes through the American landscape; and we have ended up with dirty water."[5] And yet this process has been largely taken for granted, if not actively encouraged; if all behaviors in the landscape embody an environmental ethic, a set of beliefs about what it is acceptable to do to the natural world, then the consensus seems to be that water exists to be shaped, made rational, and put to work.

Despite the commonness of this ongoing process, though, commentators and critics habitually seize on humans' efforts to tame water as perhaps the extreme example of people's domineering, antagonistic attitudes toward nature, the reductio ad absurdum of our relations with the nonhuman world. Environmental historian Theodore Steinberg's book *Slide Mountain; or, the Folly of Owning Nature*, for example, views our culture as one "determined to own nature, a culture of property," by which he means "a society that organizes its relations with the world, the natural world in particular, around the concept of ownership. Such a culture is so dedicated to control, so obsessed with possession, that it is willing to deny the complexities of nature to satisfy its craving to own."[6] As I have suggested, few things in nature are as complex as flowing water, and of the five examples that Steinberg examines to demonstrate the perversity and absurdity of contemporary relations between humans and nature in this country, three have to do with the hydrologic world. Chronicling a legal battle between the Omaha Indian tribe and white property holders over a piece of land that had evidently switched from the Nebraska to the Iowa side of the Missouri River when that notoriously fickle watercourse had carved a new path through the local alluvial soils at some point in the past, Steinberg concludes that the interested parties were dealing with "a piece of earth that just will not fit into the square hole of property" and that the relevant legal doctrines "are neat and ideal stories that the law tells about the natural world. Yet neither story, of course, can remotely capture all the complexities of river movement in the Great Plains."[7] Steinberg then turns his attention to the Louisiana bayou country and recounts a protracted legal battle over whether Grand and Six Mile Lakes were in fact to be classified as lakes or rivers; depending on the answer, either the state or private landholders would own the ground that had accreted along those lakes' shores as riverborne silt settled to their bottoms, and therefore would hold the right to pump oil from beneath that ground. In this swampy place, though, "where land and water come together in strange ways, it was to be no simple matter to determine nature's identity," and while "names impose order on a disorderly natural world, . . . that world is so fluid and chaotic that it often defies classification." "Whatever the power of the law," Steinberg concludes, "it was unable to contain the contradictions that emerged in bayou country where nature . . . pushed ownership to its limits."[8]

Finally, Steinberg concludes his discussion of legal battles over American waterscapes by examining the phenomenon of pumping water from beneath the Arizona desert for the benefit of both agriculture and that state's burgeoning urban populations. Water flows from place to place within the aquifer, though, and so while landowners thought they had title to the water immediately beneath their property, those with deeper wells and more powerful pumps could in effect steal water right from beneath their neighbors while remaining within the letter of the law. Despite legal doctrine, though, Steinberg concludes that "the notion of private property in percolating water is an illusory one. It is hard to imagine exclusive ownership over something so elusive, there one minute and gone the next, headed off toward wherever gravity might take it."[9] And yet people thought they owned it and behaved as if they owned it, just as in Steinberg's other scenarios they attempted to abstract and simplify lakes and riverbanks through the fictions of law, turning watery nature into a thing they could predictably possess despite its unpredictable behavior, enacting "the assumptions of a culture that by this point in the twentieth century had grown used to having its way with the natural world."[10] Steinberg's story is in part one of antagonism between human parties to property disputes, yet it is also a tale of antagonism between humans and the natural world, with humans struggling desperately to gain and retain control, yet never quite able to get the upper hand because of the nature of flowing water.

And yet this ongoing struggle to achieve physical, legal, and imaginative control over water in America is by no means an exclusive product of the twentieth century. Mark Twain provided a famous rumination on one episode in this difficult relationship in his 1883 book *Life on the Mississippi*, emphasizing not only how much hard work and civil engineering acumen was being applied to taming the Mississippi River over a century ago but also the specifically antagonistic character of the interaction between humans and an opponent that, in Twain's view, seemed to be doing everything it could to thwart their efforts. After commenting on the efforts of the U.S. River Commission to ease navigation on the Mississippi with dikes, levees, beacons, and other shoreline improvements, Twain cynically observes that "one who knows the Mississippi will promptly aver — not aloud, but to himself — that ten thousand River Commissions, with the mines of the world at their back, cannot tame that lawless stream, cannot curb it or confine it, cannot say to it, Go here, or Go there, and make it obey; cannot save a shore which it has sentenced; cannot bar its path with an obstruction which it will not tear down, dance over, and laugh at."[11] Twain grudgingly admits, though, that "the West Point engineers have not their superiors anywhere; . . . and so, since they conceive that they can fetter and handcuff that river and boss him, it is but wisdom for the unscientific man to keep still, lie low, and wait till they do it."[12] One unscientific man traveling with Twain, though — the riverboat veteran Uncle Mumford — has seen enough of the Mississippi to believe that even the best engineers will be hard-pressed to make the river behave as predictably and conveniently as they would like it to. As he puts it, "Four years at West Point, and plenty of books and schooling, will learn a man a good deal, I reckon, but it won't learn him the river. . . . Well, you've got to admire men that deal in ideas of that size and can tote them around without crutches; but you haven't got to believe they can do such miracles, have you? And yet you ain't absolutely obliged to believe they can't."[13] Even in the skeptical Uncle Mumford's mind, it seems, the outcome of this ongoing confrontation is largely predictable but at least slightly in doubt, with engineers continuing to erect structures to control and rationalize the river and the river doing its best to circumvent their efforts. And the engineers did in fact achieve many of their goals: James Eads's system of jetties, for instance, effectively kept the mouth of the Mississippi scoured of silt and continuously open to navigation, while Henry Shreve's innovative snag boats kept the river channel clear of obstructing trees.[14] Still, these expedients often seemed provisional at best, with the river always ready to dump more and more loads of silt and trees off its banks, and despite Twain's qualified admiration for the West Point engineers, he had seen enough of the Mississippi's ways not to award them the victory outright.

One hundred and six years after *Life on the Mississippi*, John McPhee provided what is in effect an updating of Twain's comments on the river and its engineers in the "Atchafalaya" chapter of his book *The Control of Nature*. In the years since Twain wrote his book, the Army Corps of Engineers had assiduously and energetically continued its program of river improvements for flood control on the lower Mississippi, relying primarily on levees to contain the river between its banks at times of high water. If the river managed to breach or overflow the levees, the Corps simply built higher ones in anticipation of the next flood. As a result of this practice, the Mississippi was kept more or less in its place, and as it deposited its loads of silt in the Gulf of Mexico it effectively became longer and longer, building an ever-extending delta out into the ocean. A river like the Mississippi, however — one that shifts its bed within softer alluvial soils rather than being confined within rocky banks — continually attempts "to get to the Gulf by the shortest and steepest gradient," and as it becomes longer, slower, and shallower because of sediment deposits it "spills to one side," as McPhee puts it, and follows a new path of least resistance.[15] Shifts like these happen about once a millennium, and the river has been attempting to change course again in recent years, to flow through its Old River distributary in Louisiana through the Atchafalaya Bayou to the Gulf. Not without a fight, however, as the Corps has been doing everything it can to keep the Mississippi from capturing the

Atchafalaya. As McPhee puts it, "For the Mississippi to make such a change was completely natural, but in the interval since the last shift Europeans had settled by the river, a nation had developed, and the nation could not afford nature."[16] If the river were to forge a new course, the cities of New Orleans and Baton Rouge, as well as the many riverside industries between them, would be stranded, cut off from river traffic, and no one wanted that to happen. "For nature to take its course was unthinkable," McPhee notes. "Nature in this place had become an enemy of the state."[17]

Having established this antagonistic relationship, McPhee spends much of his chapter discussing the massive control structure that the Corps had built at Old River to keep the Mississippi right where it is — a modern version of the efforts that caught Twain's notice in the 1880s. The military mindset of the Corps only highlights the adversarial quality of the story that McPhee tells: he quotes the narration of a Corps promotional film about the Old River structure that claims that "we are fighting Mother Nature" and that "it's a battle we have to fight day by day, year by year; the health of our economy depends on victory."[18] The outcome of this battle is by no means certain; as McPhee notes dryly, "From the beginnings of settlement, failure was the par expectation with respect to the river,"[19] and he not only recounts the history of floods and failed control structures on the river in Louisiana but quotes several geologists to the effect that if the Mississippi wants to capture the Atchafalaya, the Mississippi will eventually succeed — will, in effect, someday tear down the Old River structure, dance over it, and laugh at it. Still, the Corps refuses to admit this possibility despite the odds favoring it, manifesting in an especially powerful way an ongoing antagonistic relationship with flowing water, a cultural belief that it can and should be tamed and subjected to human interests and intentions, while at the same time testifying unwittingly, in McPhee's quiet estimation, to the ultimate perversity of such a belief.

As I stood on the towpath between the living Presumpscot River on one side and the stagnant Lower Kemp Lock and moribund Cumberland and Oxford Canal on the other, trying to find a way to think about and understand this complex piece of landscape, it occurred to me that perhaps I was in the presence of material testimony to an earlier episode in the ongoing effort to dominate water that these other observers have described, one that had been very successful in its day.

Redesigning the River

McPhee, Twain, and Steinberg recount the frustrations that engineers and lawyers have encountered when trying to corral flowing water on its own terms, when having to wrestle not only with the water itself but also with the natural systems of which it is a component part. To be sure, dam-builders from the early New England industrialists to the Bureau of Reclamation in the American West seem to have been quite successful in plugging rivers and making water sit still and work for them, essentially turning those rivers into productive machines, but as historian Richard White has pointed out, a river like the Columbia "is not just a machine. It is an *organic* machine. Our tendency to break it into parts does not work. For no matter how much we have created many of its spaces and altered its behavior, it is still tied to larger organic cycles beyond our control." [20] The builders of canals like the C & O, however, tried to completely circumvent those cycles as best they could, not altering and working within the river's space but creating an entirely new space right next to it, one that they could keep under their firm control; they took the troublesome water out of the river, out of its organic cycles, and converted it into a flat linear highway, and as long as river water was available — generally not a problem in New England — they were in business. This seemed to be a very clever way to overcome the liquid adversary, not meeting it on its home battlefield but diverting it into a completely artificial, humanized space.

Today, though, it is clear that something went wrong: the canal is dry, the water in the landscape confined not within its sculpted sides but within the shaggy rough banks of the Presumpscot. The canal operators have withdrawn, and the water, no longer held hostage, has returned to its natural place (fig. 15). Now largely abandoned to reforestation and collapse in those few remaining stretches where its bed and banks are still visible at all, the canal was a place where nineteenth-century ambition and technology ran up against the physical limitations imposed by the natural world. In a nice irony, while it was designed to reshape nature in such a way as to more efficiently serve the economic goals of Mainers, the canal ultimately failed in 1872 because it remained too natural, insufficiently removed from the daily and yearly processes of water and weather. The paradox can be summed up in a phrase first applied by Americans to the Erie Canal, whose opening predated that of the C & O by five years: early nineteenth-century canals were seen as "artificial rivers." [21] If the

15. An overgrown section of the Cumberland and Oxford Canal towpath,
Gorham, Maine. The canal bed — the "artificial river" — is on the right, and
the Presumpscot River is visible through the trees on the left.
2000 photograph by the author.

towpath separating the canal from the Presumpscot and Fore Rivers
also separated engineered space from natural space, the "artificial"
from the "river," at the same time that canal also retained much of its
riverness, much of that uncontrollable quality that canal builders
worked so hard to overcome in their effort to make nature better
serve humankind. Thus, as we try to reconstruct something of this
canal's past and also interpret its present ruined character, these overgrown stretches of bank and ditch emerge most meaningfully not as a
simple emblem of human domination over nature but as an intermediate or transitional landscape, one in which engineers and builders
did their best to vanquish natural limitations but in which nature had
the final word. And the abandoned canal landscape carries one final
irony as well: its present green aspect is no final triumph, but rather
an acknowledgment that the canal simply became no longer useful,
that people had found a better way to get things from here to there.

Redesigning the River

Reclaimed by nature, these canal ruins were also a way station toward an increasingly firm nineteenth-century control of nature.

Historian Ronald Shaw has referred to the years from 1790 to 1860 as the Canal Era in the United States, with a particular flurry of digging taking place between the end of the War of 1812 and the early 1830s.[22] The Erie Canal, a civil engineering project that riveted the attention of both Americans and foreign travelers and linked the Hudson River with Lake Erie, was opened in 1825, and work on the Chesapeake and Ohio Canal, designed to defeat the Alleghenies and connect the navigable waters of the Ohio and Potomac Rivers (although it ultimately reached only from Washington, D.C., to Cumberland, Maryland), was begun in 1828.[23] Within New England, the Middlesex Canal connecting Boston Harbor to the Merrimack River opened in 1803, the Blackstone Canal between Providence and Worcester opened in 1828, and the Farmington Canal between New Haven, Connecticut, and Northampton, Massachusetts, was ready for travel in 1835; in addition, a series of short canals and locks around waterfalls had made over 250 miles of the Connecticut River navigable by 1810.[24] First surveyed by Erie Canal veteran Holmes Hutchinson in 1823, opened to traffic in 1830, the Cumberland and Oxford Canal was part of a larger regional and national historical moment of intensive canal building, all pursued with the same general goals in mind: providing a more efficient means for moving farm produce and natural resources — in New England, particularly wood for fuel and building — to growing coastal cities, and promoting economic development in the hinterlands.

As early as 1791, Portland merchants had begun looking into the possibility of digging a canal to join Sebago Lake to the navigable waters of Portland's harbor at the mouth of the Fore River.[25] A canal company was incorporated in 1795 and recapitalized in 1804, but economic conditions during the U.S. embargo of 1807 against France and Great Britain and the War of 1812 greatly constrained its ability to raise money. After Maine achieved statehood in 1820, though, an enthusiastic state legislature granted a charter to the new Cumberland and Oxford Canal Corporation, and progress on the canal immediately commenced. Hutchinson surveyed the canal route in 1823, the survey was adjusted in 1825, construction began in 1828 under Hutchinson's engineering supervision, and the canal opened for business two years later. Rather than strike across country, the C & O was designed to closely parallel the Presumpscot River from Sebago Lake to Portland for much of its dug length, departing from the Presumpscot at Saccarappa Falls in Westbrook and rejoining the Fore River in Portland. The canal from Portland to Sebago Lake was about twenty miles long according to toll schedules, its twenty-seven locks combining with the canal's built-in foot-per-mile drop to negotiate the 265-foot change in elevation between the two spots. In addition, with the construction of a single lock on the Songo River between Sebago Lake and Long Lake, both these bodies of water were also opened to navigation, making a total water-transportation route of about fifty miles between Portland and the town of Harrison. Seeking the route that entailed the least amount of geographical resistance and lock construction, the canal's surveyors chose to take advantage of the path that the Presumpscot River had already carved through the landscape before it turned north outside Portland; the river was too filled with rapids and contained insufficient stretches of slack water to be used for transportation itself, but in building right next to it the canal's engineers fitted their project to the preexisting natural contours of the land, adapting themselves to the landscape as much as possible rather than fighting against it.

At the same time, in its capacity as an artificial river the canal was not meant to simply imitate the river that it adjoined; it can more properly be seen as an edited or improved version of that river, a Presumpscot that has been rationalized, made abstract and linear, stripped down and rebuilt so as to move canal boats as efficiently as possible. While closely paralleling a natural space, and while taking full advantage of the natural contours of the land, the canal also represents a firm effort to control nature both physically and imaginatively, to rebuild the river on the ground so that it resembles the ideal, convenient, obedient river of the mercantile mind. Seen as a potential highway, the existing Presumpscot was woefully lacking: it was full of rocks and waterfalls, its water level varied unpredictably according to the wetness or dryness of the season, its current discouraged upstream travel, and while it may have been good for driving raw timber to Portland during the annual log drive, it wasn't good for much else. From earliest colonial times, New Englanders had looked at rivers primarily as travel and transportation routes, providing paths into the interior and vehicles for driving lumber out of the woods, and if the Presumpscot were to increase and fulfill its potential as a means of getting things from here to there, something would have to be done.

The C & O Canal, like all canals of the period, was designed specifically to overcome such natural obstacles, emerging primarily as a simplified, streamlined version of the original Presumpscot. It had emphatically regular dimensions, thirty-two feet wide at the surface and eighteen feet wide at the bottom. Its waters were still, making for easy travel in both directions. Its depth was kept at a constant three and one-half feet, ensuring that loaded boats with their three-foot draft would not run aground under normal conditions. Wherever there was a fall on the river, canal engineers built a lock, a piece of technology that amounts to a sort of gentle mechanical reinterpretation of the rapids that it parallels. A boat going downstream would enter the ten-foot-wide, seventy-two-foot-long lock, the gates would be closed behind it, water would be released through a small iron hatch in the wooden downstream gate, thus bringing the boat down to the level of the lower canal section, and the boat would continue on its way, having achieved the drop in elevation without sustaining any damage; likewise, upstream boats could negotiate the rapids with equal ease. At one point, the canal was even carried over the Presumpscot's Little River tributary on a 100-foot-long aqueduct consisting of a strong plank-and-timber trough, two stone abutments, and three stone piers that carried the trough eight feet above the offending stream. The canal was a space where the crooked in nature was made straight, where the messy and inconvenient was redesigned and regularized. Historians have drawn parallels between the work of nineteenth-century canal builders and the post-Enlightenment spirit of rationalism, which also saw the rise at about this time of the Army Corps of Engineers, famous for their river and harbor improvements, and the Rectangular Survey, which was dividing up the rumpled landscape of the central and western United States according to the dictates of an abstract mathematical grid.[26] Remnant evidence in the landscape of how engineers applied artifice to the Presumpscot and Fore Rivers — straightening them where possible, converting them into a series of flat segments linked by locks, contrasting starkly with the water on the other side of the towpath — suggests even today the extent to which the canal was nature as interpreted and reinterpreted by the rational, abstracting, nineteenth-century mind.

While being a revision and mechanical improvement of a particular riparian landscape, the canal represented an attempt to change people's relationships to other fundamental if more abstract categories of nature as well: in particular, to the limitations and felt experience of time and space. In early nineteenth-century America, water was still the most efficient way to move people and freight: port cities could engage in coastwise and transoceanic commerce, and in some places navigable rivers allowed for exchange of resources and finished goods between the coast and inland regions, but by and large overland transportation was a slow and difficult business. The state of roads, particularly in places like Maine, was such that only people on foot or riders on horseback could move any distance with anything approaching ease; loaded wagons or stagecoaches had a much more difficult time on unpaved roads that were frequently muddy, washed out, and rock-strewn, and thus moving freight overland in inland regions was unpredictable, time-consuming, and expensive. Canal boats solved the problem of roads just as they solved the problem of rivers: sliding smoothly over still waters, they moved freight on the C & O for a rate that was about one-eighth of that charged by a teamster on the same route, and a single horse could pull much more weight on slippery water than it could on resistant land. Boats on the C & O were limited to traveling at four miles per hour so their wakes wouldn't do any damage to the canal's earthen banks, so they weren't exactly rocketing across the Maine landscape. Still, by allowing freight to move regularly, predictably, and more quickly along its route, the canal both shortened and regularized time, and it shortened and regularized space as well: Portland and Harrison, while still fifty miles apart, were now in an important sense brought much closer together, as were all the other towns that surrounded the lakes and canal. The tamed water of the canal allowed boats to move much more efficiently than could wheeled vehicles on land, a function of water's properties as a physical medium, particularly when brought under human management; as conceptual media through which people and goods also had to move, time and space were now brought equally firmly under human control.

As it shortened space and brought the hinterlands conceptually much closer to Portland, the C & O Canal also served as an agent of landscape change, altering the natural and cultural face of the earth in southern Maine in a variety of ways. Portland developed a sort of colonial relationship with the lands around the lakes: they supplied resources and agricultural products to the city, and Portland merchants in turn sent foodstuffs, manufactured goods, and other materials up the canal for rural storekeepers and manufacturers. Since Portland was both a port and a growing urban center, it had a particularly fierce appetite for wood, both for itself and for trade, and the Sebago and Long Lake region was very heavily forested. Loggers and millers sent boatload after boatload of cordwood, sawn lumber, barrel staves, and other raw and finished wood products down the canal, thus greatly increasing the rate of deforestation in the region. In addition, the increasing number of mills and manufactories that the wood trade called for led to the growth of both industry and population along the area's rivers and streams; as a convenient means of bringing in raw materials and shipping finished products, the canal created a busy corridor of villages and waterpowered factories producing a variety of products, a history, like that of local logging, that is now obscured by the landscape's green and quiet surface.[27]

I will let one brief example stand for the whole: the site of an old gunpowder mill at Gambo Falls in Gorham, Maine. Gunpowder was manufactured at this waterpower site from 1824 to 1904 under several company names, rendering it a busy and occasionally explosive spot; in fact, forty-seven men died in twenty-five separate explosions at the mill complex over the course of its working life.[28] At the same time, this particular location represents two ways in which landscape was reshaped and water was tamed for the purposes of commerce and industry: not only as a medium of travel, but also as a power source. At one time several mill buildings stood between the canal and the river at this spot, although the circular foundation of the incorporating mill is all the evidence that remains on the ground (fig. 16). Water ran from the river through a raceway that had been both blasted out of the rock and built from earth and stone. It entered the mill foundation and turned a horizontal waterwheel as it passed through and out the other side; the waterwheel in turn rotated an arm to which were attached heavy granite wheels that crushed together the charcoal, sulfur, and saltpeter that had been prepared elsewhere in the mill complex, incorporating (hence the structure's name) these several ingredients into gunpowder. Canal boats brought the sulfur and saltpeter from the Portland docks, while charcoal was prepared on site from the surrounding forests; the finished product was then taken back down the

16. The foundation of the gunpowder factory's incorporating mill, Gorham, Maine. 2000 photograph by the author.

canal to Portland for transshipment, a mode of travel that was actually much safer than overland wagons given the product's volatility. And the mill had an impressive and far-flung list of customers: it supplied approximately one-fourth of the powder that the Union army used in the Civil War, had a contract with the Russian government to fulfill its army's needs during the Crimean War, and was an important supplier to the nation's railroad builders and mining companies.[29] Related in its instrumental use of naturally flowing water as a power source to the fantastic growth of mills and factories all along New England's rivers and streams in the early nineteenth century, the gunpowder mill owes its long-term success to the C & O Canal. Rebuild this abandoned and overgrown site in your mind, with all its buildings and activity, and you get a sense of the extent to which the canal transformed the physical and economic landscape of its surroundings, linking rural inland Maine to not only local but national and international commercial networks, a manipulation of space that far outstrips the new proximity that Portland gained to Harrison.

Redesigning the River

And not only was the C & O instrumental in reshaping the land-scape through which it passed, in and of itself it represented a new kind of space within the American countryside, a space that had been privatized and regulated in a way with which Americans had only recently become familiar. What landscape historian John Stilgoe says about the many locally funded private turnpikes that were established in America in the early nineteenth century is also true of the canals that began appearing at the same time: "It passes across many neighborhoods but its route and use are controlled by none. Only its makers and owners command its right-of-way and traffic; all others pay for the privilege of walking or riding upon it"[30]— or, in the case of canals, transporting their freight on it. Canals and turnpikes were long thin corridors of private property, owned not by local folks but by corporations located in a city some distance away, that were conceptually broken out from the landscapes through which they passed in a way that was unprecedented in a country in which the right to use paths and navigable waterways had always been held in common. Unlike in the rest of the rural neighborhoods that the C & O bisected, people had to reach into their pockets in order to get inside the canal's right of way, and were kept out of it by physical and legal as well as monetary means. Having secured its right of way largely through eminent domain, once the canal was built its commissioners established that landowners could build fences no closer than twenty-eight feet from the canal's center on the towpath side and twenty-two feet on the other side, expanding the canal's regular linear dimensions into the larger space that bordered it. In many places, the canal company itself fenced the right of way where it crossed through pastures, and also built thirteen bridges to carry town and county roads over the waterway, lifting road travelers safely over the alien intrusion into their landscape and into familiar neighborhood space once more on the other side. Trespassers could be fined three dollars if they rode, led, or drove their own animals onto the towpath or opposite bank. And, of course, any boat moving goods on the canal's waters had to pay a toll in order to do so, with tolls in the 1830s and 1840s averaging about three cents per ton-mile, with a lockage fee of six cents on downstream boats.[31] Through laws and fences and fees, the C & O Canal was rendered a carefully guarded private space as well as an engineered space, one that could be closely owned as well as heavily manipulated and used. It exemplifies a culture of property just as much as does any of Steinberg's other watery examples, and in the way it privatizes and regulates space it exhibits yet another dimension of cultural control within the rural Maine landscape.

Finally, as a product of its times as well as an artifact constructed in a particular time and place, the C & O Canal gave physical form to a number of other attitudes toward the natural world that were current in segments of American culture in the early nineteenth century. I have already mentioned the canal's conceptual connection to post-Enlightenment rationalism and its abstract, mechanistic view of nature, particularly as manifested in the growing profession of civil engineering, and will briefly mention two other important connections. By building their artificial river in the pathway that the Presumpscot had already forged, regularizing and mechanizing that river in the process, and by digging across country from the Presumpscot to the Fore River in order to find the shortest path to the sea, the canal's engineers were participating in a pattern of belief that held that it was humans' God-given role to improve on the natural landscape that nature provided them, that nature was a lump of only partially formed material that people were obliged to perfect, to engineer into a final form that was the most useful to humankind. In her study of the Erie Canal and its connection to nineteenth-century notions of progress, Carol Sheriff summarizes this attitude as it played out in upstate New York: "Americans believed that they had been placed on earth to finish God's work in shaping the New World. Their destiny was to perfect the human and physical world. Where God left gaps in the Appalachian Mountains, in other words, He intended humans to create their own rivers."[32] And where He left a river, like the Presumpscot in Maine or the Mohawk in New York, He evidently intended humans to perfect that river as best they could, either by bypassing its falls or by building a new and improved version right next to it in the gap that God had obligingly placed there. Much of the Erie Canal, like the Westbrook-to-Portland stretch of the C & O, was built not in a river valley but across country, a case of finishing work that God must have intended and never quite gotten around to, but certainly foresaw: "art's ultimate triumph," as Sheriff summarizes the feeling of the time, "was that it forced nature to do what nature had neglected to do on its own: create a river where one was needed."[33] The natural landscape that God provided gave specific direction to human technological activity as part of a divine mandate to complete nature's work. In building canals, Americans explicitly enacted this perceived relationship to the natural world, their careful linear channels signaling their allegiance to a nineteenth-century culture of improvement.

In addition, canal builders saw themselves as contributing to the improvement and future greatness of the young United States as a whole, to the expansion and progressive perfection of the nation as people moved west from its eastern cultural, political, and economic hearths, a movement to be brought about precisely by internal improvements such as canals. In the early nineteenth century, and particularly in Treasury Secretary Albert Gallatin's 1808 *Report on Roads and Canals*, the national government actively promoted canals and, on a more limited basis, turnpikes as a means of cementing the various states of the young nation together as a unified republic, bound by watery threads of communication and commerce. As Gallatin put it in his report, "good roads and canals" were vital to the nation's future, as they would "shorten distances, facilitate commercial and personal intercourse, and unite, by a still more intimate community of interests, the most remote quarters of the United States. No other single operation, within the power of Government, can more effectually tend to strengthen and perpetuate that Union which secures external independence, domestic peace, and internal liberty."[34] Internal improvements like these were a recurring concern in the nation's first few decades; as early as 1787, James Madison argued in *Federalist 14* that "the intercourse throughout the nation will be daily facilitated by new improvements," noting that "the communication between the western and Atlantic districts, and between different parts of each, will be rendered more and more easy by those numerous canals with which the beneficence of nature has intersected our country, and which art finds it so little difficult to connect and complete"[35]— a turn of phrase that casts rivers as natural "canals," co-opting nature into human plans and structures and suggesting Madison's allegiance to the belief that the American landscape was provided by God and that it was humanity's divine mandate to finish and improve God's works as best they could. A national system of canals would fulfill this mandate, facilitate interaction among states and regions otherwise divided by a difficult geography, and contribute to the strength and well-being of the nation as a whole through promoting and enabling agricultural and industrial development in the hinterlands by giving them easier access to regional and national markets.

Thus leaders in the national government — not only Gallatin and Madison, but every president from Washington to Monroe — advocated canals as part of a geopolitical agenda that had as one of its goals the same compression of time and space that the C & O accomplished on a much more limited scale. As John Stilgoe puts it, plans like Gallatin's were designed first and foremost to "strengthen government through spatial modification,"[36] while critic John Seelye sees internal improvements as physical correlatives of the new country's Constitution, each working with the other as part of a unified "beautiful machine" designed to facilitate the workings of government and the health, strength, and unity of the nation. Canal advocates wanted to bring the various sections of the country closer together, to bring more space firmly under national control, and to join together places that previously felt impossibly distant. For example, the Chesapeake and Ohio Canal, mentioned earlier, was an attempt to link the waters of the Atlantic with the Ohio River and thus ultimately with the Mississippi, achieving if not a transcontinental Northwest Passage then at least a passage through half a continent. However, much of the enthusiasm for national internal improvements foundered on questions of states' rights and latter-day anti-Federalist disdain for excessive governmental activity. In fact, the Constitution contained no provision for federal involvement in and funding of internal improvements (such a provision had actually been voted down), and so the exhortations of people like Gallatin and Madison were never enacted on a national basis.[37] Most big canal projects such as the Erie were built within individual states and financed through private investment and stock sales. And certainly the C & O was built on a small scale to serve only part of a single state, and was funded largely through a lottery, the chartering of a Canal Bank, and the public sale of stock.[38] Still, the country was abuzz in the 1820s with talk of the magnificent new Erie Canal and the desirability for still more internal improvements however funded; so it is likely that the C & O's financiers and builders would have been very aware of where the canal placed them in relation not only to nature, to time and space, but also to larger national ideologies of progress.

These ideas about nature and progress were not only evident in political discourse, but also animated American landscape painting in the middle of the nineteenth century. In the case of American art, though, ideas about the human relationship to the natural world were not usually announced as blithely, self-assuredly, and unambiguously as they would have been in a governmental report or political address, but were often more subtle, more complex, and, in the case of canals, more willing to suggest some of those waterways' shortcomings and limitations as technological instruments for controlling nature. This is particularly true of the only landscape painting I know of that actually depicts a part of the C & O Canal system: Portland artist Harrison Bird Brown's *View to the White Mountains from the Locks, Naples, Maine*, painted in 1862 (fig. 17). The lock that the painting shows is not actually nestled within an excavated canal ditch, but instead stands at the outlet of the canal into Sebago Lake. Still, it is a part of the larger system of structures that fundamentally changed the nature of time, space, and landscape in the area around the lake, and as such we can contemplate Brown's scene not only within the context of contemporary artistic conventions but more specifically in terms of how people used art as well as technology as a means of thinking about nature and expressing their relation to it.

The painting's complexities begin with its title, which calls equal attention to the mountains and the lock, which stands in the lower center of the canvas. This particular lock is depicted in the early 1860s, about ten years before the canal ceased carrying traffic. While centrally located in the painting, though, the locks are depicted in such a way as to be small and not particularly obtrusive: their masonry walls and wooden gates are visible, but at first glance the structure looks more like a small rural bridge than an engineered device designed to ease the passage of boats between bodies of water. Physically, the lock is both dwarfed and contained by elements of the natural world, the relative proportions of engineered structure and nonhuman components suggesting that the human presence in the scene is rather insignificant, that the predominating impression that the landscape gives is not one of human interference: the lake's waters stretch from the lock structure into the foreground, trees stand above it on either side, and in the background the hazy peaks of the White Mountains preside over the scene as a whole. The effect of this composition is to subtly

17. Harrison Bird Brown, *View to the White Mountains from the Locks, Naples, Maine*, 1862.

shape the viewer's experience of the painting, diverting attention to its nonhuman elements: while the lock stands at the painting's center, the eye is drawn everywhere but to that center — to the arrestingly vertical trees, to the placid and mirrorlike expanse of lake, to the teasing glimpses of mountain peaks in the background. These framing natural elements provide a physical, visual, and interpretive context for the picture's center, obscuring that center's artificial quality and locating the cultural within the natural. The lock is also partially obscured by a canal boat, a constructed artifact, with another boat floating nearby, but here too the presence of artifice in the scene is muted: the vertical thrust of the boats' masts echoes the form of the trees that frame the picture, suggesting a sort of organic relation between the natural and the artificial within the scene, and the boats appear to be lightly laden if not in fact empty of cargo, appearing almost more like pleasure craft than like freight carriers. A close view of the painting reveals small human figures in the boats and on the nearby shoreline, their purpose in the landscape unclear but their small proportions again suggesting that the influence of human culture in this scene is both insignificant and subordinate to the dominating presence of nature. The entire painting

Redesigning the River

appears quite idyllic, invoking nothing so much as a boating scene within placid natural surroundings, an 1860s equivalent of the sort of enjoyment that swimmers and fishermen find near Babb's Bridge today.

Like the banks of the Presumpscot, however, the painting also obscures a great deal about the evidence of heavy human use that the scene contains; its predominantly natural character is in large part a product of artistic shaping and selection. By placing the lock in the painting's middle ground, the painter is able to make it appear relatively small and unobtrusive, whereas in reality it was ten feet wide, seventy-two feet long, and obviously the product of a complex process of construction. As noted earlier, the boats provided the transportation link in a sort of colonial economic system connecting Portland to its hinterland, whereby raw materials and agricultural produce came to the city and finished goods were returned to the communities along the canal route. By showing the boats empty or nearly so, the painted scene's implication in this economic system is conveniently masked; likewise, the small stature of the human figures in the painting obscures the fact that, in this time and place, they would likely have been boatmen and lock tenders, central human agents not only in the functioning of the regional economy but in the heavy daily use of the canal itself, that strikingly artificial intrusion into the natural landscape. In other words, while the painting may be more or less true to the painter's selected angle of vision, there is a lot about the meaning, shaping, and use of this landscape that the painting does not show, or even hint at very strongly, and yet that is fundamental to the scene.

The effect of Brown's depiction of the locks is similar to that which Barbara Novak describes regarding the presence of trains, another important transportation technology, in American art at about the time that Brown was painting. Novak notes "how remote and insignificant are the trains that discreetly populate the American landscape paintings of mid-century! The assertive symbol of the new age of steam is confined to distant twists of smoke" in such paintings, its presence "blending . . . into more bucolic murmurs," its smoke and steam often blending with the clouds in a conflation of natural and artificial presences reminiscent of the blendings found in Brown's own painting.[39] The artistic insignificance of the train at the very time of its technological and cultural apotheosis, Novak argues, is a matter of deliberate choice — "a matter of camouflage as much as announcement" that such technologies exist in the landscape, a sense of "unwillingness to deal with this new man-made reality," an instance not only of the power of a pastoral landscape convention to resist emphasizing new human inventions at odds with that convention but also of painters' "sense that the train was profoundly antagonistic to the landscape before their eyes."[40] The canal could be seen as similarly antagonistic to natural scenes, if not quite as noisy and obtrusive: it relied on tamed water, on the introduction of rational order into the landscape's naturally occurring contours, and it enabled the more efficient exploitation of the landscape's natural resources in an ever-wider area for human domestic and industrial use. By depicting the lock in the unobtrusive way that he does, Brown distracts attention from the implications of the canal system of which the lock is a part, making it a seamless piece of the landscape rather than an agent in the control of that landscape.

Despite appearances, though, that control of nature is a crucial part of the painting, if not in fact its implicit central point. At the time Brown was working, according to art historian Angela Miller, even though landscape painters in the American Northeast characteristically emphasized "aesthetic proprietorship" in their paintings rather than the physical control and ownership of nature represented by such things as trains, canals, and human settlements, that aesthetic proprietorship nonetheless carried with it an "unstated corollary of economic and social possession"[41] — that is, the very act of rendering a landscape into a carefully arranged and aesthetically acceptable artistic composition was tantamount to a more tangible kind of ownership, as it established a symbolic possession functionally similar to those acts and structures of ownership and control so often and so subtly embedded in the paintings themselves. In this view, the C & O Canal and Brown's painting of one of its locks are fundamentally "about" the same thing — the possession and control of nature, be that control legal and physical on the one hand or imaginative and aesthetic on the other. As Miller puts it, in the middle of the nineteenth century "the representation of nature, in words or in paint, embodied many of the same assumptions that guided Americans as they established economic and social control over nature. It did so in the displaced language of visual mastery — a metaphor for other types of control — in which the eye was the stand-in for the actual human presence, vicariously enacting the rituals of power, property, and custodianship by which Americans defined their relationship to the natural world."[42] Brown's emphasis on the nonhuman aspects of the landscape around the locks, his decisions about composition and scale, thus help to accomplish something that on the surface they would seem to deny — the location of human presence and control firmly at the center of what seems to be a bucolic, pastoral, largely unspoiled world.

And yet, Brown's innocuous and natural-looking depiction of this important link in a carefully engineered transportation system is not a simple smokescreen for another cultural agenda, but suggests that some nineteenth-century Americans were willing to go only so far in both their actual and conceptual domination over nature. Perhaps a depiction like Brown's was necessary in order to make the implications of technology more palatable, as Novak notes in the case of railroads, or perhaps its synthesis of nature and culture suggests how the art-viewing public actually (if not perhaps fully honestly) saw humanity's position within the natural world — as a cooperative partner rather than as a conquering hero. In parsing the term "artificial river," which was popularly applied both to the Erie and to other canals, Carol Sheriff suggests how Americans juggled and reconciled the phrase's two seemingly irreconcilable components, giving shape to a vision that ultimately located humans not only above nature, but within it as well. "With the term 'artificial,'" Sheriff argues, "men and women emphasized the human resourcefulness behind the waterway and its alteration of the physical landscape. . . . Yet by clinging to the notion of a 'river,' they also suggested that the waterway belonged to an older way of life, one in which nature, not humans, determined the shape of the natural world."[43] To be sure, the Erie Canal was seen as "a symbol of progress," that same spirit of progress that energized so many advocates of internal improvements, but at the same time canals like the Erie remained firmly located in specific landscapes even as they allowed their boats to glide confidently into a glorious American future. Art and engineering may have represented the economic and cultural possession and control of nature, but insofar as art depicted engineering it did so in a way that suggested that, at least in the case of canal systems, technology was as much a natural process as it was a cultural one.

Nine years before Brown's painting appeared, Asher Durand produced what became a much more famous work of art, one that through its programmatic manipulation of space and time provides a clear visual representation of the paradoxical, problematic qualities of canals, a transportation system conceptually placed both within nature and in opposition to it. Durand's 1853 painting *Progress (The Advance of Civilization)* provides an excellent visual summary of the nineteenth-century ideologies that excited artists, engineers, and politicians, while also returning us to the idea of reading the relict C & O Canal as an intermediate or in-between landscape, as much river as artificial, remaining too close to nature for its own good even as it engineered nature into crafted linear human forms (fig. 18). Miller claims that "no painting better exemplifies the narrativity, confidently nationalistic message, and proprietary gaze" that characterized American landscape painting in the mid-nineteenth century than Durand's *Progress*, and it's difficult to think of a more overtly didactic, conceptually untroubled piece of art than this one, based as it is on an artistic convention that was known for "incorporating a narrative dimension into landscape, imbuing the mute geography of nature with a cultural program."[44] The painting's celebratory sequential story of American material progress and mastery over nature is clear, as the viewer's eye moves not only from earlier stages of transportation and landscape development to later ones, but in the same movement drifts from scenes of raw nature to landscapes shaped by the beneficent hand of technological and economic development; the natural world, in this view, is emphatically linked to the not-to-be-regretted past. Following the painting's program, the eye moves from the tangled forest foreground (and its Indian inhabitants) to a rude farm and wagon, to boats plying a placid canal immediately below, to a train skirting the lake on its way to the city that shines in heavenly glory in the background, its factories emitting innocuous clouds of puffy white smoke, more like clouds than like industrial exhaust in their color and form. Both the eye and the narrative of American history are inexorably led to the bright center of the painting and the ultimate triumph of civilization over wilderness, as nature's limits are progressively thrown off in a proudly nationalistic story of technological, industrial, and economic perfection.

Durand's painting grew directly out of the same cultural impulses that had earlier led to the great enthusiasm for internal improvements as a way of binding the country more tightly together and expanding its westward reach, placing his narrative composition firmly within an imperialistic and nationalistic framework. According to Miller, both

18. Asher Durand, *Progress (The Advance of Civilization)*, 1853.
Courtesy the Warner Collection of Gulf States Paper Corporation,
Tuscaloosa, Alabama.

Durand and his audience "were conditioned by the utopian promise
of technological change, abetted by nationalistic rhetoric and popular
images, to view technology, working in tandem with natural features,
as the agent that would draw together the republic. They made the entire program of expansion possible by integrating the local landscape
into a vast web of space."[45] Insofar as Durand is painting a national
epic and mapping out a historical and geopolitical ideal, however, it
is significant for our contemplation of the C & O that he places the
canal in his painting as close to the foreground as he does, explicitly
leaving canals out of his utopian vision of the future. His canal is only
two steps removed from unimproved nature, already located on a by-
passed point in the American story even at a time when many canals
were still actively carrying freight. Looking back from the vantage
point of midcentury, Durand sees the canal as only partway along the
narrative thread of national progress, much more entangled with nature than is his ideal industrial city (whose visual connection to nature
is to the bright and happy clouds above the smokestacks rather than

to the forest's rough and blasted stumps). As such, in the painting's formulation of history, the canal is doomed to obsolescence, much closer to the past than to the present — as in fact turned out to be the case in Maine and elsewhere. While a canal like the C & O in many ways represented human control over nature, in other important ways, as suggested by the landscape paintings of its time, it was a technology that remained bound by certain unavoidable constraints imposed by the natural world; its artificiality, its circumvention of geographical circumstance, its integration into that "vast web of space," was always only partial at best. As such, it was eventually overtaken, in life as in art, by the next figure in Durand's visual history of transportation, a figure much more distant from the forest and from natural constraints in general: the railroad.

The canal's ultimate proximity to nature is suggested not only by art but by its own physical characteristics. While the C & O Canal, with its locks and carefully engineered levels, is to some extent a mechanized version of the Presumpscot, a river rebuilt expressly to move freight as smoothly as a conveyor belt, in other ways it still fits Richard White's description of the modern, extensively dammed Columbia River as "an organic machine, as an energy system which, although modified by human interventions, maintains its natural, its 'unmade' qualities."[46] While canal boats moved through the landscape in an unnatural series of angular straight lines — ahead through the level sections, straight up or down in the locks, moving between lake and sea level in a long series of constructed steps — the locks themselves, while requiring the expertise of skilled craftsmen for their construction, were nonetheless fairly low-tech devices, relying on the simple properties of flowing water under the influence of gravity, the same principle by which river water reached the sea. The locks were carefully built: they were reinforced with rough stone walls that held the earthen banks in place, and had inner walls of planks attached to wooden pilings, three surviving examples of which can still be seen at what was known as the Lower Kemp Lock. (Lock walls made completely of cut stone rather than of fieldstone lined with wooden planks would have been sturdier and less prone to damage in freezing Maine winters, but also more expensive.) Once the boat was in the lock, the gates were closed, and the openings in the gates were slid back, though, nature took over, the water's stored kinetic energy leading it to flow downhill until the level was once more restored on the side of the lock the boat was moving toward. Canal locks thus are very simple machines — organic machines, perhaps, given that they rely for their functioning on the same natural properties that move the untamed water on the other side of the towpath. The canal may have been highly artificial in conception and construction, but here was at least one way in which it retained the river at its core.

Moreover, while in many ways the canal seemed clearly distinct from the river that lay just to its side, it remained intimately connected to the unregulated bodies of water that lay at its ends: Sebago Lake and the Atlantic Ocean. If a lateral move across the canal represented a disjunction between spaces, a move up or down the whole length of the canal suggested more of a continuity between spaces. Looking again at Brown's painting, and particularly at the canal boats that it depicts, will help us understand the particular circumstances of this continuity for the C & O Canal. These vessels, which were in common use on the canal throughout its working life, were slightly modified versions of a vernacular regional form called the gundalow, a narrow flat-decked boat of very shallow draft used as a sort of all-purpose carrier on the coastal waters and estuaries of Maine and New Hampshire. A product of vernacular invention and modification over time, the gundalow was originally developed specifically to operate in the shallow waters of New Hampshire's Piscataqua River estuary, and thus amounts to an interpretation in physical form of the qualities of a particular natural environment, as builders and users drew on their collective experience of the New England coast to create and refine a boat that fit organically into the contours and conditions that nature imposed. As local historian Richard E. Winslow puts it in linking the boat to the shallows and coves of the Piscataqua basin, "Without this local peculiarity of geography, affording such ideal conditions for the nurturing of this vessel, the growth of gundalow transportation would have never developed to the extent that it did."[47] Thus the boats that moved up and down the C & O Canal were not developed specifically to fit the artificial river's dimensions; the model for them was already at hand, and they were suited to the canal precisely because it was as shallow as some of the estuaries that constituted the gundalow's original working environment. In their history and form, then, the C & O canal boats allude to the ocean, the muddy inlet, the salt marsh; they were developed to work in such environments, and brought a reminder of untamed places with them as they moved at their stately pace through the canal's placid waters.

The boats also provided a direct link between the enclosed waters of the canal and the open waters at either end, in that once they passed through the guard lock at either end, they went back to work in the environment for which their prototypes were originally designed. As can be seen from the painting, the boats had masts that were hinged so they could pass under the thirteen bridges that spanned the canal at various places. Once the boatmen left the canal and entered Sebago Lake, they would raise the mast and sail, put down the centerboard, and sail anywhere on the lake they wanted using wind power rather than horsepower. If they wanted to continue all the way to Long Lake, they would pole their way up the Songo River connecting the two, pass through that river's single lock, and continue sailing. At the Portland end of the canal, boatmen also frequently took to the open water, traveling to the islands in Casco Bay and to nearby communities up and down the coast just as more conventional oceangoing gundalows did. While the C & O Canal differed from the lake and ocean in being a predictable, regular, linear, engineered artifact, then, in the ways it was used it maintained intimate connections to those natural bodies of water. In the end, water is water wherever you find it, and the water that was fed into the canal from the Presumpscot and its tributary streams provided a link that, while it may have been artificially made, was still part of a single hydrologic system for the people and boats that moved along its length. To move from ocean or lake to canal and back was perhaps not so much a transition between *kinds* of space — natural and artificial — as it was a transition between *degrees* of space.

And even as it sits in its current state of quiet obsolescence, the C & O Canal speaks subtly to us about one further aspect of its intimate connection to the natural world — or, more accurately, of the connection to nature experienced by the men who built it. It brings back to mind Richard White's observations on the deep knowledge of nature attained through work that I introduced in my discussion of John Casey and Ruth Moore, that "bodily knowledge of the natural world" that workers accumulate through the repeated experience of shaping natural materials and overcoming natural obstacles: "Humans have known nature by digging in the earth, planting seeds, and harvesting plants. They have known nature by feeling heat and cold, sweating as they went up hills, sinking into mud. They have known nature by shaping wood and stone, by living with animals, nurturing them, and killing them."[48] The canal represents a tremendous amount of work on the part of hundreds of men, most of whom, like the bulk of canal workers in northern states at that time, were poor Irish immigrants who generally found a very limited range of available jobs from which to choose. These workers, now lost to the historical record, lived in shanties and tents immediately adjacent to their remote job site, a circumstance that surrounded them nightly with insistent reminders of the nonhuman world. As historian Peter Way puts it in describing a typical nocturnal scene along any American canal under construction in the early nineteenth century: "Small animals scratched in the leaves, deer made their way to the creek, owls called, water burbled along a rocky bed, frogs croaked and, underlying it all, the industrious clicking of insects warning of the morrow's labour."[49] Way's recreation of this scene helps underscore the difficulty and discomfort of the canal workers' lives, a circumstance that extends from their living arrangements to the harsh conditions of their backbreaking work. As Way later describes them, "The labourers who dug the canals were a sweating, drinking, brawling, hurting, dying mass that seemed to well up from the muck in which they worked, scorched by the sun, choked by rain, bitten by chill frost."[50] Their immersion in the natural world, while extensive, was by no means benign, but rather was a constant source of pain. At the same time, it also helps indicate the paradoxical nature of their task: charged with digging an artificial river that would efficiently overcome natural obstacles, they inevitably carried out that work in an environment that resisted and retarded their progress every foot of the way.

If nothing else, then, the canal stands today as a mute monument to the forgotten bands of Irishmen who, driven to work on canal projects by the simple need to get a living in a country marked by pervasive anti-Irish sentiment, risked their lives and health on a daily basis to forward the progress of the ditch. And they obviously knew what they were doing: the canal was operated for more than forty years, and its remnants still stand in those places where they have been allowed to remain unmolested. The canal workers were amply familiar with White's earth, mud, and stone, as well as his heat, cold, and sweat; applying what they learned under the instruction of their supervisors, they built a remarkably durable artifact, placing dirt and masonry in such a way that they stayed put and did the job that they were expected to. In some ways victimized by nature, the workers at the same time exhibited a control over nature similar to that demonstrated by the existence of the canal as a whole: confronted by intransigent natural materials, the workers tamed them and made them do their bidding. After a strip of land was cleared of trees and brush, the most difficult and extensive work on a canal project was simply digging the ditch and hauling the dirt away, a job carried out with unremarkable tools like shovels, picks, wheelbarrows, and carts. Digging took more skill than might first appear, since the canal's uniform proportions had to be maintained throughout its length. The best fill was then heaped up to build the banks and towpath, which had to be firm and level. Diggers frequently had to excavate while standing in mud and water in wet swampy areas, and also had to blast and haul away rock where necessary (as at the old gunpowder mill site). Since the canal had to be level, the canal bed had to be raised in low places and dug deep when the ground rose, another way in which earth had to be carefully controlled and rearranged. To make the canal bed waterproof, workers had to "puddle" it with rammed clay; and to construct the lock walls, stonecutters and masons had to fit large blocks of fieldstone carefully into place. All of this took a lot of work in a remote place with relatively primitive tools, and it was all done well; the workers' collective experience and evident expertise with the vagaries of the riverside landscape and the natural materials it provided give ample testimony to the depth of their knowledge and understanding of nature as it was found alongside the Presumpscot. We cannot now recover who these men were and what they thought about the job they were doing; however, if we agree with historian of technology Robert C. Post when he says that "artifactual analysis provides the single most valuable means of understanding what early American workers actually did,"[51] the artifact that is the Cumberland and Oxford Canal, like the gundalows that plied it, speaks eloquently to the particular relationship that its builders had to their natural environment, a relationship that poised them ironically between deep environmental knowledge and the use of that knowledge to extend dominion over the natural world.

While distanced from nature in concept, form, and construction, then, the canal remained close to nature in other ways, and it was this natural aspect — the "riverness" of the artificial river — that ultimately led to its obsolescence and its current state of ruin and reforestation. If you haven't guessed it already, the reason should be obvious: in a state like Maine, rivers freeze in the winter, and so do canals. While the canal was a great improvement on Maine's primitive roads, it was still unusable for four or five months a year, and so during the winter may as well not even have been there. The canal provided a great impetus to economic development in the towns along its route and around the lakes, but its natural quality, its inability to resist the effects of cold Maine weather, meant that local business remained keyed to the seasons. Mills would stockpile their output to move it out in the spring, and would have to slow down or stop altogether if they could not get delivery of needed materials. Likewise, local merchants and consumers became cut off from supplies of goods in the winter. Even the coming of spring brought its own problems: small tributary brooks usually passed under the canal in culverts, and if a snowy winter brought heavy runoff these brooks could flood and wash out the canal banks, necessitating lengthy repairs and causing costly delays in transportation. Even the mechanical locks had problems caused by their geographical location: as noted earlier, in order to save money, the canal builders had made their locks from stacked fieldstone, posts, and planks rather than carefully cut and joined granite blocks, and despite the locks' being drained and cross-braced in the winter, the lock walls would frequently heave, buckle, and cave in during winter's frosts and spring's thaw, again necessitating repairs and delaying the seasonal opening of the canal to navigation. While the canal represented to its builders and users an improvement on what nature had originally supplied, then, it was only a partial improvement: in many ways, the canal still behaved inconveniently like a river, still was unavoidably subject to the conditions imposed by its natural environment. While it shortened and regularized time and space, it did so for only part of the year; during the winter months, southern Mainers were as bound by geography as they had been before the canal opened. Ultimately the C & O Canal, and other canals like it, represented only a partial triumph over nature; in the end, there remained some aspects of local environments that simply could not be engineered into submission. For the people who came to depend on them, the riverlike qualities of artificial rivers, the organic qualities of these organic machines, were highly inconvenient and frustrating. Some other, more reliable means of moving things through the landscape was clearly called for.

The railroad, of course, was subject to none of the canal's natural limitations, and it was the railroad that led to the abandonment of most nineteenth-century canals, sometimes scant years after they had opened. Railroads could operate in all weather. They could be built far from the sorts of reliable sources of water that canals depended on. They could scale heights and pass through mountain ranges where canals would have been physically impossible to build. And if canals shortened time and space, railroads annihilated them, covering distances and moving at speeds far beyond anything a canal boat could manage. As such, the experience of being on a canal boat remained in many ways much closer to nature than being on a train: canal boats moved at the speed of a walking horse, a rate of travel that remained scaled to the limits and capabilities of flesh and bone, not to the explosive power of the steam engine. People sitting outside on a canal boat were involved in the slowly passing scene in ways that rail passengers, sitting behind glass and watching the world race by, were not. They could even hop off the boat and walk on the towpath or explore natural scenes if they wanted to — as Nathaniel Hawthorne discovered when, during a trip on the Erie Canal, he disembarked in the middle of the night "to examine the phosphoric light of an old tree" only to discover that the canal boat had continued on its way without him, stranding him for the night.[52] Of course, the glowing tree was about the only attractive thing that Hawthorne found along the route of what he called "an interminable mud-puddle — for a mud-puddle it seemed, and as dark and turbid as if every kennel in the land paid contribution to it."[53] He in fact thought the canal constituted a direct attack on nature: the phosphorescent tree, with many of its fellows, had died when the swamp that had sustained it had been drained to supply water to the canal, creating what for Hawthorne was a suggestively emblematic scene: "The wild Nature of America had been driven to this desert-place by the encroachments of civilized man."[54] The Erie Canal seemed to Hawthorne to be inimical to nature, not intermingled with it, despite its proximity to the landscapes it traversed and the way its scale and speed of travel allowed him to plunge into those landscapes on a whim.

Redesigning the River

In general, though, that distance from nature was precisely the point of railroads. In the evolution of nineteenth-century transportation systems, as Asher Durand recognized in retrospect, canals turned out to be an intermediate step on the way to railroads; if canals were still deeply implicated and entangled in the natural world, railroads were much more fully removed from nature. True, they relied for their power on the energy stored in wood and coal, but otherwise could go anyplace where rails could be laid, and with the completion of the transcontinental railroad in 1869 began to link together the entire country as a single unified space in a way of which earlier promoters of internal improvements could only have dreamed. When a rail line, with its greater reliability, speed, and carrying capacity, was built along the same corridor occupied by a canal, the canal was inevitably the loser. As railroads burgeoned across the country, canal construction virtually ceased. The canal's heyday was spectacular but short-lived. While there were only 100 miles of canals in the United States by 1816, that number grew to 1,277 by 1830 in the wake of the Erie Canal, and to 3,326 ten years after that. During the 1840s, though, fewer than 400 miles of new canals were constructed in this country, and by 1850 more canal mileage was being abandoned every year than was being built.[55] The so-called Canal Era was over by the start of the Civil War, a victim of its ineluctable natural qualities. Most active canals today, like the St. Lawrence Seaway system, are primarily shipping routes that can still compete efficiently with railways. The only reason that the C & O Canal lasted until 1872 was that rail service was relatively late coming to the Sebago Lake region. Other New England canals were not that fortunate: the Blackstone Canal, which opened in 1828, was moribund a mere twenty years later after rail lines connected Worcester to both Providence and Boston, and the Farmington Canal between New Haven and Northampton went out of business after only twelve years of operation.[56]

As a direct result of that abandonment, the experience of strolling the C & O's towpath today is far different from what it would have been 130 or 170 years ago. Aside from the rebuilt lock on the Songo River and two short stretches of canal that were widened and deepened to serve small hydroelectric plants, those pieces of the C & O that still survive along the Presumpscot and Fore Rivers have been left to undergo whatever slow changes the passing decades would bring to them. In a further historical irony, what once was a largely, but not entirely, artificial space has now taken on an almost completely natural aspect, its current green cover obscuring its earlier bustling history of construction and transportation. While a moment's reflection might lead an observer to think that the riverside ditch looks a little too regular to be the direct result of erosion or glaciation, unless one comes across something as obviously artifactual as the gunpowder mill foundation at Gambo Falls, a walk on the old towpath seems no different from any other walk in the woods, from any other experience of the ostensibly natural world. As the presence of the fisherman at the Lower Kemp Locks first suggested to me, the C & O Canal landscape today represents qualities that are completely opposed to those that characterized the canal at its creation. It's a green and quiet place governed by the dynamic processes of forest succession, by the quirks of flowing water and the mysterious ways of fish — the farthest thing, it would seem, from a controlled, engineered, and privatized place designed to rebuild and improve nature and to warp the very experience of time and space.

In fact, in places the canal towpath has been officially defined as a natural space for the benefit of people who want to take a quiet walk in the woods. The first time I went poking around the canal's remnants at Gambo Falls, becoming simultaneously excited and puzzled by the strange circular foundation of the old incorporating mill, scrambling around in the old raceway that had been blasted out of the rock so long ago, and starting to work out in my mind the technological story that the landscape was trying to tell me, I came across a sign where the old towpath left the abandoned road that led down there. The sign tried to convince me that I had it all wrong, that this was a scene of nature and not culture (fig. 19). Its words explained that the canal landscape at this point had been preserved under the aegis of the Gorham-Sebago Lake Regional Land Trust "to preserve and protect forever its natural and scenic beauty, open space and wildlife habitat." Certainly the scene amply exhibits those qualities, but in exhorting us to save the place in that state "for future generations" the Land Trust passes over the contributions of *past* generations in making the landscape what it is today. Their sign mentions nothing of the human history of this patch of earth, and I can't fault it for that, as it is clearly a one-size-fits-all placard suitable for placement in any surroundings that the Land Trust has acquired and not something created spe-

19. The Gorham-Sebago Lake Regional Land Trust sign posted where the
towpath-turned-walking-trail leaves Gambo Road, Gorham, Maine.
2000 photograph by the author.

cifically for the canalside scene. Still, any such landscape would bear at
least the indirect marks of human shaping, and in describing preserved lands in the way it does and in enjoining people to act in ways
deemed appropriate to valued natural surroundings — no fires, no
building, no cutting, none but the most transient human occupation,
basically no activities of the sort that shaped the place to begin with —
the sign strictly enforces the conceptual divide between natural and
cultural landscapes; places like this can be one or the other but not
both. Humans have a very limited and strictly prescribed place here.

Of course, just because people have exploited this landscape in
the past doesn't mean that they have carte blanche to do so in per-
petuity, and even as I read the presence of human activity alongside
Gambo Falls I'm enough of a tree-hugger to heartily approve of the
strictures imposed by the Land Trust. A little closer to home, I also

20. A visible remnant of the Cumberland and Oxford Canal as seen looking east from Congress Street, Portland, Maine. The canal bed lies between the overhanging trees on the left and the raised canal bank that separates it from the marsh bordering the Fore River. 2000 photograph by the author.

enjoy visiting a popular refuge for nature lovers within the city of Portland itself, at the Maine Audubon Society's Fore River Sanctuary, in a spot where the canal once crossed from one side of the river to the other near a boat repair basin and a toll bridge on busy Congress Street in what was once the shipbuilding village of Stroudwater. Standing at the roadside, you can still see evidence of the canal on either side of you: downstream, the canal's earthen bank still hugs the land at the edge of the river, while upstream the canal cuts an arrestingly straight path into the woods (fig. 20). Interested in interpreting this specific landscape to its public as fully as it can given the constraints of signs and brochures as media of communication, the Audubon Society fully acknowledges that the old canal is literally, physically central to this section of the sanctuary, noting that the walking trail follows the abandoned towpath and offering in their brochure's "Cultural History" section a narrative sketch of the canal's dimensions and working life. This approach, balancing natural and cultural

Redesigning the River

21. A former canal boat basin now incorporated within the Maine Audubon Society's Fore River Sanctuary in Portland. 2000 photograph by the author.

history in public presentation and interpretation, takes accurate notice of the character and circumstances of this particular landscape and, by extension, of such ostensibly natural scenes elsewhere as well. This "sanctuary" is not so much a refuge from history and humanity as a display of how natural and cultural processes work together constantly to shape the places we see every day, even the places that seem to contrast most clearly with the heavily humanized spaces in which we most commonly spend our days.

Still, I don't imagine that many people come to the Fore River Sanctuary because of their restless, gnawing curiosity about transportation history, but because they want to leave the traffic noise of Congress Street behind and watch egrets stalking through the salt marsh or ducks paddling around in the estuary. True, it's hard to miss such cultural features as the piles of rubble where canals boats used to lock into and out of the river in order to cross it, or the heaped-up artificiality of the towpath itself — or, for that matter, the railroad tracks and power lines that run straight through the sanctuary. At the same time, though, aside from a few footbridges and routine trail maintenance, the canal landscape here has largely been allowed to go green and shaggy; today, the canal and the marsh on the other side of the towpath look more physically related than they do conceptually separate, and one could be forgiven for thinking that the weed-choked pool just off Congress Street wasn't once a wayside for canal boats (fig. 21). Even the imprimatur of the Audubon Society might seem to stamp this landscape officially as "nature," and as pretty special nature at that. This spot where culture and nature blend and bleed so tightly together looks like something quite different from another angle: a place reverting to a more purely natural state, a place throwing off the heavy hand of culture, and a place to which people appropriately repair when the world is too much with them, a human sanctuary as much as a wildlife sanctuary.

Thus we are left with some final ironies in this deeply ironic landscape. What was created as artifactual space, a deliberate imposition of cultural forms and processes upon the landscape, has now been redefined as natural space by virtue of its ground cover and its physical and conceptual distance from human activity, a state of affairs that is a direct result of the advent of the nature-defying railroad. Today, that is, people in southern Maine who want to escape the busy, mechanical, high-speed world that the railroad helped create can retreat to a restorative green landscape that is itself an ironic creation of that same railroad, its current state having been caused by its quick abandonment in the face of the railroad's success. The same towpath that provides a convenient trail for the contemplative and solitary walker seeking a nature experience is there only because of an engineering project designed to control, tame, rebuild, and systematize nature — an effort that, as we have seen, was only partially successful — and remained there to fade out of public view once the engineers figured out how to overcome natural limits even more completely and efficiently. In the canal landscape today, the natural was once cultural, just as the cultural was always deeply implicated in the natural. If you didn't think this conceptual line was sufficiently blurred already, a walk along the old Cumberland and Oxford Canal brings you to both a past and present time and place where the difference between the cultural and the natural, between the "artificial" and the "river," is as vague on the ground as it may be in the mind.

SEVEN

Natural Landscapes, Cultural Regions;
or, What Is Natural about New England?

If nothing else, the experiences and thoughts and texts that have gone into the making of this book have proven to me just how physically and conceptually complicated New England is, just how varied the landscape becomes when you look at it from the vantage point of several particular places and through the perspectives provided by several different minds. To Henry David Thoreau, and to John Casey's and Ruth Moore's characters, the forest and ocean environments look very different from the way they look to a summertime beachcomber or a Maine forester. Strolling through my back yard, or through the site of Walter Hale's old family farm, brings us across many subtle edges within a relatively small compass and through green spaces whose structure and composition have been quietly or obviously shaped by past human disturbance, spaces whose presence makes us think of the dense mosaic of land-use history that constitutes the surface of Maine and its neighboring states. The old Cumberland and Oxford Canal brings the presence of the human hand and of the desire to reshape the natural world to make it better fulfill economic desires more insistently to our notice, but its inherent shortcomings and its current state of obsolescence and abandonment also remind us that nature is not just the passive object of cultural process, that the landscapes that I see in my everyday life and in my nosings into the obscure overgrown corners of New England are a result of nature and culture working together in a complex historical fugue. Over time, the conditions of the natural world here have made some choices about how to live make more sense than others, people have reshaped the landscape to put those choices into action, and nature, irrespective of human intention, has continued to go about its business, offering opportunities for particular ways of life, letting people know when to abandon farms and canals, in either case providing a strong guiding force for how the landscape looks and how it changes over time. As I've been saying all along, it's hard for me to separate nature and culture when I look around me, if it's even possible to make such a separation and if there's even any point in trying to do so.

It's also hard for me to figure out where I am. Thinking back on what I've written about reveals to me a landscape that doesn't really seem to have much coherence or unity over a broad geographical scale; you don't have to move too far through space to pass through landscapes that have each been shaped and reshaped in slightly different ways by particular people through particular methods for particular purposes, and even to sit in one spot and let your historical imagination start working makes the world shift and scramble around you, as you think about how (in my case) nonfarm changes to farm and then changes to suburban neighborhood. It's a dizzying mental exercise to sit here on the northeastern coast of the United States and contemplate just how much physical change has happened here, and how fast it has occurred at that. From the time the first English settlers arrived, the land has been largely deforested and then reforested, farms have been made and abandoned, villages and cities have been founded, human settlements have sprawled all over the place, all with such swiftness that a time-lapse movie of the region taken from a hovering satellite would reveal a rapidly pulsing and throbbing landscape: first shaggy then smooth then shaggy again, clumps of humanity popping up everywhere, always and everywhere in motion. Moreover, a closer look would reveal that very individual things were happening, and at different rates, everywhere you cast your eye. In an oft-quoted passage, William Wood noted in 1634 of the lands near the Massachusetts coast that "the timber of the country grows straight and tall, some trees being twenty, some thirty foot high, before they spread forth their branches; . . . And whereas it is generally conceived that the woods grow so thick that there is no more clear ground than is hewed out by labor of man, it is nothing so, in many places diverse acres being clear so that one may ride ahunting in most places of the land if he will venture himself for being lost."[1] How things have changed. And changed, and changed.

Looking at the landscape at the scale that I've adopted in this book, then, might confound any sense of my residing within some sort of larger bounded whole, within a distinct and distinctive place that can be mapped and made coherent and cohesive within the mind and on the ground. What, aside from the fact of complexity and change, connects all the landscapes and episodes I've been writing about? Aside from the address, street, city, and state that are listed on my official documents, a small section of a neighborhood that contains its own particular land-use history, where do I live? Where does my geographical identity lie? One linking device may seem obvious, and it's suggested in the title of William Wood's book: he offers his readers *New England's Prospect*, and so I might be seen in these pages as offering a New England prospect of my own. There are many pieces of Maine in here, and what for me is a deeply significant chunk of Connecticut, and I think I've probably at least mentioned every other New England state in these pages so far. Also, of course, this entire book is the product of a historical, topographical, and ecocritical sensibility that has been shaped by my long-term residence and frequent travels in these six northeasternmost states. I've been discussing scenes and writers who are *in* New England; perhaps this is not just a matter of coincidental common location and my having stayed physically and conceptually close to home for this particular project — perhaps in this book's landscapes and waterscapes are consistent and region-defining components *of* New England as well.

And yet "New England" isn't a term or a space that seems to have any particular geological or ecological significance or rationale. A glance at a map reveals that most of the boundaries defining the western edge of the region are surveyed straight lines, legacies of territorial conflicts between the colony of New York and its neighbors to the east that bear little if any relation to the geology and hydrology of the place.[2] The equally historically nebulous boundary between Maine and Canada was established by a nineteenth-century treaty, but its sense of geometrical and geographical abstraction is the same; aside from small segments of the St. John and St. Croix Rivers, the boundaries are surveyors' work, with those surveyors bound more by the compass and chain than by the lay of the land. The same is true of state boundaries inside the region as well: Vermont and New Hampshire are the only two New England states that are separated completely by a "natural" border — the Connecticut River — and with the exception of the Pawcatuck River separating a small piece of Connecticut from Rhode Island and the Piscataqua and Salmon Falls Rivers running between southwesternmost Maine and southeastern New Hampshire, straight lines are the rule (so to speak). Looked at on the map, then, New England as a physical space appears to be primarily a human invention, an artifact deliberately inscribed onto the North American landscape, a cultural imposition onto that natural surface that the glaciers left behind all those years ago. The only exception seems to occur in northeastern Vermont; as Christopher McGrory Klyza points out, "Lake Champlain, which forms over 100 miles of the Vermont–New York border, sits along thrust faults, indicative of a stark geologic boundary. The Adirondack Mountains are wholly unrelated to those in Vermont. . . . So, in northern New England at least, the boundary between New York and New England makes geologic sense."[3] But the same is not true anywhere else along the region's perimeter, it seems.

Moreover, looked at according to other natural criteria, not only do New England's internal and external boundaries break down, but other kinds of spaces begin to reveal themselves, both suggesting new possibilities for internal division and throwing further into question the whole idea of New England's being anything other than a cultural geographical construction. United States Forest Service geographer Robert G. Bailey has spent a great deal of time developing the concept of the "ecoregion," which he defines simply as "any large portion of the Earth's surface over which the ecosystems have characteristics in common,"[4] and producing maps of both the nation's and the world's ecoregions on a variety of scales. On his 1995 revision of his map of the ecoregions of the United States, Bailey divides up the country into smaller and smaller ecological units based on finer and finer gradations among such factors as soil, climate, flora, fauna, and topography; beginning with four "domains," he works his way down to fourteen "divisions" and fifty-two "provinces."[5] On the level of the ecological province, the territory that makes up New England divides into three different parts, not all of which are geographically continuous: the Laurentian Mixed Forest Province, which includes much of southern and eastern Maine and northwestern Vermont; the Eastern Broadleaf Forest (Oceanic) Province, which takes in coastal southwestern Maine and New Hampshire, eastern and south-central Massachusetts and Cape Cod, all of Rhode Island, and southern and eastern Connecticut; and the Adirondack–New England Mixed Forest–Coniferous Forest–Alpine Meadow Province, which includes the New Hampshire mountains and most of Vermont, north-central Massachusetts, and the Berkshire Mountains of Massachusetts and Connecticut. (And these areas refract further depending on which criteria you use to define your geographical units; working on the level of major river drainages, Klyza, for instance, further divides Vermont into four smaller pieces.)[6] And not only do these ecosystem provinces ignore all state and regional boundaries (or, more properly, vice versa), but they are naturally related to other parts of the country that have similar natural characteristics. Thus, according to Bailey's national map, the part of Maine that lies within the Laurentian Mixed Forest Province has much more in common with northern Michigan, Wisconsin, and Minnesota than it does with the rest of New England, while Rhode Island and Cape Cod are ecological brethren of areas including most of New Jersey, eastern Ohio, and pieces of Kentucky and Tennessee. Ecologically speaking, then, it seems that there's no such thing as New England at all—it splits up internally and slops over into other parts of the country. While the landscape offers dizzying variety and complexity when looked at from the perspective of individual experience, Bailey suggests that on a broader level it is possible after all to draw individual natural scenes, such as those included in this book, into conceptual geographical wholes; these wholes, however, have nothing to do with the boundaries of New England as they have been historically mapped.

And yet that conclusion doesn't satisfy me. True, New England may be primarily a historical and cultural region rather than a natural region — an "invention," as we like to say in these postmodern times — but it doesn't seem right to me to insist that it's *wholly* a cultural construction, that it has no basis whatsoever in the natural landscapes of this part of the continent. While I don't want to come anywhere near suggesting a naive environmental determinism and implying that natural circumstances *made* New England ways of life come about, cutting off all economic and architectural choice on the part of the region's inhabitants and making the region's landscapes and history evolve inevitably, I also think that location matters to a certain degree in the development of the physical and conceptual entity that we now know as "New England." In thinking about my home region, I agree with environmental historian Dan Flores when he calls for attention to "the confluence between specific ecological realities and specific human adaptations" and for the necessity of understanding "the particularism of distinctive places fashioned by human culture's peculiar and fascinating interpenetration with all the vagaries of topography, climate, and evolving ecology that define landscapes."[7] In New England, like anyplace else, the landscape is a record of times and places where human ideas and ambitions came up against topographical and ecological opportunities and constraints, altering the land and being altered in turn by that land, and the New England scenes that I experience regularly show enough of a family resemblance that the quality and texture of the interactions of nature and culture that they bear silent witness to might be thought of as constituting a collective bundle of ongoing regional stories, individual episodes in individual places that nonetheless echo each other and provide at least a thin veneer of historical and material continuity and commonality for the region.

At the same time, of course, New England is not just a physical space, not simply a geographical surface and a bundle of landscapes, but is also an idea, a country of the mind. For many Americans both within and outside the region, New England is popularly defined not by a certain set of geographical boundaries but rather by a cluster of images, icons, historic episodes, character types: the white village, the steepled church, the Revolution, Puritan times, the Yankee. Certainly, the old houses and churches in the calendar-art version of small-town New England had to be built from lumber provided by the region's naturally occurring trees — if not William Wood's behemoths, then their smaller counterparts that still remained within the region's woodlots. And smaller sections within New England such as its coastal areas, well known for their lighthouses, their seafood, their fishing industry, and their iconic figures like the Maine lobsterman, obviously have a strong natural basis for their very existence. Still, every part of the country provides building materials and exhibits distinctive landscapes and economies that depend on those landscapes and the resources they contain. And if (as many people do) we think of New England as a region made up of certain defining historical episodes and characters — those events and personages from the colonial and Revolutionary past that tourists travel to Plymouth or Salem or Concord and walk Boston's Freedom Trail in order to get a sense of — the landscape that those events took place on and that those people lived within scarcely seems to matter at all; it serves more as a stage set for the emerging historical pageant than as an actor in how those past events unfolded over time. Here too, as in our consideration of the implications of Bailey's ecoregions, there doesn't seem to be much of an underpinning in nature for our understanding of New England, a region that is well known, historically deep, and emphatically real in the minds of Americans who live both there and elsewhere. So my question remains: what, if anything, is natural about that physical and conceptual space that we call New England?

⁂

When I was living in Rhode Island, during a period when I was particularly interested in historic cemeteries, I came across two gravestones that quietly and indirectly tell what to my mind are two archetypal New England stories. Together, I think they shed some interesting light on this question of a possible natural basis for a sense of New England identity. The first one can be found in the Commons Burial Ground in the town of Little Compton. Toward one corner of the cemetery, close to the large white meetinghouse with which the burial ground shares the village commons, one particular old slate gravestone has been removed from the ground and embedded in the west face of a tall granite obelisk that has been erected there in its place (fig. 22). The original stone tells us that "here lyeth the body of Elizabeth the wife of William Pabodie, who died May ye 31st 1717 and in the 94th year of her age" (fig. 23). The newer monument, however, tells us that Elizabeth Pabodie has been deemed important for more than her marriage and her impressively long life. Moving to the north side of the obelisk, we find out why she, alone among all the other people who have been buried in this cemetery, has been given the monumental treatment: we see that she is to be remembered first and foremost not as a member of the Pabodie family of Little Compton but as "Elizabeth, daughter of John Alden and Priscilla Mullin [*sic*], the first white woman born in New England." The opposite side of the monument contains an appropriate commemorative verse:

> A bud from Plymouth Mayflower sprung,
> Transplanted here to live and bloom;
> Her memory, ever sweet and young,
> The centuries guard within this tomb.

22. The obelisk that now encases Elizabeth Pabodie's gravestone, Little Compton, Rhode Island. 1994 photograph by the author.

Finally, on the east side of the obelisk is carved the date when it was placed there: "Erected June 1882."

According to a local newspaper account dated June 29, 1882, this "magnificent monument" was erected "through the efforts and influence of the estimable Mrs. Sarah Wilbour, widow of the late Charles Wilbour, Esq., aided by liberal donations."[8] To Mrs. Wilbour, the daughter of former Rhode Island governor Isaac Wilbour (her late husband Charles was a distant cousin) and a dedicated and indefatigable genealogist and local historian, getting the obelisk built was a long-term labor of love.[9] Her transcribed diaries, now in the collections of the Little Compton Historical Society, reveal the then-78-year-old Mrs. Wilbour's feelings and reflections on June 24, 1882, the day after the monument was finally erected: "Isaac rode to the Common with me, we went to see the monument put up yesterday to perpetuate the memory of Elizabeth Pabodie the daughter of John Alden and the first white female child born after the arrival of the Mayflower at Plymouth, it is a great satisfaction to me to know that the thing is done, I have had it on my mind 35 years, I started a subscription for

23. The gravestone incorporated into the Pabodie monument.
1994 photograph by the author.

the purpose in 1847, but was not able to awaken much interest in the
subject, let it drop, two years ago I moved again with better success."[10]
The timing of this success is interesting, but not wholly surprising
within a larger New England context. In the latter part of the nineteenth century — and particularly after the nation's centennial cele-
brations in 1876 — and the early years of the twentieth century, a new
interest in New England's colonial past was kindled among the region's elites. This new historical consciousness has been seen most often as a response on the part of influential members of New England's

old Anglo-Saxon families to new economic and social conditions in the region — in particular, increasing industrialization and urbanization, and the rising flow of immigrants that accompanied them — that threatened their economic and social positions, their cultural dominance, and what we might think of as their sense of conceptual ownership of New England, their sense that, as a place and an idea, the region fundamentally belonged to them and not to newcomers. In response, many members of old New England families did what they could to inscribe a particular version of New England history prominently onto the landscape, to re-stake their historical claim on the region and remind visitors and newcomers just whose place this was, selecting and proclaiming a version of the past that specifically bolstered what they saw as their increasingly precarious position in the present. Mrs. Wilbour's town of Little Compton was a scant ten miles from industrial Fall River, Massachusetts, and while I know nothing more about her motives than the little that her diary reveals, and so cannot say for sure just how concerned she and her neighbors were about the changing character of New England, if we place the erection of the Pabodie monument within this larger cultural chronology it makes sense that she would have found more success among potential "liberal donors" in the 1880s than in the 1840s.

For that matter, I imagine that in 1847 the story of John Alden and Priscilla Mullins wouldn't have been particularly well known within the region to anyone other than local historians like Sarah Wilbour. Henry Wadsworth Longfellow's poem "The Courtship of Miles Standish" wasn't published until 1858, and it was that poem that first lodged the names of John and Priscilla firmly in the public mind, whereupon their story and images became a popular motif in late nineteenth-century American popular culture.[11] Of course, Longfellow's poem was more fiction than fact in its specifics, but his version of this colonial love triangle quickly became the de facto public record and one of the few popular stories (along with the Thanksgiving story, perhaps) that people knew and could tell about Puritan times in New England. The June 29, 1882, newspaper account provides a quick summary of the story for the benefit of its readers: "It is said that the Hon. Miles Standish, when a young man became enamoured with Priscilla Mullin [sic], mother of Elizabeth, but being rather diffident in matrimonial affairs and having confidence in John Alden, he employed Mr. Alden to negotiate with Priscilla upon the matter. Mr. Alden, faithful to his trust, broached the love-making topic, recommending Mr. Standish as a person to make her a suitable and congenial companion for life. Priscilla, with a blush and smile, said: — 'Prithee, John, why not ask for thyself?' At this introduction the courtship began and they were married." By virtue of Elizabeth Alden Pabodie's having come to Little Compton to live, then, and with an assist from the enormously popular poet Longfellow, Mrs. Wilbour and her fellow townspeople found themselves in the possession of not just an interesting nugget of local history, but of a past personage who provided them with a direct link to three of the best-known names tied to the Puritan founding of New England.

This, then, is one kind of New England story, one typical way of using history and narrative to come to some sort of definition of regional identity — a way that disregards the local, the particularities of landscape and community, in favor of placing emphasis on a small number of what are seen as major region-defining episodes and personages that occurred or lived only in a few places within New England.[12] To be sure, the Little Compton newspaper account does contain some quiet tension between local meaning and larger regional meaning. Between describing the monument and telling the Standish-Alden-Mullins story, the article notes that "John Alden, father of Elizabeth, built a house for her, at or near where Mr. George A. Gray's house now stands in Little Compton, where she and her William commenced house-keeping." By making reference to George Gray, a neighbor of its readers and evidently someone who was well known enough in town to have his house serve as a landmark, the newspaper story takes Elizabeth Pabodie out of the graveyard and places her within the local landscape and within a framework of local knowledge: if you knew where George Gray lived, you knew where the Pabodies had lived two hundred years earlier; you could place them on your mental map and enrich the substance and texture of what you knew about that patch of home ground with which you were so intimately familiar through the process of daily living. But the article ultimately places much more emphasis upon the story of Elizabeth's parents' courtship than on anything having to do with the circumstances of her own life, evidently deeming that to be the only thing that was interesting and important about her: all we know about "her William," for instance, is that he "kept house" with her.

And, of course, the monument does the same thing, effectively decontextualizing Mrs. Pabodie from her own town both physically and conceptually and locating the source of her identity (and, implicitly, the identity of Little Compton) elsewhere. Even on a literal level, she has been wrenched out of her local ground, her gravestone removed from the company of its fellows, lifted in the air, and isolated in a granite monument that implicitly devalues all of the other humble stones around it. Poor William and the rest of her family and neighbors are left down there in the grass, forming a community of the dead that parallels in its composition their community when they were living, while by accident of parentage Elizabeth has been removed from their company and elevated to lofty eminence, the meaning of her life rooted not in the stony soil of southeasternmost Rhode Island but in a well-known and highly valued historical narrative that took place many miles to the northeast. It scarcely matters that she lived in Little Compton at all: as the commemorative verse puts it, she is first and foremost "a bud from Plymouth Mayflower sprung" — the emphasis on "Mayflower" hammering home the point that she descended directly from New England's founders, a genealogical claim to distinction that was another obsessive concern of New England's old families at that time — while she was simply *transplanted* here to live and bloom," not to be seen as native to that place in any way. If the existence of the monument implies that Elizabeth Pabodie is one of Little Compton's most prominent past citizens (or, at least, historical curiosities) and provides one of the town's historical high points, then the town's identity merely derives from reflected historical glory, its meaning coming down from a tenuous link to what has become popularly accepted as one of the defining components of New England identity: the region's Puritan founding. The bulk of Elizabeth's ninety-four years, spent living within, and helping to get a living from, the landscape of a particular place and time, seems not to matter in this version of New England.

It's a version — "New England" as "the Pilgrims" — that probably seems familiar in some way to many readers: if the names of John Alden and Priscilla Mullins don't mean anything to them, they may have at least read their share of Hawthorne at some point or participated in one of those elementary-school pageants about the first Thanksgiving. It's also a version that, as I've implied, has little to do with a specific location and in fact disavows the very importance of location, finding regional meaning and definitive regional characteristics primarily in the realm of disembodied historical narrative, a narrative that takes place in a New England that serves simply as a stage set for human historical actors, giving them someplace to stand while they go about their enduringly significant activities. Certainly, it's an understanding of what's distinctive about New England, and about New England history, that has little to do with nature. And yet it's not the only version of New England that's out there, not the only pattern for thinking about and conceptualizing a distinctive kind of regional history and identity. If we go around and inspect artifacts in the landscape in order to get a sense of what New England means, reading the textual markers that people have left in the landscape in order to get clues to the place's identity and to its shaping patterns of human experience, there are other gravestones that we can look at, gravestones that are just as significant as Elizabeth Pabodie's, that are much more gripping and moving, and that show us a region whose ongoing life has been intimately tied to the natural facts of the landscape as its residents have found them. This New England is both more grounded and more democratic: figuratively speaking, what matters isn't the Aldens and Mullinses of the region so much as all those other names in the rest of the cemetery, names of the many people who got their livings either directly or indirectly from the natural resources that the region contained, from the ways of life that the landscape made possible.

One year when I was living in rural Scituate, Rhode Island, I became very fond of taking long walks along the area's back roads. One day I came across a small historic cemetery perched atop a hillside next to that day's route, and, being constitutionally incapable of walking by an old cemetery without going in and looking for interesting gravestones, I jumped onto the retaining wall on the other side of the roadside ditch and began to poke around. My attention was soon caught by a three-foot-tall white limestone marker, the only one of its kind in the graveyard (fig. 24). Its inscription, though, was even more arresting: "Sacred to the memory of Sally Ann, wife of Abner B. Rogers, who lost her life in the calamity at Simmonsville, April 13, 1840, aged 22 years." It's sad to contemplate the death of anyone that age, let alone a young wife. But I was particularly intrigued by one resonant phrase: "the calamity at Simmonsville." What could this have been? Anything described in such a way must have been a horrifying event, and the inscription's turn of phrase seems to imply that "the

24. Sally Ann (Angell) Rogers's gravestone, Scituate, Rhode Island. 2000 photograph by the author.

calamity" was a widely known local disaster, that its meaning would have been self-evident to any people (who would all likely be from the immediate locality) who would read the stone in at least the near future. For me, though, the stone was frustratingly incommunicative; it bore a layer of local history and meaning that had eroded away over the years, leaving only a tantalizing glimpse of what had happened — or, more properly, a glimpse *that* something had happened, the exact nature of which was unknown to me.

Sally Ann Rogers's marker stood in the middle of a straight row of seven gravestones that stood close together over the space of twenty-five feet, all the others of which were made of dark gray slate. The one on the far left bore an inscription that was even more chilling than the one on Sally Ann's: "Sacred to the memory of Phillip Angell, [who] was drowned April 13, 1840, aged 50 years & 3 months. The Father, Mother, and Four Children, was lost in the calamity at Simmonsville, Johnston" (fig. 25).[13] There was that phrase again — "the calamity at Simmonsville," a village within Scituate's neighboring town of Johnston, with the additional information that said calamity involved drowning and that, appallingly, it took the lives of six members of the same family. Next to Philip Angell's stone stood that of his wife, Sally, who was also "drowned April 13, 1840, aged 45 years & 4 months." Next came the grave of a small daughter, Susan, who had died in 1836 when she was eight years old. Finally, the row was completed by the four lost children, arranged in descending order of age as though they were lined up for a picture or a walk to church: Sally Ann (Angell) Rogers, then nineteen-year-old Philip, then six-year-old Emily, and finally three-year-old Benjamin. All drowned, all on the same date — in fact, Sally Ann's is the only stone that euphemistically notes that she simply "lost her life." Certainly the stonecarvers were correct to use the word "calamity" to describe whatever it was that decimated this family. Still, there's no evidence in the cemetery itself about what it was that caused this mass drowning.

This is the kind of story that can tear your heart out if you let it. It's also a tantalizing historical episode, one that grips much more strongly than the sentimental John Alden-Priscilla Mullins love story and that would seem to make at least as much of a claim on our attention as anything having to do with the life or ancestry of Elizabeth Pabodie. And yet the calamity at Simmonsville is probably the most obscure calamity I've ever come across. With one exception, it's not marked by

25. Philip Angell's gravestone. 2000 photograph by the author.

any sort of sign or mentioned in any tourist guide or local history that I've ever seen; I would never have known about this event myself if I hadn't happened to come across that particular cemetery and decided to nose around. It seems that the various people in Rhode Island who have been responsible over time for designating particular sites as "historic" never decided to elevate the Simmonsville calamity out of the realm of the mundane and ordinary, or perhaps it became forgotten so quickly after it happened that no one knew enough about it to memorialize it. The Angells simply weren't in Elizabeth Pabodie's league historically. They unfortunately had the wrong sorts of parents — or, less flippantly, they weren't connected to any widely known and regionally valued historical figures or legendary events, didn't bring Scituate any particular glory, and so remained among the vast multitude of New Englanders whose names and memories don't live much longer than they themselves do.

I should note that while the obscurity of the calamity at Simmonsville seems to be of long standing, it persists today, and somewhat amusingly at that. It turns out that fifty years ago another cemetery snoop was asking the same questions that I was. In her "Woman's Way" column in the November 17, 1950, edition of the *Providence Journal*, Esther Willard Bates notes that "one of our readers, who does not wish her name given, asks if anyone can throw light upon 'The Calamity of April 13, 1840.'" The anonymous inquirer evidently didn't look around too closely, as the column mentions the stone of "a young wife, Susan [*sic*] Rogers," with its arresting mention of "the calamity at Simmonsville," and those of several children as well, but omits mention of the parents completely. Noting that on (only) "one of the children's stones the words read 'Drowned, April 13, 1840,'" the inquirer begins to wonder what exactly happened on that date. "Were the children (Angell was their name) little brothers and sisters of the older woman [Sally Ann Rogers]? Were they neighbors? Did they set off on some picnic and come to an awful mischance? Were all drowned, and where?"[14] As far as I've been able to discover, no one ever wrote to the newspaper to provide further information on the calamity, and most people who read a newspaper in Rhode Island in 1950 read the *Providence Journal* (although not, perhaps, the "Woman's Way" column). This suggests that the nature and facts of the calamity had become largely unknown 110 years after it had happened, both within the affected community and throughout the state as a whole. As I'll soon discuss, even the anonymous writer's guess about what might have happened is completely off the mark: her tableau of a leisurely picnic lunch gone horribly wrong has nothing to do with the facts of the event as they transpired, and also suggests that she lacked the basic knowledge about Simmonsville and about Rhode Island (or, more largely, New England) history that would have allowed her to make a more informed speculation.

More recently, upon looking around more thoroughly in order to satisfy my historical curiosity, I came across a very small plaque embedded in the railing of the bridge that crosses the Pocasset River in the Simmonsville section of Johnston (fig. 26). Given my assumptions about the event's obscurity, I was a little startled to find it, but on closer inspection I decided it doesn't tell its audience very much at all. The text of the plaque reads, "In memory of all those who lost their lives in the Simmonsville Flood on April 13, 1840. May they rest in peace. Ralph R. aRusso, mayor." A person who sticks to only the historical information written on landscape artifacts and memorials now knows that the calamity at Simmonsville had something to do with a flood, but still knows nothing about the nature of that flood: its causes, its extent, the damage it caused. The plaque doesn't even include the number of people who "lost their lives" in the flood, let alone their names and ages. All it does is note the fact and date of a calamitous event and the fact that some people died — we don't know about the people, we don't know about the circumstances of the flood. It doesn't even say if the particular site where the plaque is located had anything to do with the story of the flood (although in fact it did). This too is a kind of placeless history in a way, referring to a largely disembodied event and connecting it only barely to a specific location, and not even to the physical or natural conditions of that location (although I imagine we're to assume that the Pocasset River was the one that flooded). There's no real way to connect this historical marker to that small Scituate cemetery, unless you happen to have the peculiar combination of arcane interests and landscape-reading habits that I do. The reader of the plaque has nothing larger, either geographically or historically, to connect to the information it contains. (In fact, I suspect its existence probably has something to do with self-promotion on the part of Mayor Ralph R. aRusso, the only person whose name appears on the plaque. The late Mr. aRusso, a long-time mayor of Johnston, remains best known to Rhode Islanders for having added a meaningless "a" to the beginning of his given last name of Russo in order to ensure that he'd appear first on the ballot one year.)

To find the details that didn't appear in the landscape itself, I turned to the newspaper record. A short article in the April 17, 1840, edition of the *Rhode-Island Country Journal and Independent Inquirer*, headlined "Awful Calamity," describes the terrible course of events:

> One of the most awful calamities that it ever fell to our lot to record, occurred at half past five o'clock yesterday morning, at the

26. The commemorative marker on the current bridge over the Pocasset River in the Simmonsville section of Johnston, Rhode Island. 2000 photograph by the author.

factory village of James F. Simmons, on the Pochasset Brook [*sic*] river. The heavy rains of the previous night raised the stream to such an [*sic*] height that the dam to the upper reservoir gave way, the swollen stream rushed down, overthrowing in its course four other dams, until it reached the village, when it carried away two dwelling houses, three small buildings and a building used as a store, machine shop and dry shed. The stream struck the buildings about eleven feet high, and swept them instantly about sixty feet into the channel. One went immediately to pieces; the other floated away and broke in pieces.[15]

A detailed 1862 map of Simmonsville gives us a sense of what happened and why. There were six dams on the Pocasset River in the space of about a mile and a half, holding back six accompanying mill ponds that provided waterpower for eight mills, each of which was surrounded by its cluster of support buildings and worker housing. When the heavy rains caused the westernmost dam to burst, its waters rushed downstream and joined those penned behind the next dam, throwing the dam over; by the time the sequence of dambursts reached James F. Simmons's works, four millponds' worth of water, augmented by the rains, formed a wall of water eleven feet high that then carried before it everything that was in its path — including those two dwelling houses.

The Angells were not alone in their calamity. There were five families boarding in those houses, and only one got out unscathed. "Of the other four," the article notes, "eighteen persons were drowned, and only nine saved." Six of those drowned were Angells, as we have seen — for some unknown reason, Sally Ann was staying with her parents and younger siblings that night. Not all of the family was lost, though: a "Genealogy of the Descendants of Thomas Angell, who Settled in Providence, 1636," which was published in 1872, notes that Philip and Sally Angell had had eleven children, two of whom died young, four of whom died with them, one of whom died at sea, and four of whom were still alive at the time the genealogy was put together.[16] Still, it's a tragic family story, one echoed elsewhere in the list of the deceased provided in the newspaper account. The death toll includes a "Mrs. Matilda Whitmore, aged 46 years," and her four children, aged fourteen (Maloney), twelve (Almira), ten (Julia Ann), and seven (Laurana). After giving their names, the story dryly notes that "the above are the family of Mr. Brayton Whitmore, who is absent on a visit to Connecticut." I don't even want to try to imagine what Mr. Whitmore's feelings must have been once he returned to Rhode Island and got the news, or what his life must have been like afterward. Three other Whitmores are named in the list of the dead: Martha and Sarah, the wives of Messrs. Russel and Nelson Whitmore — brothers to Brayton, perhaps? — and Jenetta, the eight-month-old daughter of Nelson and Sarah. The remaining dead were two-year-old Franklin Randall, Mr. William McAnsland, and Mr. John and Miss Lucinda Hull, perhaps a brother and sister. Adding these names, along with their implicit stories and the impacts that we can intuit their loss had on their families, only increases our sense of the rightness of the term "calamity" to describe the event, of the sobering effect it must have had on people in neighboring mill villages, and of the huge hole it must have torn in the social fabric of that part of Rhode Island. The news story ends by noting that "the spot has been visited by thousands, ready to offer any assistance which could be rendered. No language can describe the feelings of the survivors, and of those who were the painful spectators of the scene." It's a compelling story, but one no longer available to be easily read in the landscape or the written record; it's a historical event, but not the capital-H History that has traditionally been evoked in thinking about New England. (I'm glad I can write about it here. These people deserve to be remembered too.)

Most of the victims of the flood were women and children, as people were just beginning their day at that hour and most of the men and older boys in the houses were likely on their way to work at the mill. As the newspaper account notes, "The first bell had just rung, and several persons had left the houses which were swept away. Had the disaster occurred half an hour later, the destruction to life would have been much less." Here the story takes on providential overtones: the loss of eighteen lives is presented as a matter of ill luck more than anything else. Moreover, after the well-known and widely publicized 1826 avalanche in New Hampshire's White Mountains that killed the entire Willey family — they were crushed when they ran into the path of the avalanche and would have survived had they remained indoors, a turn of events that was interpreted from many New England pulpits as a lesson in the importance of having strong faith in God — I imagine that any nature-related disaster would have been thought of in similar terms by more than a few people.[17] Still, at least one potential victim was spared in an act of seeming divine providence: "Mrs. Eddy, aged about 60 years, saw the flood coming, and returning to her bed, wrapped herself up in the bed clothes. The house was borne down the stream, and she extricated herself in safety." Finally, there's a touch of melodrama in the text as well: we learn of the dam that "the first signs of its breaking away, were discovered by Mr. Samuel Randall, and immediately started to inform the people of the threatened danger, but the dam gave way before he reached the village and the flood rushed past with such fearful rapidity that the work of destruction was consummated before he could arrive." The imagination builds pictures of Mr. Randall making a brave and gallant Paul Revere-style ride to sound the alarm, falling just short of his goal. The Angell family genealogy that I mentioned earlier follows this dramatic vein in its sketch of the calamity, claiming that Mr. Randall "leaped upon his horse and hastened down to the village to give the alarm" and that, after failing to outride the flood, "he stood on the top of the hill in full view of the village when the flood struck the buildings."[18] It also claims that the houses were carried downstream until they struck a bridge abutment and broke apart, and if I'm reading the newspaper account and the map correctly I think that this unyielding bridge must have been on the same spot as the Simmonsville bridge that I mentioned earlier. At least the plaque got the location right, even if it doesn't actually say so.

⁂

While the calamity at Simmonsville is now an obscure event (although I'm sure it wasn't in 1840 Rhode Island), and while scholarly investigation allows us to build only the barest account of the event while offering tantalizing glimpses of more, this too is an archetypal New England story, one linked not to the conventional pageant of New England history but to the ongoing interplay of nature and culture in the region, the ways that both prominent and everyday New Englanders have historically interacted with the lands and waters around them. Both the Angells's gravestones and the cemetery that contains them refer quietly to some important and typical episodes in New England land-use history, pointing to both the distant past and the more recent past to suggest some widespread ways in which New Englanders have both taken advantage of and been limited by the natural landscapes in which they have lived, a complex balance of nature and culture that also typifies many of the sites I've examined earlier in this book and that seems common enough to have constituted a shared pattern of historical experience for everyday New Englanders for much of the region's history. If Elizabeth Pabodie stands for one version of New England, the world that the Angells lived in, along with that small patch of earth that remains sacred to their memory, stands for another, one that is inclusive of more of the region's people and that helps us understand the landscapes that we see when we travel through New England today and look around us — that helps us understand the particular nature of nature in this part of the country. I think back here to remarks I quoted earlier from John Elder, in which he reflects on "my experience of wilderness and culture in New England. What began as an opposition has slowly evolved into a balance," he observes, noting around him "places where human vestiges and the region's nonhuman life have begun to fade together, lost in an emerging balance of wilderness and culture."[19] I think this observation also holds true for many, many other places in New England: for

Walter Hale's old farm, for the landscape of the old Cumberland and Oxford Canal, for the coastlines and waters where Casey's and Moore's characters ply their trade, for my various back yards, and even perhaps for Thoreau's Maine woods. The physical landscape that we call "New England" reflects and reveals the region's distinctive ongoing history, and by placing a family like the Angells within their natural, geographical context we can perhaps begin to think about a new kind of regional story and identity for New England, one that is firmly grounded in — and that crucially depends on — the natural world.

According to the Rhode Island Cemetery Database at the Rhode Island Historical Society, Philip Angell and his family are buried in the Jeremiah and Benjamin Angell Lot. This name confirms that the cemetery is representative of what was a widespread practice in rural New England beginning in the late eighteenth century and extending well into the nineteenth century: the establishment and maintenance of small family cemeteries as more and more individuals and communities began to abandon the practice of churchyard burial.[20] Usually these "tiny eruptions of holiness,"[21] in landscape historian John Stilgoe's phrase, were located on the edge of an agricultural field in a place that offered convenient access but for some reason was not appropriate to use for agriculture, which might explain why so many New England historic cemeteries, like the Angell lot, are located next to roads and thus are easy to find by wanderers like me. Some family burial grounds remained open for pasturage, while other were fenced or walled in, the overgrown grass getting mowed away every so often.[22] Either way, domestic burial grounds became a common part of New England rural neighborhoods, with more than one family sometimes combining to maintain a shared cemetery; in fact, the Rhode Island database lists over 390,000 gravestone inscriptions from 2,980 cemeteries, which works out to a little less than three graveyards per square mile in that tiny state and accounts for over 90 percent of all pre-1900 gravestones. With all this in mind, we are confirmed in what we might well have guessed about a spot like this in rural southern New England: the land around the Angells' final resting place used to be a farm — and Philip Angell's old family farm at that.

The Angell family genealogy sketches out the contours of Philip's working life: "Philip Angell was a husbandman, and occupied a farm given to his father, Benjamin, by his grand-father, Richard. This farm is now occupied by Jeremiah, brother to Philip. When his family became large he moved to a factory to have his children work in the mill. They had lived several years at different factories, and four of their children were married."[23] This is a New England story, and a very common one at that: the movement of large segments of the region's population from a countryside that could no longer support it. New England farms in the nineteenth century tended to be small, and over time there was less and less free land on which to establish new farms, particularly in rural neighborhoods in the longer-settled southern parts of the region. Thus a single farm could not support all of the male children of a single farm family — to subdivide a small piece of land into even smaller sections would not have left anyone with enough to gain a living from — and so many sons became landless as they reached adulthood, particularly if, like Philip, they had growing families to support. New England farmers worked their lands as hard as they could to both ensure their own subsistence and produce a small surplus for market, but given the structure of their farms and communities they quickly came up against limits, having divided up the landscape into parcels small enough that the region's thin and stony soils could not provide a living for all the people that it had undoubtedly been meant to. Nature and culture came into conflict in rural New England, and nature ended up throwing an unforeseen wrench into the workings of culture. Something had to happen to all those extra farm folks.

Before we follow Philip off the farm and into Simmonsville — that same farm to which he returned in death to be buried in the family graveyard, which explains why he was interred a good five miles from where the calamity occurred — there are a couple of other things about this site that interest me, indications of ways in which this tiny patch of land takes part in other stories of nature in New England in addition to the ones in which the Angells participated in the nineteenth century. I don't know the extent of the old family farm or how the entire property was laid out, but I suspect that this particular site was chosen for the family burial ground because it occupies the top of a small and quite steep hill, a typical site choice for New England domestic burial grounds (fig. 27).[24] Perhaps the elevation of the spot, that much closer to heaven, had its appeal for the Angells; also, the quick change in slope meant that this piece of ground would have been difficult to cultivate, and possibly would not have been attractive to grazing animals either. Either way, the little hill evidently seemed

27. Looking up the hill toward the Angell family cemetery, Scituate, Rhode Island. The cemetery's enclosing stone wall is visible as a dark line at the top of the hill. 2000 photograph by the author.

inappropriate to press into service in the farm's productive operations, and so it was available to be used for memorial and spiritual purposes. But the very structure of the hill suggests the presence of a deeper layer of time in addition to that occupied by the Angells of the comparatively recent past. The graveyard doesn't occupy the entire crest of the hill: if you step over its boundary wall, you see that the hill extends for dozens more feet to the north and west before falling off sharply to the forest floor below. To my nongeologist's eye, the hill looks like nothing less than a drumlin, teardrop-shaped, its wide end at the road and its curved point running off into the woods beyond the cemetery — a glacial leaving, a small heap of debris left behind when the glaciers retreated from southern New England over 10,000 years ago. If I'm right, then the Angell family lot sits on ground that, in its origins, is a close relative of the Cape Cod that I wrote about at the beginning of this book, and suggests similar dimensions of geological time. That little hill has been sitting there for millennia, and will likely be there for many more, regardless of the shifting tides of human activity that ebb and flow around it. The Angells and their farm are latecomers and minor players in a far longer story of natural presence, change, and persistence, a story that tells how the physical landscape of New England got there in the shape it did and that accounts for the material underpinnings of the ways of life that have been pursued there by both indigenous inhabitants and later settlers for centuries. Despite the many changes that humans have wrought in the land, this drumlin reminds us that there are other histories and time scales present in the landscape in addition to our own, other players in the ongoing story of New England. If I'm writing in this book about the interplay and interweaving of nature and culture, then the site of the Angell cemetery stands firmly for the "nature" part of the story, those aspects of the region and the planet as a whole that owe nothing to human beings for their presence and their form.

And yet, perhaps it's not as simple as that: when I step over the cemetery wall and into the woods atop the drumlin, I am not stepping from a humanly shaped space into a purer realm of old, deep Nature, but am entering a space that's shaped by a cultural hand so strong that it almost renders nature irrelevant. The reason those woods are there in the first place is that the cemetery is notched into a tiny corner of the Scituate Reservoir watershed, the protective perimeter surrounding Providence's water supply in which trespassing is forbidden and in which almost all potentially polluting human activities are banned (fig. 28). The reservoir, which backs up behind a massive dam blocking the north branch of the Pawtuxet River, went on-line in 1923 after a construction process in which four villages in central Scituate were condemned and abandoned; as part of the construction process, millions of trees were planted in many places along the reservoir's shoreline in order to guard against erosion, and other lands within its protected watershed, like those of the old Angell farm, were allowed to revert to forest if they were not in fact forested already.[25] As I noted earlier, the structure and composition of second-growth forest in New England is strongly influenced by the disturbance history of the land that supports it, and so when I raise my eyes from the Angells' ordered gravestones and look around me at the tangled woods, I am looking at a forest that is a historic and cultural artifact, a newer arrival on the hilltop scene than the cemetery itself, one whose form and existence depend on human decisions and human actions taken in the very recent past. Here too, as with the line between woods and lawn

28. The Providence Water Supply Board's warning sign posted at the roadside immediately adjacent to the Angell cemetery. 2000 photograph by the author.

in my childhood back yard, the stone wall that surrounds the Angell lot isn't as fixed a barrier at it might seem.

These woods, then, owe their existence not primarily to a natural process but to a reservoir, a massive cultural intrusion into the central Rhode Island landscape that gave natural forest succession a place to operate. True, in one way the reservoir's presence seems as much natural as cultural. If you take State Highway 12 across the dam and look north, you see a long beautiful lake ringed by a tall, dense evergreen forest, a safe place for animals to live and birds to nest (fig. 29). I've even heard of people sneaking through the woods to the reservoir's shoreline and illegally catching some of the enormous fish that have been living and breeding there unmolested for years. Thomas Conuel has used the phrase "accidental wilderness"[26] to describe Massachusetts's immense Quabbin Reservoir and its protected watershed, and surely that phrase applies to the Scituate Reservoir as well — and yet, it's a wilderness that's strongly conditioned and contingent, as much an "emerging balance of wilderness and culture" as anything that John Elder observes in Vermont. Moreover, I think the word "accidental" is significant here, as the wild-looking aspect of the reservoir and its surrounding forest is definitely not part of the engineers' original plan — they certainly weren't trying to recreate the forest primeval as part of their job specifications — but an incidental byproduct, one meant to help keep the water clean more than soothe the eye, and one that stands at odds with the larger implications that the reservoir has for people's relationship to the natural world.

Think for a minute about what a reservoir of this type does. It gathers water from a large drainage basin and holds it in one place so that people some distance away can use it in their homes and businesses. In that sense, it's geared toward overcoming the natural limitations of particular localities; if water users in Providence can't be satisfied with wells and local rivers, then they can draw off the waters in some other part of the state (not coincidentally, one that has less population and is less politically influential). The reservoir also brings the resources — flowing water, in this case — of a far-flung area under the control of a central human authority, its contributing streams catching runoff from rain and snowmelt all over a good chunk of Providence County and feeding it into a system that leads straight to the water intakes that fill the municipal water pipes. In this country, we tend to think of the West when the subject of human control over

Natural Landscapes, Cultural Regions

29. The Scituate Reservoir as seen looking north from atop its dam, Scituate, Rhode Island. 2000 photograph by the author.

rivers comes up and of the huge dams built there in this century by the Bureau of Reclamation,[27] but those ambitious projects to store water for various kinds of human use and to supply burgeoning human populations that couldn't live where they do without them have earlier relatives in New England. The Quabbin Reservoir, which was completed in 1939 and which demanded the condemnation and evacuation of four entire towns in central Massachusetts, is the third major reservoir that's been constructed to fulfill greater Boston's water needs since the nineteenth century.[28] With its ever-growing demand for water, Boston has kept reaching farther and farther west to slake its thirst, eventually proposing in the 1960s to divert water from the Connecticut River into the Quabbin, a proposal that was defeated in large part through the efforts of environmental activists.[29] In writing about the development of waterpowered industry in the Merrimack River valley and the establishment of the new mill cities of Lowell and Lawrence in Massachusetts and Manchester in New Hampshire, Theodore Steinberg notes that the Boston Associates textile consortium controlled enough dams by 1845 to manage the entire Merrimack watershed from New Hampshire's Lake Winnipesaukee down through Massachusetts;[30] if the mill owners decided they wanted a certain amount of water to run through their power canals on a certain day, they'd get a message up to New Hampshire a couple of days beforehand and have the gatekeepers release the requisite amount of water into the river. If not on the scale of the modern West, certainly efforts like these demonstrate how New England waters have been converted into "organic machines," to return once more to Richard White's term for the modern Columbia River: naturally occurring watercourses that have been put to work doing useful things for humans.

And not just *local* humans, of course. I've discussed how the Cumberland and Oxford Canal represented an attempt to both rationalize a particular river and overcome the constraints of time and space, but the efforts to impound and control water that I've described here attempt to meet both of those goals on a much larger and more ambitious scale. Space in particular emerges as one of the prime natural obstacles that such efforts are designed to overcome, more so even than drought and other natural factors that might lead to an unpredictable water supply for industry and human consumption. If there are natural inconveniences where you are, don't make do with what you have, but bring it in from far away. Location, and the limits of location, no longer seem to matter: if you need water in Providence, get it from Scituate, and if you need to run a factory in Massachusetts, cast your eyes toward New Hampshire. (And a western city like Phoenix, of course, needs to bring in water from all over the place. That many people probably aren't supposed to live in a place with that little rainfall.) Here we see New England nature tamed on the one hand and rendered irrelevant on the other. If the site of the Angell family cemetery reminds us of the ancient natural substrate upon which the work of human culture plays itself out, the reservoirs and managed rivers of New England suggest that nature can be made to do whatever culture wants it to do if enough ingenuity, engineering, and will are brought to bear on it.

I want to come back to the implications of the Scituate Reservoir again at the end of the book — the extent to which we might be tempted now to think of New England as existing in a kind of "postnatural"

state, one in which regional life and patterns of experience seem to no longer have much to do with the conditions and constraints of nature in this part of the country. For now, though, I want to go back and follow Philip Angell to Simmonsville, to see what pulled him there in particular once he was pushed off the family farm, and to think about how both farm and factory might stand as a kind of collective middle ground between the conceptual poles represented by the drumlin and the reservoir. Angell's move from the farm to a nearby mill village represents a widely repeated story within New England, one that accounts for much of the appearance of the region's landscape today and that suggests the ongoing embeddedness of the region's characteristic ways of life within the simultaneous opportunities and constraints offered by the natural world as New Englanders found it. In an important sense, nature dictated where people went and what they did in New England, at least through the nineteenth century — not in any environmentally deterministic way, of course, but in that the characteristics of landscape, soil, hydrology and the like made certain collective cultural choices about how to live and work make more sense than others given the technologies of the time. Culture and nature, landscape and machinery, interacted in complex, mutually informing ways in the New England of Philip Angell's day, with nature being subjected to human will while still subtly reining in human action. And this whole process left its residue on the land, in the form of agricultural and industrial landscapes that have both been subject to further change over time, landscapes of the sort that I continue to come across constantly in my New England travels. Rather than standing separate from the workings of human culture, like the ancient drumlin, or being almost completely subject to the strength of the human mind and hand, like the sprawling reservoir, nature in Philip Angell's New England was and continues to be a vigorous historical actor, one that strongly shaped the visual world, economic ways of life, and shared patterns of experience of the region's past residents and that thus might be seen as unifying New England both conceptually and physically, giving us a ground — literally — for thinking about the region as a historical whole. History reshaped environment, while environment gave direction to history; while the historical New England exemplified by Elizabeth Pabodie floats free of any geographical grounding, the New England that people see today and that the region's residents have built over time would look very different had Elizabeth's parents stepped ashore into a different kind of natural environment.

To make a long and complex story extremely short, by the early part of the nineteenth century agricultural settlement had spread over as much of New England as was feasible; only remote northern Maine, with its short growing season, was not touched by this long-term influx of new settlers bent on reproducing the farm landscapes and practices familiar to them in their older home communities in England or, later, in Massachusetts or Connecticut. Looking at New England's heavily forested aspect today, it takes a great effort of imagination for us to grasp just how much of the region had once been cleared for cultivation and pasture. Christopher Klyza notes that Vermont, with 80 percent of its land surface now covered by forest, had only 35 percent forest cover around 1870, while New Hampshire has gone from a low of 45 percent forested to a current figure of 87 percent, and Maine has increased from 77 to 89 percent forested.[31] The figures for the southern New England states, while not as drastic as those for the northern part of the region, are equally impressive: about 60 percent of Connecticut, Massachusetts, and Rhode Island are collectively forested today, up from about 35 percent in the mid-nineteenth century.[32] The removal of all those trees, just a few at a time over the course of years, cut down only with ax and saw, represents a tremendous amount of dedicated work, work devoted to a single goal held by every farmer across New England in its first two centuries: the conversion of wild landscape to domesticated, productive landscape, turning the countryside into a culturally crafted artifact dedicated to producing food and supporting livestock. To some extent and on some mental level, as historians have argued, this ongoing conversion of the landscape was driven by a dislike of wilderness as both a place and a concept and by an ideology that saw nature as subservient to human will and desire, its existence justified insofar as it could be controlled, harnessed, and put to productive use. Of course, it was also driven by the fact that people had to eat and get a living and that agriculture was not just a cultural choice but also the only viable option for most of the region's families. But whatever the combination of motivations, the effect was the same: over the astoundingly short span of two centuries or so, New Englanders accomplished a drastic transformation of their landscape, finding in nature an appropriate place in which to engage in their chosen ways of life, taking a place only lightly modified by its aboriginal inhabitants and turning it into a patchwork of field and forest, a quilt of habitation as culturally designed in its way as anything sewn together with needle and thread.

And it worked for a while: nature remained adequate to the task that had been set for it. Still, that reforestation that Klyza and others describe is dramatic evidence of the decreasing viability of agriculture in New England over the course of the nineteenth and twentieth centuries; it bespeaks an economic system that had reached an effective natural limit within a changing national context. In brief, New England agriculture worked well to fulfill the subsistence needs of farm families and to meet the needs of local markets as long as the region remained relatively isolated from the rest of the country. However, the Cumberland and Oxford Canal reminds us that engineering and technology were working hard to overcome the natural constraints of time and distance beginning early in the nineteenth century, and the opening of the Erie Canal in 1825 and the development of inter-regional railroads suddenly rendered the New England landscape inadequate to the ways of life it had been so carefully redesigned to support; the overcoming of limitations in one area of the historic interaction of humans and nature, that is, created new limitations in another. New transportation networks allowed for the importation of more and more agricultural products from the burgeoning farm settlements in the lands of the Midwest, a region marked by more fertile and less stony soils and by larger farms than those in New England, and that latter region's farmers thus found themselves less and less able to compete in a growing market economy. Relative to their national competition, New England farmers' small walled-in fields meant that they couldn't easily use the new, large, mechanized farm machines that their midwestern fellows could, while their diminutive farms and comparatively thin, rocky, acidic soils meant that their yields were smaller. Moreover, historians like William Cronon have argued that, over time, New England farmers' traditional agricultural practices, particularly their failure to rotate crops and let fields lie fallow and their tendency to focus on crops such as corn which draw more nutrients out of the soil than other grains and vegetables, led to a high degree of soil exhaustion and erosion in the region.[33] Others, such as Michael Bell, refute this notion, arguing that the yields of New England farms remained relatively high during the nineteenth century compared to other states and that farm abandonment was more the result of economic competition and of the increasing appeal of non-farm life to the region's young adults than of any absolute inadequacy in the fertility of the region's lands.[34] Still, even in this scenario nature's conditions play a central role in historical process; if the landscape was still good to use for farming, under these new conditions it was no longer good *enough*. Life over much of New England's surface had reached a spatial and temporal limit, and it was time for a new phase of regional history to come along.

New England farmers certainly followed an exploitative agriculture, trying to make their lands produce as much as they could, adjusting as best they knew how to find something that would provide a living and keep their farms going. In Vermont, for instance, many farmers turned to raising sheep to provide wool for the region's growing textile industry, while others turned to dairy farming for nearby urban markets, as perishable items like milk, butter, and cheese had to be produced locally and could not be easily shipped from elsewhere. In Maine and New Hampshire, Thomas Hubka has argued, the distinctive rambling connected farm buildings that characterize that part of the region evolved in the middle of the nineteenth century primarily because of their efficiency in enabling many farm tasks to be carried out in the same building and its surrounding spaces, as farm families produced a variety of food stuffs and home manufactures to keep their farm operations running even into the early twentieth century.[35] (Here too we see natural conditions contributing at least indirectly to the development of a distinctive cultural form — in this case, a striking subregional architectural style.) Walter Hale, it seems, was certainly not the only New England farmer to try to make every inch of his farm pay as much as possible.

Still, Mr. Hale's leaving the farm was not inevitable: if his house and barn hadn't burned down in 1948 and given him an easy opportunity to leave, he might well have stayed on for many more years. Likewise, we might see other New England farmers as jumping before they were pushed, not necessarily set adrift by a grim ecological necessity. The story of New England's agricultural decline doesn't imply that the natural landscapes of New England were absolutely inadequate to support farming of any kind or that the abandonment and reforestation of much of the agricultural countryside was inevitably forced upon the region as a matter of material necessity, but rather that cultural practice was simply out of step with natural conditions in this time and place. As Cronon points out, given the quality of New England soils and the way that agriculture was carried out in the region, soil depletion "could have been predicted, and was less the fault of the soil than of the husbandry,"[36] and even farmers whose soils were in good shape found it less and less feasible to compete in the marketplace in the face of more, better, and less expensive agricultural produce flowing eastward through the compressed time and space of the nation's growing transportation network. New England's landscape had invited communities to push the agricultural frontier as far north as they could, converting much of the region into a complex of villages and farmsteads and fields; later on, within a changed context, that same landscape convinced people in the region's marginal farming areas to give up and look elsewhere, with the subsequent reforestation creating the familiar wooded face of the region as we see it today. As a result, New England's current visual identity can be seen as a direct result of this past conflict of nature and culture in the region. Historical ecologist Tom Wessels argues that "farm abandonment and the associated loss of pastures over the past 150 years has created the single most obvious historical pattern in the region's landscape,"[37] while ecologist David R. Foster claims that "New England is a cultural landscape, shaped by the interaction of human history and the natural environment," primarily as manifested in the region's reforestation.[38] In both the flow and the ebb of New England's agricultural tide, in enabling early farm settlements (and, concomitantly, the old farmhouses and stone walls and such that, along with woods, help characterize the region in the popular mind today) and in encouraging the long-term collective decision across much of the region to leave the farms behind, nature in New England has played a central role in the economy, settlement history, population movement, landscape development, and everyday patterns of life over much of the region's history.

It played an equally important role in the next major phase of collective New England life as well. The depopulation of agricultural New England began in the marginal hill farms of New Hampshire and Vermont as early as the 1830s — this in a part of the region that was really only opened to widespread settlement after the end of the French and Indian War in 1760. Many farm families followed the setting sun in search of better agricultural opportunities — Wessels notes that 100,000 Vermonters, almost half the state's population, had moved west by 1850.[39] But many members of farm families made essentially the same trek that Philip Angell did: from the farm to the mill village or manufacturing city. Since his brother was still running the farm in 1872, it seems likely that Philip left the farm because he was a landless second son in a crowded part of the region, not because the farm itself had failed. But his eventually coming to live (and die) in Simmonsville is a representative New England story, one that encapsulates larger demographic and economic movements and that is tied to a second story — the rise of waterpowered industry in New England — that took place only because of the particular geological and hydrological conditions of the region's landscape. If nature constrained agricultural possibilities across much of the region, it also opened new possibilities for entrepreneurs to build businesses and for workers to earn wages within the region's many river valleys, again transforming the New England landscape and enabling massive shifts in the region's ways of life. Certainly, these changes didn't come without a cost — the Angell family's death is perhaps suggestive of the dangers to life and limb of industrial life, and the shift from the seasonal rhythms of agricultural time to the daily and hourly regimentation of industrial time (recall the bell that had rung to call workers to the mill just prior to the Simmonsville flood) inspired occasional protests and industrial action among mill workers recently arrived from the agricultural hinterlands.[40] (The many strikes that occurred in New England factories and mill towns have been widely studied by labor historians, although such industrial action cannot be blamed on the power source but rather on the conditions under which factory owners had workers exploit that power.) Nor, as with broadscale regional agriculture, did hydropowered industry in New England survive the nineteenth century. Still, in moving from Scituate to Simmonsville, Philip Angell can perhaps be seen as a representative nineteenth-century New Englander, one whose shift of residence and way of life is intimately tied to, and motivated by, the circumstances of New England nature: the growing inadequacy of the region's lands on the one hand, the potential energy of the region's waters on the other — waters that, as it would eventually turn out, carried natural limitations of their own.

With its frequent rains, its many rivers and streams, and the many changes of elevation that those watercourses undergo as they tumble toward the sea, New England was ideally suited by nature for running large numbers of waterpowered mills and factories, more so than other parts of the country. In comparing hydrological variables across North America, industrial archaeologists Robert Gordon and Patrick Malone note that "in the Northeast, the annual variation in rainfall is smallest, and the steady flow, frequent waterfalls or rapids, and small amount of sediment in river water made it easier for Americans to start industries that used water power."[41] In a way, New England's waters even conditioned the form and location of agricultural towns within the region: in order to build homes and farm buildings and to process their grain and their timber, farmers needed access to sawmills and gristmills almost immediately, and so small waterpowered mills with dams and millponds were always among the first structures erected in new New England towns. This meant both that towns needed to contain adequate potential waterpower and that the location of mills tended to condition later patterns of settlement, with other businesses clustering around these frequently visited sites and no one wanting to live an impossible distance away from the place where they had to haul their goods and do their business. Thus "any gristmill was a potential nucleus for a community," according to Gordon and Malone, and "since people often built communities around gristmills, the distribution of sizes of water-power privileges was one geographical factor influencing the pattern of community development in agricultural regions"[42]— that is, the more mill privileges there were of adequate size to support not only a gristmill but other emerging waterpowered businesses, the more commercial villages could potentially develop within a New England town's boundaries. That is why, with apologies to Norman Maclean, when you drive through an old inland New England village center today, you find that in most cases a river runs through it.

More importantly, New England's rivers enabled the development of new kinds of urban and industrial spaces as well as rural spaces within the region, beginning most prominently in Philip Angell's own state of Rhode Island. In 1793, Samuel Slater and his business partners opened the first American factory on the Blackstone River in Pawtucket, using waterpower to manufacture textiles on a large scale. In 1797, Eli Whitney began production at his waterpowered armory in Whitneyville, Connecticut, and New England's shift from an agricultural to an industrial region was on in earnest, enabled both by the region's hydrology and the accumulation of investable capital among the merchants of the coastal cities, many of whom now became industrial entrepreneurs. (Again, nature alone cannot cause or explain these patterns of regional history; rather, it shaped and constrained the field of human choice.) The textile industry was among the most important and prominent of these industrial endeavors: by 1804, four or five new factories were opening in Rhode Island each year, and rivers like the Blackstone, the Pawtuxet, and the Woonasquatucket quickly became blocked by dams at regular intervals and lined with factories and their accompanying mill villages.[43] Even smaller rivers were pressed into industrial service as long as they provided an adequate fall of water: in Johnston, James F. Simmons opened his factory in Simmonsville on the obscure Pocasset River in 1822, and, as we have seen, by 1862 there were eight mills on that river alone within the space of about a mile and a half.[44] Of course, when people think of the development of New England waterpowered industry today, they often think of the enormous mill complexes in new cities like Lowell and Lawrence, Massachusetts, and Manchester, New Hampshire, all of which were built along the Merrimack River by 1850 — company towns that featured complex systems of canals powering several factories at once, massive buildings that lined the river with red brick and that were closely surrounded by offices and worker housing. Cities like these and like Biddeford, Saco, Brunswick, and Lewiston in Maine, like Holyoke along the Connecticut River in Massachusetts, or like the many industrial valleys of Rhode Island and Connecticut, employed huge numbers of displaced agricultural workers from New England's farms (and, as the nineteenth century went on, of immigrants from Quebec and Europe), and the opening of the Lowell National Historical Park in 1978 and the creation of the Blackstone River Valley National Heritage Corridor in 1986 helped provide this central regional story with a more prominent place in New England's public landscape.

The region's rivers were not dominated only by enormous textile factories and the machinations of large-scale industrial capital, of course; local gristmills and sawmills still had a lot of work to do, and small individually owned waterpowered factories all over the region, like the old gunpowder mill that I came across along the Cumberland and Oxford Canal in Maine, manufactured products ranging from clocks and watches to guns and swords to boxes and bobbins. Major rivers like the Merrimack or Blackstone may have been the best places to erect large mill complexes, but even their modest tributaries were put to work as intensively as possible. As a result, the flowing waters of New England became filled with dams and lined with factories virtually from end to end, which meant that much of the region's economy was directly dependent upon people's cultural interaction with this naturally occurring resource. It's not difficult to find old building foundations and fragments of dams while walking through woods along New England's streams today, or even when observing those streams from roadsides and bridges; old farm fields and pastures are not the only sites in the region that are being reclaimed and obscured by the plant growth that occurs when people leave the scene. As with the extent of forest clearance in New England through the nineteenth century, it's difficult to rebuild this old landscape in imagination and realize just how different the region's rivers looked in the past, just how extensively they were used, just how many buildings and people they supported. Gordon and Malone note that there were approximately nine hundred waterpowered mills along the Merrimack River and its tributaries alone in 1880, which suggests the enormous number of mills there were as a whole along New England's countless rivers and streams.[45] Clearly nineteenth-century New England was a region whose life depended crucially upon one particular aspect of nature. In fact, Philip Angell's experience was in some ways more typical and regionally representative than that of urban workers in cities like Lowell or Lewiston: given the region's preponderance of modest streams and brooks and the relatively small amount of power they could generate, the typical New England mill "was a modest affair that needed relatively little power"[46]— in other words, a mill like the one that called its workers to the job on that fateful morning in Simmonsville.

Not only did rivers play a central part in reshaping New England's economy, they also as a result altered the region's social and settlement landscape, determining where many people lived and significantly changing the physical face of New England, creating a new kind of regional landscape that is still evident today. The reason that places like Simmonsville and Whitneyville could be named after the men who founded and owned the mills was not simply a matter of ego, but also of the fact that there was often no preexisting community at a good water privilege and therefore no preexisting place-name. Simply put, the factories had to go where the water was; while hydropowered mills were designed to gain control over nature, to harness the energy of falling water and convert it into mechanical motion, at the same time nature controlled the factories, determining their location by virtue of the fact that they had to be located next to their power source. With the factory located in the river valley, the unoccupied higher land around it was available for other sorts of buildings, and entrepreneurs like James F. Simmons frequently built villages for their workers to live in; in fact, given the isolation of many factories, workers had little choice to do anything for housing other than rent living space from the company. Mill villages thus were characterized by a kind of concentric physical and social space: the mill, tall and long with a tower that loomed over the entire settlement, was the focus of life and work; close to and higher than the mill was the worker housing, its residents living figuratively if not literally under the shadow of the mill; and on the perimeter of the company complex, highest of all, were the houses of managers, overseers, and executives. Simmonsville was shaped like this, its houses close enough to the river to be swept away by the wall of water when the dam burst, and it's a pattern that's quite common along New England's old industrial rivers, characterizing both small factory towns and urban neighborhoods. It's also a pattern that results from the presence of New England's rivers, of the economic, technological, and cultural wherewithal to develop them for industry, and of the desire of mill owners to keep control over every aspect of their industrial enterprise, its people included. When Philip Angell moved to Simmonsville, then, he walked out of the agricultural world and into something unprecedented in New England, a fascinating and complex interaction of nature and culture that swept away much of that older regional landscape and built a new one in its place.

Just like that old regional farm landscape, though, the waterpowered world of New England industry is now obsolete, its factories either gone or converted to other sources of power or other uses altogether, its mill housing now rented or owned by people who can work wherever they want. The reasons for its fate seem much like those for the abandonment of the Cumberland and Oxford Canal: while it was built upon the control of water, the reengineering of rivers to make them work for people, ultimately it reached an end because it remained too close to nature, unable to transcend the limits put upon it by the properties and characteristics of the New England environment. As I noted above, waterpowered mills occupied a sort of middle ground between the poles of nature and culture, both controlling and controlled by their rivers. Certainly the factories tried to control, rationalize, and harness New England's waters as best they could. Developers built dams to create mill ponds and reservoirs that ensured that the factories downstream would have a steady, predictable supply of water, overcoming any limitations that might be imposed by the vagaries of rainfall and snowmelt. From the ponds, canals carried the water through the factories to turn their waterwheels or turbines and then returned it to the river downstream, where it might almost immediately enter the mill pond of the next factory. By rebuilding the river this way, entrepreneurs collectively drew as much power from their rivers as they possibly could: out of the 438-foot drop in elevation of the Blackstone River between Worcester, Massachusetts, and Pawtucket, Rhode Island, for instance, 400 feet were utilized to power machinery, rendering the Blackstone the most intensively utilized river in New England by 1880.[47] By late in the nineteenth century, many New England rivers were turned into machines as much as organic entities, regulated and put to work, transformed into industrial artifacts.

And the heavy industrial use of New England rivers had environmental effects too, of course, another aspect of the effect of industrial manipulation upon their natural condition: mill ponds built up thick layers of silt over time, the many dams on the region's major rivers blocked the spawning runs of anadromous fish, and industrial and household waste in mill cities and villages usually went directly into the river, the same river that local people relied on for drinking water, resulting in the spread of waterborne disease. These environmental effects amounted to a human-caused change in the river that was in some ways far more fundamental than its being seen and used primarily as a power source, rearranging both its chemistry and its biology. As Theodore Steinberg argues about the Merrimack River in the nineteenth century, "The economic development of the Merrimack valley helped put an end to the region's fish runs, to the ecological relations that had long dominated the area, [and] also created a new ecology of its own with far-reaching effects on the water quality of the region's rivers, and ultimately on human existence itself."[48] To some extent, this ecological transformation may be reversible in some places. The 162-year-old Edwards Dam was removed from the Kennebec River in Augusta, Maine, in 1999, opening eighteen miles of the river that had been blocked all that time; since then, according to a newspaper report, "millions of alewives, striped bass and other game fish have surged upriver to Waterville and Winslow. Bald eagles, osprey and other fish-eating birds follow in their wake. Between its densely wooded banks, the river flows cleaner, swifter, clearer. The waters support a rich collection of plants and animals."[49] While the incredible growth of aquatic life in those waters over the course of a single year is wonderful to see, at the same time it indicates just how big an intrusion into the ecology of the river that dam had been.

Despite the extent of their control over nature, though, New England factories' unavoidable dependence on rivers placed implacable geographical and productive limits on both the capacities of individual mills and on the regional growth of industry as a whole. No matter how high an entrepreneur built a milldam, no matter how big a fall of water was created and how many power canals the river was shunted through, any given mill site could generate horsepower only up to a certain amount constrained by the quantity of water available and by the shape of the river valley where it was located. Moreover, as more and more factories lined a given river, factory owners were required by law to impound and divert only a certain amount of water so as to leave enough water available for the operations downstream, placing a further limit on their productive capacity and on the number of mills they could build on any one site — another function of the fact that factories had to be clustered close together along suitable rivers and couldn't simply locate anywhere in New England that they wanted to. Limited in some ways by the nature of the region's hydrology and topography, factories were tightly hemmed in by spatial considerations as well: while entrepreneurs could *improve* rivers, they couldn't *move* rivers, and thus kept one foot in that older world where time and space were not easily compressed, but were long and wide and hard to overcome. For the same reason, it was next to impossible to locate factories in large existing coastal cities like Boston, with their convenient concentrations of capital and potential workers; lacking an industrial power source, they had to rely on getting their manufactured products from the hinterlands. While places like Lowell, or even Simmonsville, certainly demonstrate a cultural desire to control nature and subjugate it to human purposes — Steinberg says of the early industrialization of the Merrimack that it "reduced water to an instrument in the service of economic change" and that "water by the early years of the nineteenth century was well on its way to becoming a simple utility, an abstraction employed to suit economic ambitions"[50]— they also retain a certain natural quality, kept from being too strictly abstract and instrumental by the shape, size, and immobility of all those streambeds gouged into the New England landscape by glaciers all those millennia ago.

Clearly this was not a tolerable limitation in an expanding industrial economy. By late in the nineteenth century, then, entrepreneurs turned to power sources that were not as closely linked to natural limitations — first steam, and later electricity. Just as the steam railroad engine helped bring about the obsolescence of the Cumberland and Oxford Canal, so did the steam industrial engine play its part in the abandonment of hundreds of New England mills and factory settlements. Steam power and electricity are produced by burning natural materials like wood and coal, of course, and even electricity produced by hydropower depends on rivers just as much as did those old New England waterwheels, but the difference is that the power source is no longer dependent strictly on location: fuel could be brought from long distances once roads were improved and canals and railroads were built in the early nineteenth century, and electricity can flow for long distances through power lines. As a result, industrialists no longer had to locate factories in remote river valleys but could build them in urban areas to take advantage of cities' existing infrastructures and their participation in national transportation networks, and they could increase the productive capacity of their factories by adding engines that could produce many more horsepower than could a mill site on a river. As early as the late 1820s and early 1830s, mill owners in New England were producing small amounts of cloth with steam engines, often supplementing the output of their waterpowered factories. Then, the Corliss Steam Engine manufacturing works were opened in Providence in 1849, making large-capacity steam engines more easily available to industry both within the region and elsewhere. Just as the early nineteenth century saw a new kind of landscape and a new form of cultural interaction with nature begin to characterize the face of the New England countryside and the daily experience of large numbers of its residents, so did the latter part of that century witness the decline of the region's dependence on flowing and falling water. Gordon and Malone note that, by about 1870, as much industrial power was obtained from steam as from water in America as a whole, a shift that was most strongly felt in New England and that contributed to its eclipsing as the nation's dominant industrial region.[51] The many converted, abandoned, or vanished mills and factories along New England's rivers today thus join with its second-growth woods to speak to us of an important and ongoing regional story in New England, one in which the workings of culture and technology, of minds and hands together, exert their energies to control and reshape nature and get it to behave the way that people want, only to find nature calling an end to things when the region's landscape-dependent economic systems become unable to transcend their nonhuman limits and adapt to a new set of productive and technological demands.

And Philip Angell was one of thousands of representative participants in that story, even though his untimely death kept him from experiencing its full range. But Simmonsville itself continued on to witness and exemplify this profound ongoing regional process of change. Just as Philip's hilltop resting place is the only obvious extant evidence of his former family farm, so too does little remain of the nineteenth-century Simmonsville where he resettled: today, only three old stone worker houses still stand in that riverside neighborhood where a small but bustling community of people lived, worked, and died. Over time, mills and industry no longer characterized New England's watersheds, despite their astonishingly rapid rise and their former regional prominence. By the early twentieth century, Simmonsville was largely a community of Italian immigrants and their families who engaged in the truck vegetable trade, flower growing, and cider production, ironically going back to the land to get their livings.[52] Philip Angell's move from the farm to the mill village, and his work and residence in both places, thus enmeshes him deeply in two major phases of New England's ongoing cultural relationship with the natural world, phases that, perhaps more democratically than anything else, can be seen as characterizing and defining past regional life, giving New England a widespread historical identity, one still discernible in the everyday landscape if you know where and how to look for it.

At the same time, Philip Angell's move from farm to factory also shows him circulating within a New England landscape symbolically poised between the drumlin and the reservoir, between an untouched state of nature and a world totally made over according to human design. Both places reveal ongoing regional attempts to take nature as people found it and then control it, manipulate it, redesign it, make it produce, as the Scituate Reservoir does on a grand scale; both also represent instances where nature had the last word in a sense, throwing up obstacles that, drumlinlike, were there in the landscape long before Euro-Americans arrived on the scene, obstacles that were revealed only when people tried to force nature to do their bidding, just as the drumlin is an impediment to the plow. If we want to grasp and characterize the way that nature has been a central historical actor in the ongoing course of New England life, then, perhaps the space between the drumlin and the reservoir is the best place to look.

⁂

Philip Angell's life and times, then, suggest at least one way in which we can think about a natural basis for New England's historical identity, one that brings a sense of temporal, material, and conceptual unity to the region's landscape and to the everyday experience of many of its residents in the past. As I indicated earlier, though, I suspect that when many people think of "New England" they think of the region's Elizabeth Pabodies rather than its Philip Angells: they think of a much more limited selection of dramatic episodes and well-known characters, locating those events and people within a very small range of particular places and general settings. Elizabeth Pabodie's Pilgrim connections, and her burial place on a common anchored by a classic white meetinghouse and ringed by stately homes, provide a very efficient shorthand means of letting you know that Little Compton is in New England and not some other part of the country. On the surface, this way of conceptualizing what is historically distinctive and defining about New England seems wholly separate from natural circumstances and from the opportunities and limitations that people found in the landscape: it represents historical episodes and acts of building that took place *in* New England, but that seem to have little evident basis in the geological and ecological exigencies *of* New England. It comprises not stories that grow organically out of the landscape, but stories that are laid upon that landscape from some other source — not stories from nature, but stories from a separate realm of culture.

And yet, in an important but indirect way, Philip Angell and Elizabeth Pabodie are as closely connected as they are seemingly separate, in that we couldn't have the latter without the former, or at least without the things that both represent. The existence in New England of

What Is Natural about New England?   243

factory workers like Philip Angell and his historical successors and of industrial centers like Simmonsville and *its* historical successors not only possibly led to the elevation and celebration of Elizabeth Pabodie by Sarah Wilbour in 1882, as I mentioned above, but also led to the invention and popularization of the whole historical panoply that we now conventionally use to identify New England in the popular mind. On the one hand, then, the literal and figurative rise of Elizabeth Pabodie seems to represent a kind of repudiation of nature as a historical actor in the creation of a sense of New England regional identity. On the other, however, nature remained a strong but implicit historical actor in the continuing work of regional definition, driving a powerful effort among regional elites to erase a large piece of New England's ongoing cultural interaction with nature — and the social and demographic consequences of that interaction—from the region's public landscape and memory. In addition to directly contributing to the look of the place and to its representative patterns of human experience, then, nature has continued to play a crucial behind-the-scenes role in influencing what we think about when we think about New England, even those elements of regional identity that seem most firmly based in human culture and human imagination.

And it continues to do so even today. The world that Philip Angell lived in didn't survive the nineteenth century. Agriculture in New England today, particularly in states like Vermont, takes place on a greatly reduced scale and focuses on dairying rather than on cultivation, while waterpowered industry is a thing of the past except in the case of the occasional old gristmill or sawmill that has been preserved or restored for touristic or educational purposes. With the rise of steam and electric power, industries could locate or relocate in convenient places that suited their infrastructural needs: the coastal seaport of Fall River, Massachusetts, for instance, which could support only a small number of waterpowered textile mills, quadrupled its number of spindles between 1859 and 1875 after the introduction of Corliss steam engines, leading historian Diana Muir to note that "it was as though all limits on growth had gone up in steam."[53] Nature no longer seemed deeply embroiled in the patterns of New England life, nor did it place effective limits on it, a fact that remained true while much of the region began to shift from an industrial to a postindustrial economy. (The New England textile industry moved to southern states over the early decades of the twentieth century for economic reasons — particularly lower labor costs — rather than geographical reasons, and many of the old Fall River mills are now malls for the factory outlet stores of factories located elsewhere in the United States and abroad.) And yet even as a state like Massachusetts has become more economically defined by the high-tech corridor of Greater Boston's Route 128 than by farms and factories, nature retains a strong influence in how people think about the region — not as a historical actor, though, but as an aesthetic presence, as perhaps best exemplified by New England's famous autumn foliage. In one sense, then, there has been a temporal shift in how we might think of nature as playing a prominent role in regional life, with that role changing from economic basis to recreational resource over time as conditions changed within the region. At the same time, though, there have been important continuities as well as changes, in the form of both the obvious physical interactions of nature and culture that characterize the region and the much more obscure grounding in nature of some important cultural choices about what people choose to see and value in the region today. That is, not only is the natural world that New Englanders see around them a historical artifact in and of itself, but the aesthetic enjoyment that people get from the region's woods and mountains as they travel through modern New England represents an ironic flight from history just as much as does the public celebration of a figure like Elizabeth Pabodie.

None of this, of course, is to completely gainsay the arguments I made earlier about the artificiality of New England as a place and a concept — just to blur the boundaries between nature and culture in thinking about New England regional identity as I have in looking at regional writings and landscapes. Still, there remains a big difference between the six northeasternmost states that make up the physical territory of New England and the *idea* of what we call "New England," in implicit quotation marks. The territory owes its form and existence to natural forces and phenomena: hydrology, climate, geomorphology, the ranges and tolerances of particular plants, and so on. And now, of course, that landscape is thickly overlaid with a complex built environment, many of the older elements of which — the Little Compton-style village, the stone wall — are widely recognized as helping make up the visual signature that defines the region in the popular mind. To call that natural landscape, and the things built from and placed upon that landscape, by the name "New England," though, is a specifically *cultural* act, an allusion to a collectively agreed-upon set of defining elements and features that, with some shifts in emphasis and composition over time, has been maintained for close to four centuries and that implies a uniformity and coherence that stretches from Greenwich, Connecticut, to Madawaska, Maine — a uniformity, of course, that ecoregional maps like Robert Bailey's quickly confound. Books like Dona Brown's *Inventing New England: Regional Tourism in the Nineteenth Century* and Joseph Conforti's *Imagining New England: Explorations of Regional Identity from the Pilgrims to the Mid-Twentieth Century* remind us that "New England" is largely a made-up thing, a selection of historical events and personages and visual icons and collective qualities that people have consented to believe bestow cultural uniqueness on a small piece of the earth's surface.[54] Looked at in this way, the difference between natural given and cultural construction seems irreducible.

Much of what some have called the "new regional studies" focuses on the idea not only of New England but of any broadscale cultural region as being a set of meanings and ideas, a defining set of stories and characters and images and concepts that are not necessarily inherent in the landscape, that do not amount to a kind of crystallization of some essential characteristics that are out there in the ether above the six states, but that are selected and emphasized upon the geographical surface by people — often by culturally and politically powerful people — for particular reasons, and that then become accepted by the broader public at large. Cultural regions do not create themselves; human beings do the inventing for them, and under particular historical conditions at that. And as I pointed out when I first introduced her, Elizabeth Pabodie reminds us that New England provides a powerful example of that process, especially beginning in the second half of the nineteenth century. From its theocratic origins to its Revolutionary exploits and embrace of republican ideologies in early nationhood, and through its accretion over time of a distinctive rural built environment, New England had developed a strong and positive sense of identity, one that became only stronger during the Civil War as liberty-loving New England contrasted itself with the slaveholding South (a self-serving comparison that, incidentally, pretty much wiped out all public memory of slavery in colonial New England). Moreover, during the early days of its industrial development, many people both within and outside the region saw New England as the most modern, progressive, and forward-facing part of the country. After the war, though, in large part through that same naturally conditioned and enabled industrial development that Philip Angell took part in, New England began to change, at least in the perceptions and actions of its cultural elites: it became a much more backward-facing region, concerned more with preserving a particular version of its past than with celebrating its present and future. The *concept* of "New England" became reinvented as a sort of imaginative refuge from the New England of *fact*, the actual circumstances of life as found within the six states. Faced with living in a place that was not only becoming more and more urban and industrial but was also filling up with immigrants from Europe and French Canada, New England's elites began remaking the region's landscape and memory, self-consciously doing their best to publicly define New England as fundamentally rural, premodern, and Anglo-Saxon, characterizing the region's agricultural past not through the specifics of agricultural practice but through the ethnicity of the farmers — a process of idealization made easier by the increasing absence of actual farmers from the countryside. New England's elites invented a past they could live in as a counterbalance to an increasingly disturbing present.

This invention had a great impact on the landscape itself. The colonial revival and village beautification movements can be attributed in large part to this antimodern impulse within the region. Village centers such as that of Litchfield, Connecticut — whose big houses and white church ringing a village green were in fact built by early nineteenth-century merchants, not colonial farmers — were made over by affluent residents (many of whom were fairly recent arrivals in rural Connecticut) to create the impression of an ordered and stable past; in the process, their mercantile origins were conveniently forgotten in favor of a mythic story of hardworking Yankee farmers, an impression that guides the perceptions and itineraries of tourists even today.[55] Other villages spruced up their town commons to achieve the same effect, converting what had once been rutted and treeless eyesores, holding pens for cattle and training grounds for militias, into nicely sculpted centerpieces, their history of past use neatly erased; working landscape, that is, became converted to ahistorical aesthetic display.[56] The New England center-village icon, then, is to a large extent a nineteenth-century invention, a charming Potemkin village erected to block the view of the New England present.[57]

At about the same time, historic preservation efforts were intended to achieve the same goal, saving particular old structures in order to help convert New England into a sort of big outdoor museum and implicitly argue for what the *real* history of the region was, and who the *real* New Englanders were. The Society for the Preservation of New England Antiquities, still a very active organization today, was founded in 1905 as an outgrowth of successful efforts to save and preserve Paul Revere's house in Boston's North End, which at the time had already become the overwhelmingly Italian neighborhood that it remains to this day.[58] Saving this house sent the message that, despite the North End's actual condition, Paul Revere was the person whose neighborhood it really was, and his period of New England history was the one that counted. The many immigrants who rode in on the wave of industrial development that had begun in the exploitation of New England streams were thus effectively disenfranchised from membership in the region's public landscape. SPNEA moved on to focus on preserving not the urban houses of the wealthy, not the buildings where great events took place, but old rural farmhouses, extending their argument for the region's fundamentally rural, premodern, Yankee character and literally inscribing that argument onto the landscape. (In one telling episode, SPNEA director William Sumner Appleton tried to acquire a 1691 house in Guilford, Connecticut, only to see its Polish immigrant owner demolish and rebuild part of it rather than come down to meet Appleton's lowball offer; horrified, Appleton proclaimed that "this ignorant foreigner has destroyed [the house]" and lamented "the difficulties involved in trying to do business with a foreigner, whom fortune had made for the moment the custodian of a really interesting New England antiquity.")[59] Rural and village New England was the real New England, it seemed, and not only the region's elites seemed to think so. In the late nineteenth and early twentieth centuries, middle-class urban vacationers from both within and outside New England increasingly began traveling to places like Nantucket or enjoying boardinghouse vacations on working Vermont farms, using their vacation time and travel budgets to confirm and reinforce the increasing impression that New England was a place to escape from the contemporary world, an ongoing rural idyll that was somehow exempt from modern depredations and historical declension, if not from history altogether — a perception, I think, that still guides many vacationers in "olde" New England even today.[60]

While cultural preferences strongly guided the manipulation of New England history both in public memory and on the ground in the late nineteenth and early twentieth centuries, natural scenes and elements in the New England landscape have also been co-opted into this regional scenario, one in which the *idea* of "New England" represents an escape from history — the very history, in fact, that is everywhere inscribed on the actual surface of the six New England states. As I've tried to suggest, cultural regions are very useful for the people who create and perpetuate them, and nature in the region today contributes very nicely to New England's ongoing cultural usefulness. And here I want to steal an insight from historian Elliott West to help sharpen this point — he's talking here about the American West, but I think that, with some slight modification, his point applies to New England as well. West (and, in this context, I wish he had a different last name) argues that the West as it exists in the popular imagination was largely a creation of easterners, emigrants to the region. In West's words, newcomers saw in the region "two broad and opposing sets of possibilities." One of these was to make the West over so that it resembled the East from which they had come, but the other possibility is more relevant here. In this case, "the West had promise only if it remained different and fundamentally apart. It was 'there,' and it ought to keep on being 'there.'"[61] West goes on to assert that both these ways of seeing "defined the West negatively in its record of human experience. The West was the West, that is, because of what had not happened, because of the absence of human events, accomplishments, and disasters. It was the Land of Isn't, the Empire of Gonna Be. Physical geography became the stuff of pure possibilities."[62] The obvious difference here is that New England, rather than seeming empty to residents and visitors, was filled with records of human experience, with evidence of human events and accomplishments — in short, with history. But, again, that which was publicly emphasized was a carefully selected and crafted history, one designed to meet specific cultural and psychological ends. Moreover, it was a history that seemed very much cut off from the present, "fundamentally apart" in West's phrase — a static and separate sphere rather than a continuum. The nature of New England's emerging regional identity ensured that it could be seen and experienced not as a real place but as a screen that people could project their fantasies on, fantasies that allowed them to escape from the very different world they had left behind at home. Imaginative regions, be they New England or the West, don't somehow pop organically out of the ground; instead, they mean what we want them to mean.

And this is where nature comes in once again. The character and function of New England as a useful cultural region corresponds closely with the meaning and usefulness of nature and wilderness in American culture in general. William Cronon's discussion of wilderness, of natural places ostensibly untouched by the workings of human culture, might apply as well to my assessment of New England as a cultural region here. As he puts it, "there is nothing natural about the concept of wilderness. It is entirely a creation of the culture that holds it dear, a product of the very history it seeks to deny. Indeed, one of the most striking proofs of the cultural invention of wilderness is its thoroughgoing erasure of the history from which it springs. In virtually all of its manifestations, wilderness represents a flight from history."[63] As does the New England of popular imagination for over a hundred years, a fellow cultural creation that denies that it arose as a response to historical conditions even as it offers itself up by definition as old and filled with history, a history that represents a flight from the events of more recent years — a flight *from* history *into* history, as it were. The uses of that history, then, and of a regional identity defined on that particular historical basis, exactly parallel some central American cultural uses of nature. The natural landscape of the six New England states, then, because its general cultural function so neatly reinforces other aspects of the region's constructed identity, potentially stands as an important additional component of that identity — somewhat surprisingly, perhaps, given that the West is the American region that tends to be stereotypically marked by history-denying encounters with the natural world. Yet that same quest has also motivated travelers and tourists in New England as well, and the nature they have sought out has had its land-use history eradicated from it just as subtly yet surely as have the western national parks. In the end, it is this aspect of nature in New England — its status as symbol rather than as historical agent — that strikes me as lying quite close to the heart of what we think about when we think about "New England," even as that idea has sought to remove itself from the historical effects of the region's ongoing cultural involvement in the natural world.

Certainly, a moment's thought turns up numerous examples of natural scenes and icons that help make up the additional mental furniture we might have in our heads for throwing together hasty sketches of what New England "looks like." There's the famously rockbound coast of Maine, for one.[64] New Hampshire's White Mountains have been a tourist destination since the 1830s, although their early history most closely resembles Elliott West's observation about newcomers in the West wanting to reproduce the world they left behind: the point of White Mountain vacationing in its early years was to stay at resort hotels and show off one's training in being able to tell the sublime from the picturesque.[65] But perhaps most insistently, there's New England's famous fall foliage. Evidence of the iconic status of fall foliage in defining the region is insistent and ubiquitous: everything from postcards to tour guides to coffee-table books about individual New England states all do their best to place colorful autumn forests and leaves, usually maple leaves, before us and make those scenes synonymous with the region, a central component of its very essence. And tourists respond to this message as they flock to the region every fall. I am annually amused by all the tour buses I see in October from other states that surely must have deciduous forests of their own to look at. Still, it seems there's no foliage like New England foliage: a *Forbes* magazine story from a few years back notes that "Jim Warmington, 46, a home builder in Orange County, California, likes his home state well enough but laments the fact that 'we don't get much foliage here.' So last fall Warmington, his wife, and four other couples took a bike trip in New England, organized by Vermont Bicycle Touring, just in time to catch the leaves on 50-mile-a-day outings. 'That's the way to see fall,' says Warmington," and in so saying he neatly conflates the season with the region.[66]

Mr. Warmington, of course, is not alone in rendering the fall season and its attendant colors synonymous with New England. More recently, a writer in *Health* magazine confessed that "one year the demands of work and family left me so exhausted that I didn't think I could make it through winter without an infusion of *real* autumn. We flew to Maine, dropped our rowdy boys with a friend, and headed into New Hampshire's White Mountains. We wended through hills of birch and maple, the chill sun glowing gold, rust, and lemon through the leaves." After a few days of this, the writer concluded that "I'd found fall. Now I was ready for anything." [67] Not only does this writer feel that the one and only true place to find autumn is New England, she also seems to hold the conventional view that sees natural scenes as primarily sites of escape, alternatives to "the demands of work and family" if not to history altogether. And the New England states do their best to ensure that travelers like the *Health* writer have plenty of company. Maine, New Hampshire, and Vermont all maintain Web sites and 1-800 numbers in the fall so leaf-peepers can easily find out where to go to see leaves at their peak colors. Given that trees and soils and climate and so on would seem to depend for their existence and characteristics on the conditions of Bailey's ecological regions rather than on "New England" as a purely cultural invention, one might think that those forests have been blazing since time immemorial — and, moreover, that both New Englanders and visitors would have been noticing and appreciating fall foliage from the beginning and linking it to their visual definition of that part of the world.

This is not, however, the case. Not only is the New England hardwood forest historically conditioned, a product not only of ecological circumstance but of the area's history of land use and forest clearance, but its iconic status is equally constructed along a time line that parallels the elite invention of New England's defining past. Before the twentieth century, neither New Englanders nor visitors really seemed to care much about fall foliage — in part because there wasn't all that much forest to see in the nineteenth century, but also because it seems not to have been culturally useful or necessary to celebrate the forest at its aesthetic peak. When there were trees around to look at, they were visual background or economic resources more than anything, and there was not yet an emerging idea of "New England" within which to enfold them. Time and history both built the forest and created its appeal, so when today's tourists travel to "olde" New England to escape history, they also enjoy what seems to be a timeless natural tableau that equally fuels their desire not only for beauty but for flight, flight into an ahistoric realm of pure nature and pure color. Since, as it is often popularly approached, nature by definition is noncultural and exempt from historical process, the forests seem to tell nothing of their twofold story, their physical and imaginative creation. But this, too, is an interesting story, one that joins Elizabeth Pabodie's and

Philip Angell's as we contemplate nature's involvement in defining New England.

By 1956, it was second nature (so to speak) for naturalist Edwin Way Teale, in his book *Autumn across America*, to rhapsodize about the New England scene in fall, providing his readers with a glorious vision that elevates fall foliage into a central place in the region's iconography along with the conventional human-made elements:

> We could see in our mind's eye the gorgeous tapestry of its rolling countryside, the multicolored ridges curving away mile on mile, the long vistas from its mountaintops. We could see the vivid hues reflected in quiet river reaches and mirrored in the still water of the innumerable ponds and lakes of Massachusetts and Connecticut. We could see the village greens, the white-spired churches, the winding roads, all surrounded by the incomparable pageantry of the autumn leaves. . . . The birches of Maine, the aspens of the White Mountains, the sugar maples of Vermont, the long rainbow of the Connecticut River Valley cutting from top to bottom through New England, the Berkshires — mention these to anyone who has traveled widely through a New England fall and you will evoke instant memories of superlative beauty.[68]

However, Teale's imagery, ecstasy, and elevation of fall foliage to a central place in the regional image are all latter-day developments among those who have commented on the New England countryside. To be sure, the painter Thomas Cole, in his 1835 "Essay on American Scenery," does argue that "there is one season when the American forest surpasses all the world in gorgeousness — that is the autumnal; — then every hill and dale is riant in the luxury of color. . . . The artist looks despairingly upon the glowing landscape, and in the old world his truest imitations of the American forest, at this season, are called falsely bright, and scenes in Fairy Land."[69] This last point, though, helps indicate that Cole's purpose in writing is largely nationalistic rather than regional, arguing as he does that America's scenic resources are superior to those of the Old World; certainly, we might see Cole here as simply conflating region with nation, but at the same time this famous Hudson River school founder had his attention focused more broadly on the Northeast than on New England as such. In addition, the comment on autumn colors is slipped into the essay almost as an aside, as the bulk of the essay focuses on more visually prominent and artistically conventional natural elements of the landscape such as mountains, lakes, and rivers. Foliage seems not to constitute an important defining element of New England scenery at all, and while Cole includes fall colors in his many paintings of New Hampshire's White Mountains, by and large they are not the primary focus of his visual energies; rather, his emphasis remains on other, conventionally sublime and picturesque landscape elements such as mountains or rivers, those elements of wild nature that, to Cole, offer a counterbalance to "a meager utilitarianism [that] seems ready to absorb every feeling and sentiment" and a focus for those times when we "turn from the ordinary pursuits of life to the pure enjoyment of rural nature."[70] The same seems true of other "White Mountain school" artists who came after him, such as Jasper Cropsey or George Loring Brown. By and large, autumn scenes did not bulk large among their productions — and when they did paint fall scenes, and even identify them as such in titles like Cropsey's 1857 *Indian Summer Morning in the White Mountains*, Brown's 1862 *Autumn, Windy Day, View at Gorham, New Hampshire*, or John Frederick Kensett's 1854 *October Day, White Mountains*, they follow Cole in their use of conventional aesthetic categories as the basis for what they will notice in nature and how they will depict it, using colorful trees as incidental elements in their larger compositions of weather and landforms.[71] Fall foliage, it seems, still has incidental status for Cole and his followers and has not yet been elevated to full membership in that aesthetic natural realm that represents so completely and effectively a flight from the distressing modern-day world.

More importantly, and independently of the relative prominence of autumn colors in the paintings of Cole and his followers, it's likely that most viewers of their paintings would not have found those colors a particularly interesting subject anyway. In at least acknowledging the scenic value of fall foliage and in chiding his fellow citizens for their habitual "meager utilitarianism" even while living in a country of great natural beauty, Cole touched on ideas and images that would recur on the American printed page through at least the mid-nineteenth century. Many observers and commentators bemoaned the lack of interest that they felt Americans possessed in natural scenery and in the stirring aesthetic and moral qualities of the world beyond the city limits. One anonymous contributor to the June 5, 1851, edition of the

New-York Home Journal followed this line of argument while specifically using the autumn colors of the city's hinterlands as his representative example of the scenic delights New Yorkers were missing, implicitly nominating fall foliage as the sine qua non of natural beauty in the Northeast: "As a people, we are less in the habit of luxuriating in the beauties of nature than any other pretending to civilization. We neither hunt, fish, ride on horseback, indulge in rural sports or athletic exercises. The landscape may decline into the sere and yellow leaf, arrayed in all the glorious tints of autumn, within a mile of Trinity Church, and not ten of the fifty thousand patrons of art of the Bethune class will afford themselves the luxury of casting 'a long, lingering look behind.'"[72] While the writer seems personally attracted to the changing leaves, though, finding them valuable in and of themselves as an aesthetic phenomenon, he still finds himself in a distinct minority. In a complete reversal of the situation today, when steady streams of cars with New York license plates wander north into the Adirondacks or New England on fall weekends, this writer describes a scene in which the urban population stays resolutely at home, either ignorant or dismissive of what they could see if they were to walk or ride even a short distance away.

Henry David Thoreau continued to survey this rhetorical line in his 1862 essay "Autumnal Tints," in which he also takes an important literary step in firmly binding the phenomenon of fall colors, that same bright display that caught the eye and mind of the *New-York Home Journal* writer, not simply to definitions of nature in general but to the definition of New England in particular. In the essay, Thoreau tries to call his countrymen's attention to the kaleidoscope of color that filled New England every fall, indicating that by that point in the nineteenth century fall foliage, while clearly visible to the naked eye, had not yet taken up a place in the *mind's* eye of the region or the nation; in Thoreau's estimation, his fellow New Englanders were looking at it but not truly *seeing* it, and certainly not associating it with themselves. Echoing Thomas Cole's nationalistic emphasis, Thoreau notes that "Europeans coming to America are surprised by the brilliancy of our autumnal foliage." And that comment seems to apply to many Americans as well: "A great many, who have spent their lives in cities, and have never chanced to come into the country at this season, have never seen this, the flower, or rather the ripe fruit, of the year. I remember riding with one such citizen, who, though a fortnight too late for the most brilliant tints, was taken by surprise, and would not believe that there had been any brighter. He had never heard of this phenomenon before. Not only many in our towns have never witnessed it, but it is scarcely remembered by the majority from year to year." [73] Thoreau attempts to wake New Englanders up to the beauty that surrounds them, believing that such an awareness will improve the minds and lives of the citizenry; that is, he anticipates later cultural uses of fall foliage by presenting the colorful leaves as an alternative to the drudgery of everyday life. Of the yellow New England elm, he says, "Their leaves are perfectly ripe. I wonder if there is any answering ripeness in the lives of the men who live beneath them. . . . Under those bright rustling piles just ready to fall on the heads of the walkers, how can any crudity or greenness of thought or act prevail?" [74] In discussing the sugar maple, Thoreau moves on to associate fall foliage specifically with the New England village landscape, suggesting that the composite scene is a particularly regional phenomenon that distinguishes the place from other parts of the country and provides its residents with distinct cultural advantages, providing an early and succinct elevation of fall foliage to the status of New England icon. "Poor indeed," he claims, "must be that New England village's October which has not the maple in its streets. . . . Blaze away! Shall that dirty roll of bunting in the gun-house be all the colors a village can display? A village is not complete, unless it have these trees to mark the season in it. They are important, like the town clock. A village that has them not will not be found to work well. It has a screw loose, an essential part is wanting." [75]

And yet, sadly, he finds that villagers misuse and ignore these vital scenic resources: "What if we were to take half as much pains in protecting them as we do in setting them out, — not stupidly tie our horses to our dahlia stems?" [76] In Thoreau's estimation, New Englanders do not see or appreciate fall foliage, but view it only as an unremarkable backdrop for their everyday activities, because their minds are simply not trained to notice it; their aesthetic training and cultural needs are such that the contemplation of foliage serves no imaginative purpose for them, and so, unlike today, they take it for granted. Toward the end of the essay, Thoreau exhorts his readers: "All this you surely *will* see, and much more, if you are prepared to see it, — if you *look* for it. . . . Objects are concealed from our view, not so much because they are out of the course of our visual ray as because we do not bring our eyes and minds to bear on them; . . . We cannot see anything until we are possessed with the idea of it, take it into our heads, — and then we can hardly see anything else."[77] As usual, Thoreau in many ways is ahead of the game, and here he anticipates the idea that the broad cultural celebration and valuation of New England's fall foliage that is so obvious to us today is as much a collective invention as anything else having to do with New England's popular identity, an ongoing act of selecting a certain element out of the natural landscape and investing it with meanings and powers that are more properly located in the eye of the beholder rather than in the thing being beheld. Long after Thoreau's lifetime, Americans would indeed become "possessed with the idea" of New England's autumn colors, and can "hardly see anything else" when they think about the region, but certain other conditions would have to fall into place before that could happen.

As I've said, the fact of the colors cannot in itself explain the popularity of fall foliage, and neither can the development of technological means for bringing images of that foliage to a larger American viewing public. Until the mid-nineteenth century or so, understandably, it was difficult to see New England's fall colors unless you lived or traveled there in October, or if you were fortunate enough to see paintings from the region, paintings that, as we've seen, give no special prominence to the place of autumn colors in the region's natural scenery. One might guess, though, that the development and rise to public popularity of color lithography would remedy that situation, would bring to a broad American audience an appreciation of a brilliant landscape spectacle that would seem to have a lot of inherent aesthetic appeal, perfect for hanging in a middle-class American parlor. However, looking at collections of color prints from the house of Currier and Ives suggests to us that here, too, New England's fall foliage was not yet a part of Americans' scenic inventory, was not an obvious choice for the firm and its artists when they produced images of New England that they hoped would be popular and sell well; apparently there was no mass audience clamoring for the nineteenth-century equivalent of today's autumnal coffee-table books and calendar art. When Currier and Ives depicted New England rural scenes, they tended to focus primarily on human activities, on blacksmithing and corn husking and other aspects of farm life; in fact, a print specifically called *Autumn in New England: Cider Making*, which is typical of the firm's treatment of the region, includes only three small trees that have changed color; the rest of the trees in the scene are still green, and all of this varied foliage is only a scenic backdrop anyway — the eye is drawn primarily to the people in the foreground.[78] While there is clearly an emphasis in prints like these on the past, on quaint, non-mechanized, premodern ways of life on healthy prosperous farms, which links these prints to some of the later nineteenth-century impulses I've mentioned before, that backward-looking focus does not yet take in the natural as well as the cultural world; viewers are invited to vicariously participate in what the lithographed human subjects *do*, not in what they *see*.

In fact, Currier and Ives produced many more scenes of winter activities in New England than they did of autumn activities, which indicates another possible reason for not focusing on autumn subjects for their prints: insofar as Americans in the nineteenth century associated New England with any part of the year at all, it was winter and not fall. Bernard Mergen, in his book *Snow in America*, notes that as far back as colonial times, New Englanders saw their harsh winters as tests of character and opportunities to display their physical and moral hardiness, and therefore "New Englanders . . . made snowy winters the primary characteristic of their identity." Eventually they spread this association across the nation: "In scientific papers, stories, and poems, New Englanders created an image of the United States as a nation of sharply defined seasons, in which winter, with its white blanket of snow and its mysteriously complex and beautiful snowflake, was the most inspiring."[79] And perhaps more so than the kinds of written texts to which Mergen refers, landscape paintings and prints played a particularly strong role in both popularizing winter scenes as a peculiarly nationalistic phenomenon and in conflating the winter season with New England as a region. In an early response to that same desire to depict distinctively American scenery that motivated Thomas Cole and his fellow Hudson River school painters, Boston artist Alvan Fisher as early as 1815 was producing, as he said in an 1834 look back on his career, "a species of pictures which had not been practiced much, if any, in this country, viz: barnyard scenes and scenes belonging to rural life, winter pieces, portraits of animals, etc."[80] His most popular paintings combined these elements within single tableaux, typically showing a scene of sleighing or skating or other outdoor work or recreation within a snowy setting, thus bringing together features from the increasingly prevalent American fields of landscape painting and genre painting (scenes of everyday activities). At the same time, similar to our current perceptions of New England fall foliage, Fisher presented winter primarily as an aesthetic resource rather than a natural phenomenon in its own right: In art historian Fred B. Adelson's words, Fisher's paintings "do not depict the harshness and brutality of a New England winter. Rather, they show picturesque images of rural folk enjoying themselves without signs of discomfort. The snowstorm is over; the ground and trees glisten with a fresh, clean cover."[81] Fisher was still somewhat of a pioneer in this particular artistic subgenre — at the height of his popularity in 1834, an anonymous critic in a Boston newspaper could still describe his new painting *Winter in New Hampshire* as "a happy sketch of what artists very seldom attempt, a winter scene"[82] — but he had taken an important step in introducing winter into America's, and particularly New England's, defining visual vocabulary.

The popular Hudson River school played a part in keeping winter scenes relatively rare, as it reflected an aesthetic that did not find winter a congenial subject: not only did painting winter scenes entail sitting outside in cold weather, it did not carry an uplifting moral import, being associated with passivity and decline rather than with youth and energy and optimism. Nevertheless, by the middle of the nineteenth century several American painters, notably New Englanders Thomas Birch and George Henry Durrie, adopted winter scenes as an important component of their métier, echoing in their depiction Fisher's idealized domesticated scenes of a few decades earlier, even including the sleighride as a recurrent motif. Art historian Martha Hutson credits Birch and Durrie with developing "a native American landscape style," one that spread throughout the nation's aesthetic consciousness not only because of their own works but because "winter landscapes were also being painted by amateur artists at all levels of talent and training," painters who were "influenced by everything available to them in painting, prints and book reproductions."[83] And those easily available prints became the most widespread means by which not only painters but middle-class Americans in general were exposed to New England winter scenery. In particular, Currier and Ives produced and widely distributed many prints based on Durrie's paintings after his death in 1863, and the winter sleighride scene thereby became popularly imprinted on the American visual consciousness. As Hutson notes, while Durrie's name was forgotten soon after his death, "his work is recognized today, but not necessarily associated with him,"[84] but rather with Currier and Ives; in fact, if someone today refers to a scene or an image as having a "Currier and Ives" quality about it, they usually seem to be referring to the sort of sentimental, old-timey sleighride scene that Durrie helped develop. And it increasingly came to be seen as a specifically regional scene as well: in 1868, the Boston chromolithography firm of Louis Prang advertised one of their prints, based on a winter scene by Joseph Morviller, as being "as essentially New-Englandish — if we may coin a word — as pumpkin pie or Thanksgiving,"[85] neatly bundling the winter sleighride into the larger regional system of "invented traditions," to use Eric Hobsbawm's phrase, that already included the Thanksgiving holiday and feast.[86] (And I, at least, have always thought of the children's ditty "Over the River and Through the Woods to Grandmother's House We Go," with its prescient sleigh-hauling horse, as being set in New England.)

Through visual means and mental association with other regionally defining phenomena, then, winter became closely bound to New England through the nineteenth century, an association that is true to some extent even today. Moreover, with the twentieth-century development of the skiing industry in Maine, in New Hampshire, and particularly in Vermont, New England remains conceptually connected to winter at least within the minds of a significant segment of the nation's sporting population. While New England thus may be to some extent a "two-season" region today, through much of the nineteenth century the calendrical equation of New England and autumn had not yet been firmly made. Compared to winter, this relatively mild season did not make as much sense for New Englanders and other Americans to imagine — certainly Thoreau was frustrated by the lack of autumnal imagination he found surrounding him — and so perhaps Currier and Ives didn't feel obliged to produce a product that had no real cultural meaning, and therefore no commercial appeal. While the potential was there to popularize New England fall foliage for a national audience, the justification was not.

Technological factors alone, then, didn't create the popularity of New England fall foliage as a scenic resource. But another basic material factor contributed to this lack of popularity, one that may be the most fundamental of all in thinking about this phenomenon: while

Natural Landscapes, Cultural Regions

Thoreau laments New Englanders' lack of training in seeing New England's colorful forests, and while Currier and Ives didn't provide graphic images of those forests for people elsewhere to see, both these absences might be a simple function of the fact that there simply weren't many colorful forests to *see* in the nineteenth century. The foliage that people see today when driving on the back roads of northern and western New England appeared only in the twentieth century, the result of at least two waves of forest clearance activity. Even while it represents a flight from history, fall foliage itself is a product of history, the literal outgrowth of an era when New England forests were seen as prosaic resources and not inviolate, timeless icons.

We've already contemplated the large-scale deforestation of New England and its subsequent regreening after the abandonment of farm fields and pastures. By now, the proportions of forest to cleared land in New England have been roughly reversed from where they stood 150 years ago. This regrowth, however, was not a one-step process; the hardwood forests that we associate with New England today were in many cases the result of a second wave of clearing. As Thoreau first observed in his 1860 essay "The Succession of Forest Trees," and as ecologists have confirmed, abandoned fields in New England tended to first grow up to white pine. Pine seeds are very light in weight and easily dispersed by wind, and so if there was a seed source near an old field a young pine forest would quickly appear. Pine is a fast-growing, shade-intolerant species; so the young trees would grow quickly and vigorously, forming a closed canopy in a fairly short time. Under that canopy, though, an interesting thing would begin to happen: young hardwood seedlings would begin to sprout. As Thoreau observed, squirrels and birds would carry acorns and walnuts into the young pine forest and either drop or bury them. Maple seeds might blow in or also be brought in by animals. Hardwood trees like these are shade-tolerant, so they would grow slowly beneath the pine canopy, biding their time and waiting for their moment. Their moment, in general, came in the late nineteenth or early twentieth centuries, when those pioneer white pines had grown large enough to become a significant economic resource and to attract the attention of loggers. By about 1900, according to forest historian Tom Wessels, "white pine rose once again to become the mainstay of the central New England logging industry,"[87] and once the pine forests were cleared the oaks and other hardwoods were released to grow tall, in many places not reaching a significant stature until close to midcentury. And without those widespread trees, there could be no widespread colorful foliage to delight the eyes and ease the minds of New England tourists; the conditions over time, however, had to be just right in order for them to appear. As historical ecologist David Foster summarizes this broad regional phenomenon in his book *Thoreau's Country: Journey through a Transformed Landscape*, "the historical sequence of field, abandoned field, pine wood, and hardwood forest is displayed as a spatial pattern in the modern countryside," and so the view from the bus window or the armchair today is only there to be seen and photographed because of a specific, historically timed sequence of land-use history.[88] Thomas Cole, in 1835, lamented that American scenery was being destroyed because "the ravages of the axe are daily increasing — the most noble scenes are made desolate, and oftentimes with a wantonness and barbarism scarcely credible in a civilized nation."[89] Ironically, though, New England's most prized scenic resource today, far from being destroyed, was made possible by that self-same ax wielded on certain targets in a certain historical order.

This timing may be the crucial factor in explaining something else I've noticed: the broad, unself-conscious celebration of New England fall foliage that we see today emerged, as far as I can tell, around World War II. In addition to there being forests to see and a growing desire among people to see them, another conditioning factor in the popularity of foliage is that people have to have a way of getting out where the scenery is. I therefore suspect that the rise of automobile tourism in this century has been an important factor in the creation and maintenance of fall foliage as a New England icon, as magazines and tour guides from the American Automobile Association and bumper-to-bumper buses on northern New England highways in October amply confirm. Things were different in the early days of autotourism, though. Touring guides from the World War I era and before, even those that claim in their titles to be offering "The Scenic Tour" of New England (and therefore implicitly defining what real New England scenery is), tend to focus on attractive villages and historic sites in their suggested itineraries, as well as on the perennially popular mountains and lakes, indicating not only their indebtedness to earlier traditions of New England tourism but their allegiance to the antimodern tendencies of the time that saw *village* New England and a particularly noble and heroic strain of New England history as the proper imaginative resources to use in combating the downward trends of time's passage.

Other popular tourist-oriented books of the 1920s and 1930s echoed the focus of earlier autotouring guides on particular cultural destinations and older scenic traditions as they attempted to codify what was visually and aesthetically defining and definitely worth seeing in New England; even at this relatively recent date, fall foliage doesn't make the list. Wallace Nutting, in his New England Beautiful series of books on every state in the region but Rhode Island, which were published in the 1920s, hardly ever mentions fall colors in his pages, focusing instead in words and in black-and-white photographs on mountains, lakes, rivers, farm and village scenes, and views of picturesque lanes (still largely dirt roads at this point).[90] "Beautiful" New England is an emphatically old-fashioned, rural, and natural New England in Nutting's books, a place that looks reassuringly like it hasn't changed at all over the years, but the nature it includes is still that of the painters and White Mountain tourists of the nineteenth century. Even the Works Progress Administration guides to the New England states produced in the 1930s don't give fall foliage a mention, implying that it was still not self-evident enough a regional attraction to include. But things would soon change. With the continued growth of the forest, the increase in driving and leisure time after the war, the ongoing need that many people have to locate, visit, and imaginatively inhabit geographical places that represent desirable alternatives to the places where they actually live, and undoubtedly a host of other factors I haven't stumbled onto yet, New England fall foliage, over only about the last fifty years or so, has become the regionally defining visual icon that we all know and love today. The ongoing cultural meaning of New England as a history-denying region offering an escape from real life held open an imaginative slot for something like autumn foliage to fill, and once the proper kind of forest developed, it filled that slot swiftly and surely.

I suspect that there are many more historical conditions that have helped make the fall foliage phenomenon possible: the institution of the vacation; the growth over time of people's ability and willingness to travel away from home on vacation; the extension of acceptable vacation time from summer to other seasons; the popularity of the day trip or weekend jaunt by New Englanders themselves; the involvement of state tourism boards, chambers of commerce, the professional tourism industry, and mass media; and other such social, cultural, and material factors. But I've wanted to suggest here at least some of what strike me as the most important enabling factors — both natural and cultural — in the development of the colorful autumn New England forest as simultaneously a physical thing and a symbol, an idea, the embodiment of an imaginative space and collection of meanings that transcend the trees and leaves themselves and connect to other powerful ways that people have developed for thinking about and defining New England as a cultural region. Episodes like this, I think, join with our thinking about nature as a historical actor in New England to give us another incisive key for puzzling out the connections between those two seemingly dissimilar ways of thinking about this chunk of American space: the solid nonhuman landscape on the one hand, the nebulous, shifting, emphatically human-made cultural region on the other. Nature has shaped the cultural landscape of New England; cultural activity has in turn shaped the forested face of the region that we see today. And even beyond this physical symbiosis, ongoing *ideas* about nature and about the meaning of New England as an imaginative entity have reinforced each other over time, so that nature and culture in New England are *conceptually* connected as well as *physically* and *historically* connected. If we're really wondering what's natural about New England as a cultural region, all we need to do is ask people why they'd rather visit us in October than in March and I think we'll find out.

⁂

Perhaps the foregoing ruminations on the character of New England regional identity are just a very long way of saying something much more brief that Lewis Mumford wrote over sixty years ago: "The human region . . . is a complex of geographic, economic, and cultural elements. Not found as a finished product in nature, not solely the creation of human will and fantasy, the region, like its corresponding artifact, the city, is a collective work of art."[91] The New England that I discern when I look around me and when I read books, monuments, and other written and material texts having to do with the region closely fits Mumford's definition, occupying a middle ground between nature on the one hand and human will and fantasy on the other, between the irreducible givens of the landscape and the artificial inventions of culture. Molded and altered by human hands, impossible to fully understand without taking into account human activity and disturbance, nature in New England has at the same time not simply lain there passively, not been made over completely according to human design, not had its wildness utterly plowed, walled, dammed, and engineered out of it, but has guided and constrained many of the things that those human hands have done to it, acting on people just as surely, if less obviously, as people have acted on it. The New England that I see around me echoes an observation that folklorist Henry Glassie once made about Ireland: "Suddenly I realized the entire island has been touched, molded by human beings. It is an artifact. . . . Ireland is sculpture, a collective material artwork that dwarfs in beauty and conceptual magnificence the oeuvre of the proudest of non-anonymous sculptors. Let others chip stone or pat clay into representations, the Irish people have made the emerald isle. The land is art as Waldo Emerson exactly defined it: a blending of nature and will."[92]

Still, and in spite of my having equated old farm landscapes with folk art two chapters ago, I'm not sure I want to rest with Mumford's and Glassie's artistic metaphors, persuasive though they are as I poke around in New England landscapes, seeing toolmarks and fingerprints everywhere around me. I'm definitely surrounded by a blending of nature and will, but to think of a regional landscape in terms of art, and particularly sculpture, tends to locate the genesis of that landscape rather firmly in the realm of culture, with nature serving primarily as raw material upon which the designing human mind, in all its "conceptual magnificence," can do its work. Not that I want to impute intention to natural process, but it might be equally accurate to say that, at least in New England, human beings have provided the raw materials upon which *nature* has gone to work, directly or indirectly manipulating the givens of the cultural landscape into new kinds of artifacts far different in form and appearance from the ones that humans left there. Once you've ripped your way through enough undergrowth and dodged enough tree branches to get a good look at an old mill site or a particularly interesting stone wall, once you go to Simmonsville and find a quiet residential neighborhood occupying what was once a bustling industrial center, once you enjoy the view of a forested hillside and realize that not very long ago that same hillside was bare to the summit, you begin to wonder just which has been the strongest force shaping the New England scene. In contemplating the reforested Vermont countryside surrounding his home in Bristol, a landscape made possible by abandonment and depopulation, John Elder describes the scene as "the climax of a century of enhancement through impoverishment," its wild and human-made elements melding together in a unique historical balance.[93] And it's a balance in which wilderness forms the top layer and, at least in Vermont, makes the dominant impression. People have helped lay the foundation, but it's forest succession and other natural processes that have done the heavy lifting.

I think it's important to keep our minds on the vitality, ubiquity, and centrality of nature's presence in the landscape and in regional history — not only in New England, but in all regions of the country and the world. It's an attentiveness that seems particularly urgent in what I characterized earlier as a kind of "postnatural" era, one in which location, natural limitations, and the particular qualities of particular ecological regions no longer seem to matter in the decision-making and the economic lives of many Americans. The Scituate Reservoir and the application of steam power to industrial production, thus freeing factories from river valleys, represent two recent steps on the way to a post-natural New England, as does the enormous mobility offered by the automobile (even the canal-eclipsing railroads were limited in where they were able to go through the necessity of having to follow the gentle grades offered by lowlands and valleys, tied down by friction and gravity) and the importation through ships and power lines of enormous amounts of energy from other parts of the country and world, finite energy that no one seems to feel any particular need to conserve. The popularity of large and expensive sport-utility vehicles in this country strikes me as particularly emblematic these days: engineered with rugged terrain in mind, around my neighborhood most of them seem to be driven by commuters, found more often in the urban or suburban parking lot than in the Maine woods. I can't imagine many drivers wanting to scratch up those enormously expensive paint jobs, and to me the vehicles seem to express the attitude that their drivers want to use up *all* the gasoline *now*. Let future generations figure out some alternative. If we can drink water from halfway across the state and get oil from halfway across the world, surely we can find more energy someplace. We always have. Limits and locations haven't mattered much over the last century or so — why should they start mattering now?

I'm gloomy enough to think that the postnatural world is going to find out soon enough that nature does matter, and that it matters crucially. I'm not just talking about the fact that finding a tornado aimed at your poor cowering backside or having a lightning-set wildfire eat your house will make you figure out very quickly that nature is a lot stronger than you are. It's more that there's only so much water in the West and Southwest to supply the needs of all those growing urban populations. It's that proposing to drill for oil in protected Alaskan wilderness areas is nothing more than a way of buying time until petroleum is all used up all over the world. It's recognizing both limits and opportunities, looking at where you are and seeing what local and regional landscapes both will and will not let you do. Perhaps New England has a lesson for us all here, as the region bears on its surface continual reminders of instances where human goals outran the capacities of the land to sustain them. Despite recent and current rates of growth and consumption, there's no reason why other parts of the country can't and won't become Vermont, places where, in Elder's words, "failing enterprises cleared the ground for a new attempt at balance with the natural environment," even though the East's abundant rainfall "allows the landscape to assert its own agenda with a quickness unimaginable in states west of the hundredth meridian."[94] Patricia Limerick has located such places in the West in writing about that region's ghost mining towns, places where the ore ran out, ruins that are protected in part by that western aridity but that are related to New England's stone walls, abandoned fields, and relict canals and mill structures in offering "the opportunity to stand at a spot where humans once lived in numbers and to contemplate the overpowering fact of their absence" and in demonstrating "the interplay of ambition and outcome, the collision between simple expectation and complex reality, the fallout from optimistic efforts to master both nature and human nature."[95] Limerick refers to the western ghost town as a "landscape of failure," and while I think "failure" is too strong a term to apply to those many anonymous New Englanders who found it harder and harder to get their livings from the land, Limerick's observation links the West to New England in reminding us that, within broad regional if not national contexts, nature not only matters in the course and quality of people's lives, it has *always* mattered.

So maybe I should finish by giving nature the last word as best I can. Certainly, I've been doing my best here to point out the intersections and interminglings of nature and culture, and to complicate any understandings we might have of New England as a purely cultural region, a matter of disembodied, selective histories and arbitrary boundaries. And yet, perhaps I'm simply trying to substitute one New England for another, one kind of history for another, still looking at the landscape through the familiar framework of those six northeasternmost states, still mining it for a primarily human meaning. It's difficult to think about the concept of region at all without seeing it as, if not completely human, then as fundamentally human in its origins and purposes. It seems to fall into the category of what geographer Martin W. Lewis and historian Kären E. Wigen have called "metageography," by which they mean "the set of spatial structures through which people order their knowledge of the world: the often unconscious frameworks that organize studies of history, sociology, anthropology, economics, political science, or even natural history."[96] Lewis and Wigen have focused in a book-length study on what they call "the myth of continents," arguing that what most people uncritically accept as a commonsense division of the earth's land surface into seven large, self-evident landmasses is not only false to the natural and cultural groupings that those landmasses support — "When it comes to mapping global patterns, whether of physical or human phenomena, continents are most often simply irrelevant"[97] — but is also an emphatically human invention, the result of shifting perceptions and priorities over time rather than of natural divisions that were simply waiting there to be discovered on the earth's surface. Our understanding of what and where the earth's continents are is a "fundamentally visual definition," one that has "made the continental classification system increasingly congruent with the basic patterns of land and sea that spring to the eye from a world map,"[98] and this emphasis on natural divisions between continents has resulted in, among other things, the tortured and arbitrary selection of the Ural Mountains as the dividing line between Europe and Asia. Through this act of finding a natural boundary whether one exists or not, Europe provides an ideal illustration of the unnatural nature of continents as geographical entities; Europe's very designation as a separate continent is largely a result of the simple circumstance that Europeans invented the notion of continents in the first place and didn't want to be conceptually lumped in with the lands to the east and south. In fact, the current convention of there being seven continents was not finalized until the middle of the twentieth century, when geographers added Antarctica to the list and decided that North and South America were visually distinct enough to be conceptually separated rather than being collectively seen as "America," a seemingly commonsense division that didn't become widely accepted until around World War II. As metageographical entities, continents have become "naturalized, coming to be regarded, not as products of a fallible human imagination, but as real geographical entities that had been 'discovered' through empirical inquiry."[99] In the end, though, they seem only tangentially related to the natural world, an observation that would seem to apply to a cultural region like New England as well.

Like continents, after all, regions imply boundaries — an inside and an outside, a here and a there — and I don't think that boundaries are necessarily found in nature. Rather, people find something that fits their notion of what a boundary should look like and then use it as a basis for perception and action, arguing that the land on this side is fundamentally different from the land on that side and should be treated accordingly. An Isthmus of Panama does not in itself two continents make, and the same is true on much smaller geographical scales as well. A height of land between two river drainages is one thing, a natural happenstance that determines which way the rain trickles; to call that height of land a "watershed" is something else altogether, giving the basins on either side a structure and significance and name that, like the noise made by the tree falling in the forest, didn't exist until the human observer came along. Since water and gravity behave in predictable ways, watersheds, like isthmuses, would seem to be obvious and self-evident points of geographical division — notes ecologist Frank B. Golley, "The location of a watershed boundary is usually unambiguous"[100] — but the idea of a drainage basin needs to become a useful concept before a human observer will note and care about its borders. (Many Americans today, like Golley, use the term "watershed" to refer to the drainage basin itself, but the point still holds.) In the same vein, Robert Bailey is routinely acknowledged as the author of the national system of ecological regions that I mentioned earlier: in fact, according to the titles of Web sites maintained by the U. S. Forest Service and the Environmental Protection Agency, they're *Bailey's* ecoregions, not *nature's* ecoregions — the product of the scientist and the mapmaker more than of millennia of natural process.[101] For that matter, while Bailey himself notes that ecoregional boundaries "may be delineated on the basis of detailed information about ecosystems at the site level, or by analysis of the environmental factors that most probably acted as selective forces in creating variation in ecosystems," looking primarily at vegetation and soil associations and thus locating the basis for borders within the nonhuman world, the justification for delineating those "natural" regions is as a guide to specifically human actions: Bailey's goal is to "divide the landscape into variously sized ecosystems units that have significance both for development of resources and for conservation of environment."[102] Given all this, we might conclude that there's no such thing as a region that *isn't* a cultural region, that isn't simply a metageographical concept.

At the same time, however, there are some ways of thinking about regions and boundaries that are less anthropocentric than others. Kirkpatrick Sale, in his book-length argument for the diffuse social movement called bioregionalism, offers this definition of the term "bioregion": "The natural region is the bioregion, defined by the qualities Gaea has established there, the *givens* of nature. It is any part of the earth's surface whose rough boundaries are determined by natural characteristics rather than human dictates, distinguishable from other areas by particular attributes of flora, fauna, water, climate, soils, and landforms, and by the human settlements and cultures those attributes have given rise to."[103] Sale's definition still discerns boundaries on the land that can be drawn there only after humans themselves distinguish the concentration or diminishment of certain of "nature's characteristics," and members of bioregionalist groups then use those newly discerned and bounded regions as the basis for community and for human action: watershed management, say, or political organization. Here, too, cultural functions and foundations are subtly at work in the guise of letting nature play the determining role in its interactions with humans. Nevertheless, bioregionalists believe in identifying and fitting their individual and collective lives to the limits, conditions, and interconnectedness of small, intimate bioregions, usually on the scale of a small river drainage, working to build democratic, ecologically aware communities that will lead to both social and environmental sustainability. According to Peter Berg and Raymond Dasmann, two influential early figures in bioregionalist thinking, the aim of bioregionalism as a practice entails "following the necessities and pleasures of life as they are uniquely presented by a particular site, and evolving ways to ensure long-term occupancy of that site."[104] Bioregionalism, then, offers to its adherents one alternative to the post-natural world, literally grounding community members in particular places and working to ensure that life is lived carefully and responsibly within a small ecological compass. It's a vision that lets nature draw the lines and set the rules. Under this definition New England is clearly not a single unified bioregion; rather, its artificiality becomes drawn even more sharply into focus. If we can't look at New England as a bioregion, though, we can at least draw on a bioregional sensibility if we want to introduce a firm natural presence to the way people think about the region: if the land can suggest boundaries and ways of life, perhaps it can also suggest its own interpretations, its own histories, its own stories.

After all, even though I've been talking extensively about nature in this book, and while you might characterize my practice as "reading" various landscapes that I've come across, much of what I've said is based on books and other written texts. I've looked at nature at second hand through the fiction of Casey and Moore and the nonfiction of Thoreau, McPhee, and Ehrlich, I've considered maps as depictions of natural places, and the carved inscriptions on the gravemarkers of Elizabeth Pabodie and Philip Angell sent me into the archives as well as out into the field — whereupon I began to tell the story of nature in New England not on its own terms but through individual and collective human histories. And now there *you* are, reading what I have to say about all this. There are a lot of stories in these pages, to be sure, but just as New England as a geographical and conceptual entity is to a great extent a human imposition onto a natural place, so too might this book and many of its sources be seen as equally artificial intrusions, human constructions that bear only the slightest resemblance to the natural scenes on which they are based.

If this is an accurate characterization of this book, then it's particularly ironic given the way that I experience the world around me. When I take a walk in the woods, I don't hear any voices other than my own. When I stand still and listen to the place that surrounds me, I hear leaves and branches rustling in the wind, perhaps a chipmunk skittering through the undergrowth or a brook tumbling over rocks, but I don't hear anything that I can recognize as language, let alone as narration or explication. Likewise, when I look around at the patch of forest and soil and stones through which I am moving, I don't see any writing, any legible inscriptions that explain to me in words any of the meaning, history, and perspective on existence that might be lodged in the landscape. I share the perception of critic Barton St. Armand when he writes, "When I look at nature, I see something multiform, kaleidoscopic, textured — something fuzzy or rough or crystalline or cross-hatched, as the case may be, but I do not see a book."[105] St. Armand moves on to contemplate "the characterization of nature as a bound volume — the old idea of the Book of Nature," and it seems particularly ironic that this conceit, this reference to an object in which stories and arguments are laid out clearly on precise rectangular pages in neatly printed lines, is so much at odds with the actual experience of confronting the natural world in all its tangled complexity, a world free of linguistic artifice in which meaning, if meaning is inherently present at all, lies well beyond the limits of literacy and aural comprehension. It would seem that places can be represented in ways that we can read and listen to only through the linguistic intervention of human agents — through the imposition or projection of descriptions or narratives or arguments onto the natural surface, or through the attempted transcription and translation of nature's "voices" by self-appointed amanuenses. Nature does not write books unaided, and just as books consist of trees that have been chewed up, flattened into paper, and printed on, so too might we suspect that the representations of nature that appear in those books have been equally thoroughly processed by the machinery of the human mind into a form very different from the way they existed as living beings in the landscape — the constituent molecules of those pages remain unchanged, but they have been removed from the forest and rearranged into a neat symmetrical form that is particularly useful for human culture, particular amenable to human intentions and desires.

Perhaps this is inevitable: since nature does not tell or publish its own stories, human beings are left to write narratives into nature on their own, a process that leads to the suspicion that those narratives may have at least as much to do with the minds and lives of their creators as they do with anything that is objectively observable in natural landscapes. Some writers maintain the conceit that they are trying to act as invisible conduits between nature and the reader, simply wielding the pen for an illiterate entity with no hands of its own. Think back, for instance, to the quote I included earlier from Robert Finch's essay entitled "What the Stones Said," in which he shows himself listening carefully to "the hardest of all sounds in nature to hear: the silent assertion of a landscape itself," and appreciating how "nature's unstrung voices made themselves heard in the dark silence."[106] Despite Finch's claim that nature has a voice, though, and that it can use that voice to *assert* things — to speak up for itself, to make claims, perhaps to argue — what we read is Finch's own language, what we see in his essay is not so much an unmediated landscape as a literary naturalist moving carefully through that landscape with his eyes and ears peeled for sound and significance, and what we are left with ultimately is Finch's discovery of what he wanted to find there in the first place, a natural world that means something satisfying to him as a nature writer. Despite his desire that we pay no attention to the man behind the curtain, Finch's performance is little different from that of the traditional Thoreauvian nature writer, the figure who achieves temporary self-exile from the civilized precincts of the world, spends time traversing or sitting still in a natural landscape, and emerges once more to write a report to the rest of us about the course of his or her experiences and thoughts, the things that were seen and felt and heard and smelled and the meditations and realizations that those things inspired. If that report takes on the form of a narrative, it is a story of the developing course of the writer's mind, of the movement of his or her body through the landscape and through time. Nature provides the occasion for the story, the material for mind to work on, the medium for movement, the point A and point B of the writer's imaginative and experiential progress, but it does not write the story itself, nor does it determine the course of the plot.

Finch's ears must be much more sensitive than mine, for I have never actually heard a stone say anything, nor were courses in Stonish available in any school I ever went to. The only interpretive voices that I have ever heard in the woods have been those of human companions, and here too, as in the case of writing, I have learned more about human experience and history in the landscape than I have about the workings and meanings of the natural world — in the moment of listening to those voices, I have encountered the human sense of place more immediately than I have the place itself. When I accompanied Walter Hale through his overgrown former farm, for instance, I learned a lot about the natural history of that small Maine landscape, but I also heard an extensive oral history of the place, one devoted to annotating the landscape insofar as it figured in Mr. Hale's working experience. The woods came alive for me in large part because of how the land supporting them had been used in the past, before much of those woods even existed; the stories that were so thick on the ground in the forest, so inextricably bound to the landscape in Mr. Hale's mind, had nothing to do with the forest itself, were not actually about the trees I could see everywhere around me. Through Mr. Hale's personal narratives, the place was represented to me not on its own terms, whatever those might be and if such a thing is possible, but as it had been filtered through the mind and life of an individual human storyteller.

And yet, that same second-growth forest and other landscapes like it have provided me with clues to a way around this dilemma of representation, have made me recognize the possibility that places can represent *themselves* if we know where and how to look. In his article "A Place for Stories: Nature, History, and Narrative," environmental historian William Cronon argues that narrative is an alien and irrelevant concept when talking about natural environments, noting that "nature and the universe do not tell stories; we do." [107] Since nature independent of human observation and mediation does not contain plots, morals, closed linear narrative structures, and other tropes and devices by which we conventionally identify and describe stories — because, like cultural regions, these are human inventions; because, also like regions, "narrative is a peculiarly human way of organizing reality" — Cronon argues that "we force our stories on a world that doesn't fit them." [108] Cronon spends much of the article rehearsing and analyzing the historiography of the Great Plains and the Dust Bowl by way of example, noting that environmental historians have inscribed two basic plots on the landscape, one of triumph over natural limitations and one of tragic, hubristic overextension into a place unsuited to the agricultural regimes that were imposed there. These plots have little to do with nature, but rather focus on and derive moral lessons from the experiences of human actors within nature, a fact that Cronon explains only partly as a result of the human tendency to view the world through narrative frameworks; his main contention is that "our histories of the Great Plains environment remain fixed on people because what we most care about in nature is its meaning for human beings. . . . We want to know whether environmental change is good or bad, and that question can only be answered by referring to our own sense of right and wrong. Nature remains mute about such matters. However passionately we may care about the nonhuman world, however much we may believe in its innate worth, our historical narratives, even those about the nonhuman world, remain focused on a human struggle over values."[109] And historians are not alone in this. When nature writers — or old Maine farmers for that matter — represent places and tell stories, they tend to do so within a moral framework: their descriptions become advocacy, their narratives provide models or critiques of right and wrong behavior toward the natural world, their authorial personae proffer themselves as guides to thought and action. Belief in innate worth becomes the armature on which language is hung and plots and arguments are molded; as Cronon puts it, "nature does not tell us whether a dust storm is good or bad; only we can do that. Nature is unlike most other historical subjects in lacking a clear voice of its own."[110] We thus return to the problem of language, of nature's intractable muteness and illiteracy; given this fact, as historians of any stripe — from chroniclers of the Dust Bowl to essayists describing a walk in the woods to old men telling stories of a vanished farm — we confront places that echo our own voices back to us, that serve as blank pages for our writing, that fit into the stories that humans live or discern rather than telling stories of their own; the ability of telling and the idea of story, it seems, are both fundamentally unnatural.

That may be true, but a changed understanding of both the nature of landscape and the implications of the word "history" open up new possibilities for representing places beyond the closed system that Cronon describes and justifies, while still not negating its moral base. I think again of being in Walter Hale's woods, realizing that what looked to me like forest primeval had been cleared and cultivated land only decades before — and, moreover, that the way that the land had been used in the past had a direct effect on the composition of the present-day forest. The scene puts me in mind of another comment by Henry Glassie, who notes wryly that "while historians go down into the archives to mine out scraps of paper and puzzle them delicately into frail, fragmentary constructions, the land spreads tremendous, a palimpsest, the people's own manuscript, their handmade history book." Glassie goes on to admonish us all: "We should learn the landscape's language."[111] Again, the idea of language may obscure more than it illuminates, but Glassie instructively points to a larger truth, the same truth that comes to me everywhere in my New England travels: the landscape, even those parts of it that seem natural and free from human interference, is an artifact, the product of human hands shaping natural materials, even if that shaping is an indirect result of decisions made and actions taken deep in the past. Not all intervention in the landscape is caused by humans, of course — such phenomena as lightning-set fires, windstorms, or ice storms also play a role in altering the composition of plant communities. But regardless of the origins of the forces that shape and reshape natural places as years go by, the fact remains that landscapes exist in time, shift and scramble over time, are continually altered in large and small ways that are not neatly linear, perhaps, that do not necessarily conform to the conventional rhetoric of storytelling or the sorts of narratives that humans write into landscapes, but that nonetheless constitute a temporal sequence — in short, a history. In addition to understanding environment *in* history, then, as Cronon argues is inevitable for us as storytelling animals, we can also finally see environment *as* history, as changing through time instead of being thought of as static and timeless, a sort of green alternative to and refuge from the realm of historical flux in which we must all spend our days. Moreover, as Mr. Hale's forest reminds us, landscapes carry their histories within their very fabrics, taking on their present appearance only because of the nature and sequence of their past disturbances, and so themselves are texts of a sort — not linguistic texts, to be sure, but legible legacies nevertheless of the pasts that shaped them. For the informed observer, then, places represent themselves. Mutely, materially, they tell you exactly where they came from.

Think back to our discussion of landscape change in the opening sections of this book, to the work that historical ecologists, landscape ecologists, and environmental historians have done in demonstrating that there are few if any places on the surface of the earth that have not in some way been shaped by the workings of human culture, of minds and hands together — primarily through the direct or indirect effects of such activities as grazing, woodcutting, fire suppression, mining, agricultural clearing, logging, construction of irrigation works, and the intentional or accidental introduction of exotic plants, not to mention pollution. It's virtually impossible to find any spot on the earth's surface that has not been affected somehow by human activity, no matter how slight. In a relatively short time, our North American landscape has been completely transformed from its precontact state as people have looked at it, decided to put it to economic use and bring it under some shared cultural sense of what domesticated landscapes are supposed to look like, brought in their tools and seeds and domesticated animals, and made the world out there match the ideal pattern as closely as they could, getting rid of the unwanted parts and adding new things and combinations of things. In this sense, the whole continent is an artifact, a designed object, a cultural product made out of the selected and manipulated materials provided by nature: water, soil, plant life. At the time I quoted ecologist Gordon G. Whitney's observation, echoing Mumford's and Glassie's comments about regions and places, that the American landscape "represents a blend of the past and the present, of the human environment and the natural environment. The landscape is a historical document, a cumulative record of man's impact on the natural world."[112]

I want to focus more closely here on Whitney's last sentence, particularly his use of the "document" metaphor. To look at a forest or field, it seems, is to look at the end of a historical, time-bound process — each place is in some way the end result of people interacting with their environment just as much as an obviously shaped space like a yard or garden is. As such, as Whitney's metaphor implies, a knowledgeable viewer can essentially "read" a landscape as a historical text or primary source, deciphering from its structure and composition the cultural influences, both intentional and accidental, that have intertwined with the local environment to contribute to its present form. This is particularly true of landscapes that have been abandoned by people and are now undergoing a process of succession following the human-caused disturbance — like those of New England, which suggests that this model of "reading" offers a particularly salient alternative to thinking about nature and culture in New England in primarily human-centered terms. Walter Hale's New England forest provides a prime example of such a place, and further examples are both everywhere and fascinating for the complex, multilayered stories they hold. As my University of Southern Maine colleague Rob Sanford and his team of researchers have recently noted in one New England context, for instance, "Successional stages of vegetative communities can indicate the duration and nature of past land-use in Vermont. The growth characteristics and structure of a plant community reflect how the land was initially used and what occurred after that use ended." Since "successional communities are fortuitous (rather than predetermined) associations of species whose presence is influenced by how the landscape was used prior to abandonment,"[113] a forest's current appearance is in large part a function of its past cultural shaping: logged-over land, formerly plowed fields, abandoned pasture, and residential fields will all foster certain characteristic types of growth, as will lands that have seen combinations of uses — say, logging followed by grazing in the cutover lands.

Ecologist Tom Wessels's book *Reading the Forested Landscape: A Natural History of New England* is probably my favorite regional example of a history book that writes its narratives and interpretations in terms of natural processes rather than human actions and intentions. Despite his subtitle and its implication of full New England coverage, Wessels takes a bioregional approach, confining his remarks to the central "phytogeographic region" — "an area that shares the same climate and is characterized by similar vegetation"[114] — covering southwestern Maine, southern New Hampshire, southern Vermont and the Champlain Valley, and western and north-central Massachusetts. Within this bioregional frame, not only does Wessels offer drawings and explications of typical central New England forested landscapes, giving his readers a primer for deciphering how scenes end up looking the way they do — a primer in Forestese, if not Stonish — he deliberately promotes the documentary, textual metaphor that Whitney also employs, arguing that natural scenes can be read just as surely as books can, even if they are not organized according to conventional human plots and morals. Wessels presents his book as evolving from his everyday encounters with the landscapes in his Vermont neighborhood: "my favorite pastime," he reveals, "is to wander through the fields and forests that surround my home. Whenever I encounter a change in the composition of the forest, such as a dense stand of hemlock abutting an older stand of beech and sugar maple, I am compelled to solve the mystery: What created this change in vegetation?" As a landscape ecologist, he knows that "in the majority of cases, these changes will be the result of different forest disturbance histories," including abandonment of cultivated fields and pasturelands, logging, fire, and introduced forest blights, as well as other factors such as blowdowns and beaver dams. Knowing what kinds and combinations of plants to look for constitutes a metaphorical if not actual "language" to Wessels, "one that I could apply to reading the story of a landscape the way I apply English to the reading of a book."[115] The

Natural Landscapes, Cultural Regions

composition of plant communities in any climatic region is a function of three variables: topography, substrate or soil, and disturbance history, and as disturbance varies by far to the greatest degree over the central New England region that Wessels focuses on, it emerges as the primary author of the text that he explicates; thus he concludes that the forested landscape, its green and primeval appearance aside, is fundamentally "an interactive narrative that involves humans and nature."[116]

Environmental historians like Cronon, then, account for the ways in which humans have entered North American environments and sculpted them into new built worlds of their own design; historical ecologists and landscape ecologists like Sanford and Wessels demonstrate that even those parts of the landscape that we would conventionally describe as "natural" are also shaped by cultural activity — and, moreover, that the process of their shaping is inherent in their form, available for reading by those who know the code. While we must rely on language to convey to others the historical process implicit in any natural place, the story that we tell or write is not a projection of our own minds, not a wished-for echo of our own voices. This ecological, bioregional view does not impose history and narrative on the landscape — it discerns the history that is already there, constructs temporal sequence from the clues and materials at hand. It elicits the narrative implicit in the place — if not narrative in a linguistic or tightly, compellingly plotted sense, then at least narrative in the sense of one thing leading to another: the congeries of formative events that lie behind a landscape as it exists in the present. This strikes me as far different from the kind of translating that a Robert Finch claims to do while listening to stones, which may amount to little more than mistaking an echo for an original response. Interpreting places as artifacts for the historical processes that went into their making allows for a deeper understanding of those places, a richer sense of just what it is that we're looking at when we're looking at nature. Before representing nature, we can first let it represent itself, entwining narratives together rather than using nature mainly as material for stories of our own. As John Elder says of the stone walls and old stumps that he finds in his local patch of New England woods, "Such relics insist that this wilderness is no stable phenomenon beyond the human grasp but, rather, a bundle of stories."[117] We should listen to those stories.

For in the end, the two kinds of narratives, that of the tall green tree and that of the hewn stump, go inevitably together. For that reason, despite my having qualified William Cronon's discussion of nature, history, and narrative by trying to shine a new kind of light on each one of those terms, I bring him back on stage here at the end because I agree with him when he says that "historical storytelling helps keep us morally engaged with the world by showing us how to care about it and its origins in ways we had not done before," and that "narratives remain our chief moral compass in the world."[118] While I've tried to argue that places contain their own implicit narratives independently of a writer's or storyteller's experience in that place or a historian's imposition of a plot and a moral, the fact remains that humans are an important motive force in those narratives, causing disturbance, deflecting growth and development, setting fundamental conditions determining how nature's narratives ultimately unfold. If nature is a text from which we might elicit a narrative, that text is a landscape's personal history, a tale of "How I got that way," with episodes of that story inscribed in the shape of the land, the makeup of the plant community, the paths that water takes, the presence of new biotic characters and the absence of old ones.

If nature is historical, though, that history is one that is linked inextricably with our own, with choices we have made and acts we have performed. My point, then, is not that landscapes carry within them a kind of separate, parallel history to those that people inscribe upon them, a narrative of development that has little to do with the observations of nature writers and might justify us in seeing "nature" as a realm largely separate from the airy formulations of "culture." Rather, seeing nature as historical and artifactual puts us into nature's narrative instead of co-opting nature into ours, and as such, may actually increase moral obligation beyond what we might feel if we see natural places mainly as timeless, wild realms of aesthetic delight and spiritual regeneration and defend them on those grounds alone. If attending to the ways that places represent themselves materially and artifactually reminds us that our actions have irreversible consequences in the natural world, that the things we do today will live on into the future, then our responsibility for that future becomes that much more acute. If nature tells stories, we humans still play a big part in dictating the plots — and therefore have a lot to say about how the stories will end. If they end at all, that is; perhaps it's more accurate to say that the stories are still being written, will always take new twists and turns. And if we need help in figuring out how to keep those ongoing stories from becoming tragedies, particularly that Shakespearean kind where almost everyone dies in the end, then perhaps the best guidance we can find is in the landscapes that surround us every day: our back yards, our workplaces, our abandoned scenes, the woods we choose for our favorite walks. As I've tried to suggest throughout this book, places have valuable lessons to teach us if we can set aside our own words aside long enough to pay attention. The trees in those woods tell fascinating and valuable stories even before they get turned into books.

NOTES

1. BIG TREES AND BACK YARDS

1. Robert Michael Pyle, *The Thunder Tree: Lessons from an Urban Wildland* (Boston: Houghton Mifflin, 1993), xv–xvi; emphasis in original.

2. Michael Pollan, *Second Nature: A Gardener's Education* (New York: Delta, 1991), 74.

3. Gary Paul Nabhan and Stephen Trimble, preface to *The Geography of Childhood: Why Children Need Wild Places* (Boston: Beacon, 1994), ix; emphasis in original.

4. Gary Paul Nabhan, "A Child's Sense of Wildness," in Nabhan and Trimble, 7.

5. Nabhan, 12.

6. See his essay "The Trouble with Wilderness; or, Getting Back to the Wrong Nature," in *Uncommon Ground: Rethinking the Human Place in Nature*, ed. William Cronon (New York: Norton, 1995), 69–90.

7. Bill McKibben, *The End of Nature* (New York: Anchor, 1989), 47–48.

8. Meredith Goad, "Ice Storm's Legacy: Renaissance in Maine's Woods," *Portland (Maine) Press Herald*, 30 March 1998, pp. 1A, 4A.

9. Mark Twain, *A Tramp Abroad*, ed. Robert Gray Bruce and Hamlin Hill (New York: Penguin, 1997), 294.

10. Daniel Botkin, *Discordant Harmonies: A New Ecology for the Twenty-First Century* (New York: Oxford University Press, 1990), 61–62. See also E. C. Pielou, *After the Ice Age: The Return of Life to Glaciated North America* (Chicago: University of Chicago Press, 1991), 81–103.

11. Mark Klett, "Rephotographing Nineteenth-Century Landscapes," in Mark Klett et al., *Second View: The Rephotographic Survey Project* (Albuquerque: University of New Mexico Press, 1984), 37.

12. JoAnn Verburg, "Between Exposures," in Klett et al., 5.

13. Peter Goin, C. Elizabeth Raymond, and Robert E. Blesse, *Stopping Time: A Rephotographic Survey of Lake Tahoe* (Albuquerque: University of New Mexico Press, 1992).

14. Thomas R. Vale and Geraldine R. Vale, *U.S. 40 Today: Thirty Years of Landscape Change in America* (Madison: University of Wisconsin Press, 1983).

15. Donald L. Baars, Rex C. Buchanan, and John R. Charlton, *The Canyon Revisited: A Rephotography of the Grand Canyon, 1923/1991* (Salt Lake City: University of Utah Press, 1994), 2.

16. Readers who are interested in rephotography and the kinds of questions it raises about ecology, landscape change, and historical interpretation may also want to look at the following western rephotographic projects: Allen A. Dutton and Diane T. Bunting, *Arizona Then and Now: A Comprehensive Rephotographic Project* (Phoenix: Ag² Press, 1981); James Rodney Hastings and Raymond M. Turner, *The Changing Mile: An Ecological Study of Vegetation Change with Time in the Lower Mile of an Arid and Semiarid Region* (Tucson: University of Arizona Press, 1965); Garry F. Rogers, *Then and Now: A Photographic History of Vegetation Change in the Central Great Basin Desert* (Salt Lake City: University of Utah Press, 1982); Thomas T. Veblen and Diane C. Lorenz, *The Colorado Front Range: A Century of Ecological Change* (Salt Lake City: University of Utah Press, 1991); Hal G. Stephens and Eugene M. Shoemaker, *In the Footsteps of John Wesley Powell: An Album of Comparative Photographs of the Green and Colorado Rivers, 1871–72 and 1968* (Boulder, Colo.: Johnson Books, and Denver: The Powell Society, 1987); and Robert H. Webb, *Grand Canyon, a Century of Change: Rephotography of the 1889–90 Stanton Expedition* (Tucson: University of Arizona Press, 1996).

The first four of these books, as their titles indicate, concentrate on documenting and analyzing vegetation change in certain western landscapes from the late nineteenth or early twentieth centuries to the present, focusing primarily on scientific and landscape-management questions rather than historical or cultural concerns. They consist primarily of rephotographic pairs with some brief description or discussion of the change that they reveal; this change is generally attributed to anthropogenic causes—primarily grazing, logging, intentional or accidental fires, or the more recent suppression of those activities and subsequent regeneration of forest cover—or to variations in local climate from the past to the present, or to some combination of the two based on the location and land-use history of particular sites. The last two books are based on photographs taken on two nineteenth-century expeditions down the Colorado River through the Grand Canyon, and thus literally cover the same territory as Baars, Buchanan, and Charlton's book. Stephens and Shoemaker offer an album of rephotographs of pictures taken on Major John Wesley Powell's second expedition down the Green and Colorado Rivers; while the authors mention the contemporary presence of dams on these rivers (not only the Glen Canyon Dam, but the Flaming Gorge Dam on the Green River in Utah), their interpretive focus is not on dam-caused change but on the geomorphology of the riverine and canyon landscapes. Robert Webb retraces Robert Brewster Stanton's 1889–90 expedition to survey a possible railroad route through the Grand Canyon, using photographs taken on that trip as a primary source for writing what he calls "the rudiments of an environmental history of Grand

Canyon" (xix). Webb uses his photographic pairs to assess and discuss not only the specific effects of the Glen Canyon Dam and other human-caused phenomena, such as grazing by wild burros that were originally introduced into the Grand Canyon as work animals, but also the nonanthropogenic geological and botanical processes that the rephotographs reveal. Webb's book is thus much more than a photo album, and while he takes full account of the large extent to which the damming of the Colorado has changed the riverside landscape of the Grand Canyon, and echoes Baars and Buchanan's assessment of the scale and impact of that change when he says that "wilderness is almost an abstract concept between the rims" (209), his larger perspective on the long-term geological and botanical consistency that he finds within the scenes that Stanton's expedition photographed allows him to conclude that, even in the face of all these alterations, "fundamentally the canyon is little changed" (205).

17. Baars et al., 31.

18. Baars et al., 9.

19. Baars et al., 3.

20. Baars et al., 9.

21. For a good brief discussion of how the Grand Canyon came to be seen and interpreted in this and other culturally sanctioned ways, see Stephen J. Pyne, *How the Canyon Became Grand: A Short History* (New York: Viking, 1998). As Pyne puts it, "The Grand Canyon was not so much revealed as created. . . . Once endowed with significance, like a rough diamond cut and placed under light, it dazzled, and America declared it beyond price" (xiii–xiv).

22. "Flooding the Colorado River," *Geotimes* 41 (August 1996): 6.

23. Gregory McNamee, "After the Flood," *Audubon* 98 (September–October 1996): 22.

24. McNamee, 22.

25. Tina Adler, "Healing Waters: Flooding Rivers to Repent for Damage Done by Dams," *Science News* 150 (21 September 1996): 189.

26. Michael P. Collier, Robert H. Webb, and Edmund D. Andrews, "Experimental Flooding in the Grand Canyon," *Scientific American* 276 (January 1997): 88.

27. Conrad Joseph Bahre, *A Legacy of Change: Historic Human Impact on Vegetation in the Arizona Borderlands* (Tucson: University of Arizona Press, 1991), 187.

28. Bahre, 15. Robert R. Humphrey reaches similar conclusions about the reasons behind the changes in ground cover in his *Ninety Years and Five Hundred Thirty-Five Miles: Vegetation Changes along the Mexican Border* (Albuquerque: University of New Mexico Press, 1987), in which he rephotographs the monuments that had been placed along the border with Mexico from the Rio Grande to the Pacific in the late nineteenth century and interprets the landscape changes that the paired pictures reveal.

29. In addition to other sources mentioned in this section, Norman L.

Christensen's article "Landscape History and Ecological Change," *Journal of Forest History* 33 (1989): 116–24, was particularly helpful in allowing me to understand both the evolution of ecology as a discipline and the increasingly historical sensibility that the field has exhibited in recent years.

30. See, for example, Donald Worster's chapter entitled "Clements and the Climax Community" in his *Nature's Economy: A History of Ecological Ideas*, 2d ed. (Cambridge: Cambridge University Press, 1994), 205–20.

31. As Christensen puts it, a Clementsian approach "suggests that historical effects are eventually erased by succession and that the structure and composition of relatively late successional ecosystems may contain little information about their past history. To the ecologist, it also indicates that if one simply waits long enough, historical events and patterns of past disturbance will become relatively unimportant" (118).

32. George Perkins Marsh, *Man and Nature*, ed. David Lowenthal (Cambridge, Mass.: Harvard University Press, Belknap Press, 1965), 29.

33. Marsh, 35.

34. Marsh, 36–37.

35. S. T. A. Pickett and Richard S. Ostfeld, "The Shifting Paradigm in Ecology," in *A New Century for Natural Resources Management*, ed. Richard L. Knight and Sarah F. Bates (Washington, D.C.: Island Press, 1995), 263.

36. Alice E. Ingerson, "Tracking and Testing the Nature-Culture Dichotomy," in *Historical Ecology: Cultural Knowledge and Changing Landscapes*, ed. Carole L. Crumley (Santa Fe, N. Mex.: School of American Research Press, 1994), 63, 44.

37. Pickett and Ostfeld, 266; emphasis in original.

38. Botkin, 62.

39. Christensen, 119.

40. Ingerson, 45, 57.

41. Botkin, 53.

42. Emily W. B. Russell, *People and the Land through Time: Linking Ecology and History* (New Haven, Conn.: Yale University Press, 1997), 3–4.

43. William M. Denevan, "The Pristine Myth: The Landscape of the Americas in 1492," *Annals of the Association of American Geographers* 82 (1992): 370.

44. Richard White, *Land Use, Environment, and Social Change: The Shaping of Island County, Washington* (Seattle: University of Washington Press, 1992), 25.

45. See Alfred W. Crosby, *Ecological Imperialism: The Biological Expansion of Europe, 900–1900* (Cambridge: Cambridge University Press, 1986), 2–7.

46. See, for example, Daniel W. Gade, "Weeds in Vermont as Tokens of Socioeconomic Change," *Geographical Review* 81 (1991): 153–69. Gade concludes his article by noting that "like barns or houses, weeds are signifiers of human migration, technology, and livelihood," and that "even the most commonplace

natural phenomena offer unexpected ways to elucidate the culture-nature dialectic" (166).

47. Michael Williams, *Americans and Their Forests: A Historical Geography* (Cambridge: Cambridge University Press, 1989).

48. Gordon G. Whitney, *From Coastal Wilderness to Fruited Plain: A History of Environmental Change in Temperate North America from 1500 to the Present* (Cambridge: Cambridge University Press, 1994), 2.

49. William Cronon, *Changes in the Land: Indians, Colonists, and the Ecology of New England* (New York: Hill and Wang, 1983), 15, 13.

50. See Cronon, *Changes in the Land*, and White above; Timothy Silver, *A New Face on the Countryside: Indians, Colonists, and Slaves in South Atlantic Forests, 1500–1800* (Cambridge: Cambridge University Press, 1990); Jack Temple Kirby, *Poquosin: A Study of Rural Landscape and Society* (Chapel Hill: University of North Carolina Press, 1995); Dan Flores, *Horizontal Yellow: Nature and History in the Near Southwest* (Albuquerque: University of New Mexico Press, 1999).

51. Stanley W. Trimble, "The Alcovy River Swamps: The Result of Culturally Accelerated Sedimentation," in *The American Environment: Interpretations of Past Geographies*, ed. Lary M. Dilsaver and Craig E. Colten (Lanham, Md.: Rowman and Littlefield, 1992), 29.

52. See, for example, Bruce J. Weaver, "'What to Do with the Mountain People?': The Darker Side of the Successful Campaign to Establish the Great Smoky Mountains National Park," in *The Symbolic Earth: Discourse and Our Creation of the Environment*, ed. James G. Cantrill and Christine L. Oravec (Lexington: University Press of Kentucky, 1996), 151–75; Ethan Carr, *Wilderness by Design: Landscape Architecture and the National Park Service* (Lincoln: University of Nebraska Press, 1998); Linda Flint McClelland, *Building the National Parks: Historic Landscape Design and Construction* (Baltimore: Johns Hopkins University Press, 1998); Richard West Sellars, *Preserving Nature in the National Parks: A History* (New Haven, Conn.: Yale University Press, 1997); Mark David Spence, *Dispossessing the Wilderness: Indian Removal and the Making of the National Parks* (New York: Oxford University Press, 1999).

53. Christensen, 116.

54. Joan Iverson Nassauer, "Culture and Landscape Ecology: Insights for Action," in *Placing Nature: Culture and Landscape Ecology*, ed. Nassauer (Washington, D.C.: Island Press, 1997), 4.

55. Whitney, 335.

56. William Cronon, foreword to the paperback edition, in *Uncommon Ground*, ed. Cronon, 21–22.

57. Botkin, 188–89.

58. See Joan Iverson Nassauer, "Cultural Sustainability: Aligning Aesthetics and Ecology," in *Placing Nature*, ed. Nassauer, 65–83.

1. Lawrence Buell, *The Environmental Imagination: Thoreau, Nature Writing, and the Formation of American Culture* (Cambridge, Mass.: Harvard University Press, 1995), 2.

2. Scott Slovic, *Seeking Awareness in American Nature Writing* (Salt Lake City: University of Utah Press, 1992), 3, 6.

3. Henry David Thoreau, "Walking," in *The Natural History Essays*, ed. Robert Sattelmeyer (Salt Lake City: Gibbs Smith, 1980), 101.

4. Barry Lopez, *Arctic Dreams: Imagination and Desire in a Northern Landscape* (New York: Bantam, 1987), 362–63.

5. Sharon Cameron, *Writing Nature: Henry Thoreau's "Journal"* (New York: Oxford University Press, 1985), 103.

6. Cameron, 47–48.

7. Paul Brooks, *Speaking for Nature: How Literary Naturalists from Henry Thoreau to Rachel Carson Have Shaped America* (Boston: Houghton Mifflin, 1980).

8. Stephen Trimble, introduction to *Words from the Land: Encounters with Natural History Writing*, ed. Stephen Trimble (Salt Lake City: Gibbs Smith, 1989), 2.

9. Sherman Paul, *For Love of the World: Essays on Nature Writers* (Iowa City: University of Iowa Press, 1992), vii.

10. Slovic, 17–18.

11. Neil Evernden, in *The Social Creation of Nature* (Baltimore: Johns Hopkins University Press, 1992), has traced the emergence and development in Western humanistic thought, perception, and philosophy of a growing dualism, an "increasingly strict division between human and nature" (87). To Evernden, the story of how the Western mind has defined and constructed the concept of nature is one of "an ever-deepening sense of separation between the human subject and the surrounding field of natural objects" (102), a separation that helps explain—and, in his view, may have helped cause—current environmental problems: "Unless we have this absolute separation," comments Evernden, "we cannot claim unique qualities that justify our domination of the earth" (96). Thus, ironically, environmental degradation and the literary description and observation of nature may share a similarly dualistic stance. Still, the ways of thinking and seeing that Evernden describes and traces provide an additional, general backdrop to the discussion of American environmental writing in this essay. In talking about the development of postmedieval European art, for instance, he notes that "once it is accepted that the reality of Nature is devoid of patently human involvement, then what will be discerned as most truthful is that which appears free of human content and authorship" (73)—a statement that, broadly speaking, applies to much American nature writing as well.

12. The environs of Thoreau's house at Walden Pond were similarly strewn with evidence of past habitation—"These cellar dents, like deserted fox bur-

rows, old holes, are all that is left where once were the stir and bustle of human life," he notes at one point in *Walden* (ed. Michael Meyer [New York: Penguin, 1983], 310)—but, as Robert Sattelmeyer has pointed out, Thoreau deliberately obscures this aspect of the Walden landscape. The remote forest pond that Thoreau portrays is a self-conscious literary construction that ignores the fact that, by 1850, the town of Concord had been a busy site of commerce and agriculture for 200 years and was only about 10 percent forested; it is, in fact, much more forested today than it was in Thoreau's time, and thus may conform more closely in 2001 to Thoreau's depiction than it did when Thoreau was actually writing. Thoreau's cabin was itself surrounded by fields, woodlots, and second-growth forest, as well as by the cellar holes and overgrown orchards of a small past settlement of ex-slaves, petty artisans, drunkards, and other seeming outcasts from Concord society. Thoreau describes this abandoned landscape in half of the short "Former Inhabitants and Winter Visitors" chapter of *Walden*, but otherwise leaves most evidence of local settlement and past and present landscape use out of his book, describing instead a largely unspoiled landscape much more in keeping with the goals of his literary project. Literary critics have subsequently joined Thoreau in his effort to keep nature separate from culture; according to Sattelmeyer, the "Former Inhabitants" chapter has never attracted much critical commentary. Sattelmeyer made these points in a paper entitled "*Walden* and the Depopulation of New England," which he delivered at the Modern Language Association of America convention in Chicago on December 29, 1995, and I thank him here for having taken the time to confirm my redaction of the substance of his talk. For more on the agricultural landscape of Concord in Thoreau's time, see Robert A. Gross, "Culture and Cultivation: Agriculture and Society in Thoreau's Concord," *Journal of American History* 69 (1982): 42–61, and David R. Foster, *Thoreau's Country: Journey through a Transformed Landscape* (Cambridge, Mass.: Harvard University Press, 1999).

13. For a good journalistic discussion of the de- and reforestation of New England, as well as of the current debate over the Northern Forest's health and proper use, see Bill McKibben, *Hope, Human and Wild: True Stories of Living Lightly on the Earth* (Boston: Little, Brown, 1995), 7–55; on New England's deforestation in colonial times, see Cronon, *Changes in the Land*, 108–26. In contrast to modern environmentalist interpretations, John Stilgoe, in *Metropolitan Corridor: Railroads and the American Scene* (New Haven, Conn.: Yale University Press, 1983), has pointed out that far from seeing the abandonment and reforestation of rural New England as some sort of ecological triumph, many commentators in the late nineteenth and early twentieth centuries viewed it as a cultural defeat, as evidence of the region's spiritual as well as economic decay. In their writings, "the meaning of environmental representation" was "clearly presented: industrious, thrifty, moral people create and maintain neat fields, straight walls, and snug houses in the face of wilderness, winter storms, and the temptations of the

Devil—only lazy good-for-nothings abandon land shaped by their righteous ancestors and succumb to temptation" (325). Despite the return of the tangled forest to the ordered human spaces from which it had been banished, the sharp conceptual border between nature and culture was firmly maintained and policed—at least in the minds and writings of outside observers.

14. Cronon, *Changes in the Land*, 153.

15. Recent books concerning the Northern Forest debate include Mitch Lansky, *Beyond the Beauty Strip: Saving What's Left of Our Forests* (Gardiner, Maine: Tilbury House, 1992), a polemic; Christopher McGrory Klyza and Stephen C. Trombulak, *The Future of the Northern Forest* (Hanover, N.H.: University Press of New England, 1994), a forum including scholars, activists, and representatives of the logging industry; and David Dobbs and Richard Ober, *The Northern Forest* (White River Junction, Vt.: Chelsea Green, 1995), a journalistic account. For a discussion of the on-the-ground practice of logging in Maine, as well as the industry's increased reliance on clear-cutting in the late 1970s and 1980s, see two pieces by Bret Wallach: "Logging in Maine's Empty Quarter," *Annals of the Association of American Geographers* 70 (1980): 542–52, and *At Odds with Progress: Americans and Conservation* (Tucson: University of Arizona Press, 1991), 27–43.

16. Dobbs and Ober, xiii, xxvi.

17. Dobbs and Ober, 32.

18. Simon J. Bronner, "The Processual Principle in Folk Art, Based on a Study of Wooden Chain Carving," *Folk Life* 22 (1984): 60, 65.

19. John Michael Vlach, "The Concept of Community and Folklife Study," in *American Material Culture and Folklife: A Prologue and Dialogue*, ed. Simon J. Bronner (Logan: Utah State University Press, 1992), 63, 68.

20. Erika Brady, "Mankind's Thumb on Nature's Scale: Trapping and Regional Identity in the Missouri Ozarks," in *Sense of Place: American Regional Cultures*, ed. Barbara Allen and Thomas J. Schlereth (Lexington: University Press of Kentucky, 1990), 69, 70, 72, 64.

21. Mary T. Hufford, "Telling the Landscape: Folklife Expressions and Sense of Place," in *Pinelands Folklife*, ed. Rita Zorn Moonsammy, David Steven Cohen, and Lorraine E. Williams (New Brunswick, N.J.: Rutgers University Press, 1987), 19, 16.

22. Hufford, 30, 32.

23. Slovic, 169.

24. Robert Finch and John Elder, introduction to *The Norton Book of Nature Writing*, ed. Robert Finch and John Elder (New York: Norton, 1990), 22, 23.

25. Robert Finch, "What the Stones Said," in *The Norton Book of Nature Writing*, ed. Finch and Elder, 807, 810.

26. William Bradford, *Of Plymouth Plantation, 1620–1647* (New York: Modern Library, 1981), 70.

27. Robert Finch and Terry Tempest Williams, "Dialogue Two: Landscape,

People, and Place," in *Writing Natural History: Dialogues with Authors*, ed. Edward Lueders (Salt Lake City: University of Utah Press, 1989), 56.

28. Finch and Williams, 57.

29. Finch and Williams, 47.

30. Robert Finch, *The Primal Place* (New York: Norton, 1983), 79.

31. Finch, *Primal Place*, 160.

32. Finch, *Primal Place*, 184.

33. See, for example, these recent articles on McPhee: Thomas C. Bailey, "John McPhee: The Making of a Meta-Naturalist," in *Earthly Words: Essays on Contemporary American Nature and Environmental Writers*, ed. John Cooley (Ann Arbor: University of Michigan Press, 1994), 195–213; Joan Hamilton, "An Encounter with John McPhee," *Sierra* (May–June 1990): 50ff.; James Stull, "Self and the Performance of Others: The Pastoral Vision of John McPhee," *North Dakota Quarterly* 59 (1991): 182–200; Philip G. Terrie, "River of Paradox; John McPhee's 'The Encircled River,'" *Western American Literature* 23 (1988): 3–15; and Brian Turner, "Giving Good Reasons: Environmental Appeals in the Nonfiction of John McPhee," *Rhetoric Review* 13 (1994): 164–67.

34. David Espey, "The Wilds of New Jersey: John McPhee as Travel Writer," in *Temperamental Journeys: Essays on the Modern Literature of Travel*, ed. Michael Kowalewski (Athens: University of Georgia Press, 1992), 165.

35. Espey, 166, 174.

36. Espey, 173.

37. Quoted in Trimble, 4.

38. John McPhee, "North of the C. P. Line," in *Table of Contents* (New York: Farrar, Straus and Giroux, 1985), 249–93.

39. Espey, 167, 166.

40. John McPhee, *The Pine Barrens* (New York: Farrar, Straus Giroux, 1968), 4. Further references to this volume will be made parenthetically in the text.

41. McKibben, *Hope, Human and Wild*, 14.

42. John Elder, *Reading the Mountains of Home* (Cambridge, Mass.: Harvard University Press, 1998), 82.

43. Glen A. Love, "Revaluing Nature: Toward an Ecological Criticism," *Western American Literature* 25 (1990): 209.

44. Gretel Ehrlich, *The Solace of Open Spaces* (New York: Penguin, 1985), ix. Further references to this volume will be made parenthetically in the text.

3. SEA GREEN

1. Wallace Stevens, "The Idea of Order at Key West," in *The Palm at the End of the Mind: Selected Poems and a Play*, ed. Holly Stevens (New York: Vintage, 1972), 97–98.

2. Eric Zencey, *Virgin Forest: Meditations on History, Ecology, and Culture* (Athens: University of Georgia Press, 1998), 113.

3. Zencey, 118.

4. Cheryll Glotfelty, "Introduction: Literary Studies in an Age of Environmental Crisis," in *The Ecocriticism Reader: Landmarks in Literary Ecology*, ed. Cheryll Glotfelty and Harold Fromm (Athens: University of Georgia Press, 1996), xviii.

5. Glotfelty, xix.

6. Glotfelty, xix.

7. Love, 205–206.

8. Love, 209.

9. Love, 202, 213.

10. In so doing, I join a group of other scholars, many of them associated with the Association for the Study of Literature and Environment (ASLE), who are also working to expand the range of texts and genres that can be fruitfully studied through ecocritical approaches, as well as to examine settings and environments that readers tend not to take into account when they think about "nature writing." See two recent collections of critical essays: *The Nature of Cities: Ecocriticism and Urban Environments*, ed. Michael Bennett and David W. Teague (Tucson: University of Arizona Press, 1999), and *Beyond Nature Writing: Expanding the Boundaries of Ecocriticism*, ed. Karla Armbruster and Kathleen R. Wallace (Charlottesville: University Press of Virginia, 2001).

11. Aldo Leopold, "The Land Ethic," in *A Sand County Almanac and Sketches Here and There* (New York: Oxford University Press, 1949), 224–25, 204.

12. Richard White, "'Are You an Environmentalist or Do You Work for a Living?': Work and Nature," in *Uncommon Ground*, ed. Cronon, 172.

13. White, 172.

14. White, 174.

15. White, 172.

16. White, 181.

17. Dobbs and Ober, 109.

18. Dobbs and Ober, 119.

19. John Casey, *Spartina* (New York: Knopf, 1989), 47. Further references to this volume will be made parenthetically in the text.

20. Ruth Moore, *Candlemas Bay* (1950; reprint, Nobleboro, Maine: Blackberry, 1994), 5. Further references to this volume will be made parenthetically in the text.

21. For a brief biographical sketch of Moore, see Sanford Phippen's introduction to *High Clouds Soaring, Storms Driving Low: The Letters of Ruth Moore*, ed. Sanford Phippen (Nobleboro, Maine: Blackberry, 1993).

22. Ruth Moore, *The Weir* (1943; reprint, Nobleboro, Maine: Blackberry,

1986), 66. Further references to this volume will be made parenthetically in the text.

23. "Mainers Dispute Lobster Warnings," *Portland (Maine) Press Herald*, 29 April 1998, p. 1A.

24. William Cronon elaborates on this idea in his essay "The Trouble with Wilderness; or, Getting Back to the Wrong Nature," in *Uncommon Ground*, ed. Cronon, 69–90.

25. "Lobster Warning Ignored at the Peril of Resource," *Maine Sunday Telegram* (Portland), 3 May 1998, p. 4C.

4. "A LABYRINTH OF ERRORS"

1. Wendell Berry, *Remembering* (San Francisco: North Point Press, 1988), 102.

2. John McPhee, *The Survival of the Bark Canoe* (New York: Farrar, Straus and Giroux, 1975), 36.

3. Buell, 276.

4. Henry David Thoreau, *Walden and Civil Disobedience*, ed. Michael Meyer (New York: Penguin, 1983), 60. Further references to this volume will be made parenthetically in the text.

5. Walter Harding, *The Days of Henry Thoreau* (New York: Knopf, 1970), 83.

6. Harding, 235.

7. Harding, 275–76.

8. Henry D. Thoreau, *Journal, Volume 4: 1851–1852*, ed. Robert Sattelmeyer, Leonard N. Neufeldt, and Nancy Craig Simmons (Princeton, N.J.: Princeton University Press, 1992), 191–93.

9. Thoreau, *Journal, Volume 4*, 195.

10. Thoreau, *Journal, Volume 4*, 201–202.

11. Quoted in Harding, 276.

12. Quoted in Harding, 325.

13. Quoted in William Howarth, *The Book of Concord: Thoreau's Life as a Writer* (New York: Viking, 1982), 173.

14. Henry D. Thoreau, *The Journal of Henry D. Thoreau*, ed. Bradford Torrey and Francis H. Allen (Boston: Houghton Mifflin, 1906; reprint, New York: Dover, 1962), 1240.

15. I owe a great debt here to Robert F. Stowell and William L. Howarth for their having put together *A Thoreau Gazetteer* (Princeton, N.J.: Princeton University Press, 1970), which brings together images of the various maps that Thoreau drew or consulted in connection with *Walden*, *The Maine Woods*, and his other works, as well as various comments that he made about maps in his journal and published writings. I've included many of these comments here in this

chapter, and am grateful to Messrs. Stowell and Howarth for doing the legwork and bringing them to easy notice, as well as for compiling a fascinating reference work. Their book includes images of many of the Thoreau-related maps that I have referred to but not reproduced in this chapter, and readers may consult them there if they like.

16. Stowell and Howarth, 2.

17. Stowell and Howarth, 25.

18. Henry David Thoreau, *A Yankee in Canada, with Anti-Slavery and Reform Papers* (1892; reprint, New York: Greenwood, 1969), 88. Stowell and Howarth include an image of a later version of the map that Thoreau copied in *A Thoreau Gazetteer*, 28.

19. Henry David Thoreau, *Cape Cod* (Orleans, Mass.: Parnassus, 1984), 267. Further references to this volume will be made parenthetically in the text.

20. Thoreau, *Journal of Henry D. Thoreau*, 1721.

21. Howarth, 173–74.

22. Henry D. Thoreau, *The Maine Woods*, ed. Joseph J. Moldenhauer (Princeton, N.J.: Princeton University Press, 1972), 15. Further references to this volume will be made parenthetically in the text.

23. Stowell and Howarth, 15.

24. For more on the process by which early maps of Maine were compiled, see Susan L. Danforth, "The First Official Maps of Maine and Massachusetts," *Imago Mundi* 35 (1983): 37–57.

25. Theodore Steinberg, *Slide Mountain; or, the Folly of Owning Nature* (Berkeley: University of California Press, 1995), 18.

26. For a good and lively discussion of this and other questions about Thoreau's trip to Katahdin, see Ian Marshall, *Story Line: Exploring the Literature of the Appalachian Trail* (Charlottesville: University Press of Virginia, 1998), 226–49. As to the nineteenth-century conventionality of Thoreau's responses and reactions to the mountain's upper reaches, William Cronon asserts that "this is surely not the way a modern backpacker or nature lover would describe Maine's most famous mountain, but that is because Thoreau's description owes as much to Wordsworth and other romantic contemporaries as to the rocks and clouds of Katahdin itself." See Cronon, "The Trouble with Wilderness," 75.

27. Wallace Stevens, "Anecdote of the Jar," in *The Palm at the End of the Mind*, 46.

28. Quoted in Joseph J. Moldenhauer, afterword to Thoreau, *Maine Woods*, 363.

29. McPhee, *Survival of the Bark Canoe*, 37.

30. McPhee, *Survival of the Bark Canoe*, 39.

31. McPhee, *Survival of the Bark Canoe*, 108.

1. Thoreau, *Maine Woods*, 42.

2. Thomas Hubka, "Just Folks Designing: Vernacular Designers and the Generation of Form," in *Common Places: Readings in American Vernacular Architecture*, ed. Dell Upton and John Michael Vlach (Athens: University of Georgia Press, 1986), 429.

3. Thomas C. Hubka, *Big House, Little House, Back House, Barn: The Connected Farm Buildings of New England* (Hanover, N.H.: University Press of New England, 1984), 82–83.

4. Hubka, *Big House*, 144.

5. Stewart G. McHenry, "Eighteenth-Century Field Patterns as Vernacular Art," in *Common Places*, ed. Upton and Vlach, 107.

6. McHenry, 122.

7. John Michael Vlach, "The Concept of Community and Folklife Study," in *American Material Culture and Folklife: A Prologue and Dialogue*, ed. Simon J. Bronner (Logan: Utah State University Press, 1992), 65.

8. For more on the nature and significance of folk art, I find the writings of Henry Glassie to be particularly evocative and insightful. See, for example, the following essays: "Folk Art," in *Folklore and Folklife: An Introduction*, ed. Richard M. Dorson (Chicago: University of Chicago Press, 1972), 253–80; "The Idea of Folk Art," in *Folk Art and Art Worlds*, ed. John Michael Vlach and Simon J. Bronner (Logan: Utah State University Press, 1992), 269–74; "Meaningful Things and Appropriate Myths: The Artifact's Place in American Studies," in *Material Life in America, 1600–1860*, ed. Robert Blair St. George (Boston: Northeastern University Press, 1988), 63–92; and "Artifact and Culture, Architecture and Society," in *American Material Culture and Folklife: A Prologue and Dialogue*, ed. Simon J. Bronner (Logan: Utah State University Press, 1992), 47–62.

6. REDESIGNING THE RIVER

1. See the chapter on "The Canals" in William F. Robinson, *Abandoned New England: Its Ruins and Where to Find Them* (Boston: New York Graphic Society, 1976), 18–35; see also Ernest H. Knight, *A Guide to the Cumberland and Oxford Canal* (Cumberland and Oxford Canal Association, 1976).

2. Robinson, 190–91.

3. For a good and accessible scientific account of this hydrologic system, its various components, the physical qualities of water in its various states and stages, and the relationship of water to its environment, see E. C. Pielou, *Fresh Water* (Chicago: University of Chicago Press, 1998).

4. On the environmental effects of beavers and the ecological and historical dimensions of their one-time removal from much of the North American landscape, see Pielou, 136–38; Alice Outwater, *Water: A Natural History* (New York: Basic Books, 1996), 3–33; Carolyn Merchant, *Ecological Revolutions: Nature, Gender, and Science in New England* (Chapel Hill: University of North Carolina Press, 1989), 36–37, 61–66.

5. Outwater, xii. See also Pielou, 205–13.

6. Steinberg, 23.

7. Steinberg, 24, 38.

8. Steinberg, 53, 80–81.

9. Steinberg, 102.

10. Steinberg, 48.

11. Mark Twain, *Life on the Mississippi*, ed. James M. Cox (New York: Penguin, 1984), 205.

12. Twain, 205.

13. Twain, 206–207.

14. See Todd Shallat, *Structures in the Stream: Water, Science, and the Rise of the U.S. Army Corps of Engineers* (Austin: University of Texas Press, 1994), 144–48, 194–99.

15. John McPhee, *The Control of Nature* (New York: Farrar, Straus and Giroux, 1989), 5.

16. McPhee, *Control of Nature*, 6.

17. McPhee, *Control of Nature*, 6–7.

18. McPhee, *Control of Nature*, 7.

19. McPhee, *Control of Nature*, 31.

20. Richard White, *The Organic Machine: The Remaking of the Columbia River* (New York: Hill and Wang, 1995), 112.

21. Carol Sheriff explores this concept and its application to the Erie Canal in her *The Artificial River: The Erie Canal and the Paradox of Progress* (New York: Hill and Wang, 1996).

22. Ronald E. Shaw, *Canals for a Nation: The Canal Era in the United States, 1790–1860* (Lexington: University Press of Kentucky, 1990).

23. See Walter S. Sanderlin, *The Great National Project: A History of the Chesapeake and Ohio Canal* (Baltimore: Johns Hopkins University Press, 1946).

24. See Robinson, 18–35; Christopher Roberts, *The Middlesex Canal, 1793–1860* (Cambridge, Mass.: Harvard University Press, 1938); Mary Stetson Clarke, *The Old Middlesex Canal* (Melrose, Mass.: Hilltop Press, 1974).

25. The specific information throughout this chapter on the history, construction, dimensions, and working life of the Cumberland and Oxford Canal is drawn from the following sources: Robinson; Knight; Hayden L. V. Anderson, *Canals and Inland Waterways of Maine* (Portland: Maine Historical Society,

1982), 59–122; Harland Hall Carter, *A History of the Cumberland and Oxford Canal* (master's thesis, University of Maine, 1950).

26. See, for example, John R. Stilgoe, *Common Landscape of America, 1580 to 1845* (New Haven, Conn.: Yale University Press, 1982), 99–134.

27. Anderson, 86.

28. Maurice M. Whitten, *The Gunpowder Mills of Gorham, Maine* (Westbrook, Maine: Edwin Robertson, 1985), 35.

29. Maurice M. Whitten, *The Gunpowder Mills of Maine* (Gorham, Maine: M. M. Whitten, 1990), 41, 53.

30. Stilgoe, *Common Landscape of America*, 112. For additional information on early American turnpikes, along with a detailed discussion of specific examples, see Donald C. Jackson, "Roads Most Traveled: Turnpikes in Southeastern Pennsylvania in the Early Republic," in *Early American Technology: Making and Doing Things from the Colonial Era to 1850*, ed. Judith A. McGaw (Chapel Hill: University of North Carolina Press, 1994), 197–239. For a broader treatment of roads and turnpikes in the early nineteenth century, see George Rogers Taylor, *The Transportation Revolution, 1815–1860* (1951; reprint, New York: Harper and Row, 1968), 15–31.

31. See Anderson, 79–94.

32. Sheriff, 16.

33. Sheriff, 32.

34. Quoted in John Seelye, *Beautiful Machine: Rivers and the Republican Plan, 1755–1825* (New York: Oxford University Press, 1991), 254.

35. Quoted in Seelye, 261.

36. Stilgoe, *Common Landscape of America*, 108.

37. Seelye, 259.

38. See Philip I. Milliken, *Notes on the Cumberland and Oxford Canal and the Canal Bank* (Portland: n.p., 1971).

39. Barbara Novak, *Nature and Culture: American Landscape and Painting, 1825–1875* (New York: Oxford University Press, 1980), 169.

40. Novak, 171.

41. Angela Miller, *The Empire of the Eye: Landscape Representation and American Cultural Politics, 1825–1875* (Ithaca, N.Y.: Cornell University Press, 1993), 148–49.

42. Miller, 150.

43. Sheriff, 59.

44. Miller, 154, 5.

45. Miller, 160.

46. White, *Organic Machine*, ix.

47. Richard E. Winslow III, *The Piscataqua Gundalow: Workhorse for a Tidal Basin Empire* (Portsmouth, N.H.: Portsmouth Marine Society, 1983), 23.

48. White, "'Are You an Environmentalist or Do You Work for a Living?'" 172.

49. Peter Way, *Common Labour: Workers and the Digging of North American Canals, 1780–1860* (Cambridge: Cambridge University Press, 1993), 148.

50. Way, 161.

51. Robert C. Post, "Technology in Early America: A View from the 1990s," in *Early American Technology*, ed. McGaw, 25.

52. Nathaniel Hawthorne, "The Canal-Boat," one of his "Sketches from Memory," in *Nathaniel Hawthorne: Tales and Sketches*, ed. Roy Harvey Pearce (New York: Library of America, 1982), 351.

53. Hawthorne, 345.

54. Hawthorne, 350.

55. Way, 8.

56. See Robinson, 29–35; Taylor, 37–38.

7. NATURAL LANDSCAPES, CULTURAL REGIONS

1. William Wood, *New England's Prospect*, ed. Alden T. Vaughan (Amherst: University of Massachusetts Press, 1977), 38.

2. New York's modern-day boundary with Connecticut, Massachusetts, and Vermont actually represents a series of surveyed compromises between colonial land claims that were originally tied to natural features—specifically, the Connecticut and Hudson Rivers. As Dixon Ryan Fox outlines in his *Yankees and Yorkers* (New York: New York University Press, 1940), the Duke of York's 1664 charter for the new colony that England had recently taken over from the Netherlands extended New York's territorial jurisdiction east to the Connecticut River. New York never pressed this claim in Connecticut and Massachusetts, though, partly because the western sections of those colonies had already begun to be settled by that time and partly because both colonies had earlier been given charters that ran theoretically all the way to the Pacific Ocean. At the same time, Connecticut consistently and aggressively pushed its way westward, settling or claiming territory as far west as the Hudson in violation of a tacit assumption that New York held jurisdiction to at least twenty miles east of that river. The distinctive course of Connecticut's western boundary today is the eventual result of a 1683 agreement that kept the Yankee-settled towns in that state's southwestern extension within the Connecticut colony, a strip of land that reaches to within eight miles of the Hudson. After running northeast along those towns' landward borders and jogging back briefly to the northwest, the boundary line remains approximately twenty miles from the Hudson until it hits Massachusetts, with a long narrow triangle of land equivalent in area to Connecticut's southwestern extension having been added to New York by way of compensation (which ex-

plains why the border "leans" slightly northeast into Connecticut and doesn't match up exactly with the western boundary of its neighbor to the north).

Likewise, Massachusetts followed a similar pattern of establishing new towns on lands nominally held by New York, until in the late 1750s it was agreed that the boundary should run about twenty miles east of and roughly parallel to the Hudson, a line that was not actually finalized until 1787. New York had a clearer claim on what is now Vermont under the 1664 terms of the Duke of York's charter, but did little to establish settlements in the area. In the face of this vacuum, and seeing an opportunity to profit through land speculation and extend his colony's territory, New Hampshire Governor Benning Wentworth and others granted over 130 towns west of the Connecticut River in the 1750s and 1760s, making it practically impossible for New York to establish its own legal and spatial presence in those lands. Effectively shut out from its right to extend at least its northeasternmost boundary to the Connecticut River, New York withdrew its claims to jurisdiction in that area by 1790, and Vermont became a state the following year. While New York's original charter gave it a river for its eastern boundary, then, the countervailing territorial ambitions of three New England colonies led to the piecemeal establishment of New England's surveyed western border as we see it today; insofar as much of that border was set approximately twenty miles east of the Hudson, though, it still retains an implicit, if historically obscure, "natural" component.

3. Christopher McGrory Klyza, "Bioregional Possibilities in Vermont," in *Bioregionalism*, ed. Michael Vincent McGinnis (London: Routledge, 1999), 88.

4. Robert G. Bailey, *Ecoregions: The Ecosystem Geography of the Oceans and Continents* (New York: Springer, 1998), 2.

5. See Robert G. Bailey, *Description of the Ecoregions of the United States*, 2d ed., revised and enlarged (Washington, D.C.: U.S. Department of Agriculture, Forest Service, 1995). See also this Forest Service Web site, which includes maps of Bailey's ecoregional divisions:
<http://www.fs.fed.us/land/ecosysmgmt/ecoreg1_home.html>

6. Klyza, 96–97.

7. Dan Flores, "Place: An Argument for Bioregional History," *Environmental History Review* 18 (1994): 1–18. See also his *Horizontal Yellow*, 167–98.

8. Thanks to Fred Bridge of the Little Compton Historical Society for sending me a copy of this short, untitled article.

9. For a short biographical sketch of Sarah Wilbour, see Benjamin Franklin Wilbour, *Notes on Little Compton*, ed. Carlton C. Brownell (Little Compton, R.I.: Little Compton Historical Society, 1970), 102.

10. Sarah Soule Wilbour, diary entry, 24 June 1882, in Sarah Soule Wilbour diaries, 1882–1891 (Little Compton Historical Society, Little Compton, R.I.; transcribed by Sheila Mackintosh, 1993).

11. As Celia Betsky points out, for instance, "perhaps the most popular lit-

erary subject adopted by the colonial revival" was "the love affair between John Alden and Priscilla Mullins from Longfellow's *Courtship of Miles Standish*," with their story commemorated in objects placed in the New England kitchen exhibit at the 1876 Philadelphia Centennial Exposition, and with Priscilla in particular being featured in countless paintings and engravings in the 1870s and 1880s. See Betsky, "Inside the Past: The Interior and the Colonial Revival in American Art and Literature, 1860–1914," in *The Colonial Revival in America*, ed. Alan Axelrod (New York: Norton, 1985), 261.

12. For further discussion of the idea that selected historical narratives have come to constitute popularly accepted regional identities across the United States as well as within New England in particular, see Kent C. Ryden, "Writing the Midwest: History, Literature, and Regional Identity," *Geographical Review* 89 (1999): 511–32.

13. While Mr. Angell's name is spelled "Phillip" on his gravestone, it is given as "Philip" in other sources I will be quoting from, and I will use this more standard spelling when referring to him through the rest of this chapter. I suspect that the spelling on the gravestone was mainly the work of the stonecutter rather than Philip Angell's personal preference, as daughter Emily's name was also given a variant spelling—"Emerly"—on her marker.

14. Esther Willard Bates, "Woman's Way," *Providence Journal*, 17 November 1950, page unknown. In the collections of the Rhode Island Historical Society Library, Providence, Rhode Island.

15. "Awful Calamity," *Rhode-Island Country Journal and Independent Inquirer* 13 (17 April 1840), 3. In the collections of the Rhode Island Historical Society Library, Providence, Rhode Island.

16. Avery F. Angell, *Genealogy of the Descendents of Thomas Angell, Who Settled in Providence, 1636* (Providence: A. Crawford Greene, 1872), 120.

17. For more on the Willey family, the popular renown of their story, and the conversion of their house into a tourist attraction, see John F. Sears, *Sacred Places: American Tourist Attractions in the Nineteenth Century* (1989; reprint, Amherst: University of Massachusetts Press, 1998), 72–86; Dona Brown, *Inventing New England: Regional Tourism in the Nineteenth Century* (Washington, D.C.: Smithsonian Institution Press, 1995), 44–46; and Eric Purchase, *Out of Nowhere: Disaster and Tourism in the White Mountains* (Baltimore: Johns Hopkins University Press, 1999). The incident also, of course, provided the basis for Nathaniel Hawthorne's short story "The Ambitious Guest."

18. Angell, 121.

19. John Elder, *Reading the Mountains of Home* (Cambridge, Mass.: Harvard University Press, 1998), 82.

20. James Deetz, *In Small Things Forgotten: The Archaeology of Early American Life* (Garden City, N.Y.: Anchor, 1977), 90.

21. Stilgoe, 231.

22. David Charles Sloane, *The Last Great Necessity: Cemeteries in American History* (Baltimore: Johns Hopkins University Press, 1991), 14–15.

23. Angell, 120.

24. Sloane, 14.

25. Heritage Room Committee, *Scituate* (Dover, N.H.: Arcadia, 1998), 116. This book, part of Arcadia Publishing's popular Images of America series, was compiled by local historians and contains many historic photographs of the four "lost villages" and the dam's construction.

26. Thomas Conuel, *Quabbin: The Accidental Wilderness*, rev. ed. (Amherst: University of Massachusetts Press, 1990). For another study of the Quabbin wilderness, one that focuses on local reactions to the introduction of hunting into the Quabbin reservoir in order to thin the huge deer population that was able to develop in the protected woods, see Jan E. Dizard, *Going Wild: Hunting, Animal Rights, and the Contested Meaning of Nature* (Amherst: University of Massachusetts Press, 1994).

27. See Marc Reisner, *Cadillac Desert: The American West and Its Disappearing Water*, revised and updated (New York: Penguin, 1993), for a good popular history of the manipulation of western water.

28. See Fern L. Nesson, *Great Waters: A History of Boston's Water Supply* (Hanover, N.H.: University Press of New England for Brandeis University, 1983). The Quabbin Reservoir took seven years to fill, and didn't actually begin to supply water to its customers until 1946. The Cochituate/Sudbury reservoir system (completed by 1878, with Cochituate alone having been in use since 1848) and the Wachusett Reservoir (completed in 1906) were the two that preceded the Quabbin.

29. I learned about this episode from one of my graduate students, John Burk, who wrote his master's thesis about it. See John S. Burk, "Unintentional Revolution: The Connecticut River Diversion Proposal and Massachusetts Water Supply Planning" (master's thesis, University of Southern Maine, 1997).

30. Theodore Steinberg, *Nature Incorporated: Industrialization and the Waters of New England* (1991; reprint, Amherst: University of Massachusetts Press, 1994), 99.

31. Klyza, 82.

32. Douglas W. MacCleery, *American Forests: A History of Resilience and Recovery* (Durham, N.C.: Forest History Society, 1993), 40. Readers interested in more specific historic information about New England woodlands and the ways they have been used by human populations should look at Lloyd C. Irland, *The Northeast's Changing Forest* (Petersham, Mass.: Harvard Forest, 1999).

33. Cronon, *Changes in the Land*, 147–56.

34. Michael M. Bell, "Did New England Go Downhill?," *Geographical Review* 79 (1989): 450–66.

35. Hubka, *Big House*. As Hubka sums up his argument, "The connected

farm building arrangement was adopted because it met the requirements of a more commercially oriented, mixed-farming, home-industry operation, which had become the only viable means of farming in New England" (202–203). It did so by concentrating all economic operations within the efficient space made up by the barn, the "back house" (usually used as a multipurpose workshop), the kitchen, and the sheltered yard that stood just outside their collective doors and allowed indoor and outdoor work activities to flow into each other easily. People who think that the connected farm building was invented so farmers wouldn't have to go outside in winter to go to the barn are usually disappointed to hear this explanation.

36. Cronon, *Changes in the Land*, 150.

37. Tom Wessels, *Reading the Forested Landscape: A Natural History of New England* (Woodstock, Vt.: Countryman Press, 1997), 61.

38. Foster, 10.

39. Wessels, 61.

40. For an example of such a conflict, see Gary Kulik, "Pawtucket Village and the Strike of 1824: The Origins of Class Conflict in Rhode Island," in *Material Life in America*, ed. St. George, 385–403.

41. Robert B. Gordon and Patrick M. Malone, *The Texture of Industry: An Archaeological View of the Industrialization of North America* (New York: Oxford University Press, 1994), 60.

42. Gordon and Malone, 75–76.

43. Stilgoe, 326.

44. Louis H. McGowan and the Johnston Historical Society, *Johnston* (Dover, N.H.: Arcadia, 1997), 81.

45. Gordon and Malone, 99.

46. Gordon and Malone, 99.

47. Gordon and Malone, 63.

48. Steinberg, 206.

49. Dieter Bradbury, "A Year after Dam Demolition, River Surges with Life," *Maine Sunday Telegram* (Portland), 2 July 2000, p. 1A.

50. Steinberg, 49.

51. Gordon and Malone, 105.

52. McGowan et al., 81.

53. Diana Muir, *Reflections in Bullough's Pond: Economy and Ecosystem in New England* (Hanover, N.H.: University Press of New England, 2000), 178–81.

54. See Brown; Joseph A. Conforti, *Imagining New England: Explorations of Regional Identity from the Pilgrims to the Mid-Twentieth Century* (Chapel Hill: University of North Carolina Press, 2001).

55. William Butler, "Another City upon a Hill: Litchfield, Connecticut, and the Colonial Revival," in *Colonial Revival in America*, ed. Axelrod, 15–51.

56. See John R. Stilgoe, "Town Common and Village Green in New England: 1620 to 1981," in *On Common Ground: Caring for Shared Land from Town Common to Urban Park*, ed. Ronald Lee Fleming and Lauri A. Halderman (Harvard, Mass.: Harvard Common Press, and Cambridge, Mass.: Townscape Institute, 1982), 7–36.

57. For more on the New England village as evolving built environment and cultural icon, see Joseph S. Wood, *The New England Village* (Baltimore: Johns Hopkins University Press, 1997).

58. James M. Lindgren, *Preserving Historic New England: Preservation, Progressivism, and the Remaking of Memory* (New York: Oxford University Press, 1995), 3.

59. Lindgren, 87–88.

60. Brown, 105–67.

61. Elliott West, *The Way to the West: Essays on the Central Plains* (Albuquerque: University of New Mexico Press, 1995), 134–35.

62. West, 138.

63. Cronon, "The Trouble with Wilderness," 79.

64. And not only that, but the food that's caught directly off that coast also has taken on region-defining power in Maine if not in New England as a whole—at least among the people who can afford to eat it. See George H. Lewis, "The Maine Lobster as Regional Icon: Competing Images over Time and Social Class," *Food and Foodways* 3 (1989): 303–16.

65. See Brown, 41–74.

66. Francesca Lunzer, "Riding the Leaves," *Forbes*, 24 August 1987, 101.

67. Jayne Garrison, "Beyond Vermont: The Best in Fall Colors," *Health* 11 (October 1997): 118; emphasis added.

68. Edwin Way Teale, *Autumn across America* (New York: Dodd, Mead, 1956), 4–5.

69. Thomas Cole, "Essay on American Scenery," in *American Art 1700–1960: Sources and Documents*, ed. John W. McCoubrey (Englewood Cliffs, N.J.: Prentice-Hall, 1965), 107.

70. Cole, 100, 109.

71. These and other White Mountain school paintings are discussed in the catalogue for a 1980–81 exhibition originating from the University Art Galleries at the University of New Hampshire: see *The White Mountains: Place and Perceptions* (Hanover, N.H.: University Press of New England for the University Art Galleries, University of New Hampshire, 1980), and especially the essay by art historian Donald D. Keyes, "Perceptions of the White Mountains: A General Survey" (41–58), and the "Catalogue of the Exhibition" by Catherine H. Campbell (79–148).

72. Quoted in Angela Miller, *The Empire of the Eye: Landscape Representation and American Cultural Politics, 1825–1875* (Ithaca, N.Y.: Cornell University Press,

1993), 12. Miller notes that the phrase "the Bethune class" refers to "George Washington Bethune, a popular midcentury writer on landscape" (12 n. 24).

73. Henry David Thoreau, "Autumnal Tints," in *Natural History Essays*, ed. Sattelmeyer, 137.

74. Thoreau, "Autumnal Tints," 151.

75. Thoreau, "Autumnal Tints," 162, 164.

76. Thoreau, "Autumnal Tints," 165.

77. Thoreau, "Autumnal Tints," 173–74.

78. John Lowell Pratt, ed., *Currier and Ives: Chronicles of America* (Maplewood, N.J.: Hammond, 1968), 231.

79. Bernard Mergen, *Snow in America* (Washington, D.C.: Smithsonian Institution Press, 1997), 4, 2. For a look specifically at the place of winter within the New England poetic tradition, see Tim Armstrong, "'A Good Word for Winter': The Poetics of a Season," *New England Quarterly* 60 (1987): 568–83. As Armstrong puts it, "The snows of winter have become part of the ground of the American imagination, a white screen across which questions of origins and cultural differences have played" (568).

80. Quoted in Fred B. Adelson, "An American Snowfall: Early Winter Scenes by Alvan Fisher," *Arts in Virginia* 24 (1983–84): 2.

81. Adelson, 5.

82. Quoted in Adelson, 8.

83. Martha Hutson, "The American Winter Landscape, 1830–1870," *American Art Review* 2 (1975): 66.

84. Hutson, 64.

85. Quoted in Hutson, 70.

86. See Eric Hobsbawm, "Introduction: Inventing Traditions," in *The Invention of Tradition*, ed. Eric Hobsbawm and Terence Ranger (Cambridge: Cambridge University Press, 1983), 1–14.

87. Wessels, 74.

88. Foster, 139.

89. Cole, 109.

90. The antiquarian Nutting first published his books under his own Old America Company imprint (Framingham, Mass.), and they were subsequently republished by the Garden City Publishing Company. They include *Vermont Beautiful* (1922), *Connecticut Beautiful* (1923), *Massachusetts Beautiful* (1923), *New Hampshire Beautiful* (1923), and *Maine Beautiful* (1924).

91. Quoted in Donald Alexander, "Bioregionalism: Science or Sensibility?" *Environmental Ethics* 12 (1990): 172.

92. Henry Glassie, "Meaningful Things and Appropriate Myths: The Artifact's Place in American Studies," in *Material Life in America*, ed. St. George, 83.

93. Elder, 80.

94. Elder, 81.

95. Patricia Nelson Limerick, "Haunted by Rhyolite: Learning from the Landscape of Failure," in *The Big Empty: Essays on the Land as Narrative*, ed. Leonard Engel (Albuquerque: University of New Mexico Press, 1994), 43, 38.

96. Martin W. Lewis and Kären E. Wigen, *The Myth of Continents: A Critique of Metageography* (Berkeley: University of California Press, 1997), ix.

97. Lewis and Wigen, 33.

98. Lewis and Wigen, 35.

99. Lewis and Wigen, 30.

100. Frank B. Golley, *A Primer for Environmental Literacy* (New Haven, Conn.: Yale University Press, 1998), 78.

101. See, for example, <http://www.fs.fed.us/land/ecosysmgmt/ecoreg1_home.html>

102. Robert G. Bailey, "Delineation of Ecosystem Regions," *Environmental Management* 7 (1983): 365.

103. Kirkpatrick Sale, *Dwellers in the Land: The Bioregional Vision* (1985; reprint, Athens: University of Georgia Press, 2000), 55; emphasis in original.

104. Peter Berg and Raymond F. Dasmann, "Reinhabiting California," in *Reinhabiting a Separate Country: A Bioregional Anthology of Northern California* (San Francisco: Planet Drum Foundation), 217. For further descriptions and critiques of bioregionalism as a philosophy and a way of seeing and acting, see Alexander; Daniel Berthold-Bond, "The Ethics of 'Place': Reflections on Bioregionalism," *Environmental Ethics* 22 (2000): 5–24; Stephen Frenkel, "Old Theories in New Places? Environmental Determinism and Bioregionalism," *Professional Geographer* 46 (1994): 289–95; W. Donald McTaggart, "Bioregionalism and Regional Geography: Place, People, and Networks," *Canadian Geographer* 37 (1993): 307–19; James J. Parsons, "On 'Bioregionalism' and 'Watershed Consciousness,'" *Professional Geographer* 37 (1985): 1–6; and the essays gathered in *Bioregionalism*, ed. Michael Vincent McGinnis (London: Routledge, 1999).

105. Barton Levi St. Armand, "The Book of Nature and American Nature Writing: Codex, Index, Contexts, Prospects," *ISLE: Interdisciplinary Studies in Literature and Environment* 4 (spring 1997): 30.

106. Finch, "What the Stones Said," 807, 810.

107. William Cronon, "A Place for Stories: Nature, History, and Narrative," *Journal of American History* 78 (1992): 1368.

108. Cronon, "A Place for Stories," 1367, 1368.

109. Cronon, "A Place for Stories," 1369–70.

110. Cronon, "A Place for Stories," 1373.

111. Glassie, "Meaningful Things and Appropriate Myths," 82–83.

112. Gordon G. Whitney, *From Coastal Wilderness to Fruited Plain: A History of Environmental Change in Temperate North America from 1500 to the Present* (Cambridge: Cambridge University Press, 1994), 2.

113. Robert M. Sanford, Thomas W. Neumann, and Gary F. Salmon, "Read-

ing the Landscape: Inference of Historic Land Use in Vermont Forests," *Journal of Vermont Archaeology* 2 (1997): 1.

114. Wessels, 16.

115. Wessels, 15.

116. Wessels, 21.

117. Elder, 20.

118. Cronon, "A Place for Stories," 1375.

INDEX

Erlich, Gretel, 52, 61–65, 70, 138, 271
Espey, David, 55–56
"Essay on American Scenery," 253
Euro-Americans, 35–36
Europe, 236, 268, 247

Fair, Jeff, 48
Fall River, Massachusetts, 208, 244, 245
family cemeteries, 221
Farmington Canal, 169, 193
Federalist, 14, 177
Finch, Robert, 17, 52–54, 56, 272–73, 279
Fisher, Alvan, 258–59
Flores, Dan, 37, 203
folk art, 152–53
folk cultures, 47–52, 66
folk designers, 148–49
Forbes, 251
Fore River, 168, 169, 170, 171, 176, 193
Fore River Sanctuary, 196–98
forest succession, 261, 277
Foster, David R., 233, 262
French Canada, 247
From Coastal Wilderness to Fruited Plain, 37
Fromm, Harold, 69

Gallatin, Albert, 177–78
Gambo Falls, 173–74, 194–95
"Genealogy of the Descendants of Thomas Angell, Who Settled in Providence, 1636," 218
glaciation, 18–19
Glassie, Henry, 265, 275, 277
Glen Canyon Dam. *See* Grand Canyon.
Glotfelty, Cheryll, 69, 71
Goin, Peter, 21–22

Golley, Frank B., 269
Gordon, Robert, 235, 237, 241
Gorham, Maine, 158, 161, 168, 173–74, 195
Gorham-Sebago Lake Regional Land Trust, 194–95
Graf, Julia, 26
Grand Canyon, 22–29, 57; Algonkian Gorge, 23, 24; artificial flooding of, 25–27; as artificial landscape, 26–27; Colorado River, 23–24; Glen Canyon Dam, 24–26; Hance Rapid, 23, 24; Lake Powell, 6; Navajo Bridge, 23
Grand Lake, 163
Gray, George A., 209
Great Lakes, 18
Great Plains, 163, 274
Greenleaf, Moses, 109, 114, 119, 126, 131, 134; and his "labyrinth of errors," 104, 110, 123; and his maps' origins, 113, 115
Greenville, 109
Greenwich, Connecticut, 246
Guilford, Connecticut, 248
Gulf of Mexico, 165
gundalow (canal boat), 187

Hale, Walter, 139–51, 153, 154–56, 199, 221, 232, 273–74, 275, 276, 277
Harrison, Maine, 170, 172, 174
Hawthorne, Nathaniel, 192, 210
Health, 251, 252
Hefferon, Alan, 5
Hefferon, Donald, 5–6, 10
Hefferon, Lynne, 5
High Line Canal, 2
historical ecology, 38–39, 279
historic preservation, 248
Hobsbawm, Eric, 260
Hog Wallow, 58

Madison, James, 177–78

Maine: backyards of, 12, 14–16; borders of, 136, 201–202; cultural characteristics of, 204, 232; forests of, 16, 46, 47, 230, 278; ice storms in, 14–16, 30; loggers in, 74–75, 120; maps of, 103, 106, 109–16, 118, 126, 130, 132; mills in, 236; natural characteristics of, 203, 251, 253; tourism in, 252, 260; wilderness/woods of, 43, 56, 119, 120, 123–24, 129, 135. *See also* Concord; Cumberland and Oxford Canal; Walter Hale; *The Maine Woods*; specific place names.

Maine Sunday Telegram, 94

Maine Woods, The, 97, 98, 116–32, 133; as alternative mapping project, 117–19, 124–26; attitude toward maps in, 109–110

Malone, Patrick, 235, 237, 241

Man and Nature, 29

Manchester, New Hampshire, 227, 236

maps: in *Canoe and Camera*, 115, 118; Map of Maine, 109 (*see also* Moses Greenleaf); "Map of Moosehead Lake," 118; "Map of the District of Maine from the Latest and Best Authorities," 113, 114; Map of the Public Lands of Maine and Massachusetts, 109, 110; "Map of the State of Maine," 113; nature of, 96–97; "Railroad and Township Map of Maine," 109, 110, 115, 116 (*see also* Colton's maps); of Walden, 107, 108

Marsh, George Perkins, 29–30

Massachusetts, 18, 203, 245, 253; borders of, 202; forests of, 200, 230, 278; and Thoreau, 120, 123, 126; water use in, 226–28

Mayflower, 205–206, 210

McAnsland, William, 218

McHenry, Stewart, 151–52, 153

McKibben, Bill, 10, 60

McNeill, Donald, 56

McPhee, John, 52, 54–60, 65, 96–98, 119, 132–34, 138, 167, 271. *See also* book titles.

Melville, Herman, 121

Mergen, Bernard, 258

Merrimack River, 169, 227, 236, 237, 239, 240

metageography, 268

Michigan, 203

Middlesex Canal, 169

Midwest, 231

Miller, Angela, 182, 184

Millinocket, 130

mill villages, 235–38

Minnesota, 203

Mississippi River, 164–66, 178

Missouri River, 163

Mohawk, 176

Moore, Ruth, 72, 73, 75, 86, 96, 138, 188, 199, 221, 271. *See also Candlemas Bay* and *The Weir*.

Moosehead Lake, 109, 115

moral geography, 87

Morviller, Joseph, 260

Mount Katahdin, 61, 120–23, 128, 135. *See also* "Ktaadn."

Mount Tom, 1–2, 4

Muir, Diana, 244

Mullins family, 211

Mullins, Priscilla, 205, 208–10, 213

Mumford, Lewis, 264, 277

Nabhan, Gary Paul, 4–5

Nantucket, 248

Nash, Roderick, 37

Nassauer, Joan Iverson, 38, 40

national parks, 38

Native Americans, 34–35

natural landscapes: and stories, 138–39, 271–81; artifactual quality of, 9–11, 13, 27–28, 33–34, 36, 38, 46, 48–50, 66, 71, 140–41, 276–77, 279–80; as ahistorical, 28–30; as dynamic, 19, 28, 31–32; as historical texts, 11–12, 31–32, 39, 274–81; as static, 28–31

nature: as opposed to "culture," 3–8, 29–31, 44–45, 94–95, 195; as inseparable from "culture," 32, 46, 49, 52, 198; as mediated through language, 67–68, 271–74

nature/culture dualism, 9–10

nature writing, 44–45, 70

Nebraska, 163

New England: agricultural decline in, 230–33; as artificial region, 201–203, 245, 271; as cultural construction, 246–50; as escape from history, 249–50; as "post-natural" region, 228–29; forest history of, 138, 230, 261–62; land-use history of, 7, 46–47; waterpowered industry in, 234–42

New England Beautiful series, 263

New England Friction Match Company, 120–21

New England landscape: as encoding time, 150–51, 154–55; as folk art, 151–54; as historical text, 146; traditional patterns within, 146–50

New England's Prospect, 201

New England regional identity, 246; as disconnected from nature, 210–11; as historically based, 213–15, 220–21, 229, 247–48; natural basis for, 201–204, 220–21, 229, 242–45, 250, 264

New Hampshire, 132; borders of, 136, 201, 202; canals in, 187; dams in, 228; farms of, 232, 233; forests of, 47, 230, 278; mountains of, 203; tourism in, 252, 260. *See also* White Mountains.

New Haven, Connecticut, 169, 193

New Jersey, 203

New Mexico, 21

New Milford, Connecticut, 1, 7, 13

New Orleans, 166

"new regional studies," 246

New York, 47, 176, 201, 202

New York City, 57

New-York Home Journal, 255

North America, 269

Northampton, Massachusetts, 169, 193

Northeast Carry, 109

Northern Forest, 47

Northern Forest, The, 74

"North of the C. P. Line," 56

Northwest Passage, 178

Norton Book of Nature Writing, 53–54, 55

Norway, Maine, 144

Novak, Barbara, 181–83

Nutting, Wallace, 263

Ober, Richard, 47, 74

"Obituary," 63

October Day, White Mountains, 254

Ohio, 203

Ohio River, 169, 178

Old River, 165–66

Old Town, 120, 130

Omaha Indians, 163

Orange County, California, 251

Ostfeld, Richard S., 30–31

"Other Place, The," 155

Outwater, Alice, 162

Ozarks, 51

❦❧❦

A Rural Carpenter's World:
The Craft in a Nineteenth-Century
New York Township
  By Wayne Franklin

Salt Lantern: Traces of an
American Family
  By William Towner Morgan

Thoreau's Sense of Place: Essays in
American Environmental Writing
  Edited by Richard J. Schneider